MW01679080

I pray my story
touches your story.
Blessings,
Cyndy

Cyndy Sherwood

My Healing Journey

From Surviving to Thriving

Promise Land Publishing

Colorado Springs, Colorado

My Healing Journey: From Surviving to Thriving

Published by Promise Land Publishing
P.O. Box 60879
Colorado Springs, Colorado 80960-0879

ISBN 978-0-9832-424-1-3

Cover design and graphic art: SonLight Graphics by Kim Fiedler, www.sonlight59@gmail.com

Printed in the United States of America
2021

Foreword

It took me thirty years to get to the place where I was ready to write this book. It was suggested many times I should do it, but, frankly, I didn't want to. *Why would I want to dredge up all that ugly stuff? And why would anyone want to read it?*

The questions were merely coverups for my real question—how can I endure reliving it all? I knew it was a story of miracles and redemption, and who doesn't like a redemption story? Isn't that one reason why we like movies and books, to remind ourselves that things can change for the good, to renew our hope?

It's not that I hadn't tried to write my story. Eighteen years ago I started putting some thoughts together, the same year I began writing curriculum for my Bible study, Healing Journey, and my nonfiction book, Road Map to Healing. But because of the pressing nature of those projects, I set my story aside.

Six years later, I picked it up again, filling in more details, but stopped when I got busy filming and producing my next Bible studies, Resting in Jesus and Running with Horses. After that, I forgot about it. It was so overwhelming, trying to figure out how to even tell the story, that I lost interest.

Ten years later, November 2019, I was away on a prayer retreat when God moved on my heart. *Cyndy, it's time to finish your story.* I wasn't expecting that! I was in the middle of creating Freedom Journey for Teens as well as preparing to film it, and definitely not looking for another project. Even so, I agreed. If I've learned anything these last three decades, it's that you never go wrong when you do what God says.

Not only is my life a miracle, so is the writing of this book. When I began the process for the third time, I was shocked at the lengths to which God had gone to preserve the details. Opening the old computer files, documents I hadn't glanced at in over a decade, I discovered I already had nearly 70,000 words written. I was greatly encouraged!

The next surprise was even more shocking, though. I dug out an old bin full of stuff from my healing years. Wow! I had journals and letters and cards and artwork. And the coup de gràce? I had my counselor's notes. When Faith, my therapist, was cleaning out her old files, she hesitated to dispose of her notes on our sessions. She sensed that I would need them one day to write my story, something she also had encouraged me to do. Without her notes, I would never have been able to write about my memories, at least not in the same detail. I'd forgotten so much over the years. (FYI: Graphic details are not included.)

Honestly, the amount of saved material with which I had to work was overwhelming. So much so that one of the harder tasks of this process was organizing the massive volume of information in a way that I could combine into an orderly account.

COVID helped me write my book, too, as funny as that sounds. A few months into my writing, the world went crazy. The COVID pandemic hit my neighborhood and I was quarantined along with the rest of the planet. Suddenly all my events were cancelled, and I was home full time with an open schedule. Those weeks were a gift. Because of COVID, I was able to finish my book in a timely manner, and not put it off for a third time.

As I began looking through my journals (fifty in all!) I was confronted with a choice. On the one hand, it was tempting to edit my entries, fixing bad grammar and cleaning up syntax. But I decided to include them exactly as they appeared in my journals. I believe that editing them would have detracted from the honesty and realness of those moments. The only exception I made was for clarity. Whenever an entry needed explanation, I did not italicize the words, indicating that it was added later. I also left the swear words in; I hope that doesn't offend anyone but taking them out would mean I wasn't being authentic.

I did not journal thirty years ago with the intent that anyone would ever read my thoughts. The entries were for me, my private world, so they are often chaotic because that is how the mind operates when you're in a healing process. One entry might jump around to four or five issues, making it difficult to decipher at times. Nevertheless, I left it alone, trusting you'll get whatever you need to get from it. If I were writing a fictional story, I would create it in an orderly fashion, but this isn't fiction, it is my life.

It's been an interesting journey, that's for sure. And not only my story, itself, but the revisiting of it, too. God, being the God he is, never wastes anything. He is the God of economy. Through this writing process, he brought another layer of healing to me, revealing his great power and love all over again as I relived everything that happened. I'm not the same person I was a year ago. Because God is the God he is, I'm guessing you won't be the same person either, when you get to the last page.

Thanks for joining me on my healing journey. I pray God blesses you.

Chapter One

1991
February-May

I was eagerly anticipating the Christian Education convention being held at the Denver Mechanizing Mart as I drove over the Rocky Mountains in February 1991. Even though I had been teaching and leading church programs for nineteen years, I was ever on the hunt for new ideas and ways to improve my skills.

Most of the workshops I chose to attend were related to my job, so I'm not sure why I was sitting in one about journaling. However, in a matter of minutes, the speaker persuaded me to give it a try. He must have been good, because I didn't even like writing at the time. It turned out to be a fortuitous decision.

I had no idea what was just around the corner, but this would be the last few days of normal life for a very long time.

I am not sure whether to thank or blame the workshop speaker for what is about to follow, but I never would have remembered many of the details had I not made the decision that day to begin journaling.

One of the early entries was recorded on March 22: *God has certainly given me the signposts…. the knowledge that he intended for me to be a public speaker… the song of healing he gave me in July… the confirmation that he would use my testimony to help other women find healing… the ability to pray with women for inner healing.*

Signposts, for sure, but pointing to what?

Another entry came on March 27: *God wants me to give myself, the core of who I am, the naked and vulnerable self behind the veneer of cool competent confidence. Can I do it? Can I give up myself for Christ's sake so others can be set free?*

Spiritual Electricity

My first journal entry was a mere seven weeks before the "spiritual electricity" began. That is how a friend described the unusual activity surrounding me. I liken these journal entries to a photographer shooting pictures of birds, only to suddenly discover a massive train wreck through their lens. I had no idea I was capturing the opening moments of my own healing journey.

My first inkling that something profound was happening occurred while speaking at a church conference for spiritual renewal. Another member of the team, Frank, spoke prophetic words to me several times during the weekend event. His magnetic personality was captivating, and his understanding of spiritual matters, light-years ahead of me.

April 22: *Frank said that God wanted to give to me the fullness of the Spirit and that if I wanted to receive it, I had to ask for it. And I did want to experience all of it and receive all that God has for me. So he prayed with me. And as he prayed, he said that the ability to do intercessory prayer was missing and now would be in me. Then after he prayed, he said I would speak in tongues.* (Frank sensed I previously didn't have this gift, but would after we prayed together.)

And the crazy thing was, after Frank prayed, I did just that. This was not a normal encounter for me. My mainline denominational church didn't do "Holy Spirit" stuff—ever! I was intrigued, to say the least, even excited, glimpsing a world I didn't know existed.

Frank's parting words were, *"Don't be afraid."* I thought, *"That's strange. What could there be that would make me afraid?"*

I was eager to ask God to give me whatever he had planned. But honestly, it felt no more significant than receiving a delivery at my doorstep. I had no idea what I was really agreeing to or the package God was about to deliver.

A week after the conference, a man came into my office. I knew who he was, but we had never spoken prior to this meeting. Then he shared a dream he'd had about me.

April 26: *The dream revealed a car accident, people were dead, and I was praying with some survivors. And when I finished praying, I got into my own car and started to cry. And the inside of the car filled up with my tears. What he had "seen" in my eyes/face was a little girl who had been hurt very badly and abused and rejected. (How does he know these things about me?) But now I was holding a mask in front of my face—a mask of being happy and pleasing people—a mask that would come off at home to show my exhausted self.*

I had no idea why this man would have dreams about me. Unusual occurrences were one thing, but this new development was bizarre. Afterall, I hardly knew this person. Why on earth would he be having dreams and visions about me? And why would he feel compelled to share them with me? That was weird.

Like a auger, opening the deeper pools hiding in my subconscious, God sent people, dreams, and visions to deliberately disrupt me. For some, this phase might begin with an earthquake-like event, i.e. a divorce, death, or scary health diagnosis. For others perhaps a growing restlessness, feelings of fear, or disturbed sleep patterns. For me, it was a subtle sense that something wasn't right, a sense that grew to a tsunami in a matter of weeks.

The spiritual electricity didn't stop for three months. Finally, I could no longer ignore the reality that God was trying to get my attention.

The Green Light

At the same time, I began having my own strange dreams, six in two weeks. In the most significant dream, I was in the Sierra Nevada Mountains, standing on a precipice. My mother was with me.

May 1: *I was in the Sierra Nevada mountains in California talking to my mom. I was exclaiming how different these mountains were from the Rockies, but that Mount Hood in Oregon was the most spectacular mountain I had even seen. Then all of a sudden, a very strong wind came up and I knew I was going to fall down this gorge into the river—at least one thousand feet. My mom said there wasn't anything I could do because the wind was too strong. And then I fell. Once in the cold water, I was okay, but aware that my wedding ring had come off. I also saw my green wallet with my money floating a short distance away. A strange man, also in the water, approached me. He took my ring out of the water and my wallet and kept them.*

I understood the significance of the different mountain ranges. I was raised in California and had many childhood camping trips in the Sierra Nevadas. When I was a teenager, my family moved to Colorado where I started enjoying vacations in the Rockies. And the first time I had ever seen Mount Hood was two weeks earlier, because the church conference I mentioned took place in Portland. Portland—where the spiritual electricity began.

But why was I falling? The dream was deeply unsettling. These prophecies and dreams left me feeling disrupted and confused. Why were these things happening? What did it all mean?

The day after the dream, a friend shared that she had been so strongly impressed by God to pray for me she found herself weeping. She went on to share that God had told her I was hanging on to something and I needed to let go. She also saw me holding a mask in her vision. What was up with all the masks?

May 6: *God seems to really want to impress on me the need to help people. "Help" is so inadequate to express this. For God seems to want to give me—empower me—to heal people.*

In the midst of the strange occurrences, God interjected a prophetic word. He told me that he would one day use me to do a healing work of some kind. It was, however, nine years before I saw him begin to fulfill this. It was sort of a Joseph thing, God telling me the end while I was at the beginning.

I sought out an insightful friend for feedback. She was seeing unreleased ministry in me and sensing I was cutting God off, unwilling to receive what he had for me. And the key seemed to be some deep hurt that God was bringing to the surface.

But what was the hurt?

My friend's words resonated truth into my struggling, inner world. She was right, I was resisting God's work. With this realization, I gave God the green light. I chose to trust him and let go. I responded with the only thing I had to offer—my willingness to go where he wanted me to go.

As soon as I did, God's peace flooded my unsettled place. Calm replaced fear. I still didn't know what God was doing, but I was convinced he was behind everything.

Giving God permission to begin his healing work was necessary or I wouldn't have moved forward in my journey. I had to take an initial step of trust. He wasn't asking me to trust him with everything all at once; trust is built in incremental steps, steps that sometimes take years! But he was asking me to take one step.

I was beginning to get glimpses of God as the gentleman he is, never forcing himself on me, waiting for me to open the door and let him in.

Opening the Package

He will keep you strong to the end. (I Corinthians 1:8a) What comfort I received in this verse, beginning this new journey. My prior world was so ordered and predictable, my need for control insisting it be that way. I certainly wasn't controlling anything now. I had no say in the dreams, prophetic words, or spiritual electricity. They were just happening.

In a way, though, I was enjoying this phase. It was new, different, a bit of excitement. God had never moved in my life this way before.

May 10: *I am so eager to learn and grow right now. God whet my appetite with curiosity in the unusual occurrences of the past weeks. I desire for him to reveal to me the meaning of the dreams, visions and words of knowledge. It is exciting to be God's servant. He does such amazing things.*

I was about to open a surprise package that God had delivered to my door and see what was inside it.

May 17: *"No eye has seen, no ear has heard, no mind has conceived what God has prepared for those who love him." (2 Corinthians 2:9) I am really struck by this verse as I marvel at his revelation to me over the past month.*

It is true, no one could conceive of all that God has planned for one's life. What a pity for those who miss it. I am learning so much about how the Spirit works. He has revealed God to me through other people and their words of knowledge, dreams, and visions. Also, through my own dreams, Scripture, and prayer. I am learning a lot as we go, and it is the Spirit who is teaching and leading. I hope I do have the mind of Christ. I will need it for this adventure we are on together.

About the time I began journaling, my husband, Roger, and I began seeing a therapist. Our marriage has been difficult from the beginning and we had seen a number of counselors, trying to resolve the issues. Although previous attempts had failed, we wanted to keep trying and so connected with John, a pastoral counselor. After sharing the recent events of my life, John suggested I do an individual session with him to explore what was going on.

I filled John in about my earlier life, including my divorce from Tim, ten years earlier. He was surprised to learn I had never grieved the loss of that marriage. In fact, I hadn't grieved any of my previous losses. I wondered why. Why didn't I feel anything about the end of my first marriage? Why did I just shut the door and march on without ever looking back whenever life blew up? I began to detect a pattern.

John was the first person to suggest that my inability to grieve wasn't healthy. Trying to put the puzzle pieces together, he asked if I would say more about my earlier life.

Chapter Two

1971-1981

I filled John in with basic details, beginning where my memory was clearest.

High School

My newly divorced mother moved our family from Denver to Fort Collins, a small college town, to take a job as a Christian Education Director the summer before I started high school. My younger brother and sister, twins, were thirteen and I was fifteen. It would be the first time I had lived anywhere for more than two years.

My siblings and I talked Mom into buying a one-hundred-year-old house, near downtown Fort Collins. It was the coolest house we'd ever seen. The house faced a beautiful divided street with a grassy median that was nothing like the suburban tract homes we'd grown up in. We were all ready for a change.

The big old apple tree in the front yard, the expansive front porch, and clothesline in the back were like something out of a Norman Rockwell painting. We even found some canned apples in the cellar that the previous owner had left. I'd never seen homemade canned goods before. My upstairs bedroom had sloped ceilings with a dormer opening to the porch roof and a little side room, perfect for my sewing machine.

Our rose-colored glasses obscured certain details, however. Like the fact that there was only one central furnace and it was nowhere near the bedrooms. Later I learned to carefully place enough throw rugs so I could hop to the bathroom on cold winter mornings without touching the icy floor. There was only one makeshift shower and the toilet was in a closet so small you couldn't shut the door when you sat down. Nevertheless, the days spent in that house were good.

Before I even started school, boys began noticing the new girl in town—high school and college boys. One summer night, a dozen or so boys showed up at my house to hang out, many I had never met before. Offers to go out arrived incessantly. I was overwhelmed by all the attention and ill equipped to handle it. Deeply entrenched was a belief that I had to be nice to everyone, always smiling, always cordial. Saying "No thank-you," was unthinkable. In my distorted world, good girls weren't allowed to say no.

The situation was completely out of control and I didn't know what to do. I was desperate for some guidance from my mother, but she offered none. So, after Christmas, I came up with a plan. I would pick one out of the pack, one with whom I would belong. If I went steady, then the others would have to leave me alone. And I knew just who to pick—there was one boy who really wanted me.

1: High School Graduation

I met Tim soon after starting high school. He was the basketball superstar and I was the smart girl, self-condemning if a teacher dared give me a grade less than an A. Seeking acclaim anywhere I could find it, I was every teacher's pet, awarded in business competitions, chosen for the school's show choir. Perform, excel, achieve, impress—those were my goals, providing unstable scaffolding for my identity.

And it was certainly impressive to be the girl who was dating the red-headed, basketball star. He played football and baseball, too. Eventually, golf would be the sport he gravitated toward, becoming city champion at sixteen and a pro golfer after college. Sports became our world, to say the least.

I attempted to find a way to join him in that world, taking golf lessons. It was quickly evident, though, that we would never play on the same golf course. I thought, perhaps, if we tried a new sport, we might be able to enjoy it together. After several tennis lessons, the instructor pulled me aside and chastised me for holding Tim back from progressing. Forget it! Me and sports were not meant to go together.

While Tim's family was staunchly Catholic, his own faith was somewhat nebulous. I failed to notice clues that our understanding of matters of faith were not the same.

It was a rocky relationship from the get-go. We fought frequently, breaking up several times but then getting back together. I was in it for life; he was in it for fun. Nevertheless, we were married a year after graduation. I was nineteen.

2: Wedding Day: Me (age 19) and Tim

Marriage, Motherhood, and Ministry

Because my mom worked at a church, I had already been involved in Christian Education for several years, teaching a fourth-grade Sunday school class. In fact, I was in the eighth grade when I taught my first Bible lesson. I was very interested in what the Bible had to say, reading it every night; its stories fascinated me.

After getting married, I started an after-school program at my church called Pioneer Club. I had been a "Pioneer Girl" growing up and wanted other kids to have this experience, too. It had given me a foundation of truth and introduced me to Jesus. Between ministry, work, and marriage, life was full.

Tim was a year older, and already beginning his third year of college when we moved into married student housing. While he was completing his teaching degree and playing basketball for the college team, I worked at a bank to pay the bills. More than anything, I wanted a baby, but it was necessary to put that off until Tim finished college.

The bank hired me as a file clerk, but I quickly moved through the ranks, becoming a loan officer by age twenty—youngest ever and first female. I couldn't order a margarita, but I could authorize a $50,000 loan. Continuing my perform and excel patterns, I received awards for achievement in the credit industry.

Even though banking came easy to me, my heart wasn't in it. I wanted to have a baby and be a mom—that was my dream. I counted the days till graduation.

In the meantime, I cooked, cleaned, and did the laundry. Gathering up the dirty clothes one day, I found women's panties in Tim's pocket. They weren't mine. I can't even remember the lame excuse he offered. But by now I was pregnant and too afraid to rock the boat. Maybe he wasn't lying to me.

Our daughter was born six weeks after he accepted a position teaching high school English and coaching basketball in a small town in Western Colorado. The day I went into labor, I suggested it was time to go to the hospital and he asked if we could wait until Monday Night Football was over. We did.

It was a rough labor, forty-two hours long. I nearly bled to death in the first hours after giving birth because my uterus wouldn't contract anymore. I remember fading off into never-never land, feeling so peaceful as my blood pressure plummeted. After hours of nurses and family members manually massaging my abdomen, the bleeding finally stopped.

A Dream Come True

I couldn't wait to take my baby home. We had purchased a tiny yellow house for $20,000, three blocks from Main Street. I was excited to finally have my own place to fix up, sewing curtains and decorating the nursery. Motherhood turned out to be everything I had hoped for. I was a happy little clam, taking care of my home and daughter.

I frequently walked downtown to do errands, pulling Bree in her Radio Flyer wagon. Sometimes I stopped in at Comet Drug to order a fresh-squeezed limeade from their still-working soda fountain. Folks were friendly to the new teacher's wife in town who frequently walked Main Street with her baby.

We attended church in a little white chapel building, complete with steeple and bell tower. Before long I was directing the Sunday school program. A group of young moms invited me to join their Bible study and I made wonderful friends. An idyllic life... well, almost.

It turned out Tim hated teaching. So much for the five years of college. After teaching just one year, he got a job delivering packages with UPS. One morning while he was working, I answered the door to find his best friend, also a UPS driver, asking to come in for a visit. He said Tim had suggested he come over to see me. I didn't let him in, but the whole thing didn't sit well with me.

About that time, my husband began suggesting 'creative' sexual experiences that included other men. Disgust gripped me as I evaded compliance. Then I began finding Playboy and Penthouse magazines in the house, nothing unusual for him, but these latest ones had photos of my mom, sister, and me glued over the women's faces. That creeped me out. Who was this man I married?

Soon after becoming pregnant with our second daughter, my world fell apart. My husband came home late, wanting to talk. "I am leaving," he said. After serious coaxing, he finally admitted he was having an affair. I tried to find out how many women there had been during our six years of marriage. Struggling to recall, he thought maybe a dozen or so.

Shock reverberated to my core. The waves of fear, rejection, and abandonment kept coming, threatening to drown me. What would I do? Where would I go? How would I manage? I was four months pregnant, for heaven's sake! Tim moved in with his girlfriend and I moved in with my mom for a couple months, later agreeing to give our marriage another try. He had broken up with his girlfriend and wanted me to come home. That's when we started counseling with Roger.

Weeks later, Jenny was born. This birth was a lot easier than my first one, only sixteen hours of labor. The afternoon when I arrived home from the hospital, I noticed Tim was particularly detached from the moment. He just sat in the living room, watching a golf match on television, annoyed when I asked for his help with the baby.

It wasn't long before it became apparent to the therapist that my husband wasn't committed to me or the marriage. It was clear Tim didn't want to be married. He was a player, seeking out fun, women, drugs, and alcohol at every opportunity, using his sports travel commitments as a cover. A week after giving birth, the therapist, Roger, said we should get a divorce. So we did.

I continued with the counseling, feeling needy and broken by my husband's affairs. After several weeks of individual work, Roger said he wanted to have a relationship with me. So we did. Seeing each other was tricky, because if anyone found out, he would have lost his job. (It's illegal to date your clients.) Later he wanted to marry me, so I did.

At the time of the divorce, the court awarded me only $400 a month for child support and a year of maintenance support, another $200; that didn't go very far. Even so, I was reluctant to get a job right away. The girls were so young, Jenny only weeks old. I held out for a year before I had to do something. I was offered jobs, but I still didn't want to leave my girls, so I accepted Roger's offer of marriage, instead. Problem solved.

In my arrogance and naïveté, I thought all those rules about transference and ethical behavior were silly and not relevant to our situation. It didn't apply to people who were in love. He wanted me, and that was all that mattered. Besides, it solved my financial predicament, allowing me to stay home with the girls.

Today I know those ethical boundaries are in place to protect clients, just like me, who are too vulnerable to recognize they are making a serious error.

I was twenty-six and the girls were four and one years old, when I began my marriage to Roger. I was sure I was doing the right thing this time. Roger was a Christian therapist and elder in the church. He didn't use alcohol or drugs. I had fixed all the previous issues in my choice of men.

3: Wedding Day: Bree, Me (age 26), Jenny, Roger

Grieving Begins

Ten years later, as I was recounting all this to John, my pastoral counselor, he noticed I had responded to my crisis purely on a practical level. Where were the feelings of grief and loss? When my marriage ended, I lost more than just financial stability. My husband and life-partner had abandoned me. My dream of an intact and happy family evaporated. My children had no father. Didn't I have feelings about any of that?

Apparently I did, because tremendous grief welled up inside me as I began to explore the impact of my divorce. I felt pain for the first time. The sadness persisted for weeks, tears flowing frequently. *How odd,* I thought. Ten years had lapsed but it felt like yesterday. Alfred Lord Tennyson, the English poet wrote, *time heals all wounds.* I don't think so! It is ironic that I'm related to him, because I'm here to say, it ain't true.

I hope there isn't much more of this grieving stuff. I don't like it.

Chapter Three

1991
June-July

The Little White Cell

Two months into my new adventure with God, things took a dramatic turn. Several times while praying, I saw a small room, like a prison cell. Inside, the cell was pure and clean with white walls and one window blocked by steel bars. The room was empty–that is except for a little girl sitting on the floor, hunched over her knees.

June 21: *I want to find the way out of this funny room I'm in. It has been my safe and secure place for many years but I'm a grown woman, not a hurt little girl, and I don't need to be in there. I want to come out.*

I was a long way from meeting that sad, little girl; still, I felt her pain. Confusion and pain continually emerged in my journaling. Where were these feelings coming from? Why was I in this cell?

June 23: *I now see the need to leave this safe room. It has been my retreat for over 20 years. But a bittersweet retreat it has been, because I only go there to escape pain and hurt. So it is always associated with bad things happening. But I believe God wants to be my retreat. And, I know I can count on his large comforting arms being available whenever I need them.*

It seemed so mysterious. What bad things? Pain and hurt from where? Why did I feel a need to create a place of secret retreat? What was so threatening that I had to protect myself?

I told John about my little cell. The idea that God wanted me to leave the room was terrifying, but I didn't know why. I only knew I was gripped with fear when I thought about it.

It turned out John had the key that would unlock my next step. *"Next time you see the cell,"* he suggested, *"invite Jesus inside the room to help you leave."*

Days later, while camping with family friends near the top of McClure Pass, the little, white cell appeared in my mind again as I prayed. I wrestled with what to do for hours, battling hard before remembering the key John had offered me.

"Jesus, please come and help me. I'm afraid to leave." Before I could say "amen," Jesus was at the door, a door that didn't exist moments earlier. He didn't say a word. He simply held out his hand and waited while I chose between captivity and freedom. His kind face and gentle demeanor bolstered my will. He knew it had to be my decision. I can't say fear went away, but the love on his face won the day. I took his hand and we left together.

Why didn't I think to ask for his help before? Jesus made it so simple. He obviously wanted to help me all along, but he waited until I asked, until I would receive him. *I hope I will remember how much easier it is to get through difficult things when I ask for God's help.*

My life is defined by the decision I made that day, forever personally referenced according to BC (Before leaving Cell) and AC (After leaving Cell).

Once outside the room, I asked Jesus to seal the door so I couldn't return. Somehow, I knew I would be tempted to go back there, and I was certain that wasn't God's plan. I never saw my little, white cell again. Nothing could have prepared me for what happened next.

There is something to be said for blind faith. I'm glad I didn't know what I was getting myself into because I may have been tempted to turn back from the journey. And then I would have been left with my anemic life forever.

Dead in the Water

God kept taking me back to the book of Exodus, revealing the parallels to my life. I had been in Egypt, the land of bondage, all my life. But I wasn't there anymore, not since God launched my journey to the Promised Land the day I left my cell.

My season in Letting-Go Wilderness (the term I use for the season of redemption and healing) had begun. Like for the Israelites, Egypt was behind me and I was heading into the desert, feeling afraid and insecure. The Egyptians had a season of separation from the life they had known, and I was about to do the same. However, there was one way I decided I would not follow suit. Their journey took forever—forty years! *I'll be smarter than that. Surely there's a shortcut.*

After leaving my cell, I began to deteriorate.

July 2: *Today I felt like I was walking around with my feet in concrete. I could barely handle any work. I don't have the energy to do anything. I can't stand this feeling of being incapacitated.*

The pain and confusion seemed to increase by the hour. I wanted to bail on all my responsibilities. I needed to create some space. Wow! That was a brand-new thought. Me—the consummate Miss Responsibility—wanted nothing to do with responsibility.

I asked God to show me what to do and, that night, I had another dream. I was on a ship—my ship. Suddenly, a storm came up and a huge wave overcame my ship, knocking it out of commission. It didn't sink, but it was dead in the water. Fearing for my survival, I scrounged for something left to eat, finding nothing but junk food scattered about. I cried out, *"I will starve on this food!"* Just then a god-like voice replied, *"Yes, you will. You have to go below to discover the real food. There is food to sustain you on a lower level."*

When I woke up, I called John and headed straight for his office. *What was going on? What was happening to me?* I did feel dead in the water, unnerved, undone, unravelling. They don't use the term "nervous breakdown" much anymore, but it sure felt like I was having one.

John framed it as a deep, grieving process, suggesting I should expect it to last up to six months. My response was telling: *"Six months! Are you crazy? I don't have six months. I have a job. Fall programming at the church starts up next month. I'll give you four weeks to fix me. That's it!"* Obviously, I was close to delusional, believing first, that I still had some control over any of this, or second, that it could be resolved in a matter of weeks, or third, that John could fix me. Wrong on all accounts!

That night, July 2, I wrote: *Just like my earlier dream predicted, I have fallen or am falling a very long way down. The Holy Spirit has blown me over the edge. But I don't know if I have hit bottom yet. It seems like it is still getting worse by the hour.*

What I didn't know is that I wasn't anywhere near the bottom. It would be five years before my life would resemble anything close to normal. While John would be very instrumental in my healing, God would use a variety of means and many people to help restore my life. And, at this point, the situation was beyond neatly stuffing it back inside. There was no turning back.

Unpacking Boxes

With my prison cell gone, my prayer experience changed. I saw a new picture. After Jesus and I left my cell together, he led me to a hallway. Packing boxes were stacked from one end to the other, each with a label somehow relating to my life. Some had names of significant people, others hurtful events from my past. I saw nothing beyond the hallway, only boxes piled up to the ceiling everywhere I turned.

While curiously reading the labels, I heard God say, *"It is time to unpack the boxes, Cyndy."*

The hallway metaphor made sense: a passageway of sorts, dealing with stuff before I would be able to move forward. Obviously, some of it had already started. Processing my grief and loss related to the end of my first marriage had been just that—unpacking boxes. I had also begun working on the wound of losing my half-brother, Scott, four years older than me, when he ran away one night, never to return. My first sudden loss, but not my last.

As John and I continued to work, new feelings emerged. This time they were about my stepfather, Jim.

Stepfather

Jim had been a breath of fresh air when he came into my life at sixteen. After my parents' divorce, my mom picked up the shattered pieces of her life and courageously began a new one, working at a church to support her three teenagers. And, in the midst of all this, she met someone who made her heart beat again, a history professor at the local university.

*4: Jim and Me (age **18**)*

Jim spent a lot of time with our family. He and I bonded over academia and music. Taking a genuine interest in the things that mattered to me, he supported my different activities, helping with school papers and attending my events. Jim respected my opinions and seemed to enjoy our conversations. I felt valued. Our relationship was definitely a new father-figure experience for me.

One time I was preparing to give an organ performance, and I needed to practice my recital pieces on the pipe organ at my church many evenings. Jim came down to sit with me in the sanctuary for hours so I wouldn't be alone in the building. *So that's how fathers are supposed to act.* I didn't know.

Three years later, Mom and Jim married. As positive as our relationship had been for me, it was the opposite for my mom. They struggled right from the start and split up six years later. Losing my cheerleader and encourager left a large void.

After the divorce, I tried to connect with Jim and did see him one time, but my mother saw it as a betrayal of our relationship and chewed me out when I got home. Feeling forced to choose between them, I did not pursue my relationship with Jim any further. Theme repeated: Another sudden loss of a significant person in my life.

Descending into Pain

Ten years after the fact, I unpacked the "Jim" box, grieving the loss of my only good father-figure. It hurt to lose him. I loved him as a dad and missed him. Grieving allowed another piece of my heart to heal.

July 6: *I really want to be alone for a couple days. Maybe there I can finally do some crying. I sure need to. I feel the tears starting to leak out, but I stop it. I just need God to take me through this and to teach me and show me what he wants me to see and learn. Somehow, I'll get through it.*

I found the grief work difficult. I hated crying, so I distracted myself with busyness. Besides that, I was attempting to keep things as normal for the girls as I could.

I had transitioned from Christian Education volunteer to employee a couple years earlier but had been involved in that work for nineteen years. On the side, I had a practice, doing budget and debt counseling with couples and individuals through Crown Financial (previously Christian Financial Concepts).

Because Roger and I had a separate office building behind our house, we were able to be home with the girls. If I was gone, Roger was there. Even my church hours were flexible, allowing me to be home after school. Now that it was summertime, the girls were home a lot, playing with friends, riding bikes, and going to the pool.

I didn't want them to see my pain, or anyone to see it, for that matter. Hiding my emotions made me more uncomfortable, though, increasing my feelings of desperation. As much as I resisted expressing my grief, I finally had no choice. Only by letting it out did I find any peace or calm inside.

July 8: *A friend said a vision flashed before him as we talked after church yesterday. He saw silver being purified—a chemical called flux being added during the meltdown of the silver in order to draw all the impurities to the surface so that they could be skimmed off and the silver purified. Then he saw a mirror reflection of Christ. It fits. I feel like Christ is drawing out my impurities. He is pulling the grief out—sometimes bit by bit, but sometimes it is coming out in massive chunks.*

At least this vision came with a little encouragement; maybe one day I would be a reflection of Christ. I needed to hear something good would come from this. The smelting process was certainly easy to relate to; the heat seemed to intensify with each event of repressed grief.

Needing time alone, I headed for Ouray, a favorite getaway and one of the most beautiful places on earth. The small town, nestled in a v-shaped crook of the San Juan Mountain range, ministered to me. It provided what I needed to truly grieve—God's creation and privacy. Soaking in the hot springs soothed my jangled nerves.

Soon after arriving, pain lunged at me again.

July 13: *I have spent hours in the depths of despair, crying until I thought I would dry up, begging God to stop the pain. This passage of Scripture in Isaiah 55 helps. I can see God's encouragement and promise in it. Verse 13: "Instead of the thornbush will grow the pine tree, and instead of briers the myrtle will grow." That makes me feel better. I have to endure this for a while. And then the joy and the fruit will come. Verses 8-9: "'For my thoughts are not your thoughts, neither are your ways my ways,' declares the Lord. 'As the heavens are higher than the earth, so are my ways are higher than your ways and my thoughts than your thoughts.'" Now is the time to find out if I really believe those verses. Do I really trust God? Yesterday I doubted. The pain seemed more than I could stand.*

Unfortunately, I couldn't stay in Ouray. I went home two days later, my family expecting me back.

July 16: *I am reduced to such a place of dependence—asking God daily, hourly, "so now what do I do?" I'm feeling the depression more today. The last two days were like wearing a pair of jeans two sizes too small, holding the feelings and thoughts in, not letting them out, being so uncomfortable because they felt constricting and painful. It was also like treading water. It took all my strength to stay afloat, constantly working at it, no peace, no rest, no letting down.*

In some ways it's better today. I am letting the thoughts and feelings come, feeling the depression and sadness, not trying to be in a place emotionally better than I really am. God showed me something else about my hallway today. I saw clearly that every pain in which I escaped by using the room was waiting just outside the door. And my process now is to travel through the hallway and all the pain piled up in there in order to arrive at the new place.

At least I knew why I was an absolute wreck. As I said, time heals nothing. The pain of decades past was as fresh as yesterday.

July 23: *"He is like a tree planted by streams of water, which yields its fruit in season…" (Psalm 1:3a) As I think about this verse, I realize that it is my off-season, non-fruit bearing time. This is comforting. I can't remember the last time I was not producing 'good works.'*

After resisting my reality for some time, I finally acquiesced to a leave of absence from work. I was in no shape to be administrating church programming. *It's just for a little while. Like John said, just a few months.* As it turned out, though, I never returned to the job.

It had been four months since the wild spiritual activity and healing process had begun and I felt a need to bring my parents and siblings up to date. I sent them a long letter, starting with Frank's words to me in Portland and then describing the strange occurrences when people shared dreams and visions about me. I also shared my own dreams, and about beginning therapy with John and leaving my little white cell. I told them I had taken a leave of absence from my work because I was hurting, feeling weak and needy. I really needed their support. They didn't all respond, but those who did were caring.

I cleared the way to focus on my journey and began doing some serious work with John. We did two and three-hour sessions a couple times a week to speed up the process. If I had to do this, I would do it as quickly as possible.

July 26: *There is no doubt that this has been the hardest day so far. By the end of the second session I felt like a major artery had been severed and was bleeding profusely. Such horrid pain. So many losses, none fully grieved, none resolved. So many boxes to unpack. So much pain.*

Living in the Wilderness

For the first time, my life came to a halt. Even as a child, I never stopped. But now there was nothing else to do. I had no work, no commitments. My social calendar was blank. I was alone with myself.

I did little that summer except hangout in my backyard, watching my plants grow. That wasn't so bad, actually. I had never noticed the comforting display of peonies, columbines, and roses in my own yard. I observed my fruit trees as the apples, pears, and plums ripened. Days on end I rested in my chaise lounge, a gift from my kids on Mother's Day, journaling and playing my guitar. To break up the monotony I played Tetrix and Solitaire on my Apple Classic computer.

On July 31, as I was journaling, the words to an entire song emerged on my paper. I got my guitar and put them to music. *Sitting under my apple tree, feeling the warmth of a summer breeze, seeking his face and my burdens to ease, let me feel your presence, please. I don't know why it hurts so much, but I long to feel your loving touch. Sometimes it feels like I can't go on, when there's nothing left, please make me strong. I want to live as you created me, but that person you made I can hardly see. What I really need is you to set me free, heal the child, for that is the key.*

The song was prophetic, but the meaning hidden. I still hadn't met the child. It is odd today, looking back at the clues, clues that seem obvious, yet I couldn't see them. I guess I wasn't ready.

It wasn't the first song I'd written. A year earlier, I wrote another one called, "The Little Girl," describing a young girl who cried herself to sleep. This little girl was hurt by people who should have loved her. She was in constant pain but didn't know why. I was baffled when I was finished writing it, not knowing what some of the lyrics were about.

Back in therapy, John tried to gather data about my early years and family history, but it quickly became apparent that I didn't remember much. So he gave me an assignment to visit my parents and do a family genogram, a diagram depicting generational issues and dynamics.

Chapter Four

Family History

Growing Up

Certain pieces of my past were easy to recall, my memory being punctuated by the many moves and houses we lived in.

5: Me and Mom

I was born in southern California in 1956 and lived in various parts of the state for the first fourteen years of my life. Twenty months after my birth, the twins were born, Judy and Steve. My father had one son from his previous marriage, my brother, Scott.

Dad sold pianos and organs for a living, something that had a great impact on my life. While other people had a dining room, we had a music room with three organs and a piano. The Hammond B3 organ was my prized instrument. Beginning at age five, I took organ lessons for seventeen years, performing frequently at my father's trade shows and in concerts and recitals.

As a young girl, I was terrified of going to bed at night, frequently crying and complaining about my stomach hurting. I had no idea why. Even at four and five I couldn't sleep, so my mom gave me some red medicine that tasted terrible. Later, during grade school, I remember crying myself to sleep, feeling so sad at night.

My mother stayed home, ever finding ways to express her creative and artistic abilities, sewing dresses, making ornate birthday cakes, and also helping to arrange class field trips.

6: Mom with Me and the Twins

I was close to the twins. We grew up as a clump, doing everything together, building forts and playing school. And, of course, I was the bossy teacher. I felt protective of them, keeping an eye out at school to make sure they were okay.

Until my dad left our family, a pattern started each afternoon around 6:00 when my mother would tell us kids to pick up our things and get the house in order before Dad got home. The atmosphere was tense the moment he walked in the door, removing his coat and tie, pouring a glass of Jim Beam, a glass that never left his side until bedtime.

7: Me (age 4)

Mom would report any misbehavior that occurred during the day, and Dad would beat whomever needed a spanking. After dinner, Dad settled in his recliner, watching *Gunsmoke* or *The Rifleman*. Because he loved ridiculing us, tearing us down with sarcastic comments, I tried to stay out of his way. I learned early on to never to break a rule or cross my dad for fear of being whipped. I still got beatings, but not as much as my little brother.

When I was six, Scott, my half-brother, came to live with us. It was never explained why he wasn't living with his mother anymore, but clearly my mom was not happy about the new family member, angry that Dad never asked her how she felt about raising Scott. Her open resentment was hard for me, because I loved Scott and was thrilled to suddenly have an older brother.

Although my dad was a good provider and we always had our material needs met, he was out of control in many areas of his life, struggling with multiple addictions. He didn't seem to know what to do with children. He had very little to do with me. I don't remember ever having significant talks or doing anything together. The only trips or vacations we took were for the purpose of his fishing, which I detested.

As a restless, alcoholic salesman, he never stayed in a job very long. So every year or two, I found myself repacking the same stuff, getting a new address, starting a new school, looking for a new organ teacher, and making new friends.

Losses and Gains

The move from Southern California to Sacramento brought many changes. It was my third-grade year, and school had already started.

***8**: Me (age 8)*

That Christmas, my teacher launched a contest. Whoever formed the most words from "Merry Christmas" would receive a 45 LP record of Little Drummer Boy. I decided I was going to win that prize. On the final day, I produced a list of 148 words. The second-place person's list had twenty words or so. It occurred to me that maybe I wasn't normal.

Mom became sick as soon as we moved. From then on, she suffered from various ailments, including intestinal disorders, depression, and anorexia. A back disease required her to live in a hospital bed in our den for a few years and wear a back brace. At ten, my dad took me to the hospital to tell her goodbye. A tall woman, weighing only eighty-six pounds at that point, they did not expect her to live. Somehow, she turned a corner and returned home a little while later.

Because of mom's illnesses, many household responsibilities fell to me. I welcomed them, finding purpose and significance taking care of everyone. Always the good girl, I cooked and cleaned and helped with the twins.

With the move north, we were only an hour away from my Grandma Johnson. Technically, she wasn't our real grandma. Her daughter married my mom's brother, so she was my cousin's grandma. But I didn't care about that. Her grandkids were back in Ohio and we seemed to need each other, so we adopted her as our grandma and she became a regular fixture in our home.

Grandma Johnson was an oasis in my life. She was the jolliest woman I knew. One year she arrived at our house for Thanksgiving dressed as an Indian. Because her maiden name was Waters, and her first name, Minnie, we liked to call her "Minnie Ha Ha Laughing Waters."

9: Grandma Johnson

Her husband had abandoned her and her daughter, my Aunt Zoe, soon after Zoe was born. Grandma Johnson never remarried. Instead, she taught children with special needs for forty years. She was an amazing woman, teaching me to cook and sew and make crafts, the first adult to take a personal interest in me.

I'll never forget the week I got to go to her house all by myself. I thought I'd died and gone to heaven. Under her tutelage, I made my first cake from scratch. We dyed shredded coconut green and decorated the top like a nest with jellybean eggs to celebrate Easter. I was proud of my creation.

I grew up going to church. If Mom didn't go with us, she would drop us off to go by ourselves. My dad did not attend. In fourth grade I joined a Christian club called Pioneer Girls. Pursuing my "Perform" and "Achieve" goals, I earned all the badges, attending camp each summer and eventually becoming a counselor myself.

I can still remember the camp counselors, women who seemed so much older and wiser, (at least nineteen or twenty!), pouring attention and affection on all of us. I thought they were so cool. More than anything, I wanted to grow up and be like them. So, on the last night of camp, while sitting around the campfire singing "Kumbaya" (no, I'm not kidding) and "It Only Takes a Spark," I accepted Jesus as my Savior. I was twelve.

The year was one of mixed blessings, though. That same year, I woke up one morning to find my older half-brother Scott gone. He had run away during the night. Three anxious weeks later, my mom told me he had gone to San Francisco, seeking out like-minded hippies in the famed Haight Ashbury area. He never returned.

10: Dad, Me (age 18), Steve, Judi, Scott

Years later, Scott told me that Dad caught him using drugs, and threatened to have him put in jail, so he fled our home in Sacramento.

This first loss was devastating. It never mattered to me that we came from different mothers. Scott was the one person in our family who didn't seem to need anything from me. I felt accepted and special anytime he asked me to come and listen to his newest album. He treated me with consideration and would have significant talks with me; in return, I loved him dearly.

Pot and Panthers

We moved again that year, without Scott, this time to Oakland because my dad got a job in San Francisco. We lived in a fancy house on a hill overlooking the Bay Bridge while I attended seventh and eighth grade.

It was interesting, to say the least, living there during the Black Panthers heyday. Busing was forced and racial tensions high.

There were areas of town you did not drive through, areas where shootings were common. My school was attended by every color and socioeconomic level of student. The wooded path behind my house, leading down to the local junior high school, was lined with teens smoking marijuana. No one seemed to care or even notice. There was no such thing as teens going out at night in Oakland, carousing or playing pranks. It just wasn't safe.

None of that, however, was of concern to me. Wherever we moved, I just recreated my usual life, going to church and Pioneer Girls, taking organ lessons, excelling in school, and making friends.

Little did I know that being asked by the leader of my Pioneer Girls club to teach a Bible lesson would launch a fifty plus year career, but that was where the road began for me. I no longer remember the Scripture I taught on, but I do remember feeling both nervous and excited, bringing the lesson to that group of eighth grade girls.

While living here, my mom got word regarding her stepfather, the one who sexually abused her. (I knew nothing about that at the time and had only met him once). I remember standing in the kitchen and asking her what was wrong. With little affect, she simply said, *"My stepfather died."*

On my thirteenth birthday, Mom took me and my friends into San Francisco to see Fisherman's Wharf, The Cannery, and Ghirardelli Square. We had a blast. It's one of my special memories from this time.

Colorado Beginnings and Family Endings

True to form, though, we hit the two-year mark and Dad got antsy. This time his job change took us to Denver, Colorado. It was June, an unusual entry point for me, allowing me an entire summer with the neighborhood kids before starting school.

There was a good-sized group of teens who hung out every day, taking turns offering their backyards for the nightly outdoor sleepover. I had never heard of such a thing. Guys and girls were included, something I wrongly assumed my mother wouldn't go for.

One night, we slipped out of our sleeping bags, each one armed with toilet paper and *decorated* the neighborhood. I was scared to death the next day, fully expecting the police to come and arrest me. I had never done anything criminal before. Riddled with guilt, I confessed my crime to my mother. She just laughed. I was both relieved and confused. Why wasn't she mad? Why didn't I get in trouble?

Soon it was time to start ninth grade at the nearby junior high. I came home from school one late September afternoon to find my parents in the living room. Dad was sitting on one side, my mother on the other, sobbing. I was immediately suspicious. Dad was never home before six or seven. With no explanation, Dad announced he was moving out. No prior notice. No warm-up. No fighting. He just packed his bags and left.

I filled in the blanks, guessing another woman was in the picture. I eventually learned my father had had women on the side his entire life, just like his dad, my Grandpa Merrill. The theme of sudden losses was once again repeated. Dealing with devastating emotions, my mother retreated to her bedroom for the rest of the school year. *But everything was okay, right?* Because I was there to hold things together, including my mom.

Four months later, my third traumatic event occurred.

My parents were both out of state, leaving me home alone to care for the twins. It also happened to be the week of my fifteenth birthday. Wanting to feel especially pretty, I helped myself to a yellow-ruffled blouse from my mother's closet. During lunch, a group of boys, at least twenty or more, dragged me into a dark auditorium, pinning my arms and feet and sexually assaulted me, an act perpetrated on several other girls as well. When they were done, I went to science class as if nothing had happened. After all, good students don't skip class, right?

That night, my mother called to wish me a happy birthday and I explained to her what happened. She told me to report the incident to the principal. The next day, by myself, I did just that. After telling the story, the principal instructed me to leave separately from him so no one would know I had talked to him. Except for catching hell from the boys who somehow found out I told the principal, it was the last time the matter was mentioned. No follow up from my parents, either. I wasn't surprised or disappointed by this because I did not want to talk about it.

When the school year ended, my mother emerged from her bedroom and started a job in Ft. Collins as a Christian Education Director right as I was beginning high school. It was 1971 and my tenth move in fifteen years.

Chapter Five

1991
August-September

Hearing the Whispers

Just prior to visiting each of my parents, Roger and the girls and I went camping by the Roaring Fork River on Independence Pass. One morning, sitting by the river, I wrote this:

August 5: *What a beautiful and gentle river it is here in this place. The sun feels so warm on my body. The gentle burbling of the river quiets my spirit. I can smell the sweet freshness of the thick and plentiful foliage in its varied shades of green. The scene as a whole provides a splendid treat for my eyes. Only one of thousands of marvelous creations God has made and yet remarkable all by itself. And, as I literally soak in the beauty and warmth here, I begin to hear God's voice.*

This is what he said: *"At this time you must learn to be content in the moment, not living for tomorrows. I have chosen this time, not you. I desire for you to accept it, not fight it. I will remake you, but you must not be busy. It will interfere if you choose to be busy now. You must learn to hear my voice in the whisper of a quiet stream as well as in the roar of a raging river. And that requires spending more time than ever alone with me. We must learn to dance together in a more intimate way. You must be able to discern my voice better than you are able to now."*

The insight of my wrong goal is like a bolt of lightning this morning. And now I understand why I was experiencing mounting anxiety and frustration this past week. So I relinquish to God my job and all that goes with it—from the building and supplies to the teachers and coordinators, to the students, children, youth and adults. They are all his and I must trust him to care for them in his perfect way—without me right now.

God outlined the game plan. He wanted me to keep my eyes focused in his direction, leaning into him. He knew I felt the temptation to go back to my old life. The rhythm of the Christian education year filled every fiber of my being. For twenty years, I had been directing or teaching Sunday school classes, Bible studies, youth groups, retreats, Vacation Bible schools, and women's groups.

And it was August! August is the time to gear up and organize and prepare and recruit and train. But God said, *"Don't go there, Cyndy."* My work was of a different nature now. I was learning who God really was, as well as a new way to respond to him.

A thousand times, I would return to the visual of dancing with the Lord, being in his arms, letting him lead. I needed the reminder daily.

August 8: *"I will praise the Lord, who counsels me; even at night my heart instructs me." (Psalm 16:7) How true that is. Nine times God sent his messages to me at night in my dreams. He sent more information than I could even understand. In fact a lot of it is still a mystery to me.*

August 12: *"The LORD is my rock, my fortress and my deliverer; my God is my rock, in whom I take refuge.... He reached down from on high and took hold of me; he drew me out of deep waters.... You, O LORD, keep my lamp burning; my God turns my darkness into light." (Psalm 18:2a, 16, 28) I see hope in these verses as I ponder another heavy therapy day here in Ouray. I look forward to the end of introspection, looking within and desiring to feel freedom from the past pain. I long for joyful days filled with a sense of wellbeing. It was painful today, dealing with all the issues of my mother. But the most pain came when I faced the scared little girl inside me. The sadness surprised me.*

Revelation was still a long way off.

August 15: *"May the LORD answer you when you are in distress." (Psalm 20:1a) The scriptures, prayer, and quiet times with God have been such a comfort to me during this ordeal. It has really fed my soul and brought me direction. It is a tremendously good feeling to be walking on God's path—even when it's hard. Tuesday's therapy session was as painful as anything I have felt. It kind of gushed out at the end. The real pain from the destruction of my marriage reared its ugly head and griped me with the most awful pain I've ever felt. Just remembering it today brings the tears again. What an amazing time of my life this is. It is so weird being off work—at loose ends—time on my hands. It is a foreign state for me. It is not all bad. The lack of pressure is delightful. John said that now that I had relinquished control and responsibility of church work to God, I needed to act out that release. What a challenge that will be.*

And now it was time to face my assignment.

The Maternal Side

Mom was only six hours away, so I started there. As Mom reminisced, I created the genogram, drawing the details as John instructed so he would be able to read it. Her memory seemed clear, easily recalling names and information, going back three generations. The amount of tragedy and abuse on her side of the family surprised me. I could feel the pain and struggle of relatives long dead as I listened to her recount their stories.

At an early age, my mom's mother, Jesse, along with her two siblings, George and Emma, were removed from the home and split up in different foster homes. Jesse lived in seven different foster homes, a woman my mom described as chronically ill, emotionally needy, depressed, and not the nurturing type.

Mom didn't know what happened to her Aunt Emma, but her mother's alcoholic brother, George, apparently prostituted his wife, brutally abusing her and their five daughters, who were removed from the home. He was eventually murdered.

Jesse married Oscar, my grandfather, and had two boys, Dan and Joe, before my mom was born. Oscar died of leukemia when Mom was five, crushing her heart. After his death, Mom was keenly aware of her mother's grief, responding to her constant medical problems and trying to be a good girl so as to not disturb her.

11: Maternal grandparents, Uncle Joe, Mom (age 3), Uncle Dan (Back)

(Besides visiting soon after my birth, I only saw my grandmother Jesse once, when we took the train to Ohio for a visit. I was young, maybe four or five. I have no memory of her, only of running around the yard with my newly discovered cousins, throwing fallen apples at each other. I thought my dad was going to kill my cousin when Mom stepped out the back door at the most inopportune moment, catching an apple right in her face.)

My grandmother's second husband was not faithful to her. Because he sexually abused my mom, she was sent away to live with her older brother, Dan, who was already married with children. She became the maid and nanny. Dan also sexually abused mom. She was only thirteen. Mom mentioned being sexually abused by an employer, too. Mom viewed her mother as a helpless woman who chose her new husband over her daughter.

Learning of my mom's family history impacted me with sadness and horror that she had endured so much pain, although it was actually my dad, not my mom, who told me about the multiple accounts of sexual abuse. Mom left those details out.

The mother-daughter similarities between she and I were striking. I, too, tried to take care of a chronically ill mother, being a good girl so

I wouldn't make the already difficult situation at home harder. And there were more similarities to be discovered years later.

When I finished the genogram, Mom told me not to tell anyone. She said it was a secret. I remember thinking, *Who on earth would care about these stories of people long gone?*

On the Road to California

With my mother's visit behind me, it was time to head to California and get my dad's family history. I decided to take Bree along. She was soon turning thirteen, and the road trip seemed like a good opportunity for mother-daughter time. I also thought she might enjoy seeing where I lived in Sacramento and Oakland.

Bree and I spent our first night at Lake Tahoe, a place where my family had vacationed several times when I was a child.

August 22: *Tonight I look for his guidance for tomorrow I face Elinor for the first time since Dad remarried her. And I'm not sure how I will feel about it all. I'm not even sure what to do about Dad. I'm not nervous or anything. But I don't really know all the purposes for which God has planned this trip. So I need his guidance.*

The next day we drove into Sacramento, driving by my old neighborhoods and schools. Later I journaled this: *I felt less good about the* (house where I lived when I first moved there in third grade) *than the other places. I think that must have been a stressful time. I can't really identify the reason, but it felt negative for some reason.*

Next, we drove into Richmond, just outside Oakland. I was curious about seeing Elinor, the woman my father left my mother for when I was fourteen. Dad and Elinor had been married and divorced twice and were back together again. I hadn't seen her in years.

Dad kept us busy for three days, including a tour through San Francisco, seeing all the sights, including lunch at Fisherman's Wharf. We crossed the Bay Bridge to see our house in Piedmont, my home when I was Bree's age. While there, we attended services at my old church. I was having fun sharing my past with Bree.

The night before we were to head home, I still hadn't brought up the subject of the genogram, and Dad hadn′t asked, although I told him it was the purpose of my trip. Before arriving, I let him know I was going through a painful time and that my therapist had given me an assignment to gather family information.

Time was running out. So during our last few hours together, I finally got the nerve to have the conversation. He was visibly agitated.

The Paternal Side

The picture my father painted was full of one destructive, painful event after another—generations of sexual sin, alcoholism, abuse, and dysfunction. I wondered how anyone survived coming out of that family.

Several things caught my attention.

12: Paternal grandparents, Uncle Don, Aunt Gean, Dad (age 10)

My dad's father, Merrill, was one of nine boys, and dressed by his mother as a girl, because she was disappointed that she had another son. Merrill's father died young, forcing him to enter the workforce at twelve, and the navy at fourteen. Later he married Dora, my grandmother, and had three children, eventually becoming an Episcopalian priest and naval chaplain in World War II. They were stationed in San Diego.

Before the war, when the family was still under one roof, Dad said they were all aware that Merrill was raping missionary girls who were staying in their home in the upstairs bedroom. But no one talked about it or tried to stop the behavior. My Aunt Gean ran away at sixteen, because Merrill was molesting her as well. Dad never forgave my grandfather for abusing his sister Gean.

My grandfather cheated on my grandmother, unabashedly sending home photographs from the war of himself with other women.

While Merrill was away at war, Dora struggled to manage my dad and his older brother, Don, who was a wild kid. So when Dad was twelve, she sent both of her sons to a private all-boys boarding school until they graduated. Dad shared one memory of being sexually abused by Don's friend while his brother watched, resulting in resentment toward Don. As an adult, my uncle spent time in a mental institution, and ended his own life while living with my grandma.

Dad said he had no real relationship with his father; he didn't even grieve when Merrill died. (I was seven when my grandfather died.) These dynamics created a close bond between my dad and grandmother, a bond that remained until she died. I remember him saying, though, *I spent my life trying to win my mother's approval, but never did.* Dad was always jealous of Don, the one who got the attention from their mom.

13: Dad, Grandma, Aunt Gean, Uncle Don

Suddenly hearing these sordid stories at thirty-five years old was shocking. While I rarely saw my mom's relatives, that was not the case with my dad's. When we lived in Southern California, we often got together with relatives. In fact, my grandparents lived only a mile away during my first few years.

I struggled to overlay these stories on top of my childhood memories. For some reason, though, I didn't feel the same sadness I had when I heard mom's story. The feelings were more like an uncertain, internal disruption.

14: Christmas morning with paternal grandparents

Dad had one last detail as he finished the family backstory, a comment that haunted me for some time, *I am completely blacked out on my life before age twelve.* Blacked out? Why?

Hmmm…twelve…the year my dad was sent away to live in a boy's boarding school, and the same age as my younger brother when Dad walked out on our family. Was there a connection?

August 26: *"He will instruct him in the way chosen for him." (Psalm 25:12b) I'm so glad God will instruct me because I feel as if I'm in a fog. I don't know where I'm at, what I'm feeling or where I'm going. It's been a great few days with Dad. He has really wined and dined me. We've had a great time. Elinor has been very nice and generous. It has been easy to be around her and even enjoyable.*

August 27: *I'm very anxious to connect with John soon. It's been 2 weeks since my last session and I really feel a need to do more work now. I thought a lot about Dad today as I drove. I found it odd and somewhat disappointing that Dad asked not a single question about my current situation in the entire visit. Even when I brought up the genogram, he didn't inquire about why I wanted the information. He just answered my questions. I get the impression that he also has a strong need to hold me in a certain place—just like Mom does. It's almost like he can't tolerate the idea that I might not be okay—all put together—reliable and strong. Or maybe he's afraid that I'll discover some level of unhappiness or anger regarding the past and start to resent him. I don't know the real reason—but he definitely avoided the subject of me.*

As I attempted to meld the backstories, seeing these two streams feed into the next generation, the one in which I was born, the water appeared polluted from both sides. Trying to find anything good or positive was an empty endeavor. And it didn't get better from there.

Between the two genograms and the outline sketch of my growing up years, John now had a decent idea about my life, or so we thought.

Mom in the Hospital

I was home, getting back into routine when the phone rang. It was my sister. Mom had been taken by ambulance to the hospital after waking up with hysterical paralysis. She couldn't walk. *Was it a coincidence this happened right after I met with her or was it connected? Did going to California to talk to dad have anything to do with this?* My sister lived in Ft. Collins, so she was seeing to her needs.

My mom had been in a car accident just before I left for California. She called at the time to let me know she was okay. She was physically fine, just a little shaken up by the ordeal. Apparently, there was more to it.

August 31: *The road seems long and hard ahead of me now. Just days ago I felt I was almost at the end of the ordeal. But the events of the last 3 days are painting a different picture. The dilemma of my mother's situation leaves me feeling confused and overwhelmed. She needs help and I don't know what to do. Her injuries seem to be quite disabling.*

September 4: *"Weeping may remain for a night, but rejoicing comes in the morning." (Psalm 30:5b) I long for the day when this is finally over. I look forward to the morning of rejoicing. Since Saturday I have been thrashing around like a lion in a cage. I have at times been angry with God and his plan. I have been grieving terribly over the loss of my job. And all the while asking God to show me if I'm reading the signposts incorrectly. Maybe this is an Abraham test and God will give it back to me just before the knife falls for good. And maybe this is the end of my job. I really don't know the answer to that. But I still am sensing that I can't go back right now.*

September 12: *"The angel of the LORD encamps around those who fear him and he delivers them." (Psalm 34:7) With Mom in the hospital and unable to walk, I find myself struggling for survival emotionally. I feel such guilt that I am somewhat responsible. John assures me that I am not.... I don't feel ready to face her. I'm so clouded with emotions regarding her.*

September 19: *After my session with John yesterday I felt so much anxiety about seeing Mom this weekend.*

My family headed over the mountains to check on Mom while she was still in the hospital, in the psychiatric unit. Her demeanor was startling. She was like a little girl, not a sixty-year-old. She seemed so happy to be there and loved all the care and attention she was getting. One evening we stopped by for a visit, but she said she couldn't see us because she needed to go for a walk with her 'people,' the other patients. I thought that was odd. *What had triggered all this?*

September 26: *I still haven't sorted out all my feelings about my visit with her last weekend. I know my being sick was certainly related. I don't know what my goal is with her. I am so confused. It felt like the same old, same old. She was sick and I was taking care of things. But at the same time, it didn't feel like my actions were inappropriate. Yet, by Sunday night I felt all bound up and quite angry, but I'm not sure why.*

It was just like old times: mom was sick, and I was taking care of her. But this time I was angry, because I was going through a hard time and I needed her. I wanted her help, but she had none to give.

Chapter Six

1991
October-December

Revisiting My Stepfather

Lacking the usual busyness and projects, everyday functioning became difficult. Just handling home and kids at the most basic level was overwhelming. Scripture was my solace.

October 3: *"Why are you downcast, O my soul? Why so disturbed within me? Put your hope in God, for I will yet praise him, my Savior and my God.... By day the LORD directs his love, at night his song is with me—a prayer to the God of my life." (Psalm 42:5, 8) "Send forth your light and your truth, let them guide me." (Psalm 43:3a) God's word is so helpful and so timely. It is so good to hear his voice.*

October 8: *I just read a brief story about Fyodor Dostoyevsky and how he found the Lord in a Siberian prison camp with a New Testament. Fyodor said, "One sees the truth more clearly when one is unhappy." Thoughts and insights have drifted in my head these past days. More prayer and meditation are needed for that is the thing that brings me peace—which is in short supply these days. The conversations with friends are also very helpful in managing the pain level. So I must work harder at this and stop relying on John to fix it all.*

"Not only so, but we also rejoice in our sufferings, because we know that suffering produces perseverance; perseverance, character; and character, hope. And hope does not disappoint us, because God has poured out his love into our hearts by the Holy Spirit, whom he has given us." (Romans 5:3-5) The key word for me is perseverance.

So often lately the temptation to succumb has been present. I just want to give up and stop fighting with all the pain. God's word is timely. For it would be wrong to succumb—I would rapidly sink into a depression. I can feel the fingers of depression wrap around me and attempt to pull me down. It would be so easy to let it happen. But I'm not going to.

I laugh at myself, now. *But I'm not going to.* I still had no idea how little control I had. But I was a fighter; I wouldn't give in easily.

Early in my journey, God began teaching me the value of suffering, using his word, other authors, and life itself. Suffering was never on my bucket list, nor anyone else's for that matter. Dostoyevsky's comment was impactful, helping me realize its value.

October 10: *I'm aware that I have not unpacked a box in the hallway yet. It's the one labelled 'Jim'* (my stepfather). *My only feelings and thoughts about him so far have been centered around fear and anger. I don't know what I'm afraid of. I do know why I'm angry. He betrayed me. He left. He checked out of the relationship. When my dad left, there was little to miss. He was never involved in our lives and was hardly around.*

But Jim wasn't that way. He was involved in my life. He participated in things I was doing and always seemed interested. He would talk. He knew a tremendous amount about the Bible. But there were inconsistencies. Like he had filed bankruptcy and had a history of financial difficulties. And, of course the biggie—he committed adultery and left Mom for another woman. It's like his relationship with God was only head knowledge. It didn't affect him personally.

When I moved back to Ft. Collins during my separation, he comforted me. (I was 25, pregnant with Jenny, and had moved home after learning about Tim's affair.) *He* (Jim) *seemed genuinely concerned about the awful circumstances of my life. He was there for me the awful night when I got the call from Tim saying he didn't want to try anymore—he wanted a divorce. Jim held me as I sobbed and sobbed. What a shock to hear Jim had moved out just weeks after I had left.*

Mom told me a few days after Jenny was born and I just couldn't deal with it. My own marriage broke up 3 weeks later.

I found it more than coincidental that Mom and Jim began their relationship at the same time Tim and I did. Our prospective weddings occurred two months apart, and the divorces four weeks apart. What was that about?

October 10 (cont.): *It was all too much. I couldn't face the pain. I was afraid to admit that I'd lost that relationship. Rejected again. How could he* (Jim) *just walk away? How could he just disappear?*

I was learning that healing is rarely a one and done proposition. I had already had one round of healing regarding my stepfather. But my tendency had always been to quickly walk away while thinking, *Glad that's over.* With the more significant relationships, however, I could see it takes more than one healing season to fully put them to rest.

When I first processed the 'Jim' wound, my healing centered around my grief at losing the relationship. Now I was ready to deal with my anger at his rejection of me when he left my mom, effectively ending our relationship.

Grieving the End of My Marriage

Jim wasn't the only relationship where I invested healing energy. I'd been working on the one with Tim, as well. Unpacking that box allowed me to deal with an unresolved issue—unpaid child support. Roger had adopted the girls two years into our marriage, after Tim signed the relinquishment papers. At that point, however, he was in arrears to the tune of about $10,000.

I finally had the gumption to do something about it and filed the necessary documents to start receiving what he owed the girls. Soon after I got a call from Tim, saying his new wife had been crying for days because the court orders were being enforced, and would I please back off. I agreed to monthly payments, of which I never received one from him. Eventually, Tim's mother paid it off. I split the money into two savings accounts, one for each of my daughters.

In the process of filing the documents, it was necessary that I go back through the bank statements from my first marriage.

October 15: *"I will take refuge in the shadow of your wings, until the disaster has passed." (Psalm 57:1b) It was so hard to look at those statements that reflect our life together—especially the first Delta statements. We moved into our first home, getting established in Delta, Bree being born. That whole life that represents the lost dream—the shattered hopes. Even seeing his signature was upsetting.*

And then the last statements were hard. The last statement with joint signatures, the final expenditures together, my first expenditures on my own, closing the account, the first support checks. It's all there—our whole life together.

Those days were good for me. I made a good life and a good home. I feel a fondness in my heart for those days. I'm not ashamed of it. It wasn't perfect and he wasn't a full partner—but for me, there was a measure of happiness. It wasn't till the end that I began to learn what was going on.

I have had to pull back my feelings of responsibility for him in order to prepare this document. I'm only responsible for the girls now—and this money belongs to them. I need to work on their behalf, not Tim's. I'm not responsible for him. I'm not anything to him. And he is not anything to me. It's over. He's gone.

I had to stop being everybody's caretaker.

Learning Humility

My therapist, John, encouraged me to try an antidepressant to stabilize my emotions and help me cope with the stress of recovery. Initially, I hated the idea. After watching my mom's perennial state of illness, which included taking Valium and other prescription drugs, I wanted nothing to do with it. It didn't help matters, knowing my dad and half-brother were addicts.

I realized pride was in play here, too. I didn't want to need help! Drugs represented dependency to me; they insulted my self-sufficiency. Even so, I finally admitted I needed some help and started the medication. I have to say that it made a big difference, allowing me to work more effectively on my healing issues. More humility.

One day after a hurtful exchange between Roger and I, I wrote this:

October 22: *I sat in my green chair and cried. I have never been so miserable. I wish there were an island somewhere with my name on it. I cried out to God, "You said you'd never give us more than we can handle. Well, I'm at my end!" And just then I heard him say to me, "Forgive him." I couldn't believe it. So he said it again, "Forgive him." God said retribution is his work, not mine. So I did. And then something amazing happened. The dark cloud hovering over me lifted and his peace settled on me. It was such a relief.*

Right from the beginning of my recovery, God worked in my heart toward forgiveness, and not just for current marital issues. Particularly concerning Tim and my parents, there was forgiveness at every round. It helped with my healing, but because I was not fully connected to the reality of what happened to me earlier in my life, later it would be necessary to forgive at greater levels.

Understanding forgiveness was a slow unfolding of truth for me; honestly, it was at least a ten-year process before I knew forgiveness didn't mean that I thought what others had done was acceptable or that I would now forget about it or stop hurting. I was simply trusting God to handle it, rather than me. I was surrendering my burden to God.

October 24: *I'm learning that God alone is my refuge in pain. The room is gone—I can't hide there anymore. And people have no wisdom or power to make it better. Only God can help. He has the power and the wisdom.*

October 29: *"Save me, O God, for the waters have come up to my neck." (Psalm 69:1) God is bearing my burdens daily.... I want so much to live a normal life. I want to feel good. I long for this to be over.... I am already four months into this ordeal. Hard to believe. I still have no idea what is coming.... I've lost any confidence in myself to be able to function at a normal level.... Francis Roberts, Come Away My Beloved, speaks to me today: "Once you accept your limitations and settle the fact once and for all that I will never ask you to perform Herculean feats, you can begin to learn what I really have in mind for you. Stay in a place of humility."*

God wanted to be the source of power in my life. Would I let him?

November 4: *"...then make my joy complete by being like-minded, having the same love, being one in spirit and of one mind." (Philippians 2:2) I really desire to be like-minded with Christ. I realize today that the three attitudes Christ had—making himself nothing, humbling himself and becoming obedient, are exactly what I have been learning lately.*

I had known this passage in Philippians chapter 2 all my life but had never related it to how I should live *my* life. God was multitasking; he was remaking me spiritually while he was healing me.

November 7: *"Restore us, O God Almighty; make your face shine on us, that we may be saved." (Psalm 80:7) I desire to be restored, but not to my former self. I want to be recreated by God, restored to a place of wholeness and peace. But I hear God's warning to me today. I must listen to him continually and not return to my folly.*

I was propelled by the need to run from my pain. For so long I lived every day in such a way as to never feel my feelings, to never stop long enough to let them out. At such a high speed, I would go every day. My own voices were not speaking for my good, but for my destruction. Obviously, I was headed for a major crisis. This truly is a pilgrimage, on the path of God's will. I am not essential—God is essential.

God wanted to be my protector, as well as my power source. I found the thought of turning that role over to him disturbing. Relinquishment, relinquishment, relinquishment... it seemed to never end.

November 7: *He controls all things. I control nothing. As I have so painfully learned, I can't even control my own self. Last night I learned the lesson again. After stewing about something at church, I realized it was God's program, not mine. And, so I relinquished my imagined control and responsibility and prayed God would bring his success.*

November 19: *"For you have delivered me from death and my feet from stumbling, that I may walk before God in the light of life." (Psalm 56:13) "Blessed are those who have learned to acclaim you, who walk in the light of your presence, O Lord." (Psalm 89:15) These verses are so important to me. If I haven't learned to walk in God's light these past months, then I haven't learned anything. I am struggling to find that light again. And I won't take a step unless I see his light.*

They were baby steps; nonetheless, I began to give control to God. Progress was constantly challenged as new opportunities to trust him appeared in my path. When the door closed to return to my job, I realized I had secretly harbored expectations that things would improve and resolve to my satisfaction and on my timetable. My expectations set me up for disappointment.

December 5: *God's wisdom helps. "Therefore do not worry about tomorrow, for tomorrow will worry about itself. Each day has enough trouble of its own." (Matthew 6:34) All through this I have been waiting for the new whatever to come, for the struggle to be over, to go back to work, to be normal again. "Life will begin again in January," has been my most recent expectation. Yet each of these expectations has ended in bitter disappointment.*

I remember God's encouragement to me in August: "Strength for today and bright hope for tomorrow." All I have is today. Tuesday, I worshipped God and that was my service that day. Even though only he and I received any benefit, it was my service. Service, I'm learning, is obeying God and following HIS plan. That's a much broader perspective than my previous one.

The lessons kept coming. I attended a spiritual retreat and God showed me more insights. It had been months since I'd left the little white cell, but God had more to show me about that vision. There was more to the hallway, there was another door. We opened the door together to reveal a great banquet hall. It was regal and magnificent. He said that I would serve there one day.

December 10: *It hurts so much, leaving my job. Telling the congregation that I wouldn't be back was so hard.... I don't want to leave it. I still love it. It hurts so much. When will life ever get easier? When will I ever feel normal and okay? "...Strength for today and bright hope for tomorrow." That's all I've got.*

It was good to forgive the church on Saturday. I needed release from my bitter feelings.... "I tell you the truth, unless a kernel of wheat falls to the ground and dies, it remains only a single seed. But if it dies, it produces many seeds." (John 12:24) God keeps telling me this verse. Dying to self—I seem to be doing that now. It hurts a lot. I had to die to my job. But it is so clear in this verse that the dying must come before the ministry can. So I need to die to my selfish ambitions and vain conceit. And at the same time, seek the release of the Spirit in me to continue and grow stronger. That seems to be my job for now.

God was gracious at the retreat and gave me hope for the future. I got a glimpse of some future ministry. The Spirit was powerfully present. (Then God gave me verses of hope that I would desperately hang onto many times in the coming months.) *"…fear not, for I have redeemed you; I have summoned you by name; you are mine. When you pass through the waters, I will be with you; and when you pass through the rivers, they will not sweep over you. When you walk through the fire, you will not be burned; the flames will not set you ablaze." (Isaiah 43:1b-2)*

1991 had come to an end, but my healing journey had barely started.

Chapter Seven

1992
January-May

Diary Clues

1992 was a very different year. As I look back at 1991, I can see God was giving me a foundation of truth to stand on. I needed a better floor underneath me for what was coming. Those first months were almost like a honeymoon period. I was feeling and experiencing the heart of my heavenly Father in a brand-new way. Even though I was grieving the pain of past events, the time with God was sweet.

That didn't prevent my hopes from being dashed, however. When January arrived, and nothing in my circumstances changed, I found myself struggling. My identity was in crisis. I had no job or even volunteer work, so why was I here?

January 16: *For several days now, I have been thinking about having another baby…. So many times, for so many years I have prayed for a child. He has said no every time. Is he answering that prayer now? Or is it just me groping for purpose in my life?*

Motherhood had clearly given me purpose in the past, so why not have another child, I thought. My girls were ten and thirteen, and while my role with them was still important, it didn't require nearly the effort babies did. Fortunately, I didn't get pregnant. If I had a clue about what was coming, I never would have tried.

January 21: *"Turn my eyes away from worthless things." (Psalm 119:37a)*

I was spending my time reading worthless novels and playing computer games until I became disgusted and gave it up. Still pushing for my own agenda, I thought it was better if I read books that filled my mind with life-giving thoughts to renew my mind and prepare me for future ministry. In the end, however, I again resolved myself to this off season by turning down a job offer as director for the Crisis Pregnancy Center.

February 7: *"Set me free from my prison, that I may praise your name. Then the righteous will gather about me because of your goodness to me." (Psalm 142:7)*

While other people may enjoy a sabbatical, it felt like prison to me.

February 19: *"He who falls on this stone will be broken to pieces, but he on whom it falls will be crushed." (Matthew 21:44) I have been broken to pieces by Christ—but not destroyed. He is putting me back together in a new and better way. I seek the healing ministry now. I hear God's call. The how, when, and where are still unknown. But that's okay.*

March 3: *I have so easily fallen into the hole of despair and discouragement. I feel so disgusted with myself no matter what I do. If I stay in bed and rest and neglect my responsibilities, I feel guilty and overwhelmed. If I tend to the needs, then I feel compulsive and unwise. So I go back and forth, taking on the chores until I am too sick and tired to continue and then resting in bed until I am overwhelmed, and guilt ridden again. What a mess I am. I am not satisfied with myself no matter what I do.*

My old identity had been stripped from me, violently, and I did not find my new one quickly or easily. It took years. In the meantime, I was left with a painful void. I had no idea what my true needs were.

March 14: *Last Tuesday I opened my diaries and began reading them. I have no recollection of writing the diary, written when I was 14 and 15. In fact, I didn't know the diary existed.*

I remember how strange it felt, finding the diary that day. Even though I had written in it for a year, I had no memory of doing so.

March 14 (cont.): *I guess what I see in all this* (the entries in my diary) *was that I was obviously trying to do the right thing all the time. There is no sense of me—only pleasing my boyfriend, pleasing my parents. The sexuality issues were a no win. Either I did what I knew was wrong or I made my boyfriend mad. I immediately turn to blaming myself. It was all my fault. My motto was, "be perfect, do perfect, let no one down." And I failed. I was and am a failure at keeping my own motto. I guess I need a new motto—the old one doesn't work.*

I could see that my identity was all messed up, at least as far back as junior high.

March 15: *The rules in me were so powerful:*

1) *Don't make anyone mad.*
2) *I am responsible for meeting others' needs.*
3) *Be good, do right, do it perfectly.*
4) *Do what they say.*
5) *Do everything in your power to avoid rejection.*
6) *Find someone who will care for you.*

But suddenly it wasn't possible to follow all the rules at once. Again, at no point was I aware of my need for privacy, respect, and no sexual pressure in my relationships. It wasn't relevant to me or more probably—there just wasn't any room for my needs. My list of other people's needs was already longer than was manageable. I can feel my anger rising as I think about all this. I'd like to take a baseball bat to a wall somewhere.

Where did all of this come from at such a young age? This was crazy. Why did I adopt such an impossible standard? What was propelling it? As I began to see the insanity in all of it, an appropriate response began to well up inside me—anger. Perhaps for the first time in my life, I was in my honest place with this hard emotion.

March 16: *I am struck…* (as I read in my diary) *at how little feeling I seemed to have about anything. The pages are filled with schedules and activities. Several names are mentioned, but very little description of them or insight into my relationship with them.*

By age fourteen, the dye had been cast; I was a 'human doing,' not a human being. Apparently, when I retreated into my little, white cell, I became void of all feelings, not just the bad ones.

Fathers, Round Two

Sometime earlier, I had written a letter to Jim, sharing a little bit about my life and asking if he would be interested in getting together the next time I was in town. He responded right away:

Dear Cyndy: What a pleasant surprise to hear from one of my favorite people after all these years. It's hard to imagine that it's been ten years since I saw you last. And it sounds like time hasn't stood still for you—remarried, mother of teenagers (they're a special breed, eh?), going on for all that work in the financial field, and Christian Education Director, besides. It would be wonderful to get together again when you're over here. Let me know and maybe we can have another dinner out. I'd like to meet your family again. Hopefully I'll see you soon. Love, Jim

We made a plan to meet when I got to town.

March 17: *My mom has been visiting for a few days. I told her about contacting Jim and attempting to arrange a meeting with him while in Ft. Collins next week. She responded extremely poorly. She got angry and expressed her still very bitter feelings. Then she got withdrawn, packed her bags, and left for* (my brother's) *house. It is so hard for me. Why can't she be there for me? Why does it always get turned around to her problem or her issue? This has nothing to do with her. It's between Jim and me. It's always about her. My needs never matter. She's always the fragile victim, demanding that I take care of her. Since I was two years old, it's been this way. It's so unfair.*

March 19: *It's true that I have been very poor at having companionship, relaxation, and fun in my life. As a teenager, my search for someone who would want me and love me was unending. Those painful roots, of not really being wanted, go deep. It was like I was on a discovery mission and I was the subject. Who was I? How did I get like that?*

Continuing to read in my diary, I had finally arrived at the place where my dad left, the day I arrived home from school to find my parents sitting in the living room, waiting for me and my siblings.

I was expecting to read about my dad leaving but was shocked to see what I really wrote about. Twenty-two years after Dad walked out, I wrote this:

March 22: *My dad left this week* (in my diary entry of September 28, 1970). *There is absolutely no mention of it in my diary. I'm consumed with thoughts of* (another boy at school). *The day my dad left is simply blank and marked with a big "X." However, there is a full report on my weeks' schoolwork, but not one word about my dad moving out. Where were those feelings? ... I wrote nothing in my diary, yet I remember the afternoon vividly.... I left the house right away. I didn't want to watch him pack.... I went over to* (a girlfriend's house) *and we walked to a nearby elementary school to hang out on the playground. We were together for quite a while and I never told her my father was moving out. I pretended like nothing was wrong. When I returned home, Dad and his things were gone, and Mom was in her bedroom crying. She didn't come out for three days. I never cried. I felt no feelings except a fierce determination to restore order to my life.*

Today I can see how bizarrely I responded, but at the time, it felt quite normal. I simply left the house, walked to a girlfriend's house, and hung out for a few hours. The words, "Oh, by the way, my dad just moved out," never left my lips.

March 22 (cont.): *My mom said something strange* (currently, on her recent visit in 1992). *She said, "My mother gave me away when I was thirteen." That's when she went to live with my Uncle Dan. Maybe that's why I feel as though she stopped parenting me when I was fourteen. Why was I so determined to block my feelings?*

My dad's departure in 1970 was like an earthquake. The financial ramifications alone were huge. We went from affluence to poverty. We had to move to another city, which meant starting over again with school and friends. My mom went back to work, but her small salary didn't reach very far. In other ways, though, life was better.

It was like a black cloud had lifted from our home when Dad left. Things were relaxed for the first time. The four of us had fun together. My mom changed, too. She seemed to have new energy for us and became more involved in our lives. Because of the contrast both economically and emotionally, I learned that happiness had nothing to do with money. I was happier in high school than I had ever been, and we were dirt poor.

Reminiscing about all this begged the question: Why was this cataclysmic event omitted from my diary?

March 24: *Jim called today to confirm getting together for lunch or something next week. I am so glad he called. But I still feel very nervous about meeting together. My mom really tried to discolor my view of him. She hates the fact that he and I are getting together. She can't separate herself from me. The feelings* (I am having) *aren't good. The diary has been so hard to face. Will it ever get easier? It doesn't seem like it will.*

April 7: *My meeting with Jim was good. He was very happy to see me… and catch up with the girls. It is so good to affirm that relationship. However, Mom doesn't see it that way. She gave it to me good, brought out the big guns. I am so sad that she can't let me be a separate person from her. And I am terrified that she will ruin our relationship with her skewed view of things. Lord, help us both get through this traumatic time in our relationship.*

Even though it was the last time I saw Jim, the reunion was healing for me. I regained something important in connecting with him, a piece of myself. In his last years, sadly, dementia took his mind from him. His wife, the woman with whom he had the affair, wouldn't allow a memorial service to honor Jim's life, so my mom did this of her own accord. This was a great act of generosity on my mom's part, providing the needed opportunity for so many to grieve Jim's death. For me, the service was good closure on a good relationship.

Shifting Ground

April 9: *I'm so full of feelings these days. I used to think and not feel; now I feel and can't think. My eyes leak when I read, watch TV, and share with a friend—anything that evokes emotion. I feel such sadness, fear, anger, and bitterness at times…. And the worst of it all is that I am so angry with myself.*

Today it is easy to see how healing steps were occurring, how individuating from my mom was making me healthier. At the time, however, it was nothing but darkness and pain. I recognized little progress.

Rejecting my old identity initially caused stress in every relationship. It seemed like I was in conflict with everyone. I reacted with anger when others made choices that hurt me or that I didn't like. But then I immediately felt afraid because anger was scary. I was like an emotional toddler, lacking skills to deal with these things.

Later, another puzzle piece fell into place. I discovered the changes in me were impacting the homeostasis in my relationships. (That is a $5 therapy word, meaning the equilibrium of a relationship or social group.) I had come into my existing relationships as a victim and caretaker. When I dumped that identity, I upset the balance in certain relationships. It was like trying to tango with someone who was doing a waltz—it didn't work anymore.

People were upset when I found my voice, expressing my likes and dislikes. They didn't want to hear them, which in turn left me feeling disrespected.

Some relationships were so enmeshed that they just blew apart when I began individuating. They were previously balanced between my need to be needed and be a caretaker, and their need to be taken care of. Their approach was to manipulate and dominate. I couldn't do that dance anymore. Nevertheless, it was a painful, death-like time, losing these relationships.

May 5: *I guess it* (the change in the relationship with my mother) *is sort of late adolescence. It is definitely an emotional separation—not like that which precedes divorce—but more like the separating of Siamese twins—individuation—redefining boundaries.*

And so, I'm back in a "wet" cycle of tears, grief, sadness, low energy, tiredness and a stronger need for alone time. These things mark my days. It feels good to be back under my apple tree. I never tire of the warm sunshine, the fragrant trees and flowers. or the chattering birds. What a restful retreat I find in my backyard.

Chapter Eight

1992
June-December

A Minimalist's Life

God worked on many levels while my healing continued, one being areas of sin.

May 12: *"You, therefore, have no excuse, you who pass judgment on someone else, for at whatever point you judge the other, you are condemning yourself, because you who pass judgment do the same things." (Romans 2:1) It seems to be an epidemic with women and certainly true of me. I pass judgment on other people and deny the fact that I commit the same acts in my own life. When will I ever look at people with Christ's eyes—to see as he sees, to love and forgive rather than hate and condemn? What a challenge.*

During this time, I was in a group for survivors of sexual abuse led by my therapist, John. The women taught me a lot about the healing process.

May 12 (cont.): *It was good to be reminded that God has chosen a unique path of healing for each one of us. And mine doesn't look like anybody else's. The length of time it takes, the different episodes and events, the process—none of it is predictable. Right now, just getting up each morning and living each day is an act of faith. I must put feet to my belief that God has a purpose for me this day and that God has control of how it will go. What a different manifestation of faith that is for me. It is so significant.*

Finding purpose when I was accomplishing nothing was a hard lesson to learn, requiring new levels of trust.

June 7: *So much depression, so much pain, so much struggling—to even get out of bed in the morning.... It is insidious. It permeates my being like an unwelcome visitor. And nothing seems to affect it one way or the other. I feel helpless and at its mercy. I hate it. I hate how it makes me feel. The longer it continues, the worse it gets.*

June 9: *The depression is just insidious. I sleep at least ten hours every night and, in the morning, I spend thirty minutes to an hour trying to convince myself to get out of bed. Anything in my schedule bearing even a little responsibility throws me into a panic and I have to force myself to carry through. Yesterday I almost came undone in the market which was crowded and chaotic. I was so stressed out when I got home that I napped for an hour.*

This was the first time I used the word 'panic,' but it wouldn't be the last. Anxiety became my unwanted, constant companion.

June 9 (cont.): *My voices become more independent of each other and stronger. It is harder to be rational and wise. One voice keeps saying to me, "It's too hard, just quit everything, lock the doors, draw the drapes and wait 'til I feel better."*

The entry was mysterious at the time, revelation still months away. I had no idea why I heard these voices, but they didn't seem like they were my thoughts.

June 9 (cont.): *I was so worried about vast amounts of available time on my hands. What a waste of worry that was. I feel too busy for my energy level and emotional state right now.*

My own issues were plenty to handle, but, as is always the case, other life events still showed up, usually without warning. While spending a week in the mountains at a family retreat center with my father and siblings' families, my dad had a heart attack. We were able to get him down to Denver and be there during the necessary surgery. In spite of the scary circumstances, the outcome was good. A week later my mom had surgery as well. I don't even remember what it was for; probably because she has had over thirty surgeries and I can't keep them straight.

Twelve months had now passed since my healing started, the day I left my little, white cell. I was a long way off from measuring my healing season in years (truly it is a good thing we don't know how long it is going to last), but year one was done. My life had been significantly reduced. I was home, taking care of the family, going to therapy, and trying to survive. Except for seeing a few budget counseling clients, that was about it. Yet as simple as it was, even that felt overwhelming most days. Depression was no longer a visitor—he was resident.

What I didn't know was that a big shift was about to occur.

A Layer of Freedom and Healing!

July 15: *The two-day training seminar with Gary is coming up. I feel that is somehow very important to me. I'm anxious to see what comes of that.*

My pastor asked a group of ten people to participate in a training seminar on spiritual warfare. I was one of the ten. We met for over a week while our leader, Gary, taught us the basics of spiritual warfare and intercessory prayer. What an eye-opener! Even though I had been in the church my whole life, I had never heard anything about the enemy. But it was in Scripture, plain as day.

Gary, a prior church member now serving churches and pastors in Europe, did a lot of ministry with each of us, demonstrating the power and authority of Jesus to clear out the garbage in us. Then we began practicing intercessory prayer with each other. It was exciting to see how much healing was occurring in everyone.

Typical things emerged when we prayed for the other team members, like unforgiveness, sexual sin, pride, fear, anger. My list, however, was different. It included things like witchcraft, the demonic, and death. I found that weird and somewhat disturbing.

Prior to this last year, God seemed bland and impotent to me—almost removed from having any impact on my life. Not anymore. I was now seeing how God's power transcended time and the spiritual realm as he changed my life in palpable and relevant ways.

During several sessions of prayer work with the team, God removed the presence of evil from me, decades-old demonic attachments. I felt the difference immediately. Who knew the Holy Spirit was alive and well and able to work so powerfully? I am pretty sure no one in my church did.

August 3: *"Be joyful in hope, patient in affliction, faithful in prayer.... Do not be overcome by evil, but overcome evil with good." (Romans 12:12, 21) Boy, do I feel and see things differently. I have a new Independence Day—July 29. I am free of an insidious evil. I haven't stopped thanking God yet and I hope I never do.*

(Apparently, 'insidious' was my new favorite word because it kept showing up in my journaling. It's tempting to edit that, but I promised I wouldn't change the entries.)

As I experienced this new freedom, I saw another piece of God's future plan for my life. I had just witnessed crazy healing, life-changing healing, healing I never imagined could be possible. I was intrigued.

August 9: *Love, that's the point—the bottom line. Loving people in a way that helps them love God more and experience his love more, that's what the healing ministry is all about. Everything done in the name of love—binding the brokenhearted, setting the captives free, healing the sick—all so that we can know God's love and serve him better. What shape it's going to take, I have no idea. God has not given me a how or when.*

God was dropping clues about my future, but I wasn't at a place to recognize them.

August 13: *"May the God of hope fill you with all joy and peace as you trust in him, so that you may overflow with hope by the power of the Holy Spirit." (Romans 15:13) There is certainly a heaviness gone from me now. I feel much freer, lighter, more hopeful. I actually feel like doing something. It's been a very long time since I've had that feeling. I love praising God and have much to praise him for.*

It was a wonderful respite from the pain, for as long as it lasted.

The Babysitter

After the training seminar was over, our group continued in the prayer work. One day while we were praying, I started remembering something from my childhood.

September 17: *I was feeling a lot of pain and a strong memory of being four or five years old and having stomach aches and not sleeping. So we went to prayer. While in prayer, a repressed memory came up of a babysitter—Mrs. Hetrick. My mother took a job for a while. The pain and knowledge surfaced that the babysitter molested me, hit me, and yelled at me. It was pretty awful. It was shocking to find this out. But Jesus was right there with me, holding me and helping me through it. But that trauma was the source of my stomach aches and sleeplessness. So, in prayer, God did some healing.*

September 18: *I've always known about the trouble I had as a child sleeping and with stomach aches. I had to take barbiturates at night sometimes. But, until now, I never knew why I had that trouble. When I asked my mom about it, she said it was because I was such a perfectionist and an achiever, and I just couldn't relax. She also mentioned that, for some unknown reason, I was terrified of this babysitter.*

I'm thankful that God has spared me this revelation until a time in my life when healing of it would be available to me. The emotions associated have been so powerful. But God has met me in the memory. He released my fear and bitterness and trauma. He enabled me to forgive Mrs. Hetrick for her vile acts, my mother for leaving me with her, and myself for being violated. Then he took me in his arms and healed me.

It is true that when I was a child, I had frequent stomach aches, particularly when I went to bed. I remember crying because it hurt so bad, begging my mom for the red medicine. The medicine was Phenobarbital, a barbiturate the doctor had prescribed for sleep.

This new memory was strange because, as far as I knew, we never had a daytime babysitter. My mother was a stay-at-home mom. And it was also strange because I was now a mother myself and had new thoughts about the medicine. While I never questioned taking a barbiturate when I was little, now I did. Why was a four-old-year being given a narcotic? Was I really an overachieving, perfectionist at four years old? Really? I couldn't imagine giving this to my kids.

I was reeling in confusion. How could I not remember this babysitter, such a significant part of my life? Why did this surface thirty years later? It was shocking. Adjusting to the truth that I was sexually abused didn't come easily. However, with the Lord's help, I forgave the sitter and let go of the bitterness. Then Jesus healed that little girl and set her free.

Later, I asked Mom if I had a babysitter. She confirmed that she had worked full time for five years, beginning when I was three. This woman was in our home daily for at least three years. Mom added further details, telling me that I would hold onto her leg every morning, screaming, begging her not to leave. When she came home from work, I would be huddled up on the couch, shaking. When I asked her why, she said I had a personality conflict with the sitter. I don't think my mom had any idea what this woman was doing, and I opted not to tell her. But the pieces all fit.

Learning Lessons

October 16: *"I have become its servant by the commission God gave me to present to you the word of God in its fullness.... To this end I labor, struggling with all his energy, which so powerfully works in me." (Colossians 1:25, 29) I am so glad it is God's energy and that his energy is powerful. I'm learning—the process is painful at times, but I'm learning. I must keep current with people. Take out the trash as quickly as it collects. God is always the leader. My role in the ministry is coordinator—not leader. Becoming a real team will take time. The temptation to succumb to weakness lurks at every turn. Staying close to God is my only defense. And the balance between humility and authority is a fine line, yet essential to grasp.*

The lessons kept coming.

November 10: *Being here in Ouray at the retreat apartment is very satisfying and comforting to my spirit.* (John's church had a guest apartment that I frequently used for overnights when we were doing the more intense therapy work.) *I delight in being in my Lord's presence. I eagerly listen for his voice and hang on his every word when he speaks. Somehow the chilly gray snowy day heightens my security in the Lord.... Continue on in faith and patience is the word concerning my job. This seems to be an identity problem. I have no label right now. I am label-less. I am fulfilled in Christ. My time is his to use as he sees fit, just as my money and gifts are his to use. If there isn't a category for people to put me in—that's their problem. I can't fix it. I have no employment.*

The work with the prayer team continued through the fall. Many sessions dealt with the demonic, deliverance work, and spiritual healing.

December 14: *It's been five weeks since I last wrote. What a bumpy five weeks. God seems to be putting a puzzle together—piece by piece. He is working ever so slowly. Sometimes I wish he would just put the whole thing together so I could see and know what it is all about. But when I get close to it, when he hands me the next piece, I am suddenly overwhelmed with feelings of terror…. I'm praying God will continue the process giving me the faith to go with him and face whatever this is.*

As the pain increased from the therapy work, prayer sessions, and new memories, I found it hard to cope with the mounting evidence that I was abused. I couldn't get the pain to stop or even pause for a while, so much so that I wanted to die. For the first time in my life, I was thinking about suicide. It was Christmas Day.

1992 was over. I am glad I didn't know what would happen the next year.

Chapter Nine

1993
January-April

Perspective of Time

The calendar turned over again—1993. This would be the defining year of my restoration, but, of course, I was clueless at this point. It had been eighteen months since my healing journey began, and I thought I was far along. Ha! Every fiber of my being does not want to write about this year.

January ushered in new insights of truth about my identity and the hard place I was in with my healing process.

January 5: Today I gave up my need to have my schedule a certain way. I gave him (God) *permission to prune my personality and make changes where need be. I sense he doesn't want me to work. So, I want to learn to be content with no routine—and no socially acceptable identity.*

Of course, with each round addressing my identity, I thought that was it, done, finished. And, of course, it wasn't. There would be many moments revisiting this before I fully believed the truth about my value and who I was. I had lived as a human doing for a long time and the lessons didn't absorb easily.

At these earlier stages of my recovery, God not only took away my false idols and the things I used to prop up my self-worth, but he kept them away, refusing to restore them. I couldn't understand why he kept my life so hard for so long.

A frustrating facet of the journey was the fact that I never knew how far I had to go. Am I a month away from wholeness? A year? Ten years? It was hard having no inkling of what I was in for.

In more recent years, my perspective has changed. When I was enveloped in my recovery, it seemed like it was taking forever. The days dragged on. The pain dragged on. The unknowing-ness of it all dragged on. As I look back now, viewing it through a lens of freedom and wholeness, I'm struck by how quickly everything moved along. In fact, I can't believe how much happened in a matter of months.

January 9: *I hope I will soon be free of this pain of my relationship with my mother. I feel very guilty, sad, and angry. The guilt is the easiest to feel. It comes out because I am no longer fulfilling my caretaking role. When I realize that I cannot get my needs met (by taking care of my mom)—and never have—I feel the sadness. And then, somewhere lurking in the unsafe territory, are the angry feelings. God have mercy on me and give me strength.*

January 15: *The feelings of terror and pain and grief are very strong. They have a will of their own. The repressed memory fully surfaced on Monday. At first, I thought, "Oh good, it's finally over now that the memory is out." But it is just the beginning. The scab has been picked off and the wound is oozing. And I hurt.*

The Little Girl Emerging

It's interesting, going back and revisiting my entries. So much truth did emerge along the way. Long before the facts and events revealed the whole story, there were clues.

January 20: *The memories are trying to poke out. It's like I'm in an eggshell—hard and fragile at the same time—trying hard to poke holes in the shell to get out. But it's hard work. The memories are slow in coming.*

January 25: *Unending pain. It's hard for me to see the point. It's not working! Why not fix it or throw it away? Why go on and on? What's the point? But, then what's my choice? I can't fix anything—at least not in the relationship area. And I'm not about to check out of life or my marriage. So, if I can't fix it and I can't throw it away, what does that leave me? I know Christ holds all hope of healing, so I must continue to seek him. But it takes so long. When will it ever be better? And what can I realistically hope for? Will there ever be any joy? Will the effects of sin in my life ever be overcome? Patience. That's what comes to me today. My least evident fruit. Be patient, wait, worship, pray. Things will change.*

Again, I now see my perspective was skewed. The memories were not slow in coming; in fact, they didn't stop during these middle years of my healing. My issues escalated quickly as the new year began, including an increase in healing activity.

February 10: *It has been so difficult to write in this journal these past months. I don't know why I have such resistance since it has been such a help in the past. Am I bored with journal writing? Is there so little to process that it isn't worth the effort? Has the value of writing out thoughts and feelings diminished? Why do I have so much trouble being disciplined in my meditation? Am I afraid to probe what's there? Now we are getting closer to the truth. I am afraid for what I'll find and feel. I am afraid to poke at it too sharply because I will hurt. I don't want to hurt anymore. I want to live joyfully and exuberantly. I'm tired of being sullen, withdrawn, and introspective. I don't like these new secrets. I feel so alone, so isolated. I'm still trying hard to make it not true—to make it go away. But it's hard because there is some evidence, proof. Too many things add up.*

Journaling, I learned, wasn't merely a tool for recording the journey. It was a vehicle, drawing out from my inside world what I knew to be true but wouldn't allow my conscious mind to acknowledge. I would write my questions and then the answers would come from within me. Without journaling, the truth remained submerged.

February 10 (cont.): *So I opened myself up to it Sunday. And for four or five hours, the pain was intense. I was terrified, full of panic, a curled-up ball of fear. And when it got to the point I couldn't stand it anymore, I began to sing in my head "Jesus loves me this I know...." And the peace would come over me slowly. And I would start to feel safe again. Then within a couple of hours, I was sick with a fever and sore throat and spent the next three days in bed, during which time I have been unable to think about my emotional memories. What is the process here? Therapy or prayer ministry or both? How much do I need to remember? How much pain do I need to relive? There is a very, very frightened, hurt little girl inside me. She is indeed frightening to me. No one helped her then or since. I guess that explains the strong feeling I have that no one will help me now.*

As soon as I stopped resisting what was happening inside me and instead began cooperating, reality tumbled out with little effort. As is typical, the memory of the emotions arrived before the memory of the event. So I had pain without details.

I had no trouble sensing and acknowledging the little girl in my journaling. So odd, because it was a long time before I accepted her. Why did I have such a disconnect?

That day in February was just one of many times I reacted strangely while in church. While worshiping, I was overcome with anxiety and a strong desire to bolt. It was all I could do to remain there. That afternoon, it was as if some other reality within me took over. I did not feel like an adult, but rather like a small, frightened child. Feeling helpless and lacking any tools to handle the immense pain, the child sang a comforting song about the love of Jesus. How could I be completely overtaken with pain, but not know why?

It took me years to see my pain as a friend. Instead, I viewed it as my enemy—but I was wrong. Pain was my communicator, attempting to tell me where there was a problem that needed attention. Without it, I never would have healed.

Healing in Marriage

February 11: *My very repetitious prayer is that God will bring his truth and light to my life and that nothing false would be allowed in this process. It feels like my body is seized up or wanting to seize up. The terror and fear are the worst part of it all. I want to flee. But flee to where? Flee from what? It feels like I only have a very small glimpse of the picture—maybe only ten or fifteen percent.*

As if I didn't have enough to handle with my recovery, my marriage to Roger was in constant crisis. Our ten years together had been rocky from the beginning. Being married to a Christian counselor set me up for expectations that he would understand what I was going through. But he really didn't. I had no peace in my home or safety in my marriage, making it hard to do the healing work.

February 13: *The pain doesn't go away. It feels like pressure in my chest and in my throat. Roger and I had a terrible interchange Thursday after my session. I can't relate to him anymore. He is the most unkind person I know. His anger at me is relentless. I want to say there is no hope. But I know God is still working here. It is certainly going to take a miracle to ever pull this relationship together again. I wanted to throw him out of the house. I can't work on my own pain and feelings and memories with him anywhere near me because he is so angry, demanding, and impatient. He makes things worse. I feel hatred. But it is a no-win deal. It doesn't work to have him around while I am going through this miserable repressed memory stuff. But if we separate, it will exacerbate the crisis, so I won't be able to work on the issues either. I hate what he has done and is doing. He refuses to acknowledge his part in all this. Or if he does acknowledge it, he does not change one iota. He is the hardest, most inflexible, unteachable person. And he thinks it's all my fault. Just put me on drugs—or in the hospital, as he suggested Thursday. Fix me, so I'll stop being this uncomfortable problem in his life.*

Well, just when I think there is no hope and I can't take it anymore, it gets better. God is certainly hanging in here with us. Roger and I continue to be able to pray together. And that is the only positive thing between us now. When we hold hands and pray together, I feel oppression lift. I believe it deals a mighty blow to the enemy. He will not win.

Roger and I discussed the unethical, sinful beginnings of our relationship and how it laid a bad foundation from which we have continued to build poorly upon. We gave it to God and asked him to restore the foundations. I believe this is an important step.

As mentioned earlier, in 1981, my marriage to Tim was falling apart. After a three-month separation, Tim and I got back together, starting marital counseling with Roger to try and make it work one last time. Jenny was born in the midst of all that.

Shortly thereafter, Tim left our marriage for good and I continued therapy with Roger on an individual basis. A month later, Roger began pursuing me romantically. We had to keep our relationship secret so that he would not be fired from his job.

February 13 (cont.): *I continue to feel and be weepy. I long for the truth, but I'm not sure I'll ever fully know what went on. My life is so bleak. It's hard to see the point. And, it's very difficult to continue pressing on. But, I do so in faith. For nothing means anything to me except following Jesus.*

Blood in the Pool

After several weeks of unexplainable suffering, the truth emerged.

February 17: *I arrived in Ouray yesterday morning. I had two hours with John. We began some more inner healing work, trying to nurture the little girl.*

February 24: *I was unable to finish writing in my journal last week. Each day I have thought about it and have been unable to go back to it.*

April 17: *Well, I still can't—won't write about what's going on. Someday—not today.*

I never did write what happened in February. But I also never forgot. It was so traumatic that I couldn't put the words on paper.

I guess *someday* is today.

After the session with John in February, I headed over to the local hot springs for a relaxing soak. While sitting in the pool, I was suddenly triggered into a past memory and the water appeared to have turned to blood. It felt like I was in two realities at once. Panic overtook me. I fled the pool, repeating over and over, *"Jesus, help me. Jesus, help me."*

I went to the apartment and began praying to God. I began crying out to God, *"I need to hear from you. I need to hear you right now. I am remembering bits of a satanic ritual and I can't deal with this. This is bizarre and it is freaking me out. I need something from you—right now!"* Then I did something I rarely do—I let my Bible fall open and began reading. *"Yet I am poor and needy; come quickly to me, O God. You are my help and my deliverer; O Lord, do not delay." (Psalm 70:5.)* The words resonated with the cry of my soul.

I kept reading until I heard him speak. When I arrived at Psalm 71:20-21, my heart nearly stopped. As if he was in the room, God clearly spoke these words to my heart, which I personalized: *"Though (I) have made (you) see troubles, many and bitter, (I) will restore (your) life again; from the depths of the earth (I) will again bring (you) up. (I) will increase (your) honor and comfort (you) once again."*

This was key in my healing, a promise given to me by God at the moment my life was about to explode again, a promise sustaining me in the hell hole where I would soon fall.

As I read the passage, God's comforting presence settled all around me and he whispered in my ear, *"It's true, Cyndy. But don't despair. I have a plan and will take you through this to the other side."* God was giving me the end of the story at the beginning. He was reassuring me this was something we would *pass through*; it would come to an end.

God wasn't kidding when he said *the depths of the earth*! I would plummet further than I thought anyone could, and still live. But just as he promised, he never let me go.

Latching onto this hope, I wrote the Scripture on a big piece of paper and put it on the wall at home where I would see it often. A thousand times in the coming months, I went back to the passage in Psalm 71, reminding myself God promised to *again bring me up.*

A week later, it happened again. While swimming laps at the community pool, I was triggered and had another panic attack. This time I drove to my church. While my pastor and a few friends prayed, the rest of the memory emerged.

When I was little, maybe four years old, I was at home, in the backyard with my babysitter, wearing no clothes. My brother and sister were watching through the screen door, from inside the house. There were several adults wearing black robes, standing by our blue and yellow kiddie pool. The man in charge wore a heavy, silver pendant with an upside-down cross. There were vile things in the water and the smell was awful. The man said to do what I was told, to get in the water, or he would kill my siblings. I complied.

It was a ceremony for a satanic baptism.

Chapter Ten

1993
April-May

Ostracized

This latest revelation confirmed my feelings that I was certifiably insane. I felt like I was demented, perversely inventing fantasies for some unknown reason. This was all nonsense! After all, I grew up in suburbia, riding bikes, swimming, making mud pies, playing with friends. Like most dads, mine went to work every day. Mom was home, taking care of us kids. (Well, I guess it turns out that past perception wasn't true. But that doesn't mean everything else was wrong, right?)

Normal people don't do satanic rituals and we were normal people. I was certain of it.

The problem was that I couldn't shake the feelings. The terror remained. Try as I might, I could not make myself go back to normal, whatever normal was. Shame and embarrassment were my new companions. But why? What did I have to feel embarrassed about? It never happened.

Even so, I didn't want anyone to find out. Other than my support team, few knew what I was going through. The last thing I needed was judgment; I had enough of that going on all by myself. This aspect of small-town living complicated things. We were well known—the therapist and the Christian Education Director. It was hard to keep secrets in a small town.

So much for being in control; people found out anyway. And my concerns were founded. Judgment was handed down and I became the fodder of gossip. Many friends fell away, no longer feeling comfortable being around me. It was like I had leprosy or something. But, praise God, there were others who held fast and didn't waiver in their commitment and care.

I remember arriving for a beauty appointment with a friend who also attended my church. Her kids had been in my children's program. Without explanation, she told me she wouldn't see me anymore and cancelled. That hurt.

My world spun out of control at this point. I was reeling from the Satanic ritual abuse (SRA) memory. I didn't understand it; I had no reference. I didn't know whether it was true or false or who was behind it. I didn't know where it fit in with my life as I had known it. I did not want to know any of these things, either. Like an animal in a cage, I was trapped in this thing and couldn't get out.

Reviewing My Notes

Except for one week, I didn't journal for four months.

April 17: *I want to put in writing things that I believe to be true and God's promises and reminders to myself. I need some handles to hold on to during the rough times. My mind gets muddled and I can't think clearly as the pain rises. I want to survive this. I will survive this. But I need a lot of help.*

There was a vast ocean of healing still in front of me, none of which I understood. So, as I often did, I went back to what I knew for sure in order to face what I didn't know. I recorded twenty-two things I was convinced were true:

1. *Bringing all this to the light was God's idea.*
2. *He has chosen this time.*
3. *It is right that I take this journey.*
4. *God will heal all this in his time.*
5. *This is going to take a long time, so I need to be patient.*
6. *God loves me and is holding me in his arms every day.*
7. *God will provide every bit of help that I need, when I need it. He is not limited in any way except when I say no to him.*
8. *I need to cry—a lot.*
9. *I need God's help to cry.*

10. *It's okay to be in a state where my emotions are controlling me.*
11. *This journey, however long, will lead to wholeness and a really positive change in how I feel and cope with life.*
12. *This suffering will work itself to an end.*
13. *God has a plan for my life—today and tomorrow—and they are good plans.*
14. *I can count on God to be there every second of the day. I am never alone.*
15. *There are lots of people who love me and who will respond to my cry for help.*
16. *It's okay if I sleep away some days.*
17. *I am not responsible for how other people respond to my suffering.*
18. *It's okay if I don't suffer perfectly.*
19. *Productivity does not measure value, worth, wisdom, or obedience.*
20. *I am doing something when I am grieving, or crying, or meditating, or processing, or even screaming with pain.*
21. *God has a purpose for this suffering.*
22. *I want to survive, to face the past, to heal, and to live.*

I was grateful for my journals for a thousand reasons, but a big one was because they grounded me. Every time I started to feel crazy, I would go back to the beginning and review how I got here. And, every time, it brought me back to truth and clarity: This was NOT my doing. God brought me here. God led my steps. I am not crazy. This is real.

Fighting denial, however, was not a single event. It didn't give up easily; I had to return to this struggle over and over. And each time, this foundation of truth gave me strength to continue into the dark forest ahead of me.

When I recently came upon this list, today, I had no recollection of writing it, but I did have a strong reaction. I was impressed with my thirty-seven-year-old self! But, even more so, I was impressed with God for giving me this amazing list. It shows me how massively helpful it was to have God's truth in me, because, clearly, he is the one who planted it there.

Coping with Uncertainty

April 18: *I was significantly affected by a movie called "A Far Off Place."* (I'm condensing a large narrative about the movie into a brief synopsis.) *Two kids were forced to cross the Kalahari Desert in order to save their lives. If they went back, they would be killed. But going forward meant the scariest journey of their lives. At the edge of the desert, the brother turns to his sister and says, "You didn't tell me how far it was." She then responded, "If I had, you wouldn't have come."*

Like these kids, I was traveling in a far off place—a journey I would never have chosen. I was traveling in dangerous and scary places. Just like the kids had to find new ways to survive and find food or water, so I had to rely more on God's resources to survive as each day got tougher. So many times, the kids thought that their destination was surely over the next dune. But, of course, when they reached the top, they saw only more dunes. Despair set in.

I have said to myself so many times that this must be the end of my suffering. I have finally arrived. Life will be different now. Each time to be profoundly disappointed that there is nothing but more dunes to cross.

So often, I wanted God to give me the map, to show me where we were going and how long the trip would be. He never did. Today I know His silence was an act of mercy because, *"If I had, you wouldn't have come."* Some things are best not known ahead of time. He was also teaching me to trust him.

While it is true that I had paused my journaling, I was still seeing John frequently, trying to process through the meaning of the episode at the hot springs pool. And the prayer team that formed the previous year continued to pray with me. Their intercessory prayer was immensely helpful, quickly revealing the source of issues, and bringing deep healing. The prayer sessions brought healing faster than therapy.

I also went to see a psychologist in Denver, trying to get answers about what was happening to me. He said I did not have Multiple Personality Disorder. What a relief, because some had raised the question.

Real Life Doesn't Stop

Like everyone going through a healing season, real life didn't stop just because I was going through recovery. Even though I hadn't been employed for nearly two years, except for a few weeks when I worked at a bakery (really, a bakery? What on earth was I doing at a bakery? I'm still not sure), I still had my home and family. Laundry never stops.

An opportunity arose to take a part time job, working for friends at their dental practice. I felt like it would be a good fit. So I began working as a hygiene coordinator. Because the dentist and his wife were part of my support team, they knew about my healing journey and that my recovery had to take precedence.

Looking back and considering my instability, it is nothing short of a miracle that I was able to stay employed for three and a half years. God provided understanding employers who went an extra hundred miles for me. The job was a blessing.

Up to this point, I had been home most of the time. There was plenty to do, taking care of the girls, who were now eleven and fourteen and involved in school, sports, and music lessons. I did my best to keep all the plates spinning. Though still today I feel regret and sadness for how little I was there for them emotionally during these years.

In spite of all the challenges, May brought a bright spot for all of us.

Years earlier, I worked with the youth group at my church. As part of that ministry, we took a group of high school students to Washington D.C. to attend a Christian leadership conference. I had been enamored with all the wonderful sights in D.C. and dreamed of going back with my family. Five years later, my dream was fulfilled. We flew to D.C. for a week of sightseeing and then on to Orlando to visit Disney World. We had a fabulous time—one of my favorite life-moments.

However, as these things sometimes go, Jenny got sick in D.C. She had a fever and an ear infection, requiring Roger and I to take turns staying with her in the hotel room our last few days there. This was unfortunate because Jenny was a big Abraham Lincoln fan and we hadn't been to his memorial yet. So, on the last day, I called for a cab, drove straight to the memorial, half carried her up the many stairs, said, *"Okay, there it is,"* and rushed her back to bed. Desperate times…

The next day we flew to Orlando. You've never flown until you've flown with a kid who has an ear infection. All we could do is apologize to everyone on the plane. Our first activity at Disney World was to locate the medical office and get antibiotics. Praise God kids respond quickly to medication.

When we returned to Colorado, I officially started at the dental office. Just weeks later, my recovery picture changed again.

As the SRA memories began to emerge more and more, John felt inadequate to help me. My support team started feeling uncomfortable, too. My stuff was just getting a little too weird. Everyone encouraged me to find someone who understood this new world I had entered.

John was willing to stay involved (a great blessing! I did not want to lose his support), but not to do my primary work. A friend of a friend gave me the name of a therapist in Denver who specialized in this sort of thing, which I decided must be therapy for crazy people.

This is how I came to meet Faith.

Chapter Eleven

1993
June

Journaling Takes Center Stage

After meeting with Faith the first time, I knew I had met someone who could help me. There was just one drawback: the drive to therapy was five hours—one way! But I was so desperate for help, I would have driven to the North Pole at this point.

Faith was the first person who understood this strange world I had entered, who wasn't totally wigged out over what I was remembering. Strange phenomenon that seemed like insanity to me, appeared to make sense to her, allowing me to get focused help.

After our first session, I began journaling again. Apparently, I felt the need to get caught up, because the first entry was *long*.

June 6: *The newsletter* (produced by Faith's ministry) *said journaling helps move things along more quickly. It can make therapy times more fruitful. It can be a very valuable tool at no monetary cost. Those things are important to me. I don't want to use any more resources on this than I have to. Time, money, and emotional energy are the resources. I also don't have to write what I'm not ready to write about. That is what has kept me silent for most of the last 3½ months. I'm not ready, not willing to write what I am remembering. And I don't have to.*

I was referring to the incident in the pool at the hot springs, when my first ritual abuse memory surfaced.

June 6 (cont.): (After reading a newsletter for abuse survivors…) *I realized I too could write—particularly the stream of consciousness writing and dialoguing with myself. There is plenty going on in me that could be shared in my journal. And it doesn't have to make sense. It can be disjointed, weird, chaotic, and contradictory. That certainly describes my thoughts.*

I also realized that I could set aside an hour a day to do my personal work. I have been overwhelmed by all there is to do—all my assignments. There is the daily inner connecting with the little girl. Then there is the reading. I know that if I stray for long periods of time from Scripture, I become confused. The constant prayer is the easiest (assignment) *and I have been very consistent with it. And, of course, the journaling. I've always been so hard on myself. I have to do it perfectly. Statement #18: "I don't have to suffer perfectly." I really need to capitalize on what I can do rather than on what I can't. And I feel I can "show up" most days for one hour for an appointment with myself.*

(Later in the day, I wrote…) *Communion was emotionally and mentally eventful. Water and blood are very hard for me. I feel all churned up at communion and baptisms. Today I kept seeing…* (I described parts of another memory). *I've seen this several times now. As I sat during communion, I could feel the hot tears behind my lids, but I wouldn't let them out. I didn't want anyone to see me crying because I was serving communion. I kept flashing to previous scenes, memories.*

My pain level has been really high for four days. It started when I called Faith. I told her how hard it's been and the terrible effect it was having on my marriage and how I desperately needed to talk to someone who has been where I am. She reassured me and said how normal all these things are. She said it is normal to not really know what has happened to me. She told me that I'm not crazy and that it will come when I am ready.

('Normal' became my new favorite word.)

"One thing is certain—something happened." (That statement that Faith made) *jolted me out of this semi-denial I've been living in for weeks. It is like I woke up from a deep sleep only to find the pain staring me in the face again.*

She was right. Something had happened to me. There was no doubt whatsoever. I just didn't know what. I had been stalled out for months, my denial fighting against the truth, trying to not see what I had clearly seen. I didn't want to believe it. I couldn't believe it. But the more I indulged my denial, the crazier I felt and the more confused I became.

Connecting with Faith really helped me get back on track and start moving forward in my healing. Just when I arrived at a place where I needed someone else to help me continue on, God provided the right person.

June 6 (cont.): *I told the girls. I had to. They kept coming in and finding me crying. I got past the lie that I had to tell everything. They certainly couldn't handle everything. So I told them abuse—sexual, physical, mental—a long time ago—not involving grandma or grandpa. I don't know what the girls felt or thought. I told them—babysitter and some other people.*

The girls handled it surprisingly well. Bree grasped the issues with discernment beyond her years, being articulate in her feedback to me. I'm sure it helped them to be brought into the truth. I think parents too often try to shelter their kids from the truth of matters impacting their lives, thinking they are protecting them. When, all the while, their silence is increasing their kids' anger, fear, and anxiety. Kids often blame themselves, thinking they are the cause of the problem.

Kids know more than we think they do. They usually see the problems and they always feel the tension and stress. Talking is good. I should have done more of it.

Parts are Talking

June 6 (cont.): *And I spiraled down, down, down. I tried to talk to the little girl* (inside me)*, but I only saw scary monster faces, so I quit. I ran so hard the next day, just like every day for the last five weeks. There is a war in my head. I hear this voice say, "Stop! Don't do it! Stop running. Don't push yourself. It can wait. You don't have to do it all today. It's okay. I'm hurting. Pay attention to me. I need your help. Please stop. Please just stop for a little while."*

But it always loses to the other voice. It is like trying to stop the entire Marine Corps. It is powerful, formidable, unstoppable. The voice says, "I can't. It's better if I get it all done. Don't let the standards drop. You must be perfect. It's best this way. As soon as this all gets done, then I'll take a break and relax. This all must be done first—now."

And now I realize there's a third voice. She is saying, "Yes, please do it all. Please do it all right and perfectly. Hurry and get done before she sees you. Don't let anything go. Hurry, hurry, she's coming soon. She said if I'm a bad girl then the bad people will come and take me again. But they come anyway. Look! They're at the door. I must be really bad because they're here again. I see them at the door and then that's all. I don't see anything else. I tried so hard, but I was a bad girl anyway. I tried so hard. What did I do? Why won't anybody tell me? Why did the bad people come again? I'll be good, I promise, please, please, please. I don't want to go. Please don't make me. No, no, no, NO, NO!"

Friday night I sought out the little girl again. (In my mental prayer vision) *I was outside the cabin, by a bush, sitting on the ground. I soon realized I was crying. So much so that I slumped over in the dirt. Jesus came over to me and put my head on his lap. He stroked my hair. After a while, I sat up and he said he wanted me to see something. We would watch it together and he would hold me and not leave me.*

(I continued writing about a long flashback or vision of abuse involving cult people and the little girl.)

June 6 (cont.): (Still in my mental prayer vision) *I said, "I need to be washed, purified," that I wanted some more of the water. Jesus took me to the river and dipped me down into it. He said, "With this water, I once again purify you." Then I noticed the little girl, for the first time. Jesus took her into the river, too. As he dipped her, he said, "I baptize you in the name of the Father, the Son, and the Holy Spirit. By this water you are made clean." Then I took her over to a hammock and we got in together and cuddled and soaked up the warmth of the white light above us and around us.*

What does this mean? What is this stuff? I'm so tired, I just want to sleep.

What was happening to me? What was I hearing? Why was I so disrupted inside? What were these different voices that I was suddenly noticing? It was a mystery to me. I had never felt so out of control or strange.

Fighting Against Acceptance

June 7: *I feel a little better tonight, less panic and anxiety, more energy. Ran hard today. I told myself several times to do my "hour"– to keep my appointment with myself—but I didn't. I skipped it. I feel bad and guilty. So, I actually wrote the appointment in my book for Tuesday, Wednesday, and Thursday. We'll see if that helps.*

(A woman on the prayer team) *confuses me. I feel afraid about her. I tried to share my feelings, but she doesn't hear. I feel truckloads of anger from her. I try to stand and speak, "I'm not a victim anymore. I can choose what I will accept from people. I can say something doesn't work for me." But those things seem to cause further conflict. God help me.*

This person had an agenda for me, assuming what I needed and should do, and was working hard to impose it on me. The more she did, the more my alarm bells went off. I chose to back off from our relationship. It was an important step of healing for me to refuse to receive from people who felt unsafe to me. I didn't have to say yes to everyone.

June 7 (cont.): *I like work but I dread the responsibilities at home this week. I feel so fearful and inadequate regarding church things in particular—the retreat, adult education, session. So why on earth am I meeting with* (a friend) *regarding fundraising? Because I can't shake it—the ideas, the passion, the vision for it. But I can't do it! Can't they see that? It's too much. Stop! Please stop! It hurts too much. Make it stop, make it stop.*

Life was a no-win. My passion for ministry never stopped, but I was drowning in memories and pain. So I did this yo-yo routine, getting back into a few ministry things, then feeling like I was going to implode, then backing off from everything. But then the old passions would surface…

June 8: *"My life is consumed by anguish…. My times are in your hands…" (Psalm 31:10a, 15a) I have a deep thirst for truth, help, and knowledge. I need to drink deeply from God's water, his river of life. The tide of pain rises sharply tonight. I want to cry. My stomach hurts. I want to throw up. I have had a headache all day. Mostly I want to have an all-out panic attack. I'm swirling down. It's getting darker. I see less and less. I look up to God, but I don't know what he wants. Leave me alone. I can't do anything right now. Go away and leave me alone. Let me be. The compulsive pushing has stopped.*

June 8 (cont.): I drew a picture of a church and a small voice said, *"We have to go in there. I don't like the old church. It makes me feel really bad. The people there are very bad to me and I don't like it." I'm coming unwrapped. It's leaking out again. This could be very bad.*

June 10: *I'm doing better, but I don't know why. I had energy about mid-afternoon. But I still didn't want to work on church stuff—the reports, reading. It's been almost two years since I've had my job at the church. Part of me hasn't let go. I can see myself back in my old office, sorting through my files and cleaning out my belongings. Only this time I am violently throwing files at the wall. The papers are flying everywhere and I'm swearing and yelling. Why did they take my job away? I love my job. I gave my blood and sweat to it. No one appreciated how hard I worked; how much I gave. It's gone. The little girl thinks she lost her job because she was bad, and nobody wanted her. I've never admitted that. I have tried to be mature—it was God's plan. He led us all to that end. It wasn't personal. It didn't reflect on my performance or worth as an employee. That is what I have told myself. But I don't believe it. No one wanted me. No one ever wanted me. Rejection—bitterness—pain—anger.*

June 11: (I drew another picture.) *I stare at the picture of the little girl, the one in front of the fireplace. I try to know her, to relate to her, to imagine myself being her, but I can't. I don't ever see what she looks like. She is a form with limbs, hair, and feelings, that's about it.*

June 13: (After I had been reading a book for survivors of sexual abuse, I wrote the following, fulfilling Faith's assignment to check in with the little girl. Apparently, we had ice cream together.)

Me: *Did you like the ice cream?*

Little Cindy: *Yes. It was good and creamy.*

Me: *Do you know I'm reading this book?*

Little Cindy: *Yes.*

Me: *How does it make you feel?*

Little Cindy: *Very sad. There are so many little children like me. So many of us got hurt like this.*

Me: *What else are you feeling?*

Little Cindy: *My stomach hurts again.*

Me: *Do you know why it hurts?*

Little Cindy: *Because of all the bad feelings.*

Me: *Can you tell me about the bad feelings?*

Little Cindy: *I'm really worried and afraid. If I'm not good enough, the bad people are going to come and get me. I'm trying to be good. I try all the time, but the bad people come anyway. They hurt me and make me scared.*

Me: *I'm not going to let those bad people come anymore. You're safe tonight. And you can be as bad as you want, and it will be just fine with me. I'll make sure no one hurts you. So, just try to relax and be yourself.*

Little Cindy: *Will you hold me? I feel lonely.*

Me: *Yes.*

I had been hearing conversations in my head for a while. But today it was different. This time it was a distinctive dialogue between me and someone else. I recorded the conversation even though I did not understand what was happening. However, the more I acknowledge the little girl inside, the more I could hear what she needed to say.

June 14: *The visit in Denver opened up wide channels for me. I met with Faith and* (the same psychologist I saw on April 22) *later in the day. So much to write about but I'm too tired. I'll write tomorrow.*

June 15: (After the two sessions in Denver, I began to process what happened.) *It was hard. She* (Little Cindy) *came back today. And she wanted her mommy and daddy. She cried and was scared and lonely. We laid in bed for a long time with her doll. She just kept saying, over and over, "I want my mommy and daddy." I have pains—cramp like—it hurts. I couldn't move for a while.* (The psychologist) *asked her who knew how the blood got all over her. She said, "Tammy. Tammy knew." Who's Tammy? That doesn't mean anything to me.*

She was triggered when she saw the word "blood" on the church building. I let her come out. So she went to the counseling session instead of me. Faith told the Marine Corps they could step aside now for a while. She told them they had done a really good job of protecting her all these years and now it was safe to step aside. And there she was.

Years. Years. Can I do this for years? Three hours in bed. Half the day cancelled. Unbelievable pain—alone—no one is with me—scared—all alone. I want someone to hold my hand and tell me I can get through this. It's okay. I can do it. It won't always be like this. But I'm alone and confused.

She talked about the bad people and… (more memory fragments). *Parts are missing. The picture is incomplete. Who knows? I love Faith. I felt at peace. She listened to me. It's all true. She knows. She's seen it before. It all adds up. My world—false views—are caving in. I can't pretend it didn't happen. I'm at peace. I'm in pain. I'm scared. I'm dreading all the tomorrows. God help me. Don't leave me.*

June 16: *It's true. It's my life. I can't deny it. It keeps adding up—explaining things—fitting with other parts of my life.*

June 18: *Why can't I be normal? Why can't I have a normal life? I don't want to do this for years and years. God help me. A piece at a time. A day at a time. An hour at a time. A memory at a time. A stage at a time. That's enough—too slow, but enough. Will I ever get to where the pain and memories don't overwhelm me? Will I ever be able to have days that are laid back and relaxed but without pain? Will I get to the place where I don't have to work compulsively in order to have a break from pain?*

I want to sleep. I want to stop. But I have packing and food prep still to do. But I'm tired and I'm sad. And now my stomach is starting to hurt. And there is anxiety about the family gathering this weekend.

Family Reunion

My family had been having reunions for several years, my siblings and our children, with our parents alternating attendance each year. It had been a special time, being altogether in a cabin in the mountains. Watching the kids play, hiking, making meals for the whole gang, playing the guitar and singing as a group was great fun.

I was getting ready to head to the "high country" and repeat the annual event, even though it was difficult to muster up the needed energy.

My anxiety was high, but I held it together for the weekend. I was glad because the kids had a blast. Unfortunately, it would be the last reunion. As details of my recovery became known to the family, the response would be hostile.

June 23: (After a brutally violent nightmare…) *It was horrible. Such terror and fright. I drifted off again and was right back in the nightmare. I forced myself awake—repeat: Jesus, Jesus, Jesus, Jesus—don't stop till it's time to get up. Later—find the little girl—she's extremely upset—you can't go to work with her like that. She's in bad shape—so are you. I'm looking—there she is—hiding under the bed, shaking. She readily comes out—into my arms. She has burrowed herself into my chest with a blanket over her head and over me, too. I told her the bad people wouldn't come back today—she was safe. I had to go to work, but Jesus would take my place and she could stay where she was for as long as she wanted to. Three hours later—it still hurts so much—the pain the nightmare brought. I'm trying to work. But I can't seem to work hard enough to blow it out of my thinking. Finally, it recedes. How many more of these will I have? How long will it go on? What happens to the children? I don't want to know—that's why I wake up before I find out.*

I got what I wanted. I was working again, but at a price. The position at the dental office took tremendous energy to perform my expected duties with all this ugly stuff going on in my healing process.

June 24: *"For you were once darkness, but now you are light in the Lord. Live as children of light…. Have nothing to do with the fruitless deeds of darkness, but rather expose them…. But everything exposed by the light becomes visible…" (Ephesians 5:8, 11, 13)*

Me: *Little girl, do you hear these words of Scripture?*

Little Cindy: *Sort of.*

Me: *What do you hear?*

Little Cindy: *God is helping you by shining his light down on me. He is helping you by being with you so you can hear me.*

Me: *Is there anything in those verses for you?*

Little Cindy: *He's going to fix my pain and give me a better life. Jesus' light helps me, too.*

Me: *That's good. We both need his help.*

Tammy: *That's great for you guys but, what about me? When is someone going to help me?*

Me: *I'm afraid of you.*

Little Cindy: *But she's in trouble, too.*

Me: *How do you know?*

Little Cindy: *I feel her pain and confusion. She's thrashing around.*

Me: *I know. I hear her, too.*

Tammy: *Well, at least someone knows I'm alive.*

Me: *You are very confusing to me. Tell me about yourself so I can understand better.*

Tammy: *I'm fat. I hate my body. It's bad, bad. I can't handle it. I just want to zone out and go to sleep. I hate this.*

Well, I'd finally met Tammy. It's weird how my parts knew each other, but I didn't know them, none of them. What a strange world I was in. I was doing my assignments, like I was told, but it seemed surreal.

June 28: *I feel confused. What is this "little girl" work? Is it real? What are the other voices? I am curious who the girl is in the pond drawing today.*

?: *You*

Me: *At what age?*

?: *14*

Me: *What's her name?*

?: *Tammy*

Me: *I've never been called Tammy or referred to myself or thought of myself as Tammy. So how can she have this name?*

?: *You never knew about her till now.*

Me: *Who are you? Are you Tammy?*

?: *No-she's very shy. She's not ready to talk.*

Me: *So can you tell me who you are? I feel you strongly, but I can't tell who you are. You seem old, scarred, hard, worldly, a little scary, and not very familiar.*

?: *I'm the bad one.*

Me: *The bad what?*

Bad girl: *I'm the bad girl.*

Me: *Why are you bad?*

Bad girl: *When the bad stuff had to be done, I did it. Somebody had to—and you were absolutely gone—so I did it.*

Me: *Are you mad about that?*

Bad girl: *No, I don't really care anymore.*

Me: *You're lying.*

Bad girl: *The alternative is too painful. Go to bed.*

Hmmm… I wasn't even sure these parts were real, but they were beginning to identify themselves. And one was even bossing me around. Interesting. But, I'm not multiple, right? The doctor said I don't have multiple personality disorder. It was all very confusing.

Chapter Twelve

1993
July

Accepting the Letters

I settled into a pattern that would continue for three years, working at the dental office while trying to fit in regular trips to Denver for my therapy work. I typically made the drive once a month, seeing Faith every day for three to four days. When I was home, my part-time work hours were flexible, allowing me to be home when the girls got out of school.

After my first appointment with Faith, I called her. I had been having terrible nightmares and the voices were getting more involved. I told her that somebody named Brenda wanted to talk to her. Suddenly, someone else in me was talking out loud with Faith, but it wasn't me (or it didn't seem like it was me).

Despite the in-your-face-reality of different parts talking to me, I refused to consider that I might really be a multiple. In fact, I sought several opinions, looking for someone who would offer me another explanation for my strange behavior. When I met with the last therapist and she said to me, *"What is it that you don't get, Cyndy? You came into my office with a list of different personalities, each with names, ages, and characteristics,"* I finally gave up looking for some other reason and accepted my new normal. I was a survivor of abuse and I now had six letters behind my name: SRA (Satanic Ritual Abuse) and MPD (Multiple Personality Disorder). (The therapeutic community was transitioning to the new term, Dissociative Identity Disorder or D.I.D., during this time).

I was horrified about the whole thing. The SRA was bad enough, but MPD? Come on, that's ridiculous! If I felt like a freak before, I felt doubly so now. My shame was intense. Again, that whole small-town dynamic thing wasn't doing me any favors, either. Hardly anyone had ever heard of these things.

Once my inner system of alters (the different parts of my personality) knew there was someone to help, more parts quickly emerged and began telling their stories, describing different types of abuse from many different directions. It was often hard to make sense of any of it.

July 3: (When I did my little-girl work, I often saw her in my mind by a stream in the mountains, either inside or outside a cabin. While I was checking in with Little Cindy today…) *I could see three but sensed there were four. As I looked inside for the little girl, I noticed she was with someone. There were two little girls playing with the rocks in the dirt by the stream. One was the bad girl. She was bigger and stronger, tougher than the little girl. She was full of rage and I felt her desire to break things. I couldn't tell if she was older or just bigger. She could have been anywhere from four to seven years old. I saw the third girl off by herself—in view of the others, but alone. She was reading a book. I couldn't see the fourth. Jesus was by the rock, watching, overseeing the girls.*

The World of the Multiple

I would never expect a person to understand how the world of the multiple works, having never had the experience of living in it. It is sort of like trying to understand what is going on in a house by peering in the windows. You can catch glimpses, but that's about it. Only a multiple can fully know what it's like to be in the house.

For someone outside the world of multiples, it might be hard to understand how one aspect of you can communicate with another aspect of you. But, really, it isn't that different from talking to yourself, something most people do from time to time. Even today, when I haven't been multiple for twenty-five years, I say things to myself like, *"Get a grip, Cyndy. You're worrying about something that hasn't even happened. Think positively!"* My self-talk is simply trying to move my thoughts to a healthier place.

Multiple or not, there is a tremendous amount of truth and knowledge inside us, truth we never access or acknowledge because our rational brain won't allow it. We resist because we fear the truth. But if we want to know, we can find out more, simply by going inside ourselves and asking.

This journal entry is recording what I saw when I did this. I went inside and asked. Because I was multiple, fragmented by abuse, different parts of me had information and truth to share. Working with the parts was a powerful process and essential to my healing.

July 3 (cont.): *The bad girl stood up as I approached. I wondered why I hadn't seen the others before, when I had previously visited her, but the bad girl said they had always been there—I just couldn't see them. There are others, too. She wasn't angry or anything—she was quite verbal and seemed to know a lot. She told me her name was Brenda. She took me over to where Tammy was. I could feel so much pain and loneliness when I got near Tammy. Brenda said to not get too close. "Don't disturb her—she's not ready."*

I asked Brenda where the fourth girl was. So, we walked out behind the cabin. We found her high up in a tree. She wanted to see what was out around this immediate area. She invited us up. Brenda would have gone up, but I didn't want to. It seemed hard and scary to try to get all the way up there. Barbara was dazzling. She seemed older, maybe 17 or 18. She was energetic, confident, capable, and irresistible. Brenda told me she was the one who did job interviews. She reminded me of the time in Delta when I applied for two jobs and was offered both of them. Well, Barbara did it. "She's great. We can always count on her for that sort of thing," said Brenda. "She performs, too." I didn't talk to Barbara, but I couldn't help but notice how beautiful she was.

We walked back to the cabin area and found the little girl asleep in Jesus' lap. Brenda said the little girl didn't ever like to be alone, so Brenda usually stayed with her so she wouldn't be afraid. Brenda thought the little girl had probably gotten scared when Brenda left and so she sought comfort from Jesus. Apparently, the little girl frequently used sleep as an escape. I asked Brenda what the little girl's name was. She said, "Little Cindy. We've always called her that."

I hugged Brenda and told her she wasn't a bad girl. It wasn't her fault, whatever happened. I told her we would talk about what happened to her sometime when it was safe, and someone was there to help us. She seemed okay about that. I told all four of the girls that I felt it was going to turn out well. We had help now and there were safe places for us. I told them I appreciated each of them a lot. I felt loving and caring toward them. Then I left.

I drew a picture of the girls and where I had seen them. (One was sitting with Jesus, one leaning on a tree trunk, reading a book, and the third high up in a tree.) *But I couldn't draw Brenda. I don't know why. How many voices now? Voice #1, Marine Corp., Little Cindy, Teenager, Brenda, Barbara, Tammy—seven.*

I never knew where their names came from, exactly. They just came up with their names and told me.

July 5: *Finding four girls in my safe place was really unnerving to me. I wish someone would help me sort this out. I have new body things going on. The sensitivity in my mouth has been going on for a couple of weeks. I'm still feeling a strange sensation in my pelvic area. My knee hurts all the time. And now I keep seeing my arms pulling my body up onto something. It seems like I'm escaping from something. I can feel the strain of my arms trying to pull all my weight up. That's all I know.*

I was months away from knowing what this memory was about. In the meantime, I continually had this sense of needing to pull myself up by my arms, and that my life depended on it. Trying to get a memory out was like being in endless labor, feeling discomfort and pain for weeks. Except there was one big difference—I was giving birth to a monster, not a baby. There would be no relief until the memory fully emerged.

July 5 (cont.): *There was an important dream some time ago. It needs to be recorded because it is critical in nature. In the nightmare I was walking around a building toward the front of a garage. As I approached, I looked into the garage. No cars were parked in it. There were things around the perimeter but basically the concrete floor was clear except that there was a machine running—like the street construction crews use to cut up asphalt road surfaces. An unknown man was operating the machine and had already made a few long cuts in the concrete, but the concrete was still in place. However, it was moving so much it looked like canvas fabric being cut with scissors. Then I noticed there was a small opening in the concrete and underneath was an open area like the hold of a ship. The area was filled with children and I could hear their blood curdling screams coming from the opening. I was then totally freaked out. The man said he was sorry he had to show me what happened to the children. Then I woke up.*

Never before my season of healing, or afterward, did I have such strong and graphic dreams. Prior to all this, I didn't remember my dreams, but that wasn't true anymore. Now they were a vehicle God was using to get my attention and prepare me.

July 11: *I met number eight—Marianne.*

July 12: *I realize so much of my energy goes out with the nearly constant pain, traumatic memories, and new discoveries about myself that I don't have much left for other, everyday stress. Family takes some, work takes some, and those demands alone exceed what is available at times. That's why I have to keep stress to a minimum. There are no available reserves. I don't want to spend what I do have on non-essentials or negatives. Relaxing, resting, letting the hours pass gently feels good. I feel more in control. I'm being restored during these times.*

(Later that day, I was lying in bed praying when I heard my daughters and their friends playing, making noise.) *They were screaming and laughing and carrying on. Instantly, I was full of rage. I felt something* (inside) *want to scream and scream and scream. It was strong and irrational—out of character—scary. I looked inside seeking the source of the rage.*

I asked Brenda to tell me who it was that reacted. She said, "Alex." I didn't know if that was a male or female name. Brenda said they don't have much to do with Alex because he's so touchy. She said he pushed (my brother) *down once. He holds the angry feelings. He is very sensitive to loud noises and commotion. I thanked Brenda for helping. Now my stomach hurts.*

It is common for alters to be both male and female, assuming the best persona for their role in the system. Alters are usually a variety of ages, as well. Sometimes they even have different accents. For more information about alters, SRA, MPD, DID, and dissociation, see the glossary.

The list of alters kept growing. The more I accepted the parts inside, the more comfortable they became, sharing themselves. Journaling was key to giving them a voice. Artwork was another helpful tool. I have never been artistic, but neither had I ever been a writer. Nevertheless, creating drawings and pictures helped my story be told. The more opportunities I provided for my parts to share, the more progress I made.

July 13: (As I got out art paper and markers, a strong voice began to direct me while I was drawing. What emerged was a dark, scary picture.)

Me: *Alex, why did you want to draw this picture?*

Alex: *Because it tells the truth. Nobody ever told the f******* truth.*

Me: *I don't know what to say.*

Alex: *Figures.*

Me: *Are you real?*

Alex: *Would you have made a drawing like that?*

Me: *No, it isn't nice, and it isn't pretty.*

Alex: *Well, la-di-da. You make me sick.*

Me: *Why?*

Alex: *You're just so out of touch with reality.*

Me: *Are you always angry like this?*

Alex: *Why don't you go f*** yourself.*

Me: *Why are you so mad at me? I'm trying to understand you and listen.*

Alex: *Oh right. Like you really want to know the truth. You're such a useless piece of s***.*

Me: *No, I'm not. I'm doing a good job of receiving the truth. Maybe it isn't happening as fast as you'd like, but it's plenty fast for me. I'm not interested in arguing with you. Is there anything else you want to tell me about the picture?*

Alex: *Show it to everyone. I want them to know the children died and what they did to them. Somebody needs to cry for the children. Oh, by the way, I'm 14. You wanted to know that last night.*

Me: *Thanks for drawing the picture, Alex. I'll try to keep listening to you.*

"Just sign me up for the nearest insane asylum," I thought to myself, quite often.

If I was journaling, I had no problem dialoguing with my parts and listening to them. They felt as distinct as if I were talking to another human being. When I closed my journal, however, that was another story. I was confused and unsure of what it all meant. I didn't want them to be part of my day-to-day life. I didn't want them to be real.

One side of me agreeably did this work with my alters, another side just couldn't accept it. But only when I did do this work with them, did I start to improve and heal.

Self-Care, a Foreign Language

Journaling with my parts was just one of my endless assignments. This entry helped me connect to myself and my needs. Having spent my life taking care of other people, I didn't have any idea who I was or what I liked. Faith wanted me to learn how to take care of myself, particularly when the pain was high.

July 27: *Things that make me feel better, help me relax, or escape in a non-destructive way:*

Eating ice cream
Eating peanut M & Ms

Sleeping
Diet Pepsi
Reading fiction
Praise music
Cross stitch
Sitting at the park
Talking to a close friend
Being in God's presence
Worship
Bubble baths
Praying
Buying clothes
Some movies
Going to the mall
Tea
Breathing
Drinking water
Getting warm
My doll
Holding my cats
Playing my guitar
Painting
Going out to lunch
Soaking in the hot springs

Learning to relate to myself was a foreign concept. Until now, my life-focus had been to size up every person, figure out what they needed or required from me, and then give it to them. (Cult survival skill number one.) What I wanted or needed never entered the conversation. How could I expect others to see me and respect me if I couldn't see me? If I didn't respect me?

And, as I already said, real life doesn't stop just because you're in a major healing crisis. I was constantly contending with marital issues.

July 28: *When it gets hard and bad and ugly, I just stop writing.*

Roger and I were not getting along.

July 31: (I met another part.) *Teresa Lynn King, age 25, gets me out of bad marriages. She's one tough mama. "Just pack up your stuff and get in the van and go to Florida and buy a trailer. Have your lawyer draw up the papers and don't look back. Time to start over. I can't believe you've stayed this long. What a waste. Come on, wake up and smell the roses. He manipulates you, goes behind your back. You can't believe anything he says, and he never keeps his commitments to you. You can't trust him. It's time to check out of this relationship."*

*"He has controlled you all these years with his threats, rage, and psychological s*** and rules. Stop playing his game. He doesn't have your best interests in mind. He's bad news. If you ever even think about sleeping with him, so help me I'll kill you. Do you like being violated? Only you can put an end to it. Stop listening to him, stop cooperating with him, stop playing his manipulative games. Don't put the guns down; don't put your guard down. If you can't get out of here, at least stay and fight. Don't give in for nothing."*

Oh, wow! How was I to maintain in my marriage with all that carrying on inside. My marriage was more than messy. It was hard to sustain my equilibrium in any arena.

Chapter Thirteen

1993
August-September

Understanding Dissociation

August 1: *"You, O LORD, keep my lamp burning; my God turns my darkness into light." Psalm 18:28. There's that hope again. The day will be a glad one when the darkness is gone, when it becomes light. I long for God's truth and his wisdom. The information comes as fast as I will let it out. But I don't like it when it comes out.*

Someone was taking pictures—cameras—children being used (in acts of sexual abuse)*—people watching—lights—stage—cameras—Marianne was there—Barbara, was she there? She's too old to be there. Warehouse—concrete floors—pornography—*(the man in my dream recorded on July 5th) *said it had to do with pornography before he led me under the concrete to where the screaming children were. Used—abused—people watching—it was a show—souvenir pictures—the ultimate thrill—I was there—No! No! No! Go away!*

Fragments of unbelievably horrible memories were flooding out. I wasn't looking for it. They just arrived, unwanted and unexplained. I was in a living nightmare and could not find a way to wake myself up.

August 2: *Confusion, pain, doubt, clarity, answers, more questions, heaviness on my chest. It can't be, it has to be. What am I supposed to believe? Is it true? Where did it come from?*

August 26: *What to write—how to write. I'm still swimming in a vast ocean. There is still no shoreline visible. I'm still swimming from one buoy to the next. I thought this time in Ouray would be a buoy, but instead it is a storm on the ocean. I have been underwater as much as on the water. I'm sleeping half the time. In the last 24 hours I have slept 14 hours. The other 10 have been fruitful and traumatic.*

I talked with the teenager—Matilda. She is another hard one with a really negative view of her body. She is alone, isolated, unhappy, angry. But she must be hurt, too, because she disappeared when I asked her if anyone ever told her she was fat and ugly.

(I then recorded a terrible dream involving Tammy and a priest and many rounds of violent, sexual abuse.) *It was over. I was awake. All of my nerve ends were tingling. My body felt like it had really been through all this. Then Patty began talking to me.*

I now knew the roles that alters Tammy and Patty played in my system. They took over whenever there was sexual abuse. They handled it so I didn't have to. Tammy and Patty saved me.

Having come into my healing journey with zero knowledge of dissociation (unless you count Hollywood's version), I had a steep learning curve. It was on-the-job-training. It wasn't hard for me to understand it because I was living it. I was literally experiencing the cause of dissociation, the reason for dissociation, the expression of dissociation—traumatic abuse.

As I got deeper into my own story and these new levels of abuse emerged, I began to see the phenomenon of dissociation differently. There's no way a child can mentally, physically, or emotionally handle the things that evil people do to them. Dissociation wasn't insanity. Just the opposite; it made perfect sense. It was a mechanism God created to allow children to survive unspeakable abuse and horror. It was a process designed by a merciful God to protect the child.

When a child experiences something that is intolerable, they have to find a way to change the reality of their pain so they can survive. It's not so different from a doctor who induces a coma when treating a burn victim because the pain is intolerable the first days or weeks. There is no amount of pain medication that will make the burn patient comfortable, so the coma allows them to survive. Dissociation creates the same relief by putting the trauma away in a compartment.

Everything that defines that compartmentalized trauma (the physical sensations, the emotions, what was seen and heard), then takes on a life of its own in an alternate personality. It remains separate from the child, perfectly preserved as if the trauma occurred that morning, until such a time when help arrives and the memory can be resolved. This usually doesn't happen until adulthood, if ever.

Learning these things helped me understand what was happening to me. As I began reliving the memories, I understood that my parts saved me. I needed their help, because I had been literally frightened beyond my ability to endure. My parts took the abuse, so I didn't have to. Yes, it is true that my parts were still me, but they had operated independently, outside my knowledge for thirty-five years.

August 26 (cont.): *At that point, the kids* (my parts) *wanted to paint. It was really fun. We were having a good time. There were cult pictures, symbols, designs, blood, snakes. Then John* (a new part) *wanted to paint a picture of hanging from the bars and he painted snakes under his feet. That's when we all went into crisis. John had remembered the snakes. Little Cindy was terrorized. The panic escalated. John* (my therapist) *came and helped us* (mentally) *get rid of the snakes and calm down.*

Brain Changes and Body Memories

My mind was beginning to release the facts of the event causing my recent body memories. The process I was going through was textbook. The body memories and emotional memories were coming first, with the cognitive memory trailing behind.

When someone is abused or traumatized, it isn't simply a set of facts, like a news item, it is a full-body experience.

Trauma affects the thoughts because the mind continually replays the incident. It challenges our beliefs, attempting to impose lies about our value and God's love. It affects the heart, too, the place that holds the emotional pain of betrayal, rejection, and abandonment, and more.

The trauma also lives in the brain, changing how the brain processes information. Trauma literally alters the brain, changes that can be detected on a scan. It changes *how* survivors respond to perceived threats, and even *what* they perceive is a threat. A child who hasn't experienced trauma might be afraid of a man they don't know. Whereas a child who was abused by a man, might be afraid of all men. A child untouched by abuse is often afraid of the dark. An abused child might be afraid of everything outside their small, familiar world, day and night.

A child with a traumatized brain won't know how to respond appropriately to different levels of threat. A spilled and broken glass of milk might cause the same reaction as a nearby explosion. Traumatized neurological systems simply don't work correctly, making it common for survivors to live with elevated stress hormones all the time. This, then, can lead to fatigue, illness, and learning challenges. Because the brain never calms down and rests, neither does the body.

When you live with these disproportionate responses for years and realize so-called 'normal' people don't respond the way you do to life, that they aren't chronically stressed like you are, then you begin to believe you are damaged at the core of your being. It affects your identity at a deep level, and you can begin to see yourself as hopeless.

In addition to all that, the survivor's body bears the physical reality of the trauma. What they physically endured is imprinted in their muscles, tissues, organs, etc. Our bodies remember what happened to us physically, even when our minds do not. This is one reason why abuse and trauma lead to so many health problems, diseases, and autoimmune disorders—the body is holding the trauma. Intercessory prayer work is effective for this aspect of healing, as is Splankna and EMDR (Eye Movement Desensitization Reprocessing).

Accepting the facts of what happened is the most difficult part for the survivor. This is why the subconscious protects the survivor by holding the information in a compartment, effectively hiding it from them. Until the mind is ready to release the truth, clues erupt in the form of emotions and body memories. Survivors then begin to experience the same feelings they did at the time of the trauma, and the body begins reliving the physical sensations. It is a crazy-making process because the survivor has no idea why they feel certain things in their body.

If they go to a doctor, it is highly likely they won't receive any help other than a script for drugs. The medical world recognizes drugs as the primary treatment for trauma survivors, even though drugs contribute nothing to healing trauma, emotions, or memories. If this protocol is allowed to continue, drugs will become a survivor's new prison, holding them hostage to their trauma for the rest of their life.

Some doctors liberally pass out drugs to survivors—such a bad idea. Not only does it not solve anything or heal anything, it adds forced, harsh, chemical reactions in the body that can make everything worse.

Drugs do have an appropriate place in healing. If you can't sleep or you're drinking yourself to death to avoid your pain, medications can be helpful to stabilize your emotions so you can begin to work on the underlying issues. If you can't function, then you can't work on your healing. But, in this case, the medications are a useful aid so the survivor can do the real work of resolving memories and trauma.

The Abuse Picture Expands

August 28: *Pain—suffering—sadness—abandonment—guilt—despair—fear—quiet—peaceful—escape—food battle—don't eat—must eat. Exercise goals: do it to relieve the depression and be healthier, no, do it to get thin, "you're too fat." Miss my kids—feel sad—lost so much—afraid of what this is doing to them. How are they? Do they need me? Are they okay? Tired—confused—muddled—can't go back—must go back—won't work—can't take it—stay here—it's quiet and peaceful—no hassles—no conflict—no pressure—no s***—no* (husband)*—go—run—escape—it's too much—overload. Tilt! Tilt! Tired—depressed—sleepy—no hunger—unstable—in crisis—too much expense—fear—hard work—God's here—he's in charge—trust him—I can't do it—hope he can.*

My system was in conflict. Their chatter expressed the alters' ambivalence about everything. *Run! No stay!* I constantly wanted to run away but sensed there was no point. The problem was inside me. If I ran, the pain would not be left behind; it would go with me. And the brief times I did run only terrified the little ones inside.

Eat! Don't eat! This was the only time in my life I lost weight without dieting. The weight fell off. I was never hungry because my stomach was almost always in knots.

August 29: *God said, "You are my precious beloved child. I am your Father, Redeemer, King. Don't look at tomorrow. This is a really difficult part of the trip. Today has all you can handle. And when you get up each morning, I will already be there waiting for you to take you through that day. You must trust me as we walk over this scary part. I am not afraid at all. You just need to put your hands in mine each day and don't take your eyes off me. I will get you through. I love you very much." I love him so much, too. I finally feel okay now.*

God was my lifeline. He couldn't spare me the journey (he loved me too much to do that), but he would hold me and not let me go for one moment during my ordeal.

September 8: *As usual the gaps in my journal represent the times of greatest trauma and pain.*

I wrote nothing from August 29 to September 8, but someone else did. I had been in Denver, seeing Faith. Of course I knew she took notes. The surprise came when she handed her notes over to me a few years ago, thinking I might need them one day. It was a prophetic gesture because now I have her perspective on my healing journey, in addition to my own journals.

On September 1, Faith documented emerging details about my parts: John was 6-8 years old, Barbara 17-18 years old, Marianne, 4-7. Judith Ann, 37, was a tattle tale, but also wise and helpful. Marilyn was only 3 and either couldn't or wouldn't speak. Patty, 17-19 handled the sexual abuse, including unions with the high priest. Joey was the one whose knee hurt. Sarah had the shoulder pain. Cinderella was abandoned in the first marriage. And Marie, 10 years old, was the little mother who cared for the twins, cleaned the house, and took responsibility for taking care of mom.

Mom's chronic illnesses had a great impact on me, so I wasn't surprised to meet Marie. With Mom laid up so much of the time, many responsibilities fell to me. It wasn't uncommon for me to make dinner or handle other household duties.

I remember one evening when my dad told me to clean the bathroom. Being only five or six at the time, I had no idea how to go about it. Nevertheless, I grabbed a washcloth and a bar of Ivory soap and went at it. It was my only reference to cleaning something. I knew better than to back-talk or ask questions because that meant incurring my father's wrath.

I don't remember being taught or shown how to do things, just ordered to go do it. Good thing I was a quick learner.

In my next session with Faith, a memory emerged, linking the babysitter with the cult people and the Phenobarbital. The sitter told me, *"It's time to take your medicine. Go to sleep."* Information was coming to light, revealing a network of evil people. The alter sharing this memory said she woke up to find herself in different places: a room in the church by the bathroom, the school gym, the room with the shiny bulb.

Then, finally, on the third day of therapy, the memory that I had felt pushing inside me for so long, tumbled out. Young John told about the memory involving snakes.

A few weeks after this memory came out, I remember stepping out of the shower and noticing a scar of an upside-down triangle, a cult symbol I had never noticed before. I stood paralyzed in front of the mirror for what seemed like an interminable amount of time. Evidence. I wouldn't allow myself to see if before, but now I did, clear as day.

Something else came back to me with this memory. When I was seventeen, I made an appointment with a gynecologist because I was experiencing spontaneous bleeding. After an examination, he told me I needed minor surgery to heal some scar tissue on my cervix. Using a freezing instrument, he said, would cause the damaged tissue to slough off and allow healthy tissue to grow. The uncomfortable procedure took only a couple minutes and solved the problem.

As I thought back to that time, I was curious about two things: Why didn't I tell my mom about the bleeding, the doctor, or what he discovered? And why wasn't I curious about the cause of the scar tissue?

I've known enough survivors to know that we all go through hell, toggling between believing and not believing what we're remembering. And, honestly, I don't know which is worse. *Oh, wow! Supporting evidence! Maybe I'm not as crazy as I thought I was. Maybe I'm not demented, inventing sick fantasies.* But moments later the deep and dreadful revelation sets in that this means it did happen. We really did go through these horrible things.

Child Porn

Back to Faith's office, apparently, I wasn't done recalling abusive memories, because another one came out on our fourth day together. Barbara, the beautiful performer, shared about doing the scarf dance on stage, in front five men in chairs, with cameras rolling.

Child pornography. Wow, these people don't miss a beat. They've got evil covered in every form imaginable. I don't know who these men were, or what happened to the filmed footage. But the likelihood that it was distributed has haunted me for years.

Brenda, my tough girl with the tender heart, came out to talk to Faith at the end of the session. She was scared, her heart beating too fast. *"They are going to hurt me if I talk. If I'm quiet, I'm safe. The babysitter said, "Don't tell."* Then Brenda told Faith why Marilyn doesn't talk, and how bad people hurt her.

After the four days of therapy, I made the five-hour drive back to Montrose, back to my family, and back to work. I hadn't even begun to process any of these memories or try to figure out what they meant. But that's the thing about being multiple and a survivor of abuse—you know how to survive.

Reflecting back, it is hard to believe I was still maintaining my job at the dental office through all this. But, then, that's the *gift* of dissociation; it allows you to carry on, even during the unbelievably brutal times.

September 8 (cont.): *So much, too much. I can't even remember all of it. I hate my life! I hate all of it. I hate my days. I hate what I've been reduced to.*

I hate how I feel. I feel like I've been banished to my little padded cell in the attic. I feel like a blithering idiot. I just want to go back to bed and sleep 'til it's over. I don't want to do this anymore. I don't want to be who I am. I don't want my life! I hate it.

Panic attacks—fear—terror—loneliness—abandonment. It's awful. I can't stand it. I don't want it. (I then described the event with the snakes.) *Come on! It makes me sick. I don't believe it. I don't believe any of it. My stomach hurts. How am I supposed to deal with this? I do NOT understand. I do NOT understand why this happened to me. I do not understand how this happened to me. It's unbelievable. They want me to believe these things happened to me. I did all this work and I still feel like s***. I faced the memory. I let it out. I did my part and I feel like s***.*

They say in the book (about healing from traumatic memories) *it takes years. And I said: "Well, I'll work hard and stay focused, and not give up, so it won't take me so long. I'll be smarter and work harder and beat the system." But then I read last night about a lady who tried to do the very same thing. And she said she learned the hard way—it takes years for the highly motivated, hardworking, focused people. For all the others it takes forever.*

I can't take this anymore. It is too desolate a picture. My life is pathetic and disgusting. It's trash. From beginning to end—trash. I have only 2 redeeming (things) *to the whole miserable mess—*(my daughters). *If it were not for them, I don't think I would continue. It's TOO hard.*

Just what exactly am I supposed to do with this new information? Just how does one deal with the knowledge they have been (graphic descriptions of sexual and physical abuse)*, terrorized, brain washed, drugged, threatened, and witnessed murders. What category does one file such stuff in? What was so bad about the "Missing" file category? Is this really better?*

Do you really expect me to do this over and over and over? Do you really expect me to retrieve more memories? Do you really expect me to wallow in this wreckage for years? My epitaph: A miserable life, what a pity.

At least a million times, I said I did not understand how a human being could endure this much pain. I wanted out, but the only way out was to go forward.

Well-meaning people said thoughtless things to me all the time. I know they were only trying to help, but some of the comments made me crazy. Several times someone (who knew what I was going through) said that I didn't need to worry and stress about remembering the abuse. The actual abuse was over, and I survived, so this would be much easier. They were wrong. *I* did not go through the abuse. *I* was not aware of any of it. *I* was completely separated from what was happening to me. Ask any trauma survivor, "What was worse, the original trauma, or going through the healing process years later?" The current processing is far worse. It is only in the present day that the terror, pain, betrayal, rejection, and physical pain all occur simultaneously.

Despite the pain of the healing process, continuing to live without healing leads only to deeper and further pain. Walking this road to its end is the only thing that leads to a better place.

Battling Avoidance

September 12: *My dad's 65th birthday. I wrote him a letter this week. I might mail it soon. I'm trying to break the news gently. I hope he'll receive it okay.*

I experienced something different this weekend—an intense desire for privacy. I really didn't want anyone to talk to me about my situation. I was irritated and close lipped to all who made inquiries. I feel like I'm in a fishbowl. It has been so hard to go back to the artwork, journaling, dialoguing. I never feel like I do enough. But when I get active with the work, I quickly get overwhelmed.

I still haven't recovered from the intense work I did in Denver. I want so much for that to be the end of it. I don't want to recount the memory, think about it, feel it, process it. It's too painful. But I have to. I have to make myself talk about it in therapy next week. I can't keep ignoring the remembered memories. I have to process them.

I have an undated conversation recorded where I asked my parts why I resist accepting the memories. An alter responded, saying: *Not believing keeps some of the pain locked up. It keeps you from receiving the full impact of the abuse. It avoids the pain. It's like a wall with a leak. You allowed a crack wide enough to leak the memory, but the wall is still there.*

Pain is the issue. Accepting the pain means losing your dignity, losing control.

Self-protection was the reason for my avoidance, but also the simple fact I am a human being. No one wants to hurt.

September 15: *I rewrote and mailed the letter to Dad and feel okay about that. I've had a new body memory. I have had the pain and sensations of being kicked in the head. I think it's related to feeling like I was bad last Thursday. I have had a headache—sharp pain on the side of my head—dull pain in all the bones in my head—distorted vision—fogginess in thinking—dizziness—flashback of laying on the floor in a fetal position and someone kicking me over and over in the head—voice telling me "we were kicked and the reason was that we were bad, disobedient, and were being punished." I don't know if it is connected to the next memory or not and, if so, how?*

September 16: *Feelings. I am so afraid of the "feelings" work. The feelings are worse than the memories. The facts of abuse don't do me in as much as the feelings of the abuse. When I dissociate it is like my brain says, "Hey, I'm not doing this. I've got a way out and I'm taking it—immediately." How do I resist dissociating?*

September 23: *What did I think about and talk about before ritual abuse and MPD consumed my life? Was there life before all this? It doesn't seem like there is now. I am reduced to initials, labels, and diagnoses. I am hanging onto God—each minute. Devotions, study, spiritual reading, meditation—where are they now? Where do they belong now? Distracted—unfocused—contemplative—reflective—unable to focus—consumed. Will I get my mind back? My intelligence back? Consumed. Will there ever be room for other thoughts, interests in other subjects, learning, or growth?*

Sadness—grief—anger. Why is this my life? I've lost so much—so much I've never had. Why? We have all suffered and continue to suffer each day so much. Why? Will it end? At least lessen?

I continually lived in confusion, never fully understanding what was happening to me. The ongoing thoughts of not wanting to continue to live were beginning to concern me.

Chapter Fourteen

1993
October

Processing the Pain

October 1: *All I can say to myself is ouch—ouch—ouch—ouch—ouch. It hurts so bad. I can hardly think, it hurts so bad. How can I keep going? Keep living through this? Faith said the pain has to come out—be felt—be processed through. But it's too frightening. It's too hard. I don't want to do this. It's fouling up my life. I have obligations this weekend. What do I do? How do I get through this? It hurts so much. I'm in crisis. I need to not push myself. Only do what I feel I can do, when I feel I can do it. Once again, I must back way off. I have to get through this weekend. What's it going to take? Reduced stress—prayer support—wisdom—sleep—journaling—dialoguing—someone to talk to each day. She said to not suppress the pain—it might be why my head gets so foggy.*

So, I ask myself what will happen if I feel the pain fully? (These responses came first) *I will be embarrassed—humiliated to be so out of control. I will be out of control and so I will need help. No one can really handle that level of intense emotion, therefore I will be alone—abandoned—undesirable. They will all leave me.*

As with every survivor, feeling alone was my reality. Because no one helped when the abuse was occurring, the sense of aloneness went deep, to the marrow of my bones.

One of my parts, created to handle abuse by the cult, responded next.

October 1 (cont.): *Belonging depends on cooperating. Cooperating means staying in control so that I can keep complying. If I lose control I can't comply, cooperate, belong. I will be discarded like trash. The ones who lose control will be discarded—killed.*

This was my complicated reality. If I processed memories, I scared all the parts who were tied to the cult. They feared for their life. If I didn't process them, I started to feel crazy and out of control. It was a no-win. Another part chimed in on the question.

October 1 (cont.): *What will I do with myself if I feel the pain fully? I will hate myself. I will not respect myself. I am fearful of that inner reality. I will repel my friends/helpers. I will be at their mercy—and no one has ever held me when I truly needed them. Staying in control means I won't be too needy. As long as I keep a lid on it, I can have friends/helpers with me. I don't want to be alone. God help me, this is going to be a bumpy ride.*

October 2: *I can't do this anymore. I'm coming apart at the seams. I can't live and do this work. It's a crisis. I'm being yanked in opposite directions. One voice is trying desperately to keep up—sneakily trying to get it all done in the midst of being in crisis—compelled to do it—laundry—bookkeeping—cleaning—errands—dinner party.* (That part) *agrees to the crisis as long as all the work gets done. I listened to that voice and cleaned, did laundry, but I felt I was going to explode. It was contrary to my real needs and using up my energy. I was angry. Another voice wants to stop the crisis, to tell me it isn't real, that I'm just crying to get attention. Stop it! Act like nothing is wrong because nothing IS wrong. Stop being a baby. Buck up. Act your age. Stop making yourself miserable. You might as well get some work done because this phony crisis is wasting your time. But a third voice is screaming: How can you say that! We were raped! It hurts like hell! We're falling apart. This is finally getting to reality. You can't pretend anymore. The feelings are out. We have to take care of this now. You are hurting yourself by fighting it.*

But I can't do it. It's too hard. It hurts too much. Nobody can help me, and I can't do it alone. I don't know what to do. I'm too dependent and there's no one to be dependent upon. Home is horrible. I can't take care of them. I'm going crazy. I can't be there, but I have to be there. I live there. I am a wife—mother—but I need to cry, and I can't do that at home. I can't keep spending money to be away. Where are the answers? I don't have what it takes to do this. I'm going crazy. I'm falling. Somebody please catch me.

The pressure was building up inside me. I could no longer find a peaceful place to rest. I could not make every part of me happy; it was impossible. I lived with constant failure. No matter which direction I went—ignoring my healing or ignoring my life—there was tyranny in the ranks, unending fear, pressure and despair. It's no wonder I ended up where I did early the next year.

October 5: *Well, I survived another round. Tammy finally got her pain out—not all out, but a big portion. I finally did what I was needing to do to fully connect with the pain and feelings in Tammy's memory. She remembered and expressed what it was like being abused. Not much fun, but important—so they tell me. I don't know where I go from here. This morning I woke up full of pain, but not so much I couldn't work. By noon I was feeling pretty good and tried to do some journaling, but I fell asleep. I'm feeling okay now—that is a gift. I know that I have to keep pressing on. It is terrible when I shut down. The pain wells up and I get in trouble fast. But the last thing I want to do is delve into something new and painful.*

So, what do I do? I could write about the abuse. But that's scary. I have written very little so far. Faith says that writing about the abuse helps the process. I could try, but I don't want to feel bad. I could write until it gets uncomfortable—but it's already uncomfortable. Well, maybe one page would be okay.

I was on a shiny table—stainless steel. There was a round light over the table. The floor was checkered tile squares. There were men and a woman or two dressed in black robes. The man in charge wore a shiny silver necklace with a symbol on a chain. He said I was a curse to all men. That I deserved this. It was what I was made for. I was terribly frightened. (I went on to describe the physical and sexual abuse.)

Seeking Evidence

October 9: *The 11th anniversary today—18 since I was first married. Why is it so hard? Well, I know why. Too much garbage has made it hard. Out to dinner tonight—that should be fun. We hardly talk. What should I say? Is it worth marking the occasion? I suppose so. For some odd reason we both hold on to a slight hope that someday it will be better—even good. But how do I know that?*

What does it mean that I married my therapist? that we had a relationship weeks after therapy was terminated? Why doesn't anybody in my life act the way they're supposed to? Where will rebuilt trust come from? His word means nothing. What will change? How will it change? Will the abuse issues in me heal sufficiently to allow a normal/good relationship? If so, how long will it take? Months? Years? Decades?

I've already been in a painful healing mode for two and half years. And the end is not in sight. The waiting and uncertain future might be a little more tolerable if I knew for certain the memories were true, and that the path I'm on is the right one. It torments me, so. It is all so incredible. The memories are horrific. The pain feels life threatening. The gap between when the events occurred and when I remembered is so big.

If Faith is right, I was taught and trained to forget and dissociate. They deliberately reprogrammed my mind to not remember. My rational mind is killing me. This is beyond what I can truly understand. I know—trust in the Lord with all your heart and lean not on your own understanding. I have got to surrender more to God—believe he's doing it—let him tell me when I've gone the wrong way. I'm operating in the dark.

I asked God for more evidence and only a few days later I talk to my dad and get details that confirm that I was alone with the sitter at night and for extended periods. But I want to say, "that doesn't prove anything!" Just because they were gone doesn't mean it happened—only that it could have happened. Why is it that even when I get outside confirmation it doesn't help? Will I ever know for sure? Will I ever have peace? Will the doubts ever stop tormenting me?

I'll never forget the shattering information Mom shared with me, two years earlier, when I met with her to gather information about my growing up years and she confirmed I did have a daytime babysitter.

I had been fighting that memory for months, the memory of being abused by an older babysitter, a woman maybe in her forties. It simply made no sense, at the time, because I didn't remember having a babysitter. All I could remember was the occasional teenager watching me and the twins while my parents went out to dinner or clubs with friends. I had no memory of a daytime babysitter. Besides, Mom didn't work; she stayed home with us.

Not true, I came to find out. Dad owned the Hammond Pianos and Organs store in Ventura and Mom worked with him at the store every day. They both confirmed this. Mom was the one who was able to give me the sitter's name: Mrs. Hetrick. Dad added more pieces to this puzzle, saying he and Mom would even go away overnight, occasionally driving up to San Francisco to catch a musical performance and leave us with Mrs. Hetrick.

That changed my picture. Now it appeared my parts had a better grasp on the truth than I did. How come I did not remember someone who babysat me for years? I didn't want to know the answer.

Disclosures from Dad

October 13: *Well, I'm in Denver again. I went to my first survivor's meeting last night. It was helpful and I hope I can go again. Faith and I worked together for an hour and a half. Today is the big session. I'm worried about money. I'm anxious about how it's going to go. Will it level me like the last time? I'm in a better place today. Does that mean it won't be so hard or does it mean I won't be able to access my feelings? I feel somewhat cut off from myself. I feel afraid, a little bit desperate. Wendy* (an alter) *shared some more yesterday about being in a cage. I didn't know that. So many thoughts and feelings are swirling around—violence, danger, the darker days of fall and winter. My dad's tape and phone call saying he had no memory when he did have a memory—that confuses me. Where are we headed today?*

I still have the tape. Dad found writing difficult, so preferred to *write* by using a tape recorder. After receiving my letter in September, he recorded this:

Dad's Letter: *I don't know whether it's alcoholism or what, but my memory is really very, very bad and as I have read this letter over and over again, not only can I not remember anything about this, I can't even remember the babysitter. And, unfortunately, I'm sure* (my mom) *had her reasons, but through our lifetime, she really never shared anything with me about what was going on with the family unless it was absolutely necessary. I'm even sitting here totally surprised to find out that when she came home from work, when we were living in Ventura, that you were trembling in the corner. In fact, I guess that sort of makes me a little angry because I should have known that. I wish I could be of some help to you in my memory back then, in trying to give you some insight as to what was going on, but I can't. I'm really sorry.*

I probably never told you about this, but when I was younger, I was also molested by my brother's best friend. My brother knew about it and let it happen. That is one of the reasons I had such a dysfunctional problem with my brother, along with a lot of other things.

You have to understand, honey, that if I can help, the only way I can help is to share my own experience, strength and hope. I hated him and I went through an awful lot in ACA (Alcoholic Children Anonymous), *trying to get to the bottom of it and finally, of course, my program tells me that whenever anybody get into me that way, gets into my head that much, that there's only one way I can ever get rid of it, and that is that I have to pray for them. And every day now, I pray for my brother. I'm sure this sounds almost Pollyannaish to talk like that, but I really believe the process is one of uncover, discover, and discard. From what you have told me in your letter, there just isn't any way that anybody could do more than what you're doing. You're in the process of doing it. You've already uncovered it, you've discovered it, and now, through your various therapies that you are going through, you are in the process of discarding it. And I can tell you that if you keep doing it, you'll get rid of it, you really will.*

It's a question of balance and you're balanced. You're doing what can be done as far as the scientific community is concerned and at the same time you are also doing what you can do for yourself spiritually. And there isn't any more that you can ask of yourself than that, other than to continue and not lose the faith because it will work, and you are a highly intelligent person and you also have a good heart. What you are doing is also the best thing you can do for your family.

Apparently, he had forgotten that he had already corroborated the story with the babysitter, so his sudden lack of memory about her was confusing. It wasn't the last time I would catch him in a lie. But at least he believed me. He said, *I was also molested.* He accepted that something had happened to me.

It was unusual for my dad to share about his past painful events, but knowing these things helped me begin to understand why he was an alcoholic and had lived a self-destructive lifestyle.

Dad talked a lot about his Higher Power, verbiage from Alcoholics Anonymous. When I pressed in to find out what that meant to dad, he explained a relationship with a distant being who gave him comfort but without any personal relationship. And Jesus was just a guy who did a lot of good with his life.

Telling Mom

October 19: *Why is my mother coming now? I'm going to tell her. I don't know what exactly, but I can't pretend any longer. I'm angry. I have protected her all these years. For months now I have kept the truth from her to protect her from pain and to protect me from her punishment. But, it's too much to keep up the charade. I'm too depressed to hide it. My turf, my territory, with my support people. That's better than doing it at her house. "Stoney Martyr" or "Sick and Wounded" or "Raging, blaming, disappointed, belittling Monster," which response will I get? What do I tell her?*

It was just as disappointing as I feared. Before she arrived, I asked someone on my support team to be there. I was anxious. I didn't know what to expect, but I expected it to be difficult. As I shared a non-graphic overview, my heart was beating hard and my chest constricted to the point it was hard to breathe.

I was longing for her support and hoping she would offer to help and be part of my healing. I wanted Nurturing Mom to be there, but Stoney Martyr Mom came instead. She was unable to see me, only herself. There was never any concern expressed for me. Not then and not now, three decades later. She never asked how I was doing. She did not want to know what I was remembering. It was a closed subject.

October 27: *I told mom. She took it well.* (Who knows why I said that? She obviously didn't take it well!) *She's gone now. She didn't respond much. What does it mean that she validated part of my memory? I want to go away for a while. I want a break—a vacation—a ticket for a boat ride going anywhere. But I feel stuffed, shut down, backed up. Trying to be nice, friendly, open with my mother—meeting her needs, not mine. Guilt—broke the family rules—telling secrets. As soon as my mother left yesterday, I began to feel. I had no feelings while she was here except terror and dread for the confrontation. Why can't I cry? Where are the feelings? Where did my heart get put?*

During her visit, she wasn't too bad, but weeks later, Raging, Blaming, Monster Mom emerged. She was livid. She never denied anything, but neither did she admit anything. She blamed Faith for all of it, and still does. When I reminded my mother that my abuse memories started returning two years before I met Faith, she dismissed it as irrelevant. It was still Faith's fault. Faith had planted everything in my mind and manipulated me to believe it.

Mom began researching "False Memory Syndrome," going so far as to join their society, a group that espoused the theory that all repressed memories were false, and even sent them monthly donations. That was incredibly hurtful. As if I didn't have enough trouble working through all these painful memories. Now my mom had joined the enemy camp. So much for telling the truth.

Sadly, I've learned that everyone in the family plays a role in keeping the family secret. It isn't just the perpetrator. No one wants to admit what is really going on. Children have no voice, no power, nowhere to go. Their very survival depends on living with the secret. So, whatever is heard is denied. What is seen is justified, ignored, or forgotten.

In twenty years of working with survivors of sexual abuse, I've heard a few stories from victims who've told the truth, however, most do not. But I've never heard a story of a survivor telling the truth and then being believed, supported, and protected by their perpetrators and others directly involved. They are either blamed for what the perpetrator did, or rejected and abandoned for revealing the family secret. The latter was me.

I would often try to imagine being the mother of a daughter who was seriously traumatized in the same ways as me, hearing her tell me she had been sexually abused and victimized in cult ceremonies. And in no mental scenario does anger enter my picture. I would be devastated for my daughter, grieved, concerned for her well-being, offering any possible help and support. Isn't that how mothers are supposed to respond?

Throughout my healing, my mother remained an enigma. On the one hand, I knew she loved me. I was a loved child. On the other hand, she didn't seem to see me or truly know me. I existed only as a reflection of herself. This made me feel unsafe around her.

Today, I know a paradox always exists in close relationships because people are human. Jesus is the only one who loves perfectly. The rest of us love others within the midst of our woundedness; it is love tainted with self-deception and selfishness. Healing reduces our selfishness and increases our capacity to love more fully.

At the time, I knew nothing of this, so my only recourse was to shut down whenever I was around her. And, always the question in my mind, *Where was my mom when all this abuse was going on?*

Chapter Fifteen

1993
November-December

Alters Are Struggling

November 8: *In Denver again. Visit #6, five months since the first with Faith, ten months since the first memory came. How many 'til it's over? 'til it's better? 'til I no longer pay people to help me? How long until I can plan ahead knowing I'll be okay enough to follow through? How long 'til I don't feel like I'm dying every day or 'til it isn't such hard work just to be? Job 6:2-3: "If only my anguish could be weighed and all my misery be placed on the scales! It would surely outweigh the sand of the seas—no wonder my words have been impetuous." Where am I today? What is happening? What needs to happen? I am feeling. I am afraid of just that. I run all day from it. I clench my jaw to keep it from coming out. The pain is unbelievable. Trusting God with the unknown—with the terrifying. It takes my faith to new dimensions. His thoughts and ways are much higher than mine—actually they aren't anything like mine. No wonder I can't figure anything out so much of the time.*

November 11: (Patty wrote today's entry.) *So many feelings again. I have lost so much. I hurt really badly inside. I wish somebody would help me. I don't like to be alone; it hurts more. I feel really sad tonight. I feel like something got taken away—some part of me was stolen. It is so hard. Lost—where am I? Will the lost part be returned? Will I always be alone? There's no mommy and daddy. I wish there was some place I could cry. I am swollen with tears. I wish the tears would flood out because they might wash me off. I wish they would melt me and make me into somebody else. It is awful to be a little girl nobody wants. Where do I belong? I don't belong to the priest anymore. He's a bad man. Faith said so. He should never have made me do those things. I am mad at him. I would like to throw darts and arrows at him. He is very, very terrible. So maybe I don't belong to anybody. Maybe I am the lost little girl. Maybe I will melt all away like the wicked witch. Nobody wants me anymore. Sad, sad, sad, sad. Signed, Patty—the terrible little girl.*

The priest was part of the cult, but because cult members deliberately infiltrate positions of influence in society, sometimes the priests were also part of a church.

In therapy, Patty had been talking about the forced sexual unions with the priest, which was one of her roles. The purpose was to convince Patty that she belonged only to the cult, part of their pattern to control people through lies, deception, and manipulation.

November 12: (Another part was writing, again.) *Go to hell. You said we would do it. You said we would hit the tree. You said you would let me paint. You said you would let me smash the tool shop. You never let me do what I want! You said you'd let me talk. What the hell's the matter with you. I hate you. Stop doing this to me. I'm going crazy. You know you won't let me do this at home. Faith is my only chance. Or of course we could wait another month. You'd like that, wouldn't you? You'd like to never do this wouldn't you? Stuff it back in. That's what you want. Ignore it. Do everything except help me. Fine! Go away. You make me sick.*

Alex held my anger. I frequently walked this tightrope of trying to meet the needs of my parts while staying within healthy boundaries. Alex is an example of this balancing act. I didn't think smashing my car into a tree met the latter condition. At the same time, Alex did need to somehow express his anger. Journaling and artwork helped somewhat, but it wasn't enough for him. I scored big points one day when I let Alex hurl eggs in a vacant field, five dozen of them.

A couple times, following through on an assignment, I let Alex whack pillows with a tennis racket. It made a huge, satisfying noise without doing any damage. That was hard for me, though. I was terrified of anything remotely resembling violence, having grown up with a violent father. It wasn't uncommon for my little parts to be uncomfortable when I was trying to meet Alex's needs.

Complicated! Everything was so complicated!

The Power of Being Seen and Heard

Through it all, I was learning volumes. As I began accepting my alters and valuing their contribution to my survival, I started to understand what it took for my system to heal.

The first thing each of my parts needed was to be seen and heard. They were there for a reason. What was the reason? Alex witnessed the violations and torture of children, knowing it was wrong, but feeling utterly powerless to stop it. With every episode, more rage was added. Somebody needed to care about his feelings and hear him. Sometimes that was Faith, but usually it was me.

My job, as the host in my system, was to hear their story and honor their pain. Each part needed respect, something communicated by believing their story. The children were never believed. After accomplishing the important work of seeing, hearing, and believing, the next piece was to meet their needs. Sometimes that was simple. Often all the alters wanted was to get their own stuffed animal or baby doll, or to make paper dolls, or swing at the park. And sometimes their requests were impossible, complicated, or unsafe, like smashing our car.

Many parts hated my husband, including Patty. She constantly felt abused by him and wanted out. It was difficult navigating this with her because her perspective on him was right on the money. She saw his abusive, unhealthy manipulation, and cried *foul.* Roger didn't see us or respect or value us. His choices created an environment that became more toxic time went on. Home never felt safe.

By this time, I had had close to four decades of experience with not being seen or acknowledged as an individual with her own thoughts, ideas, and needs. I had been a pawn to be used by people for their own selfish purposes for longer than I could remember.

For the first eighteen years, I had no control over this dynamic. The abuse just kept happening to me. However, I was responsible, to a degree, for the next twenty years. I willingly agreed to two marriages simply because the men wanted me. I say *to a degree* because I hadn't received healing then. Without healing, I would continue to operate from a predictable playbook; I would make bad choices in relationships, setting myself up for a reenactment of earlier dynamics from my life.

From the time I could understand words, I was told I was beautiful, smart, and special. Today those words make me cringe. The truth is that I was not any more special than anyone else. Nevertheless, the perpetrators told me I was chosen because I was special, something that satisfied my basic human needs for significance and belonging. It felt good until I discovered what I was chosen for.

I was chosen for the cult, and then chosen for marriage.

Playing a Role

My first husband grew up in a legalistic church. It wasn't a bad church, but he adopted a perverted, unintended consequence of that church's teaching, having witnessed his father doing the same thing. In order to meet their standards, Tim needed a wife who would bear his children, keep his home, stand by his side, and faithfully attend church. He needed the appearance of godly living. He needed a front to cover the despicable behavior of his secret life. The affairs, the drugs, the alcohol, the pornography, the unspeakably perverted actions, all had to be kept hidden. He had no mental or emotional buy in to God's Word or his ways, no relationship with God. He just didn't want to be in trouble with his church.

I fit the bill. Once again, I was in a relationship where I wasn't seen or valued. I was chosen to play a role.

I wouldn't have recognized my needs if they had been tattooed on my hand. As far as I was concerned, I existed only to meet other people's needs. It started with my mother—she needed me to take care of her. Then there were the people in the cult who needed me to perform certain rituals. Even my beloved half-brother, Scott, I've come to realize fifty years later, just needed someone in the house who would notice him and like him. He never really saw me, either. Then dating and two marriages repeated the dynamic again.

My needs and my alters were closely tied together. My parts held my unmet needs. I was learning that if I made an effort to meet their needs, they would heal. If they healed, they would no longer need to be separate from me and we could start working toward integrating. But that was miles down the road.

At this point, my work was to let my parts give me glimpses of my needs. They were teaching me that I needed safe ways to express my anger, and also needed safety in relationships, particularly in marriage.

Getting Run Over

November 19: *God help me. I don't think I can get through this. The multiplicity makes more and more sense and gets more confusing and more overwhelming. The pain is never ending. The range is from "tolerable but significant" to "I'm out of my mind and gone." It has been at the higher end today. It's a good thing God never leaves me. I feel alone, but I know I'm not. God is here, right with me, all the time, every second of the day. I forget to reach out and take his hand—to crawl up in his lap—my safe place—the only place where I won't get hurt.*

I'm supposed to let the feelings out. But nobody told me what to do after they come out. (I had unleashed on Roger.) *I was so angry, it came flooding—bursting—exploding out. It was very, very different than the usual smoldering, tightly bound, calculated speech. Now what will happen? What will he do? Will he blame me, rage at me, excuse his behavior, leave, punish me? All are possible.*

I hate having to watch my back all the time—everything he does, everything he says. Is it true? Is he lying? Is he stealing? Is he doing something that will hurt me? It is no fun. I can't relax for a minute. I have to constantly watch out. What an awful way to live.

God help us both. Without him (God) *there is simply no hope. I guess that's why he keeps telling me to just keep my eyes on him. Everything else is too frightening. There is danger on every side. Hope only lies in his eyes.*

If my first marriage was bad, the second one was even worse. I never felt unsafe with Tim. Not true with Roger. And it wasn't just *my* safety. Because he was emotionally abusive to my older daughter, I was on high alert all the time.

The pressure I felt in my marriage made this recovery work harder. There was no tenderness and comfort, no understanding and support. Being a therapist, I thought my husband would understand what I was going through. But his concern was how hard this was for him, which it certainly was. It was a long, painful ordeal for him, too. His only reference, though, was what this was doing to him, no concern for what it was doing to me. I did not exist.

If I wasn't being triggered by memories, I was being triggered by Roger. Even though I knew he had been clinically diagnosed as narcissistic, it didn't help me cope.

The healthier I got, the harder he pushed back. He married a victim. He married someone who asked nothing, who needed nothing. But that was changing. I was coming alive, becoming human, discovering my identity. And he didn't like that. I was like a sapling, trying to emerge from the asphalt of an interstate and then getting run over.

November 26: (Tammy needed to write, again.) *Alone at last. They're gone and everybody is starting to feel better. I like my bed and my electric blanket and my gorilla. I like it when nobody talks to me and bothers me. I like being quiet. I like it when nobody makes me do anything—it is easier that way.*

I like the flower (amaryllis) *that Cyndy bought for us. I can't wait to see it bloom big bright red flowers. It will be so pretty. I like Christmas because of the colors and the music and the yummy smells. I'm glad it is Christmas time. I wish it could be Christmas all the time. I wish we could live here alone all the time.*

I just don't want anyone to ever bother me again. Please be quiet and let me be quiet. We don't want to work anymore. Please just leave us alone.

Peace. I craved peace and quiet. It was hard to find.

Navigating Alters

November 27: (Tammy, who held a lot of the sexual abuse, had more to say.) *Please help me. Somebody please come find me. I feel all alone. Nobody loves me, nobody cares about me. It hurts really, really bad. I wish somebody would hold me so I could cry. I want to cry and cry.*

Our thoughts are negative all the time—we hate our self—we are so bad—so shameful. Everyone would be better off if we just died. We are too much work. Nobody knows what to do anymore. Nobody has time for us. Nobody cares. We have been bad.

(Tammy left and I started writing.) *It's too hard. There are no answers. I'm not strong enough. I thought I was, but I'm not. I'm dissociating all over the place—can't hold a thought. Why doesn't it get better? Why doesn't it get easier?*

(I decided to check in with Patty.) Me: *Patty, how are you feeling about Peter?* (We had just gone through a painful interchange with a friend and I wanted to know how Patty was feeling.)

Patty: *I thought he was going to be my friend. He scared me. Now he's going to be mad at me and hurt me. He's really angry.*

Me: *You sound pretty frightened, Patty. I'm sorry it was so hurtful for you. I believe that Peter was trying to help Alex and really cares about Alex but didn't know the right thing to do. How would you feel about seeing Peter or talking to Peter?*

Patty: *Oh, I don't know. It might make us hurt worse. What if he attacks my body?*

Me: *Patty, Peter would never do that.*

Patty: *I just wanted to please him, but he never would let me.*

Me: *Peter is pleased by our friendship, Patty. That's what's important to him.*

Alex: Like hell it is.

Me: *Hi Alex, glad to hear from you again.*

Alex: *Don't you dare invite him over here!*

Me: *It sounds like you're pretty angry with Peter.*

Alex: *He lied to me. He said he liked me and wanted to be my friend. B*** S***.*

Me: *Alex, what do you think we should do?*

Alex: *Go blow up his house.*

Me: *Alex, you have a right to be angry. You should never have been talked to that way. Peter was wrong. He didn't know how to help you.*

Alex: *What do you care?*

Me: *I care when you're hurting, Alex. I'm very concerned about you. So is Faith. What do you need?*

Alex: *A gun so I can go shoot someone.*

Me: *What else do you need?*

Alex: *A father.*

Me: *What else?*

Alex: *Go f*** yourself. I'm never going to get what I want.*

Me: *I'm going to keep trying, Alex, because I care about you and how much pain you're in.*

If I had trouble navigating my parts, it was doubly hard for my friends to do so, those on my support team who wanted to help me. Peter was just trying to help and got caught in a messy exchange with Alex.

My parts were journaling regularly now. Their chatter didn't necessarily add anything to my story, but they were making themselves known and heard more often, even talking to each other.

December 1: *What's going on today, that's what I want to know. Why do I feel so sick at work? I want to sleep, and the pain is high. It is so uncomfortable. I wish I could enjoy work—feel good. Will I ever feel good? I feel fluish again. Does that mean I'm in a memory? Does Sarah know? Why do I keep thinking about boils? I had them when I was a little girl. I remember my mother putting bacon on it* (the boil) *on my arm. Do I need to spend more time in the memory? I don't feel good—that's a pretty good sign* (that a memory is emerging). *But I don't want to. Maybe somebody else could write now.*

(Sarah began sharing with me.) *My stomach hurts. My eyes are heavy. I don't want to go there. I don't like it there. The people are scary to me. It makes me feel sick when I'm there. Can't I take a nap? It's the big house with the basements and lots of closets and stairs.* (Sarah went on to share a memory.) *I was so very afraid. I stopped crying but my stomach hurts really, really bad.*

December 9: *I don't like this feeling in me. It's terribly uncomfortable. The chaos, confusion, unpredictability is very hard for me. I really don't handle well all the bad feelings about myself. I feel so dependent on Faith and John* (my first therapist). *The uncertainty of the team* (my intercessory prayer team) *is frightening to me. I have a strong urge to cut loose from it altogether. Sort of like, "Who needs it—I'm out of here—see if I care."*

Some parts of the memory today feel vivid, others vague. I doubt myself. Now we have to try to get some more detail on the memory. Somebody cries, somebody screams, somebody is desperate, somebody despairs, panic rises up from my belly. This is now, that was then. I am safe. We are all safe. We are protected. There are no bad people here. The bad people are not going to come. They are long gone.

1993 was finally over. What a horrible year.

Chapter Sixteen

1994
January: Part One

Running with Horses

Because I was so entrenched in painful memories, it was hard to see light in any direction. I couldn't see the end. I couldn't see a way out. I couldn't see healing occurring. Only pain. Only darkness. Praise God for my kids and compassionate employers. They gave me a reason to get out of bed, a reason to keep going.

Along the way, God relentlessly encouraged me with Scripture. One in particular gave me hope. *"If you have raced with men on foot and they have worn you out, how can you compete with horses?" (Jeremiah 12:5a)* No question—I was worn out. I desperately did not want to be in this near nonfunctioning place. This verse resonated in my soul, becoming a single flame of fire that drew me forward. I longed for the day when I could run with the horses.

Wanting to hang onto this hope, I found a poster of horses running in a field and mounted it on the wall, at the foot of my bed. Each morning, I woke up seeing the horses and prayed, "*God, I want to run with the horses. Help me get there.*"

Trauma, Anxiety, and Struck Speechless

I was back in Denver on New Year's Day. Over Christmas, a new memory began pushing. The memories always started in my gut. I would have a sick feeling and lose my appetite. Feelings of fear, dread, and anxiety became daily companions. Mysterious pains surfaced in various parts of my body along with a sense that I was caught by something.

Sometimes I would have memory flashes. One afternoon, wanting to decompress after a therapy session, I drove over to a mall in Denver. Out of the blue, I saw myself, three or four years old, pulling up my dark colored, corduroy, elastic-waist pants. I was instantly triggered back into the past. I saw it clearly for several seconds, followed by horrible feelings of violation.

Spotting a public phone, I ducked into a hallway and called Faith as I descended into full-blown panic. I could not get myself grounded enough to leave the mall and drive home. For three hours I sat on the floor, clutching my knees until she called back and talked me down to a safe enough state in which I could leave.

Words fail to describe the discomfort of a panic attack. It feeds on itself, escalating as your chest begins to tighten and breathing gets harder. After the incident at the mall, I began carrying an anti-anxiety medication with me, afraid to be in public without it.

With the memory pushing hard, I made an appointment with Faith to try and help me get at it. The words, the verbal acknowledgement of the details of what happened in a memory, were always the last part to emerge because the content of the memories was so horrific.

The reason memories are repressed in the first place is because the trauma that took place was intolerable. The heart, mind, body and soul could not deal with it in any manner, so it was shut down, pushed away. It only took about five minutes of being back in the pain and you clearly understood why you dissociated. Pure survival.

It is the unbearable nature of the event that makes talking about it difficult. The body literally resists speaking the descriptions of the trauma. It intuitively knows that if it is spoken out, denial will be much harder. There's something about telling the story that forces the survivor to accept their truth. Survivors will do anything rather than accept it. It can take an act of God to get us to speak our truth.

Another aspect that makes speaking about the trauma so hard is the intense feelings that often lunge back at you like a tiger. Remembering the details and feeling the feelings can take you right back to the moment and make it seem like it is happening all over again. There's a word for this phenomenon: abreaction.

For all these reasons, I was reluctant to go to Denver. I did not want to know what this memory was. I didn't want to know about any more abuse from anyone else. At the same time, I knew I wouldn't be free from the gripping pain until I faced the truth.

After several hours of working with Faith, I remembered what had happened. It was another satanic ritual. Another sacrifice. More sexual abuse, this time with mutilation. They manipulated me to 'help' with the sacrifice, leading me to believe I was to blame.

Unless you are in the world of ritual abuse, it is hard to fathom sacrifices being done without proper authorities knowing about it. It is important to be aware that the cult is a system, one that is deliberately created to facilitate the evil they perpetrate. And they've been doing what they are doing since time began. This is the false idol worship God condemned time and time again in the Old Testament.

Children are bred for the cult's use. Kidnappings are arranged. They know how to identify people who have no attachments or family. They prey on lost and vulnerable souls. And, they deliberately place their people, cult members, in positions of influence because it allows them to literally get away with murder. It is a well-honed system.

Tell? Or Don't Tell?

For a long time, I struggled with the knowledge that I had participated in the rituals. I kept asking myself whether I was responsible for someone dying. And if I was, should I tell someone what I did? But to whom would I share this information? And what would I say? *Oh, by the way, I think I may have participated in a ritual sacrifice, but I don't know who it was or where it happened or when it took place.* That's not a lot to go on.

It was crazy making. Tormenting. But I finally realized the truth: I was a very young child. I was not there of my free will. It wasn't my decision, I was forced. I was just as much a victim as the victim. And, besides, everyone is manipulated to participate, that is how they play the game.

People wonder why the children don't tell someone what is going on when they are experiencing trauma. There are many reasons. In the cult, they program you to dissociate and forget. You are programmed to compartmentalize the memory, so you will guard their secrets and go on with the so-called normal part of your life. Evil doesn't like being exposed.

Programming kids is easy. Their suggestions to suppress information are powerful, brainwashing their young victims.

The cult identifies a child's talents and abilities, then trains them to use their gifts to their benefit. Whatever you are good at, they call that forward. It is the same with a child's weaknesses. They find what causes fear or pain and use that to keep them in line. Because they know the child's vulnerabilities, like fear of losing their family or a pet, a simple threat is enough to get them to do anything they want them to do.

Threats and intimidation are always used. I was told my siblings would be tortured if I didn't comply and that I would never see my parents again. Pretty powerful words to a five-year old. I wanted to protect my siblings at all costs, (something I was utterly powerless to do, but you don't know that when you're five).

Motivating a child through reward or punishment is something parents and teachers regularly do, but in appropriate ways (hopefully). The cult's tactics are obviously inappropriate. A child will do anything for a treat or even a word of affirmation, *You are such a special and gifted child.* When the child doesn't comply, that's when the cult leaders do torturous and frightening things.

The catch, though, was that the torture went on regardless of whether you were good or bad. But a child is trusting, believing what they are told, even when it is a lie. All they have to do is occasionally give the reward or skip the torture once in a while and it is enough to gain obedience.

There is constant indoctrination going on, too. The cult's evil message is repeated over and over to brainwash the child. This is done in hopes the child will choose to believe and accept their ways as their own.

Even in non-ritual abuse, perpetrators tell their victims not to tell anyone or they will be further harmed. Not only that, but when you are living in a culture of abuse, no one is safe. There is no one to tell. Children have an innate sense of fear and shame that keep them muzzled for life, or at least until their desire for healing surpasses their fear. It is human nature to avoid pain, and sharing the secrets is painful.

Further complicating matters is the fact that children ALWAYS feel responsible for the abuse. Somehow, they did something to invite this atrocity to occur. *It is my fault. If I tell someone, I'll get in trouble.* That may sound nuts to those who haven't endured abuse, but it is a universal truth. Then if you add verbal threats from perpetrators—game over. I was told it was my fault because I was *a girl and a curse to all men.*

Those who do try to tell an adult or parent are usually disbelieved, blamed, or told to never speak of it again. That only needs to happen once for a child to never again bring it up. For all these reasons, children typically will not tell anyone what happened nor will they ask any questions.

With my latest memory finally out, it was time for me to make the five-hour drive home. As awful as it was, remembering the abuse, I felt much better afterward. The anxiety and anguish were gone. I could eat again. Now if I could just have a 3-day nap.

Everyone Needs to be Heard

January 5: *Things are definitely better. We are home again. The memory is out. We don't feel sick anymore. 1993 is over. We got a good night's sleep, finally. We have a new schedule.* (In an effort to better meet the needs of my parts, I made a schedule.) *Things are better.* (The chatter of parts began.) *No, not perfect. I'm still tired. Yes, I'm sleepy. Why did you tell them last night? It's so embarrassing. Nobody will do anything anyway. What's the point? You should've kept quiet. Let's just stop talking. It's better that way. I want to go to the zoo today. I don't want to work.*

Me: *I'm wondering how everyone is feeling about our new schedule?*

JoAnn: *It seems pretty complicated to me. There's too much work involved. Can't we just go somewhere and have fun? We used to know how to do that. This schedule is a real drag.*

Me: *Thanks for sharing JoAnn. I hear that you have some different ideas about how our time should be spent. Does anybody else have something to share?*

John: *Does this mean we get to play more?*

Me: *I'm glad you spoke up John. What do you like to play?*

John: *I like to build things and play with trucks. I like to ride my bike.*

Me: *Let me see what I can do. But this does mean we get to play more.*

John: *Then I like it.*

Teresa Lynn King (TLK): *I wish we could be like normal people. I wish we didn't have to do any of this weird stuff—nurture time, personal work, hours of therapy every week. Please. Is this really necessary? Can't we just live a normal life?*

Me: *I'm really glad to hear from you, Teresa. It sounds like you wish we weren't so different, that we could have a schedule like other people do.*

TLK: *You got it. This is weird.*

Me: *Thanks for answering my questions, Teresa.*

Marie: *I'm just not sure we can do it all just right. There is so much to do. There never is enough time to do everything. I'm so afraid. We have to do the personal work so everybody can get well. But there is never enough time. It makes my stomach hurt. I'm afraid of how hard it's going to be.*

Me: *This is obviously very hard for you. Marie, I would really like it if you would let me be responsible for the work and the schedule. There are several of us who can handle that, and you don't even have to think about it. Can you do that? Can you think about playing instead of working?*

Marie: *I can try.*

Me: *What would be fun for you?*

Marie: *Baking cookies and cakes, singing, and going to movies.*

Me: *Let's focus on those things for you, Marie. Let the older ones be responsible for the schedule. Who's mad? Alex?*

Alex: *Stop talking to people. I mean it. Stop it. Keep quiet.*

Me: *Alex, what do you think of the schedule?*

Alex (with his usual sarcasm): *It's cute.*

Me: *What do you mean?*

Alex: *You think you can solve everything by lining out a nice, neat, tidy little schedule with everything in its place. Well, life isn't like that. You're dreaming. It'll never work.*

Me: *You sound pretty skeptical. How would you do it?*

Alex: *Just take it as it comes. Do what seems right at the moment. Don't plan so much.*

Me: *Thanks for sharing, Alex. I appreciate it. I'll consider your opinion, too.*

When I wasn't in the middle of another memory, my work was to acknowledge and respect my different parts. The temptation was to ignore them, but that was a bad strategy, dragging my recovery out even longer.

Even though I felt like a freak and was embarrassed that I had parts, I had come to accept that they had saved my life. They did the pieces of life that I couldn't do. They handled the hard stuff.

And while it was true that they were operating independently, they were still all me. Separate, but not separate. If I was going to heal, I had to invest time and effort into meeting their needs. This had never happened in the past. Hence, the reason for the schedule.

The work was complicated. The needs of some conflicted with the needs of others. And the list of needs could be quite long, requiring a fair amount of creativity. I just did my best to do little things with each part. A friend with a young daughter came over one day and we finger painted together—a happy moment for both of us!

Negotiations

January 7: *I hate January. It is so cold. It's dark, too.* (My parts began dialoguing.) *Well, look at the bright side—25% of it is already over. Oh, that's helpful. As if that makes it any warmer. So, are you happy? You got your way. Here we are at the elder retreat. Well, I am glad it has worked out. I'm really glad the kids got to play tonight. That was an unexpected surprise. JoAnn, how are you doing with all of it?*

JoAnn: *Well, peachy keen. Here we are with my favorite person.*

?: *Where are we? I miss my bear. Why didn't we bring my bear? My stomach hurts. Are we going to stay here?*

Me: *Yes, we are going to stay here one night. I'm sorry that we didn't bring the bear. I'll try to bring it next time.*

?: *Why did you talk so much? I thought we had agreed to no small talk and there you go blabbing. You said too much. Didn't you see her watching everything we did and said? Who can relax around that?*

Me: *I'm sorry. I tried to do the right thing. I didn't want to seem unfriendly. I just wanted to be nice.*

?: *That's just great. Like being nice does us any good.*

?: *I'm tired. Can't we go to sleep? I don't want to be here anymore.*

Me: *We will very soon. But I need to check in with Brenda. How's it going for you, Brenda?*

Brenda: *Oh, it's a laugh a minute. I thought someone was going to talk to me. Forget it. I don't care. It was NO BIG DEAL. GO TO SLEEP. GO AWAY.*

Me: *Brenda, what's happening inside?*

Brenda: *What do you think? The kids are uncomfortable. Who knows what's going to happen?*

Me: *Brenda, could you help calm the kids down for the night? We are alone now and should be 'til morning. It's quiet and we're warm. I think we'll be just fine now.*

Brenda: *I suppose I could give it a shot. But I'm not making any promises.*

Me: *Thanks for trying to help, Brenda. I appreciate you.*

I was an ordained elder in the church I attended, serving a three-year term. And this was the weekend for their annual retreat. Never one to shirk my duties, I felt I needed to be there, but it caused issues with my parts. Being in groups was always a minefield for certain alters. Their only experience with groups was in cult rituals, so they were on high alert whenever we were in a group setting.

I was forever negotiating, trying to keep everyone safe and make my parts happy. When journaling, I didn't always know who was dialoguing. At times, I just heard comments and recorded them. Their fears, requests, or attitude sometimes tipped me off. Brenda was particularly sassy. I liked her spunk.

Where was Cyndy?

Impactful dreams were still a regular occurrence, but not every dream had something worth recording. This one did.

January 12: *Why are we dizzy today? What's going on? We had a dream Tuesday night. I was in Ward's. I was trying on an outfit—tan pants, double knit with a similar colored shirt and cardigan. For some strange reason I didn't want to use the dressing room, so I was doing this on the sales floor. I was trying very hard to get the clothes on without anyone seeing me. Finally, I had the new outfit on.*

My mother was there with me and it didn't fit. The pants' waist was about 6" short (preventing me from pulling the pants all the way up). *I knew I didn't want the clothes, but I wasn't willing to go through changing out in the open again. I also didn't want to tell my mother I didn't want the clothes. I knew there was another clothing store around the corner. So, I decided to wear the new outfit to the other store, find something I liked better, change into the new clothes and then take the Ward's outfit back and hang it up before anyone knew it was gone.*

I went out the back door of Wards to an alley-like area. It was late at night and very dark. I could see the store I was headed to—maybe 100 feet away. But halfway there I realized how foolish it was to be in this back alley. I got fearful and turned to go back into Wards. That's when I noticed 4 or 5 people—older teenagers or young adults. It was obvious they weren't "nice" people.

I tried to not be noticed. I turned and was faced squarely with a young man holding an automatic weapon aimed right at me. He was around 5′11″ or 6′ tall, slight build, sandy brown hair cut short on the sides and longer and curly on the top. The details get vague at that point. Either I attacked him and grabbed the gun and tossed it aside or he threw it aside. Then he grabbed me and threw me to the ground. He may have had a knife. I'm not sure. I'm sure that he then raped me, but I can't remember any details except that I was afraid because the clothes were ruined, and I would get in trouble because I hadn't paid for them. I woke up after the rape.

That was just like me. I had just been raped, but my only concern was that I would be in trouble for ruining the clothes. Just like the sexual abuse at school on my fifteenth birthday, my first thought was getting to science class on time. It never occurred to me that I needed to get help for the trauma I had just endured. But I'd learned long ago, there wasn't any point in telling. Nobody would listen.

My sense of self had long since disappeared. My needs were a foreign language, one that I didn't speak or understand. My single focus was to do everything I was told so I wouldn't get in trouble, so bad things wouldn't happen to me or those I loved. *Where was Cyndy?* No one knew, including me.

The problem was, even now, when I was trying to address my needs, I couldn't make everyone happy. If I let the little ones play, the adult parts felt ignored. If I rested, the diligent parts were frustrated. If certain parts talked about what happened, others were terrified. If I didn't work on the memories, I started feeling crazy. If I did work on them, then I was certain I *was* crazy.

Chapter Seventeen

1994
January: Part Two

The Bookkeeper

I had always liked numbers, excelling in math throughout school. I was the one who paid the bills and did the taxes, even keeping the books for Roger's counseling business and several service organizations. Numbers were my friends. They never betrayed me, always acting in a predictable manner. Today, I finally met the bookkeeper.

January 14: (Cynthia) *I feel perfectly fine at the moment, thank you, so leave me alone. Can't we go back downstairs and get the rest of the work done? We're on a roll. Things are finally getting caught up. We could get all our chores and the budget done today—maybe even the January taxes which would eliminate one more item from our "behind list." Instead, we're up here picking scabs off again. Can't we just leave well enough alone? Why do we have to go looking for trouble?*

Me: *Well, actually, the goal is more along the lines of heading off trouble. There are so many of us that it is hard to satisfy everybody's needs. But I certainly hear you. You would feel better if you could get some more work accomplished. Could you tell me who you are? Is this mother? JoAnn? Judith Ann? Somebody new? I can tell that you enjoy the work, particularly the budget. It makes you feel good about yourself to accomplish things. You have a positive feeling about yourself and inner strength. But I just don't know your name. How do you feel about my description of you?*

Cynthia: *Fine, I like it. You can call me Cynthia. Why is she playing Christmas music? It's January.*

Me: *I guess Jenny likes it. You like order, don't you?*

Cynthia: *Oh yes, I thrive on it. Can we go balance the checkbook? I would really like to do that.*

Me: *Would it be all right if I first checked it out with the others inside?*

Cynthia: *I suppose so. Could you give me a time when we will do it at the very latest?*

Me: *Yes, it's 3:15 now. Would 4:00 be okay?*

Cynthia: *I guess.*

Me: *Thanks for introducing yourself, Cynthia. I'm glad I finally got to meet you. I hope to get to know you better.*

Two Train Rides

January 14 (cont.) Me: *Is there anyone else who would like to talk today? In particular, I would like to know how each of you are feeling about the upcoming trip. Also, I'm wondering how the process of the newest memory is going?*

Marianne: *I don't want to go on the train, please. Could we please stay home?*

Me: *Marianne, why don't you want to ride the train?*

Marianne: *I don't like where we're going. It's too long. It's safer at home. We should just stay here, please.*

Me: *Marianne, are you remembering about the other train ride a long time ago?*

Marianne: *I don't want to think about it please.*

Me: *Marianne, it is really important for me to explain to you about this train ride. It is going to be very different than the other one you are remembering. We are going to a different place—Denver—to see Faith. Do you remember Faith? She helps all of you with your memories. She really loves us and cares about us. And we will only be on the train a few hours this time, not a few days. And I will be there to help you all day. Marianne, it's not going to be anything like the last train ride. How are you feeling about it now?*

Marianne: *What if we get lost or don't know what to do?*

Me: *You and the other little children will be safe because the big people and I will be in charge of everything. Marianne, we are going to see John tomorrow and Faith on Wednesday, in 5 days. Would you like to talk to one of them or both of them?*

Marianne: *It doesn't matter to me.*

Me: *I'm going to stay with you the whole time, you won't be alone.*

Marianne: *I'm afraid.*

Me: *I know. Well, I will check in with you tomorrow about how you're doing. Is there anything you need right now?*

Marianne: *The memory is still in the rain barrel?*

Me: *Yes, we will keep it safe in there until John or Faith can help us with it.*

Marianne: *You won't forget?*

Me: *No, I promise.*

Brenda: *Don't leave her alone now. She's very upset.*

Me: *You are right. Who is this?*

Brenda: *Brenda.*

Me: *Brenda, would you stay with Marianne now and keep her company?*

Brenda: *I guess. But you better take care of her now. This isn't going to be easy.*

Me: *Thanks, Brenda. I'll do my best.*

Another memory was pushing, causing Marianne to be afraid. Our planned train ride to Denver was triggering something from the past. Because I was buying a used car in Denver, I bought a train ticket, knowing I would have the new car to get home. It wasn't the first time, however, that we had travelled by train.

Ohio

My mom was from Ohio, and her family still lived there. While living in Southern California, she took me and the twins on a 3-day train ride to see her mom and stepfather. I was probably about five. It was the only time we visited those relatives.

I only have a couple memory fragments from the trip. The adventure of traveling on a train was exciting. I can still see my sister and I, standing in the station, wearing our matching, fake-fur pink coats, holding our new boxy, luggage carry-ons, full of activities and snacks.

After we were underway, I remember making fast friends with a brother and sister, sitting between them and playing for hours. Later, I heard my mom tell someone how she looked back and found me fast asleep between two black children. I hadn't noticed the differences between us.

In my journal entry, I didn't know why the train ride was upsetting Marianne. But we had learned how to put memories in a safe place when we couldn't get help for a while. The place we created was a cabin in the mountains where our parts lived. Next to the cabin was a rain barrel. When we had to wait before we could get it out, we put a new memory "in the barrel" to reduce our stress and fear.

After assuring Marianne the memory was in the rain barrel, I again called on Brenda's help. She was an amazing child, only seven, but so adult-like. Later, I would miss her more than any other part.

We soon boarded the train leaving for Denver.

January 18: (I'm not sure who this was, but possibly Marianne.) *I'm afraid to write for fear of what might come out. What a horrible experience. It's better now but I still feel so scared. I was very afraid of the train station. I really was hoping someone would be there to meet me and no one was. Then we had to go outside all alone and find a cab with a man driving. I was so scared, and I just wanted to cry. I kept wondering if cab drivers rape their passengers. I wished I could cry. Then it cost so much money. My chest got really heavy. Can't we just go home—this is awful. No one understands how this feels. Where's my mommy? I have been asking for her all day. Where's my mommy?*

So much for making careful plans. Some friends in Denver let me stay at their house while I was in town seeing Faith and they had agreed to pick me up downtown, at the train station. But when I arrived, no one was there. I called from a pay phone around eight or eight-thirty. They had decided it was too dangerous to be downtown at night and told me to take a cab. They would pay for it.

Already triggered from the train ride, already struggling with a new memory pushing, now I went into full blown panic. I went into survival mode, or, at least someone inside did. I spent the cab ride assuming I would be raped or murdered.

The next day, I went to see Faith. We worked for seven hours over four days. Patty shared the memory, along with the fact she was the one who handled the scary cab ride the night before. She said the train to Ohio was fine, but things weren't fine when we got there.

We were staying in my grandparent's farmhouse. During the night, my grandpa (mom's stepfather) got me out of the room I was staying in and took me to the basement where he sexually abused me. It was a shame-filled memory.

I was now pretty sure I was just making all this stuff up. *Come on, like everyone is an abusive monster? Really? What's wrong with you?* Doubts constantly tormented me. Then I remembered a conversation with my father. He told me that my mother was sent away to live with her older brother because her stepfather had molested her. Once a pedophile, always a pedophile. Frankly, though, I would have preferred my theory that I was demented rather than accept this was true.

Not a Happy Birthday

Because other issues were emerging in therapy, Faith gave me an assignment. My birthday was coming up, and parts were starting to freak out. The assignment was to find out who was uncomfortable and why.

January 20: *I just have a couple questions tonight. The first is can anyone tell me why we are so anxious about our birthday next week?*

?: *Bad things happen on our birthday. We don't want any more bad things to happen. It's safer if we just skip the birthday. That way nobody gets hurt.*

Me: *I really am interested in hearing what you have to say. It sounds like you want to protect us from being hurt more. That is really a caring thing to do.*

Me: *Let's talk some more about this tomorrow. I want to hear what else you have to say.*

In my session the next day, this part shared a memory of abuse on her birthday. It would be years before I could relax about my birthday. It was always something I had to endure rather than enjoy.

January 26: *What a dreadful day. What dreadful feelings. What incredible pain. I wish I could make birthdays disappear forever. I don't want to ever have a birthday. I hate Roger for ruining my birthday dinner. I am so angry. I don't want to speak to him ever again. This pain is horrendous. I lay here like a lump, paralyzed. I wish I could act like a raving maniac. I want to break things. I want to yell and scream and thrash. My head hurts. Mostly I wish I could cry and cry and cry and cry. I have buckets to fill up. I'm full of tears. I want to cry, but they won't come out. And so, I lay here, numb, paralyzed. Nothing happening—frozen.*

Waiting—watching—holding our breath 'til it's over. Will it happen again today? Or will something else happen? Are we going to get hurt? No—it's over now. We didn't get hurt today. It's over and we survived. We can relax. We had good friends today to help us get through. Beth sat with us for hours and took us out to dinner. Susan sat with us, too—and then Diane, Sylvia, Cassandra, Chris, Grace and Marie took us out for dessert. Weren't those wonderful gifts? They were so fun. Won't it be great to use all those gifts?

I no longer remember the gifts, but I will never forget the friends. God blessed me with incredible friends who came alongside and supported me many times, including special occasions like my birthday. Because they knew what I was going through and that I was multiple, it felt safe to be with them.

January 26 (cont.) Little Cindy: *My head hurts and it feels funny. I'm sleepy. My stomach hurts, too. I miss Faith. I want my mommy.*

Me: *Little Cindy, what is making you feel so bad tonight?*

Little Cindy: *I get scared when I have to go to bed. What if the bad people come? We never know when they are coming.*

I had only been home a few days, and things were already ramping up. I was a mess all the time.

January 27: *Pensive, anxious, the chest is very tight, the heart is beating fast, the head feels tight and slightly throbbing, lost, where are we now? I feel scared. I don't know what I'm supposed to do now. Why do I feel so lost? I am unfocused. Should I be okay today? Should I have gotten up early and gone to work? Should I be okay today?*

Little Cindy: *Mommy—where's my mommy? Why did she go to work? My insides hurt today.*

Me: *Little Cindy, what would make you feel better today?*

Little Cindy: *I don't want to stay with the babysitter.*

Me: *I promise you that the babysitter will never ever come to our house. She is gone for good. What else do you need today?*

Little Cindy: *My doll and blanket.*

Me: *Okay. We have the blanket and the doll. What else can I do for you today?*

Little Cindy: *I don't want anybody to come to the house today.*

Me: *If anybody does come, they will not be the bad people.*

Little Cindy was going back to the babysitter, Mrs. Hetrick, who abused us. She seemed to be present in several memories, including one involving abuse on my birthday when I was very young.

Something else was pushing. I didn't know what it was, but Faith began talking to me about hospitalization.

(Later that day, at night) *I want to scream. Please let me scream. I want to cry, please let me cry. I want to hide in a closet, please let me hide in a closet. I want to let go, please let me let go. It's so hard, it's too hard. I'm tired of handling everything. I'm tired of managing everything every day. It's just too hard. Please let me know what I am supposed to do. Please make it obvious and clear. I can't go on like this. I feel so defeated.*

I tried so hard to not go into the hospital, to do all the right things, to do the work and manage my life—my family—work—church—job. But I can't do this level of pain here. I can't do it at home. There's no safety and no support. I can't do it in 2 hours of therapy—the time is constraining, and John (my therapist) *doesn't seem to know what to do with me. And my friends can't help* (me with my memories).

God help me. Inpatient—that's what John is pushing for—inpatient. I need a safe environment—I know. This isn't safe here. I gotta get safe. Where will the tears and screaming go if I stay here? What will happen to me? Could I possibly make it without going inpatient?

I was backed into a corner, never good for a survivor. I couldn't stay in my unsafe home environment with my troubling husband. But the idea of going into a psych hospital terrified me. I was starting to lose it.

January 29: *It's almost over—January. Only 2 more days. I will be so glad to see it go. Everything gets easier when January is over. I'm so tired. I wish this was over—this fighting for survival—this incredible stress—this overwhelming decision. I'm so tired. It's so hard here. Roger doesn't get it—what is going on with me?*

Chapter Eighteen

1994
February: Part One

The Psych Unit

With my birthday behind me, Faith arranged for me to go into the hospital in Denver. I was scared to death. She met me there, staying with me through the entire eight-hour intake ordeal. It seemed like the interviews, testing, and questions would never end.

I would not have been more frightened had I been processing into a prison, so I was relieved Faith was there. My mental flashbacks to the movie *One Flew Over the Cuckoo's Nest* weren't helping matters. She finally had to leave when they led me back to the women's quarters.

Things were so bad at home that I wasn't sure I would be able to return after my discharge. For that reason, I had an inordinate amount of luggage with me. The other *guests* snickered as the staff person showed me to my room, multiple large suitcases in tow. They also got a big kick out of learning who my roommate would be—Ann.

Ann was at least ten years younger, black hair, black leather jacket, and sporting a look of death when I walked in. She didn't speak a word to me and immediately walked out. *Oh, this is going to go well. I wonder if she has homicidal tendencies.* The only saving grace was that Ann was released the next day and I had the room to myself for the duration.

One of the other women told me not to worry about Ann; that was just one of her alters, trying to protect her from the stranger moving into her room. *Oh, another multiple! She's just like me.*

February 1: *I hate it here. I knew it would be hard, but this is much more horrible than I imagined. I am so lonely. I don't know what to do with myself. I feel like I'm being threatened to adapt in 24 hours or else. But I hate it here. They asked me 1,000 questions and at each round they asked the same questions over. I'm so tired. I could sleep for a year. All the new faces were a total overload—they really make it hard to adapt. Every time I turned around, I had to deal with a different staff person.*

God, please help me. I can't make it here. This is pain to die for. Tomorrow I have to start work. I have no idea what's going on with the parts. We just need sleep. I can't believe I'm here. I can't believe I've done this. It's so scary. It's so painful. It's so lonely here. I miss my girls. I miss (my girlfriend). *I miss Faith. God, give me strength. God, get me out of here as soon as possible. God, get me well. God, get me a life, please. I don't want this one.*

My parts were confused and disoriented, seeking answers, needing different things. Journaling gave voice to their concerns. After one part prayed, she heard God respond.

February 2: *Dear God, why did you put me here? You know I fear being in the hospital as much as any fear in my life. Why do you always make me do things I don't want to do? Why do I have to try every minute of the day? I'm tired. You know I didn't want to come here. Wasn't there another way? Why is this my life? I hear you—for today this is the best way—you want the best way. You want a different life for me now—and this is the way to get there.*

So why did you put me here? I think this is a very good question. Please answer that question soon. And as long as I'm here—let's do it. But, save me from myself 'cause I will get in the way at every chance. (Parts are chattering.) *I'm sleepy and my head feels dizzy. How come? Can't we go play? I want to nap. I want to get a blanket. My tummy hurts. Go away. Let's go. Stop it.*

Because Faith didn't have privileges at the hospital where I was staying, her husband, David, also a therapist, and up-to-speed on my work, came to the hospital to do my therapy.

Later that day: *Well, it is getting a little easier. I wouldn't want to buy real estate here, but I think I can stay and do some work. I made a lot of progress getting acclimated, trying to be with people, trying the groups. I did a lot—therapy—one more intake—3 medical exams—4 groups. I TRIED.*

David said 1) journal with my left hand, 2) stay out of my head, 3) don't care-take. (The doctor) said take the sleeping pill one more night and take Prozac—aaugh! I hate taking medication. The treatment plan says 1) identify feelings when suicidal, 2) do 3+ groups a day, 3) eat 2+ meals a day, 4) sleep 6+ hours a night, 5) journal 40 minutes day, 6) meet with (the doctor) or David every day, 7) have fun once a day. That sure seems like a lot to remember.

Because the protective mechanisms in survivors are fierce, it is hard to discover what exactly happened to them. No one inside wants to tell. This is why David encouraged me to try different things to get my parts to release their truth. Writing with the non-dominate hand was one of these techniques.

Sure enough, as I began journaling with my left hand, a new part showed up. Zora identified herself as a gypsy. She was very colorful—in clothes (I discerned this by the clothes she chose to wear), ideas, and language! She latched onto our assignment to have fun, suggesting we find a man and sneak him into the hospital unit. She did not appreciate my lack of cooperation.

The Assignment

I met with a new therapist and she gave me an assignment to write about unfairness.

February 7: *I am proud of myself because I was able to face something that I was afraid of. My anger terrified me. I wanted to get through it and I did. My panic feelings were high, my head and chest were tight, my abdomen was cramped. But now I feel peaceful. I faced my anger and now I don't feel sick. I did a great job, too.*

I focused my anger on the three people who betrayed my trust. What they did was unfair and I deserve my feelings of anger. It was unfair to be born to parents with chemical dependencies and sexual abuse in their backgrounds. It was unfair that my mother left me in the care of an abusive woman. It was unfair that I had to live with her day in and day out. My anger has been in a box for over 30 years but I let it out. I expressed it. It no longer has mastery over me. The secret is out.

(One of my parts began writing.) *I feel good now. I don't deserve to feel good. I am over the crisis and so I shouldn't stay here anymore. I should go back home now because I am doing better. Why do I feel so bad about myself? I don't believe anything good will ever be a part of my life. VICTIM S***! What's the matter with me? Why am I like this? Why am I sad? Home is so hard. I had forgotten what normal, peaceful feelings were like—but today I remembered. It was so good to be relaxed, calm, no bad feelings bombarding me, no backed up/overwhelmed feelings.*

But all day I feel guilt. I am not justifying my stay here. I spent 3 hours watching a movie. I could have been drawing or writing or sleeping. Why do I feel as though I have to justify my every hour of the day? Why do I feel so guilty for being here? Why does feeling good make me so sad? What is going on here? Maybe it was God's idea that we take the evening off. I wonder…

Exhibiting anger had never been an option growing up. Dad was too big and scary, and all-too eager to whip us with the belt if we did something to upset him. So I learned early on to keep it stuffed. As an adult though, this was holding me back. If I continually refused to allow or acknowledge my anger, I wouldn't get past it and heal.

The hospital gave me a safe place to do this work. There was no way I could tackle it at home, not with a rageful husband in the house. And a few hours of therapy didn't cut it either. Intreatment gave me the support and extended safety I needed to get at it, and I finally connected to and felt my anger. (And I didn't get a beating afterwards!)

While I could celebrate doing this great work, some of my parts couldn't. Breaking out of the old patterns and ways of thinking was hard work. Any victorious steps toward healing were met with internal punishment. My system knew how to operate in the old ways. New ways scared everyone, even if they were good and healthy ways. The fear of reprisal was ever present.

My alter's journaling made it apparent that I still had no sense I was a valued human being, of having needs, of taking appropriate care of myself. Clearly, I felt I didn't deserve anything good for myself. Making a new way was so hard.

The Letter

The same therapist gave me another assignment: write a letter to mom, a letter for my own processing, but not to mail.

February 8: *Dear Mom, this is a very very hard thing for me to do. In 38 years I have never felt safe enough to speak honestly to you without fear of repercussions. The few times I have stood my ground you have blasted me. I am not going to be blasted by you again. You may try—but I am not going to be there when you do. This healing journey I am on is the toughest thing I have ever done. When you tell me that I am your precious daughter, I just want to scream. It feels like you are smothering me with false love so I won't wake up to what really happened. But, it's too late—I did wake up. I am remembering. The cat's out of the bag.*

I know I was abused—over and over and by lots of people. But the worst thing for me right now is that I remember that I told you. Maybe not in clear, verbal language. But in my very best 5 year old way—I told you. I told you with tears and stomach aches and sleepless nights and nightmares and fear and panic. And who knows what else that I still haven't remembered.

You told me—in your words—that when you came home from work you would find me huddled up on the couch shaking. Why didn't you try to discover the reason for that? You said I had a "personality conflict" with the babysitter. Well, let me tell you, it was more than a personality conflict! This woman hurt me. And you hired her! You arranged for me to be with her. Day after day after day. The terror I felt being left in her care was unbearable. The pain became a private prison of hell for me—trapped inside for years and years. All the while I pasted my happy, caretaker, no problem, I can do it all, face on. That was unfair.

The abuse was unfair. But how you treated me was just as abusive. I needed to be listened to. I needed to be cared for. I needed to be believed. I needed to be defended and protected. I needed someone to fight the bad people for me. And you never did. You gave me barbiturates to sleep –that's no different than what the bad people did to me—drug me! Why didn't you pay attention? Why didn't you get it? Why didn't you stop it? Why didn't you help me? Why didn't you tell the truth? Why did you let me take the fall? Why is protecting yourself more important than protecting me? Why did you manipulate me into being your caretaker? I needed to be myself. I needed to be a kid, responsible for nothing more than cleaning my room—not responsible for your health and survival. I am not responsible for that. You are! Not me.

I am going to be me now. It isn't a pretty picture right now. But I am not going to push it away. Someday, the picture will be pretty—no thanks to you. Thanks to me for working my ass off—thanks to God for never leaving me alone—and thanks to many friends who are helping along the way.

It would take a lifetime to unpack everything in that letter. However, I came to the heart-breaking realization recently, twenty-five years after writing this letter, that confronting my mother never led to anything good in our relationship. It led to good in me, in getting freedom from the horrible bondage created in my childhood, in becoming a real person, in living a healthy life. But, sadly, my mother was never able to see me as a person separate from herself, with my own voice and my own needs. To her, I was never more than an extension of herself. And because of these realities, we never had more than a superficial relationship. My mother never knew me.

For me and every survivor, one of the most damaging aspects of traumatic experiences, is not being seen, heard, and believed. It is worse than the abuse itself. Physical wounds heal. But being ignored, accused, and blamed sends the message that it is your fault, you don't matter, and you deserve to be treated this way. Those lies create a Mount Everest-sized identity hurdle to overcome. That wound took forty years to heal.

Healing hinged on my willingness to do for myself what others didn't do so many years ago. I had to see my parts and hear them and believe what they were telling me. I had to find my voice and use it. I had to value myself and acknowledge that I didn't deserve the abuse I received. No one else could do that for me.

The letter was a vital piece of my healing. It did not change my relationship with my mother, but it did begin to change me.

I now knew why God wanted me here, in the hospital. He wanted to move a mountain, or several, actually.

Unexpected Blessings

While there, a camaraderie began to develop with the other inmates—oops, I meant patients. (However, this unit was locked down.) I began connecting with the women, one in particular. Sandi was from Australia. Having been diagnosed with DID (Dissociative Identity Disorder), her husband's research to locate the best place Sandi could get treatment landed her at the same hospital as me. I am forever grateful.

When I left the hospital later, I quickly lost track of everyone except Sandi. She stayed in Colorado for five years before moving back to the Sydney area. Since then, visits have been few and far between. Nevertheless, even an ocean between us hasn't stopped our friendship.

Like the other women in the unit, Sandi had alters, too. Living with other multiples, hearing them share about their life and struggles in group, watching them cope, made me realize something. This was real! I really did go through this trauma. I really did have parts. I really was multiple.

Seeing a dozen or so women whose lives looked just like mine, blasted my denial into oblivion. It was such a weird line I had been walking the previous three years, discovering my inner parts, acknowledging them, working with them, living with them. Yet, at the same time, always in the back of my mind, the thoughts: *This isn't real. This isn't happening. I'm making this up.*

Living isolated in a small town, not knowing a single person like me, surrounded by people who didn't understand anything about what I was going through, made it difficult to accept what was happening. But here I was now, in a community of women who were dealing with the same stuff. Our journeys looked the same. It was sobering, encouraging, and devastating, all at the same time. I would have preferred to be crazy than for my memories to be true.

In spite of the cold splash of reality in my face, this was one of many gifts God gave me during my ten-day stay. In the past, whenever I took a short vacation back into denial, I would get more and more uncomfortable and stressed. My parts would go nuts. And I actually felt crazier. But now that I had been around other trauma survivors, I rarely questioned my diagnosis.

As I made friends, they affectionately told me what they were thinking when I arrived—what a sight I was with all those suitcases! They couldn't figure out what I was doing there. I stood out as someone who was not from their world. It didn't take long, though, for the barriers to dissolve. Our outer worlds may have been different, but our inner worlds were not.

Evenings were the best. When the day's work was done, therapists and clinical staff gone, we played games, talked about our lives and laughed and joked about things only multiples could understand. Sandi introduced us to Vegemite (a savory spread for bread or crackers) and strange Australian words like whinging (whining), Sheilas (girls), eskies (ice chests), and walkabouts (hikes). It loved it whenever she said, *Good on you, mate!*

I soon became attached. I was with people who knew all about me and still accepted me. I felt safe. The thought of leaving them and returning home filled me with dread.

The day finally arrived when I was to be discharged. One of the diagnoses they slapped on me during the intake was *anhedonia*. I'd never heard of it. I had to look it up: *The inability to experience pleasure in normally pleasurable acts.* In other words, I sucked at having fun. I was greatly offended, although I could see the truth in it.

Wanting to prove them wrong, I cooked up a plan to be carried out on the eve of my discharge. However, still being the rule-following good girl, I sought permission first from the staff. They agreed, aiding and abetting my scheme by sneaking in the needed supplies. We had a big party, including shooting silly string all over the common areas of the unit. I felt quite victorious. And happy—a rare moment those days.

But then I had to go home.

Chapter Nineteen

1994
February: Part Two

The Separation

The day I was admitted to the hospital, Roger began seeing another woman. It would be six months before anyone told me. Once back from the hospital, however, I suspected nothing.

I was on my own again, juggling the complexities of my outer world and my inner world. Both John and Faith felt Roger and I needed some sort of separation (even without knowing about the affair). I never felt safe when he was in the house, creating a state of constant hypervigilance. My parts were a wreck, either terrified or full of rage. I had to leave home to find any peace, which was the primary reason I had gone to the hospital in the first place.

Because of the uniqueness of our property, the separate four-room office behind our house seemed the logical solution and Roger moved out. Our pastor helped us negotiate terms of a marital agreement, because we both wanted the marriage to ultimately work. (At least that was my assumption, at the time.)

The agreement spelled out the rules and expectations, the goals being to bring the tension level down and create an environment of safety. Every night, we would have dinner together with the girls, discussing only their lives. Everyone in the family would see a therapist. Roger and I would meet with our pastor each week to work through problems, updates, and financial decisions.

The Dysfunctional Family

It was a good idea in theory, but it never worked. At some point, John told me Roger was a sociopath, meaning he was narcissistic and then some. John's observation, having done marriage counseling with us, was that Roger could not distinguish other people's needs, only his own. His own tragic childhood had him locked up into extreme selfishness and patterns of retaliation when he didn't get his way. This explained why he sabotaged any healthy plans or agreements.

And, honestly, I was too absorbed in my own world of traumatic memories to be helpful or supportive of his issues. My healing wasn't just hard on me, it was hard on everyone who cared about me too. As always happens, my healing issues exacerbated my husband's. All I could do was hope his therapy would be a vehicle of true healing for him.

My poor girls, what a mess their parents had become. Bree was fifteen and Jenny twelve. If I could have one do-over in life, I would use it to be a better mother to my girls through all this. Such hard years, and their home life was awful. Neither parent was focused on how they were doing or what they needed. In some ways I was reenacting my own childhood, but now as my mother. I hated that.

The girls had opposite relationships with their stepfather. When Tim and I started therapy with Roger, Bree was two and I was pregnant with Jenny. The pregnancy was key to his attraction to me, taking him back to a time in his life when he felt important and valued. When he was fourteen and living with his mother and stepfather, his mother had her second child, Tom. His stepfather left soon after, resulting in Roger having a significant role raising Tom.

Roger was just as interested in raising Jenny as he was in me, maybe more so. Jenny became the object of his affections. So she got all the goodies from Dad and Bree was left out. A later therapist suggested that Jenny was the designated wife in our family system. It was very messed up.

Roger made no place for Bree in his life, seeing her as a threat to himself from the beginning. His preference for Jenny was blatant. To

Bree's credit, she fought her way to adulthood, screaming for her rights and needs to be met. Unfortunately, that just made their relationship worse. Bree had no good alternatives, nothing she did would change the situation. After having been abandoned by her biological father at two, the relationship with Roger dealt a deathblow to her self-esteem.

My frequent trips to Denver and Ouray left the girls in Roger's care, with no one to mediate and buffer their relationship with him. It wasn't good. I don't know if I was oblivious or just too overwhelmed with my own mess to respond appropriately. But I was little help to the girls.

Hearing My Parts

I had only been home from the hospital two days when we started the pseudo separation. It was February and I was not looking forward to the fourteenth.

February 14: *Not a very happy Valentine's Day, that's for sure. The pain is so high. Roger moving out to the office feels like abandonment. Every time I turned around something was gone from the house. And he seemed so happy about it. This feels too hard to live with. I want to cry, but the tears won't come out. My chest is tight and heavy. I feel so sad that our marriage has slipped apart one more notch. So much has been bad, painful, frustrating, and now this "in house" separation. The physical reality of him living in the office emphasizes the loss and failure for me. I've lost so much. Why do I keep losing? It just keeps getting harder and harder. The harder I work, the more the pain increases. Sadness—dripping sadness—it's like my heart is leaking big drops of blood. I just wish my eyes would leak—maybe it would ease the pain and heaviness. I need to remind myself that this arrangement is only temporary. We will be able to have something more normal eventually. And this will give me space to continue recovery. It is the best thing for now.*

It wasn't long before my inner world started coming undone again. I was having nightmares all the time.

February 23 (morning): *I need to write. I need to ask some questions. I need to find out how things are inside. But still the word this week is containment. Try to keep the memory/pain/intensity contained at least through this week. I want more time here—more rest—more time to stabilize home—more time to work before I do memory work again.* (I went on to describe a nightmare involving sexual abuse in my home with an actor who reminded me of my dad. My mom was there but didn't think anything of it. The dream triggered feelings in my seven-year-old part, Marianne.)

Me: *Does anybody want to write to me about this dream or talk to me about it?*

Marianne: *I don't like it.*

Me: *What don't you like?*

Marianne: *I don't like the dream, the man or the mother. They are icky.*

Me: *Why are they icky?*

Marianne: *He was old and big, he didn't belong in my room.*

Me: *I agree he didn't belong there. That wasn't right at all.*

Marianne: *I want to see Faith.*

Me: *You like Faith a lot, don't you?*

Marianne: *Yes. She takes care of me. I miss her.*

Me: *Me, too. You know we are going to see her in March. We are going to go back to Denver and work with her again. This week we are going to stay here and rest. We talked to her yesterday. Did you hear her on the phone?*

Marianne: *Yes, but I didn't get to talk to her.*

Me: *You sound so sad, Marianne.*

Marianne: *My Mommy doesn't help me. She doesn't understand. I am very sad today.*

Me: *That makes me sad, too, Marianne. I'm so sorry that Mommy didn't help you.*

The dream felt very real to Marianne.

February 23 (evening): *Who would like to write tonight? Who wants to talk? I really want to listen if someone has something to say. How are you doing? I am wondering if anybody has thoughts or feelings about when we should go to Denver to see Faith again.*

Cynthia: *I want to stay home for a while. I want to have* (a girlfriend's) *birthday lunch before we go. I want to get caught up. It's lonely in Denver. My friends are here. I don't want to change things yet.*

Marianne: *But I'm starting to get sick to my stomach. I miss Faith and I am afraid. A lot of people hurt inside. It's hard to be a grownup and take care of things all the time. I feel sad and lonely. My stomach hurts.*

Alex: *I hate myself. Nothing is right. I don't want to be here or there. I don't want to be me. I don't want to do this. I'm an embarrassment. We shouldn't have called Faith again. We bug her too much. Go away. Leave me alone. I don't like you. I don't like me. I don't like any of us.*

Me: *Thanks for sharing everybody. I'm going to pray about this and think about what everybody said. Thanks again.*

As always, trying to listen and respect my parts was complicated. It was impossible to give each of them what they wanted. The best I could do was let them know I heard them and that I cared.

Whenever a part told me their stomach hurt, I knew another memory was likely coming up. For me, it always started there. Even when I was a young, I carried my pain in my gut. I had no idea what Marianne was remembering, but it wouldn't be long before I did.

February 28: *Another month almost over—good. The pain is too deep.*

(A new part emerged named, Thomas): *I hate being trapped in this body with this person. I hate this soft squishy female body. It is so out of shape. We should have swum today—but no—we slept in instead. Give me a break. Then would somebody explain to me why in the hell we signed those loan papers? Are we totally off the deep end? We start to stand up and then we cave in. Shut down, that's what we do. Hopeless—we are hopeless. And you are pathetic. And he* (Roger) *is bad news. He will never get it. Too deceitful, too manipulative. Well, the feelings are out tonight. We are crazy! Angry at being lied to about the banker. Angry at him twisting the truth and trying to make me out as a bad communicator, and white washing his lie by saying he was just sharing his perceptions. Angry that he tried to use the banker to manipulate me to sign the loan papers. Angry at Marissa for getting scared and signing the papers. Angry at John* (my therapist) *for not being more confident and aggressive in his work with me. Angry at the money problems because we can't afford what we are doing. Angry at my dad for imposing a visit on me at this time. Angry at my life cause it's such a mess.*

I guess the hospital stay did help, at least I could get in touch with my anger a little easier.

For exercise, I had been swimming laps for several years, and was trying to keep it up during recovery. I had limited success, to say the least. I don't remember what the loan was for, but finances were tight. Roger loved spending money and buying new things, something that added to my anxiety. I was no longer working, and therapy wasn't cheap, not to mention the $7000 hospital bill we had just incurred. Our insurance covered none of it. We were drowning in debt.

And now my dad was coming for a visit.

Chapter Twenty

1994
March: Part One

Therapy: Day One

It was time to once again make the five-hour drive through the Rocky Mountains. I knew my dad was coming for a visit, but I had already scheduled a full week of therapy with Faith. Besides, I was in no shape for a visit. He showed up anyway, spending the week with Roger and the girls.

The night before I left, someone inside made a pencil drawing of tall weeds and plants. On the ground were tiny ants. Whoever drew it said they felt worried and troubled. I didn't know what it meant.

March 5: *Long day—very exhausted—want to sleep. Should I write? Should I draw? Should I check-in? Should I read? Should I forget it all and go to sleep? Check-in—that seems most important. Jacob is nervous about being here. Sarah wants to play. What would anybody like to do while we are here in Denver?* (My parts shared a list of things they wanted to do.)

Me: *Those are some really great ideas. We will do as many as we can while we are here. It's kind of scary to come back. Are the girls going to be okay?*

Patty: *My stomach doesn't feel good. I'm lonely. It hurts. Please don't leave me alone.*

March 6: Patty: *The pain is coming out. Why am I losing my voice? Why did I draw boxes? I didn't see boxes. I saw explosions but I drew boxes. What is going on here? Talk to me! Please tell me the truth. Pain is coming. I can't stop it. I don't like it. I'm afraid of the pain. Will you help me? What if I can't take it? Will someone come to help?*

Drawing or painting pictures throughout my healing was a great aid to my parts, giving them a safe way to express their memories and pain. Sometimes I knew what it was about, but often not. I didn't know what the boxes were about, but on the back of the picture, Patty wrote that she felt angry and frustrated and her pain was contained in the boxes.

Several parts did significant work during my two-hour therapy session that day. Jacob handled the steps in the ritual, sworn to secrecy on threat of losing his tongue. Now I understood why he was so reluctant to talk. Zora, a self-proclaimed gypsy and one of my most colorful parts, described a cult ritual involving sexual abuse. She survived by focusing on the ants on the ground, trying to imagine herself crawling away with them. She must have been the one who did the pencil drawing.

My dad always told us we were part gypsy and that's why we moved all the time. That might explain why Zora latched on to the gypsy identity. Always the salesman, my dad had an excuse for everything. We weren't gypsies, but we did have English, French, German, and three Native American tribes in our genealogy. He liked to say we were little savages.

March 7: Zora: *What a day. I hate this memory. God must hate me. I've been such a bad girl. Why did I make this up? I'm such a bad girl.* (Having sex with) *men—that's what I am good for. Nobody does it better than me.*

Me: *Now what? Why is the denial back? Why is this one so hard to believe? Why is it any different from the others? Why do I feel so bad about this?*

I called home that night to see how things were going. Roger said my dad was acting strange. He was jittery and nervous, and asking a lot of questions about my therapy in Denver. In particular, he wanted to know what I was remembering. He asked Roger, point blank, *"Is Cyndy remembering whether I abused her?"* Roger had no response.

Therapy: Day Two

The second day of therapy would be pivotal. As is the normal pattern for memories, the safer, easier memories emerged first. That's why I remembered the abuse from the babysitter. I had no current relationship with her, making it less painful. The satanic ritual piece was harder. But the memory today would be the worst piece of my puzzle.

Because the rituals were so traumatic, it was normal that several parts held the information. But getting them to talk about it was nearly impossible. There is something about speaking it out loud that makes it seem more real, making silence or denial the preferred route. The subconscious reasoning is that maybe it isn't true if we don't talk about it.

Zora, Jacob, Tammy, and Thomas all described parts of the memory that day, and the man who sexually abused me. They said he was strong, tall, with dark hair and oily skin. But they didn't know who he was. No one did, at least not until John shared. John fancied himself as invisible. He watched what was happening, but no one knew he was watching, making it safer for him to hold the truth.

John joined the therapy session: *I am not happy to be here. I know something. I know what the man looked like. He looked like my dad. He smelled like my dad. His skin was oily.* (John went on to describe a ritual with a goat sacrifice, chanting, dancing, calling on the gods, and snakes.)

John was my first alter to say the word 'dad,' but even he couldn't come out and just say the obvious.

At the end of the session, while praying with Faith, I heard Jesus' voice. His first message comforted me: *I love you.* The second sent me spinning: *This is true.*

When we were finished, I was a miserable mess, confused and disoriented, looking for relief somewhere, but not finding it.

March 8: Judith Ann, my wise, inner, self-helper: *Don't judge it, just let it be. Let it be out there for whatever it is right now. It's not all clear and that's okay. Don't judge it—let it come. Let it be told—the truth. The truth always comes. You know it does. We don't need to be afraid of the truth. There is nothing we can't get through at this point. God is constantly with us, helping us, guiding us, protecting us, bringing truth to us. We have Faith's help all week. Better to let it come out here rather than at home. We have support. We aren't alone. So, relax—let it come—don't fear what's coming. Don't block what is coming or sabotage or deflect—go with it. Trust yourself and the Holy*

Spirit within you. Pray and God will bring his light. You can count on that, you know you can—he has never let you down. He will redeem the evil done to us. He will restore us to a place of wholeness we've yet to experience. Remember what he told you—"When you pass through the waters, I will be with you. They will not overwhelm you or cause you to drown." You can do it. I know you can.

After my session, I decided to drive to the other side of Denver, to the suburb where my family lived when I was fourteen and visit my old neighborhood. This was the last place I lived with my dad and the school where I was molested by the gang of boys. Apparently, Alex was doing the driving.

Therapy: Day Three

Alex had some words to share when we returned to Faith's: *I hated my dad. He was either gone or he was mean. There wasn't anything there to love. He treated Mother like dirt. I went back to that house yesterday, the last place he lived with us. I sort of felt sad. I wanted to know if memories can be trusted. I wanted to see if my house, neighborhood, and school was like I remembered it. It was exactly as I remembered it twenty-three years ago. My memory was right. That's where we lived when everything fell apart.* (The high school) *Boys—all the things that happened—parents gone—hurt over and over. Nobody cared. On our own from then on.*

When we finished day three of therapy, Faith wouldn't let us leave without making a contract with Alex, ensuring he would not drive back to Arvada. He said he wanted to drive fast and wreck the car, after he got drunk. Alex was scary. I still remember moments of careening down the interstate in Denver at high speeds in cruise control with my feet on the dash. We were not stable, by any means. Fortunately, we cooperated with the contract that night and returned to our friend's house.

March 9: (Unknown part) *I want my mommy. Will somebody please come and help me. I am so lonely, and my stomach hurts again.*

That night Alex drew a picture of a cliff above a rocky ocean. We were standing on the edge. Filled with pain and fear, and very suicidal, he wrote, *"Will she hit the rocks or the water?"*

Alex: *I hate this place. I hate all of this—every bit of it. I can't go to Arvada. I can't drive fast or wreck the car. I sure as hell don't want to go see our f****** father in Montrose. Stuck here doing nothing. Hating myself and not doing anything about it. Die—let's die and get this over with. Dying can't feel any worse than this. It's gotta be better. Then everybody inside would stop suffering. It's how I can help. I'm strong. I can do it. Just give me a chance—let's get this over with.*

Me: *Alex, I really appreciate you and how much you care about our suffering. I'm sorry that you are so frustrated tonight. But, Alex, we shouldn't die for this. As bad as it is—we will get through it and be okay. We should live and not die. We didn't do anything wrong. I need your strength, Alex. I need you to help us all see what is true and face it and keep living while we are in pain. That's how you can really help. I need you. Will you stay and help us get through tonight and tomorrow?*

Alex: *Yea, I guess I'll stay and help.*

Me: *Thanks, Alex.*

Always negotiating. Trying to keep everyone calm and safe. It wasn't easy. Suicidal ideation was never far away. If thoughts of dying weren't in my mind, it was like they were sitting on the other side of a door, waiting until I let them back in.

Therapy: Day Four

Another memory emerged. I was in the hills above Ventura, the area where I lived from ages three to eight. There was a beat-up, rusted, white truck along with a black and white van with the words "Hammond Organs and Pianos" painted on the side. That was the delivery truck for my dad's music store. There was a goat in the back of the truck, along with robes, pieces of wood, and other things.

The adults began setting up for the ritual. A Native American woman had a robe for me to wear. She told me to be very quiet. I was given a glass of water to drink. Things got blurry after that. I had to sit down. Someone was playing drums, a Native American man. The women waved scarves as they danced around the fire, showing me what to do.

My dad was there. His friend from the store was there, too. And I also saw my grandfather sitting there, watching me, telling me how pretty I was. The scene quickly descended into another ritual sacrifice and sexual abuse. The rituals always ended the same way.

When they were finished, they took me part way down the hill, where my bike was waiting, and told me to ride home.

Afterward, I struggled to believe the memory. The Native American stuff made no sense to me. Just because we had Native American blood from generations past didn't mean this was true. Seeds of doubt burrowed into my mind.

March 10: *I just need to write for a while tonight without thinking or being careful about what I'm writing—stream of consciousness writing. I feel clear in my memory yet confused because it doesn't seem to be over. Something's still happening in my head. A drugged feeling so strong I thought I was going to pass out. Can I keep going on like this? My schizophrenic lifestyle. I can't stay here. I'm imposing. I feel guilt. I don't help enough, pay enough, cook enough. I don't earn my keep. But I'm working here—hard—really hard. I'm not done. I want a break. But I have to hurry so I can keep my imposition as short as possible. I have to hurry so I can get home to be mom again as soon as possible. But I don't want to hurry this. It's hard. I'm scared. I'm hurting. I don't know if I'm ready. Don't rush me.* (The friend who I stay with) *says don't feel rushed. Things seem to be okay here. I'm scared. I just want to stop everything now—take a break—rest—process—let things begin to gel. I don't know what I think about my grandfather being in the cult activity. What do I feel? Where are the feelings tonight? Should I cry? I want to cry. I want it to come out. I want my feelings. I deserve my feelings. I didn't feel so much today during the session. But there are feelings. Please come out, feelings. Please come out, truth—all truth—please speak. Please share—it needs to be told—please don't hold back. I want to hear. I want to know. You will be believed and heard. Then healing can come from all of us. Come out, truth—come out, memory. Zora, please come and share tonight. Write to me. I want to hear from you.*

Zora: *So what do you want to know? How I am? I am fine. I am beautiful. I am tired. This memory work is no easy thing. It's hard you know, and you fight me on it. You know you do. Let me flow and I'll tell you the truth. I agree—it's a story that needs to be told. We must all share. My feelings? I do what I have to do. And I do it well. I get pleasure where I can. I take what I can get. The rest doesn't matter to me. The other feelings are no good. There's always more to tell—when the time is right. I can't afford to think about the grandfather. It's over now. Who cares? Yes, we can still talk about the father.*

The abreaction of the memory wouldn't let up. I still felt drugged. My body was remembering everything. I hurt everywhere.

Therapy: Day Five

Patty confirmed we were raped by Dad.

I knew I wasn't safe to be alone. For the first time in over thirty years, I was fully connected to my truth. The truth was no longer compartmentalized, and I wanted to die. I could find no reason to live anymore. The knowledge that I was incested by my own father was threatening to destroy me.

Faith let me rest on the sofa in her office for the next five hours so she could keep an eye on me. When I was finally able to pull myself together, I returned to my friends' house. There was no journaling for several days.

Therapy: Day Six

On my final day with Faith, I was trying to pick up all the pieces before returning home—an impossible task. Patty was feeling the effects of the rape. Her insides hurt immensely. Thomas was raging at the idea that Dad was visiting our home this week, wanting to kill him, or at the very least, end the relationship. Alex was crying, afraid of what Thomas might do, feeling abandoned by Dad, and still wanting to crash the car. Zora was taking all the blame since she was the one who did the dance to entice the men. And who knows about all the others.

Faith and I finished up a little after one o'clock, having done fourteen hours of therapy during the week. I headed back over the mountains, exhausted, but eager to see my girls.

Unbeknownst to me, while my dad was visiting my home, he recorded a cassette tape. He left it on the kitchen counter.

Chapter Twenty-One

1994
March: Part Two

The Model Family Tape

The purpose of Dad's tape was to give me his version of our family story, his response to the things I shared with him, including the memory of being sexually abused by a babysitter. The week he recorded the tape, he didn't know that I had literally been remembering that he had abused me himself. My dad's taped message was confusing, to say the least.

On the one hand, his recording confirmed some of my recollections. We lived in the San Fernando Valley, California, when I was born, relocating to the Ventura area when I was three. When I was eight, we moved north to Sacramento; that was the point Mom became ill. Weighing only eighty-seven pounds, she was hospitalized frequently, nearly dying more than once. At a height of 5′ 8″, she was nothing but skin on bones. Dad said, because she was ill, *"You were called upon then to be an eight or nine-year-old mother."* Yes, that was my memory, too.

The doctors were baffled as to what was wrong with my mother. Dad said, *"Her body would not digest food and she was starving to death."* I wondered, though, whether she was anorexic and choosing not to eat as a response to decades of unresolved trauma in her own life. She had countless diagnoses over the years, more than thirty surgeries, and even wore a full body cast for two years. For my mother, pain expressed itself through illness.

Other parts of Dad's taped story, however, did not line up. *"Your mother really never did work.... I'm sorry if that isn't the way you remember it, but my memory is very clear on this."* That was an interesting note since Mom already told me she worked every day from the time I was three until I was eight, and that Mrs. Hetrick was the babysitter for at least three of those years. My sister remembered Mrs. Hetrick, too. And early in my recovery, my father already admitted that Mom worked, and we had a babysitter. Why would Dad lie about this?

Then there were things he kept repeating, like saying four times we had a very wonderful life together. And going on and on about me: a beautiful baby, a model child, a loving, wonderful girl who never complained, unquestionably the most competent, brightest young person he'd ever known. (Let me tell you, I wasn't *that* good. I had an ornery streak when it came to my brother and sister, not to mention that my rebelliousness landed me in the principal's office more than once.)

What was *not* included in the letter was also disturbing. Especially since Dad said, *"To the best of my recollection and without doing any embellishing or trying to candy-coat it, I've told you what our life was like. It wasn't that bad."* There was zero mention of his chronic philandering, walking out on the family to marry another woman, or the wild drunken parties at our house. He even denied being an alcoholic, *"just a moderate to heavy drinker but certainly not an alcoholic."* (He was in Alcoholics Anonymous for over forty years!)

His words were carefully crafted to paint the picture he wanted me to see. Just enough truth to try and get me to buy his distorted version.

On the tape, he referenced my mother's *"horrible issues having to do with abandonment and molestation,"* assuming she had told me about these. She hadn't. In fact, she never told me anything about the many times she was sexually abused. With her, everything was a secret. Anything I knew about my mom came from my father. He then went on to say, *"Both parents* (meaning he and my mom) *were dysfunctional and came from dysfunctional backgrounds."* His perspective, though, was that *"there weren't really a lot of problems."*

By the time I was done listening, I had whiplash.

I think one of the things that most hurt me, having remembered the abuse, was the lack of interest and concern on the part of either my dad or mom. Being a mother myself, I was constantly putting myself in their shoes, imagining one of my daughters telling me she was remembering childhood abuse. My own mental scenario never came close to the reaction I got from my parents. I would be horrified, asking questions, concerned for their welfare, offering help. Not with my parents, though. None of that. Every time I brought it up (and, quickly I stopped doing so, realizing there was no point), I was met with denial and defensiveness, at best. And at worst, blame.

Years later, my mother called me to wish me happy birthday. Let me tell you, after that call, it was anything but a happy birthday. She started screaming at me, ending her tirade with, *"When are you going to recant of the horrible things you have done to this family!"* At one point or another, everyone in my family blamed me, because I accused Dad of incest.

The other strange thing is that no one in the family asked me to tell them the story. Over the years, they've heard bits and pieces when I occasionally dropped a fact or two. But, to this day, they've never heard the whole story. Nevertheless, they are quick to tell me it isn't true (whatever "it" is, because they don't know).

Three or four years after Dad made this tape, I got a call from my grandmother, the only time she had ever called me. She was quite upset with me for suggesting her wonderful son could ever do such a despicable thing as to sexually abuse me. I said, *"Grandma, but he wasn't the only one. Grandpa sexually abused me, too."* I was dumbfounded at her response. *"Oh, that doesn't surprise me in the least. He was an evil man and did horrible things."*

Really? So my dad's father, the man who raised my dad, was an evil man, but his son was an angel. Why did no one's stories add up? Why was it that anytime someone tried to convince me that the abuse never happened, they ended up confirming my story, or at least some part of it?

Processing the Tape

March 17: *Please, I don't want to feel any more pain tonight. I am tired, weary to the bone. I have worked so hard this week to keep it together. I have tried to meet the needs of the most needy—in therapy, smashing eggs, sleeping all morning yesterday, re-contracting to keep us safe, calling Faith, driving with* (a girlfriend)*, telling my story. And I am tired. It is all so much work. On top of all that I have worked at the office, done the budget, cared for the kids and household.*

And now I have to deal with this tape. The "model family" tape. It describes the perfect family. I know it's not true—so why agonize over it? Why not smash the tape and forget it ever existed? It's not worth spending even a moment of pain on. Like John (my therapist, the godly Christian pastor) *said, "Bull s***!" That is what it is. He could tell it was fiction regardless of my memories. Is this some sort of counter-play by my father? Is he thinking that since I'm having memory problems that he can invent a nice story about our family and present it as truth? Will I be gullible or compliant enough to buy into this fiction? So where is truth? If I know his little story is crap, why even give it a second thought? Why feel any pain or confusion or doubt? I don't know why.*

All I know is that my memories are wild—almost incredible. They are bizarre, weird, torturous, unthinkable. But I can't deny the pain, the agony that I feel. Why is he doing it? Is he trying to cover up the truth? Is he trying to lead me away from something he doesn't want me to remember? Is he frightened? Did he really do it? Are his memories repressed, too? Or is he right? Was everything hunky-dory? Am I making all this up? Maybe I'm delusional.

*Am I bad? Is something wrong with me? I don't want to do this anymore. I don't want to have any more memories. I want to stop all this now. I don't want to go on. I'm embarrassed. Smashing eggs with my friends is embarrassing. Being so needy so often is embarrassing. Having 28+ personalities is embarrassing. I don't want to have any more. It's too many already. Maybe I don't have MPD. Maybe every bit of this is s***. I hate myself. I'm too tired. Why is everything so muddled tonight?*

It was always the same thing. After another horrendous memory emerged and the feelings began to dissipate, the doubt would start to set in. I had been dissociative all my life, compartmentalizing the abuse from the rest of my so-called normal existence. Trying to meld it all together, thirty-five years later, wasn't easy.

Healing was Happening

I had a lot to be angry about, and anger was never a safe emotion to express at home. As a child, showing anger resulted in a beating, one of the many reasons I learned to act like a "model child"—to escape the beatings. Since being in the hospital, I was trying to do a better job of acknowledging and expressing my anger. Smashing eggs in an empty field helped a little. (I always seemed to run out of eggs too fast, though.) Destroying a plastic toy toolbox was a little more satisfying.

March 22: *How does everybody feel about the toolbox destroying exercise? How are you doing, Alex?*

Alex: *Just dandy! Well at least you let me do it—finally. Yes, I liked doing it. It felt great to heave that sledgehammer down on that box and hear it crack and see those pieces fly everywhere.*

I didn't know how to take care of myself. I'd never done it before. I could administrate anything at church, run any program, care for my home and kids with ease, but when it came to meeting my own needs, I was clueless. Figuring it out required the laborious task of talking to my parts, making lists of their ideas, negotiating, evaluating, etc. But it was the only way I could think of, to learn how to be human.

This was a rare day, because no one was home except me.

March 26: *I could just eat junk food all day—no problem. Pepsi and chips are good. We could move on to Blizzards, French fries, hamburgers, popcorn, candy. We could eat ourselves into oblivion. Wouldn't that be fun? I wonder what that would be compensating for? Fear, sadness, loneliness, abandonment, that the girls are gone, anxiety and fear that Roger is coming home. I don't want to feel anymore. Let's eat instead of feel. I don't want to feel and be alone. It's too hard.*

We could be responsible. We could swim laps, eat leftovers, type up new song sheets, file recipes. Then we would feel good about ourselves. We would be using our time wisely—getting things done. We would be able to attach value to the day because there would be tangible evidence of accomplishments—things to cross off the list—busyness to keep us from feeling.

We could do personal work. Another responsible choice because we would be not only accomplishing things, but meeting needs of alters. We could play, color, sing, paint, draw, and throw eggs. We would be using the time wisely because those things are hard to do when the family is around. It would alleviate guilt because I have done little or none of that lately. But chances are, feelings would come up. And we would be alone with feelings—again. Bad, bad, bad. I don't want to be a bad girl anymore. And of course, I feel very much like a bad girl most of the time. That reminds me of something else I could do—write letters to parents—cousins—aunts. Yuck!

Well, we could always go for the total distraction route—go to the play—two plus hours of compelling drama. And since that doesn't start until 8, we could combine that with other ideas already mentioned. We could read some journaling exercises and try them out. That would feel like we accomplished something. Then there is the extremely tempting offer of (my girlfriend) *to go out to her house and have dinner, visit and watch a movie which is the ultimate in safe, positive distractions, but accomplishes nothing.*

So, what do we have on the list? Binging and writing letters are not good—let's forget them altogether. I don't want to be alone the entire evening, so let's skip the play. We will save money. So, what could we do before we go to (my girlfriend's)*? Personal work—color, sing or paint. Journaling—pick one exercise. So, let's prioritize the list and then get started. OK? OK!*

When all was said and done, I seemed to be making some progress in understanding my needs and feelings.

March 26 (cont.): *I'm alone and it's:*

Okay because I'm safe

Sad because my kids are gone

Fun because I got to paint

Freeing because I got to pick what I wanted to do

Scary because I feel so vulnerable

Unique because I rarely am home alone

Peaceful because no one is fighting

An opportunity because what is inside comes out much more easily

Pleasant because I like my house

Focusing because no one is here to distract me

On March 29, I was back in Faith's office for three days of therapy. Now that the worst secret was out, Dad's abuse, other memories began tumbling out quickly. One part processed how much she loved her daddy, but that he never saw her or loved her back. Another part shared more about the babysitter, remembering how she would watch a soap opera and then take me into the bedroom and abuse me.

Someone talked about grandpa waking her from a nap, telling her to be *"be quiet and don't say anything,"* as he put a pillow over her head and abused her. It turned out this would be my earliest memory, seemingly to take place around age two. This led me to believe in the likelihood of the abuse beginning at birth.

One more part processed a ritual memory that took place in the church, recalling the threats toward her family if she didn't comply. It was a ceremony to celebrate the death of God. This part knew that wasn't true, because God was inside her and held her.

By now, my parts and I had had numerous encounters with Jesus. Whenever a memory emerged, Faith would invite the alter who held the memory to see Jesus. Without exception, they always did. Then we would pray. Afterward Jesus always came and took care of little Cyndy. I saw it in my mind and felt it in my heart. Each time he took care of the bad people, standing up for me and punishing them. Then he would take me away with him, somewhere safe. He cared for me in many ways: bringing warm robes, dressing the physical wounds, rocking by the fire, swinging together, holding me while I cried.

Words don't exist to express the restorative power of this process. It healed my heart, mind, body, and soul. These were the things that needed to happen at the time of the abuse, but never did. After dozens of these encounters with Jesus, embedded in my soul was the truth that Jesus saw me, knew me, cared about me, valued me, and that he had all the power I needed to be safe. Healing was happening.

Chapter Twenty-Two

1994
April

Pain

There was never a moment when I didn't feel pain. I hurt all the time.

This next entry was an exercise I read about in a book about journaling.

April 2: *The pain is great. It cuts through my heart like a knife. I'm sure if someone checked they would find internal bleeding. Is it fatal, I wonder? It is certainly monstrously large—like a cancerous tumor the size of a grapefruit pressing against my heart muscles. How can an emotional hurt cause so much physical pain? Can I dialogue with the pain? Will it speak to me and share its secrets with me? Can I learn anything valuable from this horrendous hurt? Talk to me, pain. What are you like?*

Pain: *I am like the ocean—vast, beyond what the eye can see—surging up onto the shore of your consciousness in large, cold, harsh waves—beating against the rocks of your mind and body relentlessly.*

Me: *Why is the surging and beating so harsh and difficult to endure?*

Pain: *Because the water has been under pressure for so long, it pushes hard now to finally come out. Also, because the vastness runs so deep.*

Me: *But it feels like it will kill me if it continues because I couldn't possibly live through it. Will it kill me? Can you kill me?*

Pain: *I can't kill you. But your response to me can be one of defeat and discouragement. Don't lose hope and you won't die.*

Me: *So, if your mission is not to kill me, what then?*

Pain: *To restore you. Just like your memories, I too must be brought to the light. All parts must be heard, accepted and healed. I am one of those parts. You are hearing me and now trying to accept me. The healing will naturally follow.*

Me: *So, how can I make peace with you and live through this?*

Pain: *Take it easy. I take lots of your energy. Do at least one nice thing for yourself every day. Talk to at least one person about me every day. This writing is good—do more of it. Draw pictures of me. Hold Jesus' hand a lot. And know that I will change, just as the ocean constantly changes.*

Me: *Will you ever end?*

Pain: *In a way, no, and in a way, yes. The surging and beating will become calm in time, but some of me will always be with you.*

Me: *Are you my friend?*

Pain: *I'm so glad you asked that question because I want to be your friend. I'm here to make real the magnitude of your experiences, to convince you of truth and help you believe. Even though my salt stings, it is also a preservative. I have preserved this part of you for over 30 years. Below my surface I am indeed teeming with life. And that part will be revealed to you as we go along.*

Me: *So that is the learning part?*

Pain: *Yes.*

Everybody has repressed memories, no exceptions. No one remembers everything that happened to them every day of their life because our brains have a natural filing system. They put certain information in places that are harder to access for a variety of reasons, usually because it isn't needed. If our brains aren't trying to manage too much information at a time, they work more efficiently.

Sometimes, however, our brains move details to cold storage as a form of protection, as in the case of trauma and abuse. When the information is so painful you can't cope with everyday life, the brain may move it to a subconscious level. But the information never disappears from our brain or body. It is still there; it is just harder to access.

Knowing this helped me understand my memories. The truth of my past life was in me. A ton of truth was in me, but I had been running too hard all my life to listen to it. God's truth was certainly in me, too, giving me a trustworthy foundation. But *my* truth was also in me. Everything that had ever happened to me was imprinted on my being, in my mind and body. Nothing was lost; it was all perfectly preserved until God started my healing journey.

And Pain was the messenger, doing its best to relay my hard but necessary truth to me. It was my job to listen.

Losing Hope

Despite the healing I knew I was experiencing, the events of the past months were beginning to take a toll.

April 8: *"Hope is the anticipation of specific good, the conviction that life is on our side and is ready to shower its blessings and treasures upon us."* (The quotes are by Morton Kelsey.) *I can clearly see that my "hope tank" is dry. I have become pessimistic and even fatalistic. If something bad can happen—it will. Things will get worse. I have to sacrifice everything I love and care about. "Hope is the way of the courageous, those who venture into the darkness are sure of the light on the other."*

I could not say with certainty that I was sure there was light on the other side of all this, nor could I say I understood my heavenly Father's love.

April 9: (Kelsey again) *"It is wicked and sinful to despise myself." "We are silly little people locked up in the call of our own self-abasement." So now I'm wicked and sinful for hating myself. Well, that fits. Of course, I know it's wrong to hate myself. Of course, I know God has created me and that he sees me as precious—loves me as a daughter. Now that's an interesting thought. God loves me as his daughter. Am I really supposed to compare that to being loved by my father? What a polluted concept that is. Maybe we are onto something here. Self-hatred—where are its roots, really? I'd like to know.*

I went to Denver for another five days of therapy. More memories of abuse emerged, all of which included Dad, sometimes being drunk.

Remembering the smell of alcohol on his breath made me want to wretch.

April 13: *Faith wants me to dialogue with the man in my earlier dream where I fell off the cliff into the water. The man swam up to me and gathered up my wedding ring and wallet which had come off in the fall. He said, "Now I will tell you what this means." But I didn't want to know, and I woke up. So, now I want to know. What does this dream mean? Please tell me now.*

"The fall was a long way down because the truth was very deep inside of you. The water feels so unpleasant because the work is so painful. But notice the fall hasn't destroyed you. I am Wisdom and I will be your companion during this journey. You have lost possession of who you are and of your relationship with Roger. They will never be the same again. You must trust me with these things for a time and then I will return them to you. It was God's Spirit that lifted you off the cliff and brought you down. Your mother has known all along that this time would come. The river is long, but you're not alone."

Of the ten dreams I had at the beginning of my healing journey, three years ago, I was most impacted by this one. It felt startlingly real: Mom standing with me, falling from the cliff, landing in the water. All I could do was sit with it, much like Daniel in the Bible when he had his visions, stunned but not knowing what to do.

April 15: *I hate this. I hate all of this. I hate me. I hate Denver. I hate home. There's no place to go that feels good. There's no place for me. Nobody really wants me. Nobody. What a fool I am. When will I ever learn? I'm still trying to get there by being the good girl. It's never worked in the past. Why in the hell do I keep trying? What's the point? Give it up. Stop trying. It's never going to get better. My life is s***—always has been, always will be. Stop looking for rainbows. Life is s***. Nobody is going to make it right. You got screwed. Nothing's going to change that. Wake up! Being good doesn't cut it. Stop being afraid. Don't do what anybody tells you ever again.*

I was sick and tired of it all, constantly looking for the exit ramp but never finding it.

Faith and I were beginning to talk about the possibility of me coming to Denver for the summer to work on my recovery full time. It was a difficult decision. The more I worked, the faster my recovery moved forward. But leaving the family and going away for months came with a high price tag for everyone.

April 15 (cont.): *I belong at home, but nobody wants me there. At least Roger doesn't want me. I hate me. I don't want to be with me. How do I get away from me? What makes me think I want to come here for the summer? This is awful. This is hell. I'm so lonely. I can't do this. Why did I make up all those lies? But how can they be lies? I can't explain too many things. God showed me again how he has led me here. So, I can't deny it anymore. What's my family going to say? I'm going to get in so much trouble. I should just go home. I can't do anymore therapy—it's too hard. I don't want to go to therapy tomorrow. It's too hard. I can't do this anymore. God help me.*

Family Life

Reentry was difficult when I returned back to the family. Whenever I was home, I went back to work at the dental office, playing catch up. Roger was spending money recklessly, leaving me anxious about our finances. And now he was starting to make noises about divorce. My teenage daughters were struggling. My younger daughter was acting out in scary ways. The pain in the household was taking a heavy toll on them, and their needs were not being met by me or anyone.

April 18: *It's out of control. We can't stand the pain. It feels like we're going to blow up inside. It can't go on. It's getting worse by the hour. We're desperate. Pressure, too much pressure. I want to kill Roger for* (spending money). *I want to throw the bills and the books at him and say—it's your problem now. You solve it. I can't take it anymore. Jenny scares me to death—losing her. I can hardly bear the pain of that. My heart is cracking. My heart hurts. I can't take it anymore.*

Where do you go when you're going to explode? What do you do when you can't take it anymore? What happened to God's promise to not give us more than we can bear? I'm breaking under the burden. I'm giving up. It's too hard. I can't find anything to hold onto anymore. This is the last straw. Where do I go? What do I do?

There were no respites. I was careening at high speed toward a breakdown. I wasn't sure which was worse, dealing with the crises at home or doing memory work with Faith. I was home only four days before returning to Denver, this time remembering a ritual sacrifice. It was horrible. Shocking. Heartbreaking.

And I still hadn't dealt with my dad's tape.

Chapter Twenty-Three

1994
May

Responding to the Tape

I spent weeks writing and rewriting a letter to my dad. This was the letter I did not send, nevertheless it felt good to write it. A towel might be helpful to mop up the sarcasm dripping from my words.

May: *Dear Dad: I'm so glad you set the record straight. I'm delighted to know that you have fully recovered your memory—in only five short months! It was only last September that you had no memory of those early years due to your heavy drinking. And now you not only remember it all "clearly," but the alcohol abuse has been pushed back by at least ten years. Not bad for a mere five months. Please feel free to send tapes anytime. They are so interesting—particularly when played one right after the other.*

During this same period of time the story about the babysitting has also changed dramatically. Mom went from working a lot to working only very minimally. And, I guess, all those evenings and weekends away have just been erased from history because the current story is that there were few times we were left with a sitter.

I'm only sorry that you didn't set the record straight eighteen months ago. You could have saved me thousands of dollars in therapy, not to mention sparing the pain and grief (of this process for) *me and my family. If I'd only known we were the model family then I never would have bothered with all those silly panic attacks. Nor would I have dreamed up all those hideous nightmares. I certainly wouldn't have had all those annoying body memories.*

But where I really wasted my energy is in living all these years with multiple personalities. Gosh! If I'd only had this tape thirty years ago when most of them were being developed, I could have played it for them and then they would have known that we were a model family, and everything was fine.

And, of course, had I only known this information sooner I could have saved myself a very expensive hospitalization in a PTSD (Post Traumatic Stress Disorder) *unit for dissociative people. I guess I need to take that tape to the hospital, too, because they are all under the mistaken impression that I am a trauma survivor. Then there are all the psychiatrists, psychologists, social workers, therapists, and nurses who have diagnosed me, too. Maybe they should all hear the tape because they must all be wrong. After all, MPD only develops as a result of severe early childhood trauma. So, now that we all know there was no trauma then it must mean there is no MPD. I can't wait to share the good news with my parts.*

I was finally finding my voice and learning to express my anger. The unsent letter was useful in processing my growing rage toward my father, siphoning off the larger feelings so I could form a more constructive letter. If my goal had been to simply end the relationship, or to attack him, I might have sent the first letter. My desire, however, was to invite my dad into an honest relationship.

After many rough drafts and conversations with Faith, I got the courage to mail the following letter. I stood up to my father and spoke my truth. Even so, using my voice left me terrified of repercusssions. Here is the version I mailed:

Dear Dad: It has taken me awhile to write because I haven't known exactly what to write. Some things are really mixed up for me now and some things are really clear. I know you meant to be helpful with the tape, but, frankly, it has brought more questions than answers. What you shared with me on the tape was quite different from the tape you sent last September. The information about your drinking, the amount of time with a babysitter, and your ability to remember things is in direct conflict on the two tapes. This leaves me quite confused.

Not all of my memory has been repressed. And there are significant differences in your version of our family life from what I remember. I am not sure that it is important at this point to figure that all out. Because there is one thing I am very clear about: I was severely and repetitively abused from 1959-1962, and possibly in 1958 and 1963, as well.

I am having a hard time believing that you were totally unaware of anything going on. There must have been signs of something suspicious. Do you really believe we were a model family?

Here are some facts for your consideration: I have been diagnosed with multiple personality disorder by several professionals. MPD only develops from severe early childhood abuse. I have been abused in a variety of settings including satanic ritual abuse and abuse by relatives and acquaintances.

I feel devastated that something so horrendous could occur in my life and you cannot offer any information. I don't understand.

I don't agree with your statement, "You were the model child." What I was, was deluded. I wasn't a perfect child, I was a dissociated child who repressed negative emotions and disagreeable thoughts to please her father and everyone else.

I am becoming a real person now. I feel anger and shame and pain and grief and abandonment and rejection. I am working very hard to process these difficult emotions. I am angry with you for criticizing Bree. I am proud of Bree for standing up for herself against an unreasonable and unloving father. It hasn't been easy for her and she is protecting herself the only way she knows how. It is much healthier than my approach as a teenager which was to acquiesce and make everybody happy regardless of how I felt.

It is imperative to me that you and I speak honestly about what went on thirty years ago. I will not live with lies, half-truths and distortions. I am worth more than that. I deserve better than that. I will not pretend anymore. Nor will I play the game of perfect, dutiful daughter.

So, the ball is in your court. You said, "I want to help in any way that I can." If you mean that then please hear me and respond to me. For now, please communicate through letters or tapes.

I mailed the letter and waited.

Timeline of Abuse Changes

May 3: *Let's just write whatever—whoever wants to—but please take credit for your work—it's important. Isn't it nice to not be so screwed up? Yes. It was wonderful to work today—Let's work all week—see, it makes us better (Cynthia). Easy for you to say—you haven't been screwed over—you're getting your needs met—how selfish of you (Brenda). I'm tired. Can't we go to sleep? Let's not have a fight tonight. I miss Faith (Marianne). I know it's hard to be away from her and yes, we will sleep soon—just a few more minutes of writing (Patty). Can I sleep with Polly* (our cat) *tonight (Wendy)? No, because she doesn't like to be in here all night—but you can hold her for a while (Marie). I hate Roger. He's awful to us. I don't want to live with him anymore (Alex). But we have to keep trying—it's important to be a family—isn't it nice to be home with Bree and Jenny all week (Marissa)? You're delusional (Teresa)! I don't want to do this hard work anymore.*

With every movement, someone was happy, and others were not.

The ongoing discussion about moving to Denver for the summer was stirring up trouble for some of my parts. Marie was remembering something that I wasn't aware of. I happened to be thirty-eight at the time I wrote this entry.

May 5: *I can't do this anymore. I want to die (Marie). Okay—let's all listen and remember what we're supposed to do. Don't panic. There's no need for worry. We will be okay. We need to take it slowly, but we also need to start hearing from those of you who are in pain. Is someone remembering something? Does someone know why our body hurts so much? What is going on?*

Brenda: *It's s*** in here. It's like a bloody war zone. We're being banished to the Far Country—that's Denver. No one wants us here anymore.*

Marie: *I don't want to leave our home. My mom was 38 when my dad left her. Is that going to happen to us? Are we going to lose our house? My mom was 38 when we moved to Denver.*

Me: *Marie, please hear me—this is very different now. What happened to Mom is not the same as what has and will happen to us. We are safe. And Marie, please remember that we have wonderful friends who do want us here. And even though we have problems in our family—I think they basically want us here. The reason for going to Denver is to get more healing for the abuse. No one is banishing us—I promise you.*

I made a quick trip over to Denver, May 10-11, logging in nearly six hours of therapy. Memories of sexual abuse in my original home surfaced, one memory changing the picture yet again. In the memory, my parents were entertaining my dad's boss. Later that night, Dad brought his boss down to my bedroom, who then molested me. I was thirteen, six years older than I was in any other memory.

I could count on chaos with my parts anytime new memories surfaced. Because Alex was the one closest to dad, I knew he'd have something say. And so would Patty, since she is the one who shared the memory.

May 12: *Alex, how are you? How are you feeling about Dad tonight? Are you afraid or anxious? How is this latest memory affecting you? Would you be willing to write some tonight? I'd really like to hear from you.*

Alex: *Life is s*** and you're not helping anything. This is hard enough without your doubts. I hate him. He wrecked everything. He's an a** h***. He hurt me. He hurt everyone. He ruined everything. Somebody should lock him up for what he did. Somebody needs to know what's going on. I want someone to finally know the whole truth. The truth needs to be known. Someone needs to believe us and stop that man. Nobody knows except us. Please, let's get this stopped. It's crazy. He's crazy. Someone needs to fix him so we can have a daddy. We don't really have one. We never have, but we need one. Someone needs to be our daddy. It's so sad that our daddy is such a bad man. Nobody really knows but us. Please help us.*

It was such a bind for Alex. He wanted a relationship with his father so badly, but the father he had was an evil man and not capable of being one at any level.

I was making it harder for both Alex and Patty, because my old friend Denial was back. I didn't want to believe the abuse went on until I was a teenager.

Me (May 12 cont.): *Thanks Alex. I'm glad to hear from you. I'm sorry it's so hard for you right now. Patty, how are you tonight? What's going on with you?*

Patty: *My tummy hurts. Somebody please help me. This pain is so terrible. I just want to die. I wish somebody would help me. It was a terrible time. My mommy wouldn't come. No one will ever believe what happened to me. It is too terrible. I can't go on like this. I have such a sick feeling in my tummy.*

Me: *Patty, I know this is a terribly hard time for you, but please remember you're not alone. We have lots of friends to help us and Faith and John. It is very difficult for me to accept this newest memory, but that's my problem, Patty, not yours. I know for certain you are very honest and truthful.* (My girlfriend) *and Faith really do believe you. You are loved—please remember that. Bad girl, how are you tonight? How have you been feeling? Are you okay?*

Bad Girl: *uh, huh. It doesn't hurt so much now.*

May 16: *God, please help me. I need you so much today. The weight of the stress is crushing me. The lack of a home is the worst. Will I ever be able to relax? Will there be peace anywhere? Where do you want me to be? Does anybody want me? I feel so unwanted, so frightened. Where will I stay this week? What about next week? This summer? Does anybody really want me? God, is this last memory true? Are any of them true? Are all of them true? Why does everybody believe me? This last one seems too far-fetched. Is it? If it's true, do I have abuse to remember during all the in-between years? What does this mean? Please heal me, Lord. Please keep working. Please restore my life. I need you. I want your help. I want you to do this and do it your way. Reveal your light and your truth. Thanks for being my God. Without you I'd be hopeless. Love, Cyndy*

Another Unhelpful Letter

A hand-written letter arrived from my dad. He denied any family problems or dysfunction, simply repeating the whole "model family" version of his story, adding other pointless details and making excuses. He did apologize for judging Bree and then said he *understood anger, pain, grief, abandonment and rejection. Thank God you are getting at it now.* That was a confusing statement. If my memories were lies, why would he understand my feelings?

The end of the letter was disturbing: *Cyndy, this is happening to you at a time when your dad is also dangerously close to the edge. I am not looking for any response to my stuff from you. Just to let you know I can't chance stopping in Montrose without you there.* (I told him I might be living in Denver for the summer.) *My last visit was a disaster and left me done in. I hope you understand. All my love, Dad*

It was just like Dad to make it about him. It sounded like he was trying to make me responsible for whatever disintegration he was experiencing, which he didn't explain.

I remember Roger recounting to me how agitated Dad was while at our house in March. I couldn't help but wonder why he was so 'done in,' if there was nothing to hide.

Moving to the Front Range

Back in Denver, May 18 and 19, Faith and I discussed the letter and my plans for the summer. My parts reacted with anger, fear, and confusion.

I would soon have to decide whether I was going to move to Denver for a few months. A friend from church who knew about my situation, mentioned that his mother had a house in Longmont, only a half hour from Faith's office. Since his father's death, his mother had been living with his sister and the house was empty. I was welcome to use it.

I wrote out my thoughts, listing reasons why it would be good to make the move:

To heal

To shorten (possibly) the recovery time

To function more normally, sooner

To focus more exclusively on therapy

To have one on one time with the girls (part of the plan was for the girls to come over, one at a time, and spend extended time with me)

To learn how to take time for myself

To reduce driving

To even out the pace of therapy

To take a break from family stress

To reduce the back and forth transition times

To take the path God seems to be directing me toward

Because that's where Faith lives

It all seemed to be falling into place and I felt peaceful about moving temporarily. Not only would it make it easier to do my work with Faith, but Sandi, my friend from the hospital, was living in Boulder, only twenty minutes from the house I would be borrowing.

My pastor helped Roger and I come up with a contract for the three months I would be gone. We agreed to write to each other once a week, and respond to what the other wrote, along with phone calls twice a week. Arrangements were made for how the finances would be handled. And we both agreed not to spend any time alone with someone of the opposite sex. (Obviously, it never came up that he was already having an affair.)

I packed up what belongings I could fit in my Ford Taurus and headed over the mountains, recording the following journal entry the day I arrived in Longmont.

May 31: *It's been 2 weeks since I've journaled. What a long time. But I'm not surprised. I am very aware that I have been in a shut down—don't feel anything—compulsive—don't stop for anything—survival mode. Hmmm. That's how I used to live every day of my life. Well, at least I'm now aware of what I'm doing. Mostly tonight we just need a whole bunch of sleep. So, I just want to reassure everybody that we are safe.* (The owner of the house) *is a very safe person. Her house is safe. Jesus is right with us and so are his angels. Everything will be fine.*

My first days in Longmont were hard, including the radiator going out in my car, followed by an accident the next day when I rear-ended another vehicle (totally my fault). It made me aware of what a wreck I was, literally. Bree was with me for both incidents, unfortunately. We did manage to find a bit of humor, laughing at the absurdity of driving down the Boulder Turnpike on a 100+ degree day with the heater blasting, trying to prevent the engine from blowing up.

I was hoping nothing else would blow up.

Chapter Twenty-Four

1994
June

Summer Solstice

As the reality of living in a new place began to settle in, my inside world responded with varied reactions. The little ones were frightened and lonely, finding the house too quiet, missing the family. Other parts were relieved to be away from the stress of our home life, feeling calm for the first time in a while. They were happy Roger wasn't around. One part was ecstatic, feeling like she had been released from prison. Alex was freaked out, certain this meant the end of our job, marriage, home, and family. He was convinced we had ruined our life for good.

My employers were incredibly supportive, holding my job at the dental office while I was away. It was a blessing to have the work, when I was at home—a mixed blessing, because it was difficult to get up and go to work many days, but a blessing, nonetheless. I appreciated their sacrifice for me.

For the most part, life was better after I moved. My stress level went way down. I had space to think and process and rest and let the little ones play while still meeting my own needs. We went back to playing the guitar and singing, which was always a great healing tool for us.

Now it was time to get back to therapy.

I did fourteen days of therapy in June alone. With one exception, it was more of the same—more memories of rituals with the cult, more abusive memories of life with the babysitter. However, on June 21, the picture changed again.

Throughout the many memories that had returned, I frequently wondered where my mother was. This day, for the first time, I saw her in a memory involving a cult ritual. The fact it was June 21, the summer solstice, probably wasn't a coincidence. I have no way of knowing, but it is possible the original memory took place on this date.

There are a number of high holy days in the religion of Satan, not just Halloween, although that is certainly a favorite. Easter is as well, but with a very perverted version. The change of seasons is always marked by rituals, too, including both the spring and fall equinox, and the summer and winter solstice. I was hyperaware today was the summer solstice.

Throughout my healing journey, I would unravel whenever we came to a ritual day. I couldn't tolerate anything orange and black for a long time, refusing to have things in my home that reminded me of Halloween. I dreaded fall. When the seasons changed, I had a deep sense of sadness, often feeling a sense of death.

With this memory involving my mom, my heart was soaked in grief again. Even now, I am not sure of her role in the ritual abuse, although this memory was clear and quite detailed. But in many memories, I did not see her.

In the session when I remembered my mom's involvement, my spunky little part Brenda shared her hurt about Mom. *She wasn't supposed to do those things—she's different. She was supposed to be the one we could count on. It's a great big pain, very sharp, black and big.*

I never wanted to think of my mom as being part of the abuse, so the memory was disillusioning and devastating.

Brenda then began remembering her Grandma Johnson, and how much she missed her. Faith asked her to share her feelings and Brenda began sobbing. I think it was the first time I'd grieved her death, even though she'd been gone nine years.

Art Therapy

With extra time to myself, I worked even harder on my recovery. I recorded twenty-one dreams in June, a practice I started when I began seeing Faith. Writing down the dreams brought another level of healing, almost a form of resolution.

The dreams were usually dark and violent, often on themes of abuse. The feelings of betrayal and abandonment that I struggled with during the day, played out in nightmares. It was rare to have a night without a horrific dream.

I continued my artwork as well, supplying my parts with an array of mediums to encourage them to express their reality through drawing. We had big paper and little paper, regular crayons and glitter crayons, pencils, paint, and markers—scented, of course.

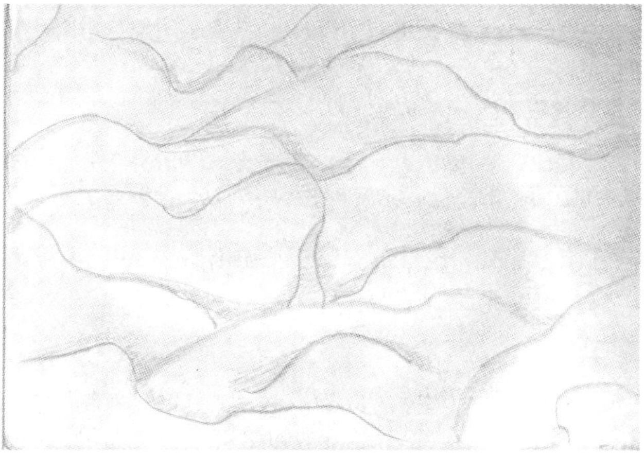

Having spent some time with an art therapist, I was taught to include a "TTAQ" (title, theme, affect, question) on the back of each drawing. I got more healing mileage when I did. One pencil sketch looked like hills with some shading. On the back, I wrote, Title: Far Country. Theme: Sand Dunes. Affect: Hopeless, discouraged. Question: "Why do I have to go?"

Art was an excellent tool for me. Anything that would pull out the trauma and grief was good. A huge part of my healing involved getting it out, telling the story, feeling the pain, expressing my truth.

As was typical of me, after the fender bender I marched on without thinking much about it. But journaling revealed some definite fallout. Parts were triggered.

June 3: *We were in an accident. We were very bad for not calling the police. I was so confused. I was a bad girl for smashing the car today. I was bad because I didn't go right home. I hurt my new car. What's going to happen to us now? We were bad to just keep going with the afternoon plans and not stopping. Faith will be disappointed with us because we didn't take care of us at all. We shouldn't have gotten so tired. We will never learn. God help us. We can't seem to figure it out ourselves. Will we sleep tonight?*

June 4: *I just think we all need to check in. How's everybody?*

?: *You didn't do what Faith said. You got tired and sleepy and didn't take a nap. Why don't you do what you're told? God was punishing us. He let us wreck our car 'cause we weren't taking care of ourselves. We were too tired. Maybe now you'll learn.*

?: *I don't want to see Roger tomorrow. He's bad to us. He made us feel worse about the wreck. Why does he always act like such a b*****d to us? This is hard enough without his so-called help.*

?: *When are we going to deal with the wreck? That's what I want to know. Huh? Tell me that. Is our car going to be ugly now?*

The toll of the previous months had caught up with me. The level of exhaustion was beyond curing with a good night's sleep. I needed weeks of sleep.

June 5: *I'm soooo tired. I think I am flunking "self-care." The pain is here again. What am I doing here? This is weird living in a stranger's house—sleeping in her bed—parking in her garage—driving miles and miles every day—no friends—no church—no job—what am I doing? I don't know—but whatever it is I'm doing it wrong. I'm sleepy—exhausted—dissociated—broke. I should be working harder. I wrecked the car. In a memory—I know it—I can feel it—it's coming up. My wreck on Friday—my mother on Saturday—Roger today. Hum—no wonder I'm screwed up. I don't want to do this anymore.*

Another part emerged, one whose role had been exclusively to participate in the cult rituals. She did not want to share anything, a common problem since there were always threats from the cult members for those who talked.

June 8: *I can feel you more and more. You did an important job and are to be respected for your efforts. It's time to meet you and listen to you and try to get your needs met. I'd really like to get to know you. Can you share your name? How old are you? Would you like to write?*

?: *My name is a secret. It is never to be spoken outside of the cult or I will die.*

Me: *Okay. I understand that they told you to never speak your name. I also know, though, that they lied to you. They can't kill you because they don't even know where you are.*

?: *My father could tell them where to find me. He could lead them to me. It's not safe. They know everything. They are everywhere.*

Me: *Do you know that 30 years have gone by since we were in the cult? That's a long time. Most of those people are probably dead by now.*

?: *The cult goes on forever and my father is still alive.*

Me: *What do you need to feel safe enough to talk about yourself?*

?: *You have no idea what you're dealing with here. This isn't some game or therapy exercise.*

This new alter was afraid the cult people would come after her. While that is a reality for many SRA survivors, it wasn't for me. The rituals ended when my grandfather died. I was seven. However, my abuse continued for another seven years because of the incest from my father.

Panic at the Ball Game

I was glad Bree had come over with me for my first days in Longmont. It was wonderful having some time alone with her. At fifteen, she seemed so grown up now. We enjoyed what the city had to offer, sightseeing, new restaurants, and shopping. (Shopping in the Denver area was a big deal when you came from a town of ten thousand!)

After Bree returned to Montrose, Jenny came to stay for several weeks. Between sessions, Jenny and I found fun things to do. One day we went to the local amusement park. I asked her about taking in a Rockies game too, and she got excited about the idea, more big-city fun we couldn't do at home.

June 24: *I got triggered tonight. It was very hard, tense, flustering. Jenny and I were at the Rockies game. A nice couple sold us tickets at a reduced rate on the way in. We got $10 seats for $7.50 each. The night was beautiful and warm and clear. The couple we sat with were nice and friendly. We had hot dogs and peanuts and cotton candy. The sun set and we saw this huge gorgeous moon rise up over the skyscrapers. It didn't matter that the Rockies were losing. It was just fun and pleasant to be there.*

Then things started to change about 9:15. I wanted to leave. I was very, very apprehensive about dealing with traffic after the game. So, I told Jenny we would have to leave before the game ended and no later than 10:00. She balked. She was really enjoying the evening, but agreed.

Then at 9:42 I knew I was starting an anxiety attack. Lots of people were leaving. I was afraid of traffic. I was tired from the hard work in therapy. Many times during the evening I had floods of grief feelings and blasts of reality. Jenny asked why so many policemen were around. Did that trigger me? Was it the lateness? Darkness? The crowd? The moon? At 9:47 came the 7th inning stretch. I turned to Jenny and said, "Let's go—now." I rushed to the van—parked a long way off. Jenny was sad to miss the end of the game so I told her we could find the radio station broadcasting the game and listen to it on the way home. The driving was terrifying even though the traffic was minimal. The radio stations blurting in and out as we searched for the game was doubling my anxiety. I desperately wanted a Xanax but couldn't because I was driving. I wanted to bite Jenny's head off. I was so irritable. My back, head and arms hurt from the tension. Finally, the game ended about 15 minutes before we got home. I turned off the radio. I had my eyes on the rearview mirror all the way home fearful a cop might be behind me. I got home safely, but jittery, frazzled, irritable, wired. What happened? Why did this happen to me? Who freaked?

I hated the panic attacks. I was angry that I couldn't just enjoy a pleasant summer evening with my daughter, watching a baseball game. As hard as I tried, I could not control my anxiety. It had a life of its own and I was its victim. I regularly felt like a freak.

While Jenny was staying with me, it became evident she was acting out in different ways. Why should I be surprised? Just being an almost thirteen-year-old was hard enough, let alone everything else going on. She was trying to survive in the midst of family hell. There was nowhere for her to turn. Her acting out brought more stress.

Jenny wasn't the only one acting out, so was I. I had a part that decided that drinking alcohol was a good solution to our pain. I hadn't had more than a few drinks in my entire life, so this was totally new, and totally not helpful.

June 25: *Somebody screamed all day, "Call Faith, call Faith." But I can't call her all the time. She needs a break from me sometimes. Then I began to have waves of grief wash over me. I just wanted to stop and stare and veg and sit and feel. But* (the owner of the house) *was here and chores had to be done—laundry, cleaning. It felt like my mom was watching—I hate that. She had no mop, so Jenny and I got on our hands and knees and wiped the floor. I had no appetite—I made myself eat. I was angry with Jenny and short tempered. I didn't want to respond to her constant questions. My anxiety kept increasing and increasing as the clock ticked away. He would be arriving any minute. Panic—panic—I need help!*

Roger was coming over for the weekend before taking Jenny back to Montrose. My parts were flipping out. Not only that, but I was getting an increasing sense that the lady who owned the house was uncomfortable with us staying there but I had no idea why. Maybe it would help if I gave the house an extra cleaning.

Chapter Twenty-Five

1994
July

Evicted

After a painful weekend with Roger, he returned home with Jenny. Bree had been away on a trip with a friend and was now home, too. On July fourth, my loaner house in Longmont was empty.

That morning the owner dropped by the house with a stunning announcement: She told me to pack my things and get out immediately.

She was angry that I had turned the air conditioning on at night, although she hadn't said anything previously about that being an issue for her. I'd had it on to help me sleep, as it had been so hot. I rarely had a good night's sleep, being hypervigilant once it was dark, constantly listening for sounds. The cooler air helped, as did the constant humming noise the air conditioner made. Opening the windows only increased my fear and insecurity.

Obviously, the owner had been coming by the house at night without me knowing it, or she wouldn't have known I was using the air conditioner. She was also upset about the way the house was cleaned. I was aware Jenny's twelve-year-old way of cleaning wasn't stellar, but rather than criticize her sincere efforts, I decided to wait until she left before redoing it. However, I didn't get that chance.

My parts were coming unglued, especially the one named "Bad Girl." She wrote to the landlady: *You hurt my feelings very very bad. You made me cry and my heart break. I tried to be very nice to you and do everything you told me and keep your house neat and tidy and be very quiet and polite. It was very hot and the air conditioner helped me sleep better. You said, "I don't care." Don't you know those are the very worst words to say to me? Am I not worth being treated in a nice way?*

The timing was terrible. Because the constant memory work left me internally disrupted, I was vulnerable to the slightest suggestion of an offense or negative word. And this woman's hostility was anything but slight. She blasted me, full-on.

I quickly packed my personal belongings and was gone within minutes. I had no idea what to do or where to go. I literally didn't know where to put myself. Faith and her husband were attending a holiday event and were kind enough to invite me to join them. At least it gave me a place to land for the day.

15: Sandi and Me (2017)

Later, I called my friend Sandi, and told her what happened. She was living in an apartment in Boulder, only a few minutes from the house where I had just been evicted. She invited me to stay with her for as long as I wanted. For the millionth time, God provided what I needed.

Pulling out Endless Memories

The next day, I resumed therapy. I logged in thirteen days of therapy in July. It was a constant concern as to how we would be able to afford that much counseling, particularly now that all four of the family were seeing a therapist. Our medical insurance offered a little help, but not much. Fortunately, the hospital and therapists worked with us, helping us manage the costs, reducing bills and fees, and offering payment plans. Back then, counseling wasn't as expensive as it is now. Nevertheless, the bills were significant.

Living with my friend Sandi was wonderful. But the initial transition to her apartment was a bit rocky since my parts were terrified we would mess up again and have to leave.

July 5: Bad girl: *I'm afraid. What if I get in trouble? I moved lots of things. I changed things. Why did that lady get so mad? I was going to clean that bathroom before I left. Why was she so angry? Why didn't she tell me she didn't want the air conditioner on at night? I would have turned it off. I'm so afraid. I'm going to get in trouble. I feel like I'm taking something that's not mine. What if someone finds out I'm here? Why can't I do anything right? We should have just left everything the way it was. We shouldn't have moved things.*

Me: *Bad girl, please try to hear Faith's words. We have permission to be here, to make ourselves completely at home, to use everything that's here, to enjoy it completely. We have permission from Sandi. She welcomed us here. God has provided this. It is a gift. Please don't feel like you are doing anything wrong. You are doing just what Sandi wants.*

Brenda: *I'm sick of these f****** memories. I hate them. I hate that hole. I swear if anyone ever tries to put me in a hole ever again, I'll cut their heart out. And if anyone ever touches Marianne in a way that hurts her, I'll do that same to them.*

Me: *I'm glad you shared, Brenda. We'll share this with Faith tomorrow. You are really entitled to your anger—it's very appropriate. We'll keep working on ways for you to get it out. I love you.*

The cult memories were still emerging. I was remembering moments of being put in dark holes with bugs and dead animals, temporarily buried, trapped with little air, freezing cold in damp spaces. I now understood why the feeling of not being able to catch my breath delivered instant panic. As an adult, I had tried to snorkel once. After putting on the mask, I lasted about five minutes before being gripped with anxiety.

Another memory that emerged that month involved some kind of testing being done on me, intelligence or mental tests. If I answered correctly, I was rewarded, if not, I received an electric shock. Nearly every memory included sexual abuse and often sacrifices, too.

I didn't want to remember anything else. I didn't want to know anymore or see anymore. I couldn't bear the burden I already carried; how would I carry more?

There was one dream that recurred frequently, dozens of times. In the dream, I had a mass of hair (or sometimes scarves, tied together) lodged in my throat. And I would begin pulling the hair out, but it just kept coming. I would pull and pull but could never get to the end, leaving countless yards of this tangled mass lying on the ground.

The frequently repeating dream was not a mystery. It felt like I would never get to the end of my memories, my recovery, my healing. It seemed like I would be pulling the story out forever.

Zora, the Magnificent

Faith worked quite a bit with my self-described gypsy part, Zora. I admired Zora, even though she was a little scary to me. She was so free and unencumbered. She enjoyed who she was and fought for the freedom to express herself. She liked physical contact and being sensual; this is unusual because survivors often don't like being touched. Unless the other person is completely safe, being touched is triggering. As my work with Zora continued, just like with every other part, my job was to hear her, respect her, and make an effort to meet her needs.

With Zora, that was a little tricky. More than once, she wanted to walk into a bar and pick up a guy. We had some close calls, but we never did. There was one request I was able to honor. Zora hated my wardrobe. So we agreed to visit an import store and buy a new outfit. Zora had no trouble finding what she wanted. She picked out a long, flowing skirt of bright blues and purples, along with a coordinating peasant blouse. She added earrings and a multistrand beaded necklace. Gypsy clothes! Of course. Whenever Zora wore her outfit, she was happy.

All Zora wanted to do was have a little fun. She wanted someone to hold her and touch her. But most of all, she wanted to be desired, someone to choose her. That piece she had in common with all of our parts. We all just wanted to be genuinely wanted for who we were.

As I learned to respect Zora, something interesting began to happen. I felt my heart begin to beat again. My body started to come alive. As I healed, I became connected to my physical self. Less and less I saw my body as an instrument for evil and wickedness. Instead I began to see beauty and goodness. I was beginning to thaw.

As the sheer volume of memories began to rack up, denial also continued to dissolve. I could try to convince myself I had made up one or two of the memories (although, God only knows why on earth I would do that!), but there had been dozens by now. Besides, maybe a mind could invent stories, but the feelings of extreme terror? Physical and emotional pain? Body memories? No one can make that up. I was running out of excuses to doubt my memories.

Then there were other moments that brought confirmation, like a random conversation between Roger and my brother, during which my brother shared his aversion to blood and body parts. That's not typical chit chat. Why would he say that?

I slowly resigned myself to my new reality. My childhood was not what I had thought it was. Neither were my parents.

It Never Happened, Says Mom

Now that I was living on the Front Range of Colorado, my mother was an hour away instead of six. Because the girls were often with me, we had frequent contact that summer, driving kids back and forth, facilitating visits between her and the girls, meeting for an occasional lunch. The stilted conversations were uncomfortable.

Mom made it clear that she didn't believe me or accept the fact Dad had abused me.

I asked her once why she didn't believe me. She said, *"I was a good mother. If those things happened, then I wasn't a good mother. So it didn't happen."* Circular reasoning, I guess. It hurt beyond words that she never believed me or supported me, but, in a way, I understand. Her life had been horrible from the beginning. In her mind, the one good thing she had going for her was her three children. And she was devoted to her family, pouring herself out for us, to the extent she could. That is the truth.

But it is also true that I was sexually abused by Dad. She, however, could never reconcile those things, so she made up her mind that it never happened. And if there is anything I've learned in walking this road for thirty years, it is that you will not see something you don't want to see. The mind has an incredible capacity to justify and explain away that which it is unable to face. Just look at any addict to see that is true.

Because trauma survivors live in survival mode, it is a tremendous reach for them to be attuned to the needs of others, including their children. All thought and energy throughout the day is focused toward making it to the end without serious casualties. There is no pause button that allows the survivor to register the needs of those closest to them. This isn't fair to the survivor and it isn't fair to the children, but it is reality, and one reason why trauma and abuse become generational problems.

Understanding my mom, however, didn't diminish my pain. After I initially told her in 1993 that I was remembering abuse, she never even *tried* to hear me or my story. Not even once. She simply maintained it never happened. I found it hard to believe Mom never saw or heard anything or noticed any unexplained wounds on my body.

My little part, Marianne wrote a processing letter to Mom. It didn't get mailed.

Dear Mom, once upon a time there was a little girl who was horribly abused by a lot of grown up people. And her mother didn't notice people were hurting her. A very long time later, when the little girl was a woman, she told her mother about it. But her mother still didn't believe her. And her heart was broken. It's a very terrible thing to not be believed when you are telling the truth. It's almost despairing.

So I sleep and sleep and sleep. And when I wake up, a horrible pain covers my whole body. So, as soon as I can, I go to sleep again, because that's the only time that I can't feel the horrible pain. And Faith says to me that one day the pain will go away. I hope so. Maybe I can be awake more then and feel good. Marianne

Not being believed was one of the worst parts of my healing journey. I've heard the same from many survivors of abuse. No one in my family believed me. Not then. Not today. And many friends took the same position. I understand the seeming unbelievability of it all.

Prior to my healing, if a friend told me a similar tale, I would have been polite, but thought to myself, *That's nuts.* If you haven't been in that world, it does seem unbelievable. And that's a good thing; it means you can't even conceive of the idea that people do this to children.

But they do. And they have—since the beginning of time, as the Old Testament has recorded for us. There are plenty of references to child sacrifice and abominable rituals. God hated it then and he hates it now.

I added a little more to Marianne's letter. *This situation just isn't working for me. I am in agony whenever we talk or meet. I have a personality who calls herself Marianne who comes out and tries to be cheery and friendly. She doesn't want to make you unhappy. But inside I'm miserable because it is such a reenactment of the past. Everything had to be a secret. And you didn't believe anything was happening to me. And I couldn't talk about it.*

As Marianne made herself more known to me, I connected something from my childhood. As a little girl, every time we went somewhere in the car, for more than a few minutes, I immediately went to sleep. Sleep was my escape when I was trapped in the car with my dad. When I was eight, I slept my way across Canada and the United States while my family was on a seven-week road trip. It was such a programmed response that, later, when I got my driver's license, I became drowsy as soon as I got behind the wheel. That wasn't good! It took me a couple years to overcome that reflex.

I wrote another unsent letter to Mom that summer. *God help me. I can't do this. It's too hard. You seemingly don't believe me or aren't interested in my diagnosis or my difficult recovery process. You ask no questions—have not taken up my offer to read the materials I have. It is not spoken about when we are together. You either don't believe or don't care. Either case is non-supportive of me. I've always been there for you, during your recent trauma and past illnesses and hospitalizations. But you're not there for me. This recovery is taking every ounce of strength and courage I have. I have no energy to spare to play games with you and pretend it's not happening.*

You validated part of my memory about Grandpa (my dad's father). *If even 10% or 20% of my memories are completely or partially accurate then there were some very serious problems in our home back then. It's not a secret anymore. Neither you nor Dad will tell the truth. You have both lied to me and changed your stories. This hurts me terribly. It is such a betrayal and the opposite of support—you are making it harder for me and more painful. As long as you are going to take this position I would rather not try to get together or talk. If you will tell the truth, please write.*

Early on in my recovery, I shared a memory with my mom about my paternal grandpa. I told her I remembered being in a kitchen with him and walking through a door with a screen to a small garage. In the middle of the garage, taking up a large area, was a workbench. (He was a carpenter, by hobby.) There was a stool to the side. Grandpa put me on the stool and sexually abused me. Afterward, he showed me the vice on his workbench and said if I told anyone, he would put my head in the vice and squeeze my brains out.

After sharing this, my mom said, *"That was your grandparent´s house. It was exactly as you described it."* I was probably five or six at the time of the memory. Shortly thereafter, Grandpa died, and Grandma moved to a senior living complex, so I never returned to that house.

One after another, family members claimed the abuse never happened, but then they would say something contradictory to their version of the story, validating my memories.

Chapter Twenty-Six

1994
August

Preparing for Reentry

While not weekly, as our contract specified, Roger and I did write back and forth several times over the summer. I didn't save copies of the letters I sent, but I do have Roger's.

He kept me up to date on how the girls were doing while with him, along with his latest projects. He described a mountain climb with Jenny and some friends where they got lost coming down from the hike. Roger said his therapy was going well and seemed to be helping. Even though finances were difficult, he affirmed the need for me to continue in my recovery.

Roger confirmed my plans to return home on the 20th, acknowledging his nervousness about it. He mentioned that he would set up an appointment with our pastor to talk through issues regarding reentry to home life. He said, *"I love you and want to reform our marriage when you can get beyond survival mode in your work."*

The letters gave me some hope that maybe Roger did care about me and would be willing to make changes so our marriage could work. The quickly approaching homecoming would be a good test of whether or not that was true.

Crossroads

August 6: *I can't believe that I haven't journaled for a month! I am remembering that this was this very date 3 years ago when God and I had a little chat by the Crystal River near Independence Pass. It was as though he and I were seated there together on the rock talking together. It seems just as real 3 years later. I remember that he told me it was time for me to learn to hear his voice when he whispers—and to learn to dance with him. I asked him tonight, while I was in the hot tub, "Have I learned any of this in 3 years?" And God began talking to me in a quiet voice. This is what I heard:*

"It's not time yet to leave the crossroads. There are things you still need to learn about the crossroads. I never would lead you to self-destruction—so the path to the left is not one I will join you on. The path straight ahead no longer fits for you—you have grown beyond the need to travel that direction. It is time to stop living to please everybody else—the blind obedience and following all rules. Defining yourself by everyone else's needs and expectations is a role you have outgrown." Suddenly, I realize this. The path to the right is the one that promises life for me. But, I'm not ready. It frightens me. I need to wait for God to lead me there. In his time.

Faith and I talked quite a bit about the crossroads in our next session. (My *Healing Journey* class includes a teaching on "Temptation Crossroads," but the crossroads in my journaling at this time had nothing to do with that later teaching.) I was well acquainted with the road to the left: self-destructive choices, drinking, staying in bed, isolating, thinking about suicide all the time. It was painful all the time.

I never drank very much for three reasons: my body couldn't tolerate it, I didn't like the feeling of being out of control, and it reminded me of my alcoholic father. Wine coolers were all the rage then. So a binge for me was more than one wine cooler. Once I drank four and couldn't even stand up. I was definitely a cheap date.

Thoughts of ending my life were never far away. I tried to stay away from suicidal ideation, but the effort to do so was enormous. With Faith's help, we were still able to disarm the crisis whenever it hit that level. It wouldn't be long, however, before that changed.

Between my destructive thinking and the ongoing violent dreams, sleep was nearly impossible. I never felt rested or peaceful or that I was generally okay, not even for a moment. Faith made a cassette tape for me, recording soothing, encouraging thoughts. I listened to it every night on my Walkman. I played a Kenny Loggins' song, too, "All the Pretty Little Ponies," a lullaby he wrote for his kids. It worked like a charm to calm me down at bedtime.

In our therapy sessions, Faith continued to process the crossroads and asked me about the road in front of me. I knew that one, for sure. It was the path of blind obedience, being the good girl, doing what everyone told me to do. That was the road God said I had outgrown. Good news!

The road to the right was less clear since I really hadn't travelled there much. Part of it was external choices, exploring my gifts, spending more time in the mountains, connecting with friends. The internal part had to do with learning who I was and my purpose, as well as figuring out what I thought about things instead of being controlled by everyone else. I had come to understand that I was a truth-speaker; it was part of the way God created me.

The road to the right was all new territory.

As this crossroads became clear, I felt that things would be changing soon. The road to the right intrigued me, the road that promised life. I was eager to travel that road and experience new things. Apparently, though, God wanted me to stay put for the moment.

Until I knew more, I just needed to stay the course, but I knew I couldn't stay in Boulder forever. The plan was just for the summer. The thought of returning home, however, was terrifying. Decisions would need to be made soon.

Processing Parents

Even though I was only on the Front Range for twenty days in August, I managed to get in eleven days of therapy. Faith and I made good use of my remaining time.

The memory work went in a different direction now, more toward my home as a child. I remembered spankings and beatings with a belt by my parents. One of my parts colored a picture of us hiding under the bed, behind a chair, in a cupboard, and inside a closet, trying to escape our dad's physical abuse. She drew Dad as large and scary like a monster, while I was small and faceless. Another memory was with Grandpa, taking me into the bathroom and abusing me.

On August 17, I reached a place of clarity and wrote a letter to my mom. It was a symbolic letter, a letter turning away from the forward path, the one of the obedient, good girl.

Dear Mom, I hereby submit my resignation as your official caretaker. From this point on, I will no longer be responsible for your health, your well-being, your decisions, your happiness, your financial stability, your future, your relationships with Roger, Bree, Jenny, my siblings and their families, your accommodations, your possessions, your surgeries, your legal problems, or your house cleaning.

I didn't want to hurt my mom, so I didn't mail it, but it was time to live differently in response to her.

Besides journaling and drawing, another incredible processing tool for me was making collages. The collages were large, some a yard wide and just as high. As I arranged pictures and words cut from magazines, a story would emerge, a story I hadn't read yet, the truth of my alters.

The hardest part of my healing was processing the reality of my childhood home and parents. The collages made the story and feelings quite visible.

On July 29, my collage depicted a tiger, sad little girls, dead bodies, wrecked cars, and a can opener, surrounding a core of raging fire. Then there were phrases: *missing out on life, think of the impact, when does the burning stop? take a look, unraveling, snakes, civil wars in the soul, whose little girls is this? lost time, deceit, growing up fast and frightened.*

One glance at the collage, and you knew exactly how my parts were feeling. They had so many emotions to process. With the memories coming so frequently, it was hard to feel like we ever finished processing anything, so the collages were helpful outlets of expression.

Home Fires

It was finally time to go home. I was glad to be back with the girls; I had missed them. Being in my own home, sleeping in my bed, holding my kitties again felt good.

I arrived just in time for Jenny's thirteenth birthday. We were both happy to be together for her important day. It was also time for the girls to start school, Junior High and Senior High.

Two days after arriving home, I had lunch with my friend, and she told me Roger was having an affair. In fact, he had been flaunting the relationship all over town while I was away. It seemed that everyone knew except me. She had hoped Roger would tell me, but after six months, it was apparent he did not intend to do that, and she felt I had a right to know.

The other woman was a friend of mine. Ten years younger and married, she was someone I'd connected with because we were both dissociative and working through traumatic memories. The similarities didn't escape my notice. Her dark hair and pale complexion reminded me of myself. And just like me, at twenty-six (the same age I was when Roger and I married), she had a toddler, a little girl.

While I was away, they were frequently seen together publicly. Roger even introduced her daughter as his own on at least one occasion. Many people knew, but were afraid to tell me, adding even more trauma to my already difficult situation.

Roger readily confessed when I confronted him. He admitted their relationship became sexually charged the night I went into the hospital, six months earlier. Roger swore they never did anything more than talk. *Was that supposed to make me feel better?* I didn't know what to believe, especially since his girlfriend was six months pregnant. I didn't even know whether he intended to end the relationship. It was her husband who apparently put a stop to it. (Nine months after my hospital stint, she gave birth to a boy and named him Roger.)

I was reeling. I didn't even have an inkling about the affair. This was not what I expected when I returned home.

When Roger and I met with our pastor, my girlfriend went with me for support. Suddenly the agenda switched from *What do we need to do to restart this marriage?* to *Do we need lawyers and separation agreements?* It would take more than a year to answer those questions.

On August 29, I headed back over the Rocky Mountains for three days of therapy. I was all over the map: fearing for my survival, wondering how I would take care of the girls, how I would finish my recovery.

Spiritually, I knew God hated divorce. How would I reconcile that with the reality of Roger's affair? I'd already been through one divorce; I certainly didn't want another one, nor did I want to disappoint God. I would struggle with those questions for a while and then swing to pragmatic matters, such as wondering whether I needed to start working full time again or if I needed to sell the house.

August 30: (One of my parts journaled to me.) *I just want to die. Why didn't you let me call Faith back tonight? Don't you believe me? I really want to die. I don't want to do this anymore. It's time to make a plan.*

That was predictable. This new layer of trauma landed on a mine, one that was about to blow up. I was confused and did not know where to turn or what to do. It was too much to bear on top of the recovery work I'd been doing all summer.

I was just starting to emerge as my true self, but Roger wasn't interested in living with that person. Because of his own dysfunctional childhood and family, he had a strong need to control and belittle me, to push me down. It wasn't possible to be my real self with him. If I lived as the stronger, more confident woman I was becoming, he would up the ante, growing more rageful.

Then there was the issue of Roger's dishonesty, which was pervasive. I'd been deceived my entire life. I needed honesty in our relationship. Obviously, that wasn't his goal. I was in a quandary.

George

While still in Boulder, I recorded this entry.

August 31: (Many parts began responding to Roger's affair in a chaotic manner.) *I feel very, very mad. I hate what is happening. His voice and concern on the phone tonight made me very, very confused. Why does he seem like a monster but not sound bad? Maybe I'm crazy. Bree cried and cried. She's missing me and needing me. Who wrote in the journal last night? I'd like to know. No more drinking. I hate it when I'm away* (not home) *at night. It's so terrible and lonely. My head feels like it's being squeezed and my stomach hurts. All this is very, very bad now. I have to be alone. I hate it when we pretend. We always pretend in front of other people. I wish we would just stop pretending.*

I'm afraid to go to Wisconsin. It's a long way away. What if George is mad at us for making such a mess of things! (George was the pastor of my church in 1991.) *What if he tells us we have to go back to the bad, bad man? I can't do that. I want George to tell me it's okay to leave him, in fact, I should because it's the right thing to do. I'm glad we're going away. Life is total s*** here. Nothing is right. I'm mad that we have to make a decision about being married. I'm mad that so many people are bad to us. I'm mad that we can't figure it out until after we've been hurt very terribly. I'm just mad. Why doesn't somebody just take care of me? It's too hard!!*

I met George when he and his wife, Mozelle, came to Montrose to be our interim pastor for a year before moving to Wisconsin. The son of a Virginia tobacco farmer and youngest of nineteen, George was a kind soul and spiritual rock. He was the loving, fatherly figure I needed, and the same age as my parents.

He began pastoring my church three years earlier, when I was just starting to unravel.

After George preached a few times, I made an appointment to talk to him, although I wasn't entirely sure why. I'll never forget what he said to me: *"I looked out into the congregation and saw your face, and said to myself, who is this sad young woman who seems to carry the weight of the world."* I wept. Someone had seen me. Someone saw me as a real person, a human being who was hurting.

***16**: George*

George said more than once how I reminded him of his daughter, one whom he missed deeply. We filled an emotional void for the other. We frequently took walks together, chatting away about many things. He wanted to know why I was sad. And I just wanted to be with my spiritual Dad. The relationship felt Christ-like, a new thing for me.

Three years later, I needed George. Like I had never needed George, I needed him now, to share everything that had been going on in my life and get his perspective. I booked a flight to Wisconsin.

Chapter Twenty-Seven

1994
September

Violence in the Laundry Room

I spent Labor Day Weekend in Wisconsin with George and his wife, Mozelle. Their hospitality and beautiful wooded property were food for the soul. I caught them up on everything that had happened, while taking time to rest and find some perspective on recent events. It was good to be with my pseudo-parents.

Honestly, George did not know what to make of this strange world I had entered. He had never heard of Satanic rituals, cults, or multiple personality disorder. It was Greek to him. But I didn't need him to understand all that, I needed his love and acceptance, and those he supplied liberally. He was careful not to tell me what to do, but listened well, as I tried to sort out what to do about my marriage.

Sunday afternoon, the phone rang. It was Bree. She was crying hysterically. It was difficult to figure out what was happening in between her sobs, but she eventually got the story out. After church, Roger, Jenny, and Bree stopped by the house, before their plan to meet friends for lunch. There was an argument and Roger started yelling at Bree, escalating into a tirade.

Jenny later shared that, while waiting for them outside, she heard Roger screaming, followed by several loud booms. Next, Roger came flying out the back door, grabbed Jenny and left without saying a word. Jenny told me she thought Roger had killed Bree.

Bree said Roger had her pinned to the wall in the laundry room, just inches from her face in a full-on rage. Then, at the last second, he turned away from Bree and began beating on the washer and dryer, denting the metal. She told me she thought he was going to beat her to death.

While his anger toward Bree had not previously reached this level, Roger had never treated her with kindness and affection; not when he met her at age three, and not that day, at nearly sixteen. Those things were reserved for Jenny.

On the phone, Bree was greatly distraught, feeling alone and afraid, not knowing where to turn. I felt like the world's worst mother, more than a thousand miles away, not there when my daughter needed me. I had put her in this situation, marrying Roger in the first place, then I left her with him for extended periods while I was working on my recovery. I may not have been responsible for Roger's rage, but I wasn't innocent, either. I was plagued with guilt and concern for Bree.

The incident flipped an internal switch for me. While I wasn't strong enough to set limits on Roger's bad behavior toward me, I finally was able to do that for the sake of Bree. I came home and told him he had to leave and get help. I was willing to give him time to seek help for his issues, but, in the meantime, the girls and I needed to be safe.

(Roger had moved back into the house while I was away for the summer, but now I asked him to find somewhere else to live.)

For the first time in my life, I put my foot down and said, "No more." It was a long journey to get to that place. I was finally seeing the truth that my daughters and I were entitled to be safe and to be respected and valued. I couldn't take that step until I began to value myself. God had been revealing his love to me for three years and it was beginning to take hold.

Memories + Family Crisis = Overload

When I was able to get back to Denver, I began processing Roger's affair and his terrifying behavior toward Bree. It was overwhelming. I was confused about what to do and how to handle my parts who were having strong reactions. Several were terrified of Roger or enraged, pushing hard to get me to divorce him.

At the same time, in these latest therapy sessions, more memories emerged involving the cult, snakes, and sexual abuse. Then I had another flashback involving my dad and his father. It would have been okay with me if we didn't do any memory work right now, but I didn't get a vote. They just kept coming.

After the latest abuse memories involving Dad, I created a telling collage. Among the pictures of a fishing boat, fish, cigarettes, Jack Daniels, an Indian, and pipe-smoking man (all descriptors of Dad) were phrases: *the home front, nix secrets/truth to tell, children are present, a question of rape, dirty, violent, news, fiction parenting,* and, in the middle, the word *atomic* next to a picture of a bomb exploding.

As with so many times over the past months, it seemed like too much to handle all at once. The recovery work coupled with my personal crises seemed absurd.

In addition to Faith and John, I sought counsel from friends, trying hard to make the right decision about Roger, the girls, and our home. Feedback was mixed, to say the least. Several judged me, citing Bible verses, saying God was against divorce. They could not hear that I wasn't seeking a divorce; only trying to create some space where my girls and I could be safe and live in peace while Roger got help. The emotional and physical violence had to end, not to mention his affair.

Others, closer to the situation saw the situation as hopeless, suggesting restraining orders and retaining lawyers.

I knew every Bible verse on marriage and divorce. And, having been through one divorce already, I had no illusions about *greener grass* should I go through another one. I knew the full reality. No one comes out a winner in a divorce, except maybe the attorneys. The kids are never the same. There's carnage in every direction. It is miserable, devastating, and sad.

But I also knew God is a God of love and grace and mercy and redemption. He understands we live in a fallen world and cannot control anyone other than ourselves. And he will heal any heart that turns to him for help. I didn't see the situation as hopeless. At the same time, I wasn't confident Roger would get healing. Clearly, he saw me as the designated patient. He once told someone that living with me was like living with a sick animal.

While all of this was hard on me and girls, it was hard on Roger, too. Besides all the wounds he brought into our marriage from his childhood, my recovery added to his pile. I was a challenge to live with these past three years—messy, unstable, with little to give to him.

I contacted a Christian reconciliation ministry and they agreed to come alongside our family to help us find restoration. My goal was to see if we could find enough healing to be able to safely live together. My prayer was for new life to emerge in our family. The way the old family functioned was diseased and needed to die. My hope was for new relationships and a new start.

I made my decision. I would wait—wait on God and see what he might do in the coming months.

In the meantime, I was home with the girls full time and back at work at the dental office. Roger moved in with friends. And we all continued with our respective counselors, along with the added sessions with the reconciliation team.

Chapter Twenty-Eight

1994
October

Letter to Patty

In the aftermath of September's memories, Patty was struggling. She was both part of me, yet still separate, as were all my alters. The composite of now over twenty alters comprised my system, each one with a role and responsibility to the whole. Having been the one who received most of the sexual abuse, Patty's role in the system was vital.

I wanted Patty to hear the truth about her value and real identity, so I wrote her a letter.

October 1: *It was so very good to hear from you, Patty. I am hearing your pain so loud and so clear. Your tears inside are being heard now, too. I hope that soon you will be able to let your tears come out because I believe it would help you to feel better. They really need to come all the way out. It is important. Maybe you could tell me what would make you feel safe enough to let the tears come out.*

I know you are lonely and feel as if nobody is caring for you. But it is important to remember that Faith and our friends really do care. And they are all helping in their own special way. The pain about not being touched and held and caressed is hard. The hugs from friends help only a little. The aching is hard. It may change someday. It may get easier as time goes on, but now it truly is hard.

Patty, you are special in a way that you never knew before. Not because you belong to a man. Not because your body is being used for their pleasure. You are special because you are God's daughter. And he has taken away all the dirtiness and all the evil of what happened. And in its place, he has made you pure and holy. You are the beloved daughter of God and totally acceptable to him. He no longer sees the past when he sees you. He only sees a pure and lovely daughter who he knows completely and loves completely.

God will give us what we never had. Not only is he your daddy forever and ever, but he has given us George to be like an earthly father. You are right. We must believe and tell the truth from now on. And it is still unknown as to whether Daddy will tell the truth, too. Patty, you really are loveable, just as you are, and not for anything you do. You never have to belong to another person. You never have to again be hurt or have your body used. Those days are over forever and ever. You are not trash. You are a princess because he is the King. Hold onto that Patty. Don't forget. God is with you and loves you constantly.

I'll never know exactly how many times Patty endured sexual abuse for us. She took this role in our system so that we could survive. Until she stopped blaming herself, though, and instead saw the truth that she was victimized, that it was the perpetrators fault, not hers, she would not heal. Truth would set her free. I crossed my fingers that my letter helped her.

It turned out to be a month for letters. Finding the courage to stand up to Roger in September, by defending my need and the girls' need to be safe, buoyed me to confront my parents. I knew too much to remain silent any longer. Many of the letters I wrote were for my processing only. This one, however, got mailed.

Letter to Dad

October 5: *Dear Dad: This is a letter that has been a long time in coming as I have worked and processed through many, many things. The recovery has been hard to face, but it has brought me far enough along to write at this time.*

I know the truth now about my past. I may not have remembered everything, but enough memory has returned to have a very good idea about the early years of my life.

You have said a lot in the last year through your tapes and letter. Yet there is no mention of me, i.e., what kind of a young child I was, what our relationship was like, how we related, what you remember of me personally.

That coincides with my memory in that I feel there never was a relationship between you and me. I feel as though I was merely an inconvenience to you. In fact, you referred to your children as "little monsters." I never felt like you were very much a part of my life. I never felt like you had any use for me. I felt like I was basically an unwanted appendage.

I don't remember any special father-daughter times. But I do remember fear of you. I was afraid of you venting your explosive anger on me and of being hit. This fear came from watching Steve and Scott receive your rage and from receiving it myself a handful of times. I learned early on that the pathway to the least punishment was pleasing you because my voice was not going to be heard nor were my needs a consideration beyond food, clothing, and shelter.

It never seemed like you had patience enough to teach me anything or help with something I was doing or that you even wanted to do so.

There are other areas of my memory that have come back, as well. Those are the memories of horrendous abuse. My earliest memory is about age 2. Grandpa Tennyson repeatedly raped me and forced me to have oral sex with him.

I remember evil ceremonies with Indians, sacrifices, and outrageous sexual behavior. I have not had just one memory, but many. Grandpa was heavily involved in these evil rituals and I remember you being there, too. I remember you taking me with you. I was used and abused repeatedly.

Added to that was the daily terror of being under the care of the wicked babysitter who abused me sexually and physically every day. I was so afraid that I would cling to Mom and cry uncontrollably every time she would leave. When Mom returned, she would find me huddled up in a corner and shaking. Then at night, when the worst feelings of terror would come, I would cry and experience terrible stomach pains.

But the worst part is the emotional abuse. I remember being forced to keep everything a secret. I was threatened with physical harm to me and my family, death, kidnapping, and other such horrors if I should tell anyone what happened. So, I could never talk about it. All the vile acts being committed to me were repressed deeply inside. I could not ask anyone for help.

I was programmed to forget each incident through dissociation. It was very effective. I not only dissociated but developed separate personalities to cope with the unimaginable things I was experiencing. Their personalities saved my life by holding the pain, the secrets, and the truth. These personalities made it possible for me to get up each day and act as if nothing had happened.

I was also programmed to feel dirty, guilty, and that it was my fault such things were being done to me. That abuse has plagued and colored my life for over 30 years.

But now I can talk about it and I am talking about it. I am getting help and support—finally! And, as a result of this help, I am becoming that person God originally created me to be.

I would like to continue a relationship with you but in a new way. It must be based on the truth of what has happened in the past. I am getting my life back and it will no longer include living with lies or pretending. You are accountable for what you have done, and I am holding you accountable in our relationship. It is not acceptable to me to pretend as though it never happened. It did happen, it was real.

My hope and prayer for you is that you will come to terms with the full reality of those years so that you may also be released from the bondage such evil brings to our lives. Only God can redeem such devastation and only if we own the truth and allow him in to heal us.

The expense of my recovery has been staggering. Roger and I have spent, out-of-pocket, $20,000 in 1994 alone. If you can assist with our expenses, I will appreciate it greatly. Love, Cyndy

Writing the letter was a major victory. I had to stand. I had to find my voice and use it without fear. I had to speak my truth. These were all movements toward healing, toward wholeness, toward becoming a human being. Secrets meant fear, bondage, darkness, lies, and defeat. I wanted nothing to do with those things now. Telling the truth was flinging open the prison door and letting the light in and being free.

Processing my relationship with my dad wasn't the only thing going on this fall.

Like a world war, battles were being fought on many fronts. Recovery, memories, and therapy were showing no signs of letting up. Efforts with my parts, listening, validating, and meeting their needs, were ongoing. Nightmares were frequent. Keeping my job was vital so I could pay the bills. Parenting two teen daughters included its own challenges. Then, added to the mix was figuring out how to navigate the separation.

Roger and I agreed on a weekly visitation plan, one that was agreeable to the girls. Once each week, the girls would have dinner with him, and Jenny would stay overnight.

Making a visitation plan brought back memories of another plan fourteen years earlier when Tim picked up Bree for a few hours. At the end of the evening, stoned out of his mind, he brought her back to the house, reeking of marijuana. She was two. I was livid. At least the girls were now old enough to tell me what was going on.

And then, in the midst of life's struggles, there was one delightfully bright moment, the joy of celebrating Bree's sixteenth birthday. She crossed the rite of passage by going down to the motor vehicle department to get her driver's license, a moment she had anticipated for months. It was hard to believe she was driving. Wasn't it just yesterday I was pulling her in the Radio Flyer wagon?

Before long, I was ready to write my next letter. I mailed this one, too.

Letter to Mom

October 17: *Dear Mom: It seems funny to me that after living at my house for such a long time (9½ years) that I would all of a sudden begin to notice and take an interest in my yard.* (I then shared detailed plans to restore the flower beds around my house.)

Mom, our relationship is like one of the flower beds in my yard. And, it is going to require all of these steps to bring it to a state of health, beauty and order.

I am ready to rip out the dead and ugly stuff. For me, they are the hideous secrets of the past. I remember now. I have a very good idea of the reality of my early years. It's time to rip out the secrets and get rid of them. They are marring the garden. They don't belong there and never have.

I was severely and repeatedly abused by many people in many different circumstances, primarily up through the age of 6, but even later in some cases. The abuse varied from perpetrator to perpetrator, but included physical, sexual, emotional, mental, and spiritual abuse. This is true. I now remember. I know that not every detail of my memory has returned, but a large enough part of it that I can make these statements with absolute certainty.

I will not tolerate anything but the truth being spoken between us. I know that is a deeply painful thing to do. But nothing at all will grow in our relationship until it happens.

You were involved. You were my mother, my guardian, and yet you allowed these atrocities to go on. Some of them went on right in our home. You must have seen the physical evidence on my body and perhaps even treated it. You were aware of my emotional pain to the extent that you took me to the doctor to get something to settle me down at night so that I could sleep. I cried to you over and over how badly my stomach hurt to the point that I couldn't sleep at night. Why did you choose to not protect me from these atrocities being committed? Why did you look the other way? Why didn't you stand up to them and make them stop or take me away from them?

The other main part in which I remember you being involved is at home during the day when it was just you and the 3 of us kids. I remember you being out of your mind with how overwhelming it was to care for newborn twins and a toddler. I remember rages, being forced to stay in my room for hours, being drafted as your assistant in childcare, and being made to feel responsible for your wellbeing. I remember your despair, loneliness and even daytime drinking which would suddenly turn your affect to rage, beating me if I did the slightest thing wrong.

Then, as if someone pushed a button, as soon as Dad was due home, you would change. You would pull yourself together and the household and make sure we did nothing negative to interfere with his nightly arrival. It was a daily ritual. Then there were your escapes: working and shopping. We all need our escapes, but your escapes meant that I was being left in the care of an evil woman who absolutely terrorized me with abuse. You have told me yourself that you would come home only to find me huddled on a couch shaking and unable to speak. You told me that I had a personality conflict with the babysitter. Well, I can assure you that that was not the case.

There is much more that could be told. My memories are too numerous to count now. And it is not important to share the ghastly details. It is only important to me, at this time, that you face this truth I have mentioned. It will sadden me if you can't or won't do this. The ground will freeze until such a season when you are able to face the truth. It will delay the work.

I must also ask that you refrain from any questions, comments, inquiries or anything regarding me when you communicate with Bree. Do not triangle our relationship with her. That is really a bottom line for me. It is only appropriate that questions and comments be directed to me.

There is nothing God cannot redeem if only we speak honestly and truthfully. I desire and pray for you, that you may also be set free from the bondage such evil brought to our lives. I feel compassion for what you have suffered, as well.

I thank God he is setting me free. I hope you will allow him to set you free, too. I sincerely hope you will work on our flower bed with me. I believe it is not too late to create one that is healthy, orderly, and beautiful. I know there are beautiful bulbs in our bed, as well. They will be so much prettier when the dead, ugly plants are gone. I'm willing to take the time to work the flower bed because I believe we can make it a thing of beauty with God's help. I hope you are, too. Love, Cyndy

Everyone inside held their breath, anticipating reactions from Mom and Dad. There was fear that we would lose them for good and forever. But a tiny bit of hope held out that maybe they would respond with love and truth.

Creating collages continued to be a great processing outlet for me. That week I made one with a mother theme. Among the pictures of cats, adult women, and girls of various ages were the phrases: *rapists, devil worshipers, pedophiles, what in the world does a mom do all day? it looks different because it was different, savage child abuse, who invited them into your home?*

One of my recent ritual memories included horrifying images of killing cats, something that was expressed in the collage, along with confusing messages about mom.

After writing the letter to my parents, telling the truth, there was fallout with my parts. The inner chaos made them anxious and needy. The cult consistently threatened torture, death, and family separation if you told anyone about the rituals. There were a lot of reactions, like this one:

October 24: *I'm the one nobody loves. Nobody loves me and I just want to be left alone. I'm very used to it now. Sometimes others pretend that we are loved, cared about, but I really know the truth. It is at the very bottom. The others can try all they want, but the moment they stop trying, there it is—the truth—nobody really loves us. If we stopped asking for help, if we stopped initiating contacts and relationship, if we just stopped—then everybody inside would see the truth, too. I prefer not to pretend.*

I prefer to be left alone. I like it quiet. Don't ask me questions or bother me because I have made this little world inside where it's okay—just me—but I'm good company. It's better this way. I don't get hurt here because nobody outside matters. I came out for a few minutes tonight and almost drowned in the pain. You see, outside my world is the pain and grief and sadness of being a little girl nobody loved. No one should ever have to be such a person, but I suppose there are many like me.

It's not really hiding you know. It's just being someplace where the truth can't torment us. We like being with ourselves. We bring music in and do things with our hands—like the flowers. Just so it's calm, peaceful, no fighting, no questions, no demands. I can sit for hours and hours and hours. Please don't disturb me, because I might drown if you do.

I'm not sure which little part wrote this, but her words offered a perfect answer to the question, *Why do people dissociate?*

Retreat. Retreat inside. It seemed like the only viable option for survival.

Chapter Twenty-Nine

1994
November

Navigating Parenthood

Time has always been a precious commodity for me. With the girls in school and only part time hours at the dental office, I wasn't sure how I was supposed to use my surplus time. Lacking any schedule or obligations made it difficult to tolerate the pain and easy to succumb to sleep and depression.

November 4: *Dear God: I'm really at a loss tonight. Things seem so hopeless and it's hard to see the point. However, it's beginning to look as if I am a root problem in all these relationships. After all—I'm the common thread—lost dad, lost mom, lost husband.* (I describe struggles with the girls, including Bree's justified and understandable anger toward me.) *It feels as if I'm losing her and I don't know what to do.*

So, what have I gained? I am supposedly in recovery and it seems as if all I've done is alienate those who were close to me. I feel lonely, unloved, and without a future. I've lost my role in the church—failed again. Projects—I've filled my time with projects—yard renovation—flowers—yard sale—house overhaul. In a matter of weeks they'll be over. Then what do I do? Find more things to keep myself busy? Why, because there's nothing else to do?

God, I just don't know what to do. I don't know how to get (Bree) *back. I don't know what loving her and loving myself looks like. I'm out of ideas and out of hope. God, I can't pull myself up. I can't figure this out. I can hardly get myself out of bed in the morning. Part of me wants to give up. But I'm looking to you for solutions, hope, change. Otherwise, I'd just give up right now. What's the point and where's the future?*

Bree was angry with me and it wasn't hard to figure out why. I had not been there when she needed me. I was off taking care of myself, leaving her to believe she didn't matter. Having Roger out of the house helped somewhat; it was less stressful for Bree. But that also gave her space to feel and express her feelings. And I was the target.

November 5: *I don't feel so hopeless today.* (A psychologist friend) *said whenever a person recovers, it causes a shift in everyone around him. They respond with positive change/adaptation or with rebellious, antagonistic rebellion. So, maybe I was only partly right last night—I am the common thread—but it's not because I'm bad but because I'm recovering. Maybe I'm not the root of all evil after all. But I still feel inadequate, ineffective and powerless to improve our relationship or make effective changes. It seems like nothing I can say will get through to her. I feel like she hates me and that pierces my heart. Faith said I must be willing to lose her altogether to get the abuse stopped—for both our sakes. But, God, that is too much. I've lost my parents, husband and now my daughter? Will there be nothing left that I care about when this is over? Is there no torment that I will be spared? Will nothing good come into my life when recovery ends?*

Is this another place that I must simply say yes to you, not knowing how it will come out? To surrender all control over her to you? Please take the reins here. So much is at stake and only you can do it.

My friend's remark about my healing causing a reaction and response in everyone around me made sense. The old physics truism described it well—*for every action, there is a reaction.* I had not factored that in when I started my healing journey. I was beginning to see that every relationship would be changed, because I was changing.

November 6: *Dear God, thank you for giving me some clarity, focus and strength today. Good will come from setting the boundary at respectful behavior. Then you can work in both of us and help our relationship. It is so clear. It was the only way. But I still need your help, Lord. My limits must be wise and appropriate. And I must have strength to withstand her tests on this. But today was a victory—with your help. I stood up for truth. Keep holding me up—I need it. I love you.*

No one likes being out of control. And kids don't respond well when there are no boundaries or limits; it leaves them feeling like no one cares enough to parent them. I hadn't done much parenting lately, and

God helped me get back on track. I think I was afraid of losing my daughter if I took a stand and asked for respectful behavior. In not doing that, however, I made it worse for both of us.

The risk paid off.

November 8: *Dear God, it's amazing to see that Bree's attitude and behavior to me have actually improved. She has been less hostile and more calm, reasonable, and respectful. I praise you! You led me to the truth and strengthened me to follow the truth and blessed the results. I had to jump off in faith—once again—fearful that I'd lose her altogether, that I would alienate her further and that doesn't appear to be the case at all. Thanks, God.*

November 9: *Dear God, I am still extremely thankful that Bree has responded so well to my limits. I told her so tonight. And I feel so much better. I feel like I've had a break for 3 days. Thank you for a break. But now I must prepare for another trip for treatment and I'm pretty darn disconnected from my system. I really need my time with you in the morning. Please help me wake up and be able to get out of bed. And please protect the time from distractions. As always, I ask that your light and truth penetrate my mind, heart and emotions. I pray that for my parents, too. Thank you, God. I love you.*

My parts were chattering and reacting to the things that were going on. Sometimes I knew who was talking, but not always. It was interesting that even though I hadn't received a response from either parent, my parts seemed to know what was going to happen when I did.

November 10: *How do we feel inside? Does anybody know? Does anybody care? Does anybody want to say something? Is anybody even in here? The pain is back. The loneliness is terrible. I'm out on a limb and it's thin. We're headed nowhere.*

I hate my life. Don't you get it? It sucks. It's empty, loveless, pointless, sexless, fun-less. I don't even know what I'm doing anymore. Is this really better than a stinking marriage? There's nothing to focus my life on. Work—so I work—it's what I do. Feel, you want me to feel, why? So my life can be more pathetic? So I can lose the functioning that I've fought hard to gain back? So I can really emphasize how alone I am when there's nobody to hold me when I cry? And here come the holidays. I don't even want to shop. I don't want to buy presents or cook candy and cookies or cut a tree.

My favorite time of year and there's nothing except Christmas music that I look forward to. It's pathetic. It's my life.

I was back in Denver for three days of therapy. One thing was a lot easier now. Whenever I returned to the Front Range, I stayed in Boulder with Sandi, getting time to enjoy our friendship.

Doing three days of therapy instead of twelve or fourteen days a month was a big change from the summer months.

I processed my anxiety, anticipating the responses from my parents, and also did some prayer work after another memory came up. The feelings resulting from the memory echoed my present-day life—feeling unwanted, unloved, and bad. So I sought the comforting arms of Jesus, looking for his healing. In prayer, I told Faith, *Jesus is holding me. I belong to him. I need to remember that. I have always belonged to him. I'm not an orphan. He loves me the way I am.*

Mom's Response

My mother's response to my October letter arrived first:

> *Dear Cyndy, I just want you to know how much I miss you. You are the love of my life—the firstborn. I have done my very best to always be there for you. I miss our telephone chats, and our visits. To know you are as close as you are at times and have no desire to see or talk to me is not only my loss, but I believe yours, as well. The years move along quickly and time is irreplaceable. Others may try to chip away at what exists between me and my daughter, but they will never be successful.*
>
> *Powerful prayers are being offered up here—lifting this situation up to God. These are my prayer partners. I do not believe God works in ways to create chaos. I will continue to hold you up to God for His will to be done.*
>
> *The whole family is waiting to be put back together—and right now, one is missing. We will always all love you—that I know for sure, and we are each waiting for you with open arms. This is my response to your letter. Confrontation is fruitless and I will not enter into that. My steadfast love is solid and firm and standing by. Loving you always, Mother.*

When the letter arrived, I was void of compassion or grace. I felt like her tentacles were trying to wrap themselves around me and force me back into my silent and submissive position in the family, while she ignored every point and question in my letter.

I felt like I was living in a land of crazy people as I narrowly viewed her comments through a lens of profound disappointment. I was enraged by Mom's *confrontation is fruitless* comment. How convenient! Maybe there was nothing good to be gained for her, but it left me with nothing. For her, entering into the truth only meant bursting her bubble of denial. Of course, she wouldn't want to do that.

Never was there any concern or support for what I was going through, no questions, no interest in understanding me, nothing. Mom denied anything took place and stuck by her story. The bizarre thing about my family is that at no point did any of them ask me to tell them my story, knowing nothing except what few tidbits I occasionally tossed out.

It begged the question, *What are you afraid of?*

Trying to understand my parents was complicated and confusing. I would have much preferred to believe their version of our family. The problem was, I couldn't. I had remembered too much.

Mom's background and past were not lost on me. Sexually abused by many people, abandoned by her father when he died, sent away by her mother to live with an abusive brother, I could easily understand her desperate need to deny knowledge of any abuse so as to hang onto me and a fantasy version of our family. She'd lost everything and was alone except for her three kids. She didn't want to lose me, too! And I didn't want to lose her, either!

I knew Mom's love for me was real—when I was little and today, as an adult and the mother of her granddaughters. Her letter was not a lie, not at all. Frightened to the marrow of her bones that she would lose me, and being unwilling to deal with the truth, she did the only thing she knew to do—declare her love.

It was such a paradox, though, trying to reconcile declarations of love with the long list of atrocities I'd experienced. How can my parents both love and abuse me? How can they say they love me and also lie to me, repeatedly?

Today, more is clear. My parents were simply grown-up victims of horrendous abuse, themselves. Abuse never drops out of the sky; it always has a backstory. Because they had never received an ounce of healing, they muddled through their lives, making many mistakes, trying to survive while shackled to their wounds. They were the epitome of parents whose efforts to care for their kids did more damage than good because they never dealt honestly with the abuse they endured as children. Their walls of self-protection became agents of abuse.

Understanding that did not excuse my parents′ choices, however, or minimize the damage.

Relationships are never entirely good or entirely bad. They aren't black or white; there is always some black and some white, an understanding that took me years to arrive at.

Our efforts to love others, even those closest to us are always tainted with selfishness. Only Jesus loves perfectly. The rest of us are on a continuum, hopefully moving further toward sacrificial love, every day. My parents never grew in their ability to love because they were trapped in the secrets of their pasts. Nevertheless, they did love me. If that were not true, then they would have been apathetic or hateful toward me. They loved to the extent they could.

Within days of Mom's letter, Dad's arrived.

Dad's Response

In the opening paragraph he referenced his friends who helped him figure out what to say, including psychologists and attorneys. It was apparent he had help drafting the letter. It wasn't written in his usual style. Not only was handwriting difficult for him, he had never typed a letter to me before and this one was typed.

The following are excerpts from his very long letter.

Dear Cyndy: I tried to walk in your moccasins and tried to understand what you might be feeling, knowing that the father you had loved and respected for the first 38 years of your life, all of a sudden has become this horrible monster that perpetrated these heinous atrocities on you. It must be devastating. I don't know how you have been able to survive those feelings.

It also occurred to me that there is still another set of feelings that you may have yet to feel. You will feel those feelings when you finally, I hope through God's intervention, come to your senses and realize that I didn't do those things. I know I didn't do them. I'm not depending on repressed memory. I'm thinking of conscious memory and I remember that time in your life and in no way did I do these things. They just plain didn't happen. When you finally realize that, you're going to make amends to me and carry a heavy load of guilt and I just hope that happens while I'm still on this planet because if you come to your senses after I've left, you're going to have a problem. You'll have to carry that guilt with you to your grave and I don't want you to have to do that.

I also know from talking with all my friends that there is absolutely nothing I can do that will change your mind. I've even been advised not to respond to this letter other than to just simply say that I received it and that I didn't do those things, but you have asked a lot of questions and most of these things, questions you've asked and statements you've made in your letter, I've already answered in tapes. But, the one thing you've done here now, you've made this a family issue by saying that you watched me abuse Scott and Steve, and I also know that you've talked with your siblings about what you think I did to you, so I have to tell you that I'm going to send a copy of your letter and my response to the family. It's important to me that the family understands my feelings and understanding of the truth.

He went on to refute every point and justify his parenting, basically saying that my memory of his involvement with me and the family was wrong on every point. He said we were *"an ideal, traditional family."* According to his letter, he never raged. He never hit anyone. Also, he was certain Grandpa never sexually abused me or was involved in rituals.

He's the last man in the world who would have ever involved himself in these kinds of non-Christian, horrible rituals you're talking about. He was a Christian minister and very much a believer in Christianity. He'd be the last person in the world who would have done these things.... You were not a fearful child hovering in the corner. There is no way you could have acted those things. Had you actually been the way you described yourself as being in these paragraphs, I would have known that…

During the time-frame you're talking about, alcohol was not a problem in my life and my memory is very clear….The things that you've said in this letter didn't happen…I've given you the truth….from here on, it's in God's hands and I will be praying on a daily basis that we will be brought back together in a loving and respected relationship. Until that time, I have to ask you to please not communicate with me any further unless, of course, that communication is that you want to restore our relationship based on your making amends to me for the allegations you have made in this letter…. With all my love and prayers, Dad.

In a handwritten postscript, he let me know I was no longer the executor of his will. My siblings received a copy of the letter, along with a cover letter announcing the termination of our relationship.

And that was the end of our relationship for seven years.

The comments about God were always perplexing to me, particularly Dad's. My dad was religious, worshiping his higher power, but was not a Christian. When my brother or I would try to talk to him about it, he would always say, *Me and my god are just fine.* He had no use for Jesus or salvation or church or the Bible. He would read his AA (Alcoholics Anonymous) books in the morning, finding a measure of peace and help in reading religious ideas. But he didn't have a relationship with God.

Mom's relationship with God was a little more confusing. No doubt she knew Jesus and was his child. It was certainly important to her that her children know Jesus and go to church, but she gave up church for herself about halfway through life. She would speak of God as *The Good Lord*, a phrase my aunt and others of her generation often used as well. But as time went on, I realized those who used that reference often did not have a personal relationship with him. God was a comforting concept, that was about it.

I guess desperate times call for desperate measures, because they both called on the name of God when they responded to me. It's ironic that everyone prayed for God to fix Cyndy. And he did! But it wasn't the way my parents had in mind.

It had obviously slipped Dad's mind that he already described grandpa as a monster and sexual predator, because, suddenly, he is the *last person in the world who would have done these things.* He forgot that he was the one who told me Grandpa raped his sister and other young girls.

Oddly enough, the thing that made me realize the letter was a lie was his comment about *a fearful child hovering in the corner,* a reference to the abuse by the babysitter. I guess he and Mom needed to get their stories straight, because she is the one who told me about that. It wasn't a repressed memory or even my memory. I only knew it because Mom told me.

Today it is easy for me to clearly state these matters—Dad lied. Back then, not so much. Back then it was torment and confusion and disappointment and rage and trips back to denial.

These were my parents, my deepest, longest standing relationships. And no matter how hard I tried, I could not remove from my heart a desire to be known and seen and loved by them.

I hated the fact that I still loved them. I cannot use the words rejection or abandonment to describe my feelings about the letters. It would be like describing an atomic explosion as a campfire.

Thanksgiving

Sorting out the holidays seemed impossible. With the separation being so fresh, I didn't know what to do or where to go, so I was grateful to receive an invitation to spend Thanksgiving with my sister's family in Wyoming. It provided a safe place to go and the diversion the girls and I needed.

Unfortunately, though, recovery was waiting for me when I returned. My parts were struggling to find their next steps.

November 28: *We must try to find out our needs and meet them. Whoever can't get out of bed needs to be heard. The pain is too much. The work is too much. The reality of life is too much. I'm just so tired and I just want to be left alone. I wish everybody would go away and leave me alone. When I sleep it is the only time I get relief. When I'm awake I feel pain and confusion. It's all just too much. I feel deep, deep pain and loss. There is just so much suffering. We tried to do what was right and tell the truth and we've just about lost everything. It's like there's nothing left to hope for. The betrayal and abandonment are awful. I just keep praying. I don't know what else to do, but I just keep praying.*

November 29: *There seems to be a disagreement about how to get through the holidays. Someone doesn't feel like celebrating at all or even going through the motions—I think that's you who would like to sleep the day away. Someone wants to keep up as many of the usual things as possible or at least try—for the girls and the kids inside. Someone doesn't want to give anything up—all the trimmings—all the music—all the gifts and baking and keep up with the usual commitments, too.*

What's it for? Our heart isn't in it. There seems to be nothing to look forward to. No future expectations of happiness, joy, contentment. Why go on like this? Why are we doing this? Why do we suffer day after day after day? To whose glory? Why focus on the monumental effort of getting through the holidays? For January? For February? Like there will be something better or even different then?

Life was just plain hard.

Chapter Thirty

1994
December

Processing the Response from Mom

I wrote a processing letter to my mom, a letter to help me work through all my feelings, but not one that I mailed. I started this letter, but other parts took over and wrote, too. Here are excerpts from the five-page letter.

Dear Mom: I can't believe my own mother will not do anything to support me through this, that you have no desire to hear my journey and my process.... It's like there is not one crumb of help and support that you will give me. And even worse—you ask me to go back to that awful way of living—in lies and denial. For three and a half years, I have prayed for God's truth to be revealed in my life and he has answered that prayer. For three and a half years, I have fought to keep up enough courage to walk through this difficult recovery. And you want me to give it all up and go back? I just can't believe it!

(A little part started writing.) *I miss my mommy. I need my mommy. I want my mommy. I don't understand why my mommy won't help me. I want nice Christmas presents from my mommy. I want my mommy to say nice things about me again like she used to. I want her to say I'm doing the right thing because sometimes I'm just not sure. I just want my mommy to be there for me no matter what. And I don't understand why she is acting this way. It feels like she doesn't really want me at all. She only wants me to help her play her games. My heart is all broken into pieces. It is bleeding and hurts really bad. It's like I'm an orphan now....*

(Another part takes over.) *How could you* (Mom) *do that to her* (to the little part who just wrote)*? How can you be so self-centered? How can you* *be such a liar? You're worse than Dad. You try to hide your lies in syrupy sweet declarations of love. You think we're too stupid to see that there is no real love there. It's emotional blackmail. Keep the secrets and come back and you'll have my love and adoration again. That's sick. You're sick. And we aren't going to do that….*

(I start writing again.) *It's lonely being the only one in the family outside your web. It hurts. I'm in pain. It hurts that you won't help one iota. You'll buy me nice gifts if I play along. But will you spare a dollar for my recovery? No. Because I'm not playing right anymore. Well, at least we both know that. That's the only truth you have—that I'm not playing the game anymore. I find your behavior toward my daughters malicious and insidious. If you think Bree and I don't see through your thinly veiled attempts to come between us and undermine me as her mother, you are a fool. We both see it. This is the lowest of low—my own mother trying to take my daughter away from me. I hate you for doing that. It's inexcusable. You actually have made my life more difficult and more painful than it already was. How dare you say to me your love is there for me always? You may want to rethink your goals here. Because, right now, you stand to lose all of us.*

My mother had been communicating with the girls, without my knowledge, writing letters, making phone calls, and talking to them during visits, all aimed at getting them to choose her side and turn against me. She realized she was losing me, and feared that meant losing her granddaughters, too. I had not been blocking her relationship with the girls in any way. But when I found out what she was trying to do, I felt betrayed all over again.

Getting Through Christmas

Roger and I planned how the holidays would be handled, including Christmas morning when all four of us would be together to open gifts. I hoped this would help normalize things for the girls, at least a little.

Using tickets purchased months earlier, I took the girls to Denver to see *The Phantom of the Opera* over the weekend, working in a therapy session while I was there. The dark themes and pipe organ music were triggering for my parts, making it hard to sit through it. At the same time, other parts were enthralled at the incredible production and the music. The girls loved it.

When I arrived at Faith's office, the subject of Mom was prominent. My parts were confused, trying to sort out who she really was. While we were growing up there were so many sides to her. One moment she was syrupy sweet, the next yelling and swinging at us, not caring who she hit. Some moments she would be engaged with us, at other times it was like she wasn't even present. Which one was the real mother?

To one of my parts, she was like a black widow spider and we were caught in her web. One thing was universal—we were all afraid of her. Our efforts to be the perfect daughter were motivated by fear of reprisal, rejection, or abandonment if we failed to please her.

I also brought up the subject of Christmas, sharing my dread of the holidays with Faith. In the past, Christmas had always been a special, even magical time, particularly when I was little. I loved putting on a big Christmas every year, making gifts, baking goodies, and decorating the house, including a live tree. Christmas music played constantly. Every Sunday we lit the Advent candles while reading Scripture. And Christmas dinner looked like it came from a Norman Rockwell painting.

But this year I couldn't imagine doing any of that. I was broken, depressed, sad, and afraid for my future. There would be no presents under the tree this year with my name on them. Money was tight. I would be lucky to afford a few small gifts for my girls.

I was definitely playing the victim, so Faith gave me an assignment to buy myself something, turning a deaf ear when I balked about having no money. When the session was over, I went to the mall to search for just the right thing. Later, I wrapped it in beautiful paper with a lovely bow and put it under the tree.

With Christmas only a week away, Roger informed me he was taking Jenny and my car out of town to see another woman. When I protested, his anger escalated quickly. He threatened me with unnamed consequences, calling me crazy and psychotic. He went anyway, but in his own car. I began to get clues that maybe I was the only one working on healing and reconciliation.

When Roger returned, he said he was changing the Christmas plans. He would be having Christmas with the other woman instead of us. It was so disappointing that he didn't care enough about the girls to be there for them.

I made three attempts to arrange emergency mediation for me and Roger, but he refused to cooperate. He did, however, cancel his plans with the other woman at the last minute and ended up staying in town on Christmas.

December 21: (My parts were chattering.) *Feelings. Where are they? What are they? Let's assess the damage. How bad was the last hurricane? Who's been wounded? Who needs help the most? How can we best manage tomorrow? Any ideas? Any information? Any feelings? Exhaustion—I'm tired and I want to sleep and be left alone—all day—don't bother me about anything else. I want to play. Can we make some decorations or some special candy or cookies or something? Let's do something fun. We'll have to get our work done first, you know. There's cleaning and bookkeeping to do. That will keep our mind off things—that's what we really need. But what about Mom and Dad? They are so confusing. And we're going to be alone. I'm scared about the coming days—being alone—no family—sad feelings—piercing pain. What will it be like? How will I feel? How bad will it get?*

December 22: (The dental office closed for the holidays.) *Well, work is over for 12 days. That's a mixed bad bag. Pressure to work more—desire to work more—uncertainty about what the next phase of recovery will look like—no work or distraction—7 days at home. Leave it in God's hands. He knows what's best. Maybe tomorrow can be fun. Faith said I need plans for tomorrow night. What should we do? Dinner and a movie? Alone? With Bree? Someone else? I don't know what's happening inside. We really need to start recording dreams again. Things are getting very active at night. Sad—lonely—fearful of the future—hanging on—hanging tough. Pain, pain, pain—alone.*

Christmas morning arrived. It was simple and quiet, just me and the girls. While the girls were opening their gifts, I picked up the box I had wrapped and opened it. I removed the lid and pulled out the plush pink robe and put it on immediately. It was so cozy and warm.

My therapist was right—the gift made me feel special, even if I had been the one to purchase it. I wore that robe for years, and, every time, it brought back a warm memory. It was truly a victorious moment for me.

I learned a lot from that robe. I learned self-pity and living as a victim were a choice. Rather than focusing on the absence of presents, I could do something out of the norm to improve Christmas morning. Was I still grieving the loss of my marriage? Was the future still uncertain? Yes! While I couldn't do anything about that, I could do something that would bring a moment of joy, something that would brighten the holiday.

Before the dental office reopened, I made a quick trip to Denver for three days of therapy. My parts and I did some memory work, but for the most part we were grieving our marriages—plural. Being separated triggered more grief from my first one. All I had ever wanted was to be married, have babies, raise kids, and take care of a home. I had invested everything I had toward that dream, but Tim and Roger dreamt of something entirely different for themselves.

I had no desire to be single or to be dating. Nada. The last thing I wanted was to be on the "meat market", which is what the dating scene felt like to me.

The Portrait

After Christmas, I created another collage, one that told a slightly different story. Among the pictures of a stormy sea and a torn face were these phrases: *mom and dad, I don't know how to tell you, but listen! muddling through motherhood, the last few years have been crazy, is it worth it? where is the finish? secrets often oppress those they were meant to protect.* The collage helped me process the pain I felt about my parents.

But that wasn't the whole story this time! The collage also included pictures of beautiful women and butterflies, with these phrases: *Bring your color back to life, Indulge your passion, Intelligent,* and *Just perfect.* Life was beginning to emerge.

On December 29, I wrote something I titled, "The Portrait," describing the process of my parts.

> *Blending—yes. But not like cake batter in a mixer or like sugar cookies running together on a sheet. Blending like the colors in a portrait. Each color present, vital, contributing, individual but part of one painting. More and more our parts are finding their places in the portrait, whether it be strength, or passion, or compassion, or music, or other talents, or wisdom, or work, or play, or bubble baths, or check balancing. Each part is a beautiful color, slowly finding its place on the canvas—not to lose its value but to blend in harmony—to create our new portrait. I believe the portrait will be stunning and captivating when it is complete. If you look closely, each color is there, but from a distance it is a portrait in progress. As more parts escape their individual hells, bondage, past abuse, they too, will find their place in the portrait where their color will most enhance the final painting.*

In nine months, the portrait would be finished.

Chapter Thirty-One

1995
January

Being a Perpetrator

With the holidays behind me, my employers let me know that I needed to begin working full time. They had certainly gone an extra million miles for me the last eighteen months, accommodating my frequent trips to Denver. I understood their need to increase my hours, but this would be a big change for me. Could I manage it?

My parts began chattering as they processed events from the past couple of weeks.

January 2 (by one of my parts): *The pain is enormous. Is it the shock of seeing my mother? The pain of spending an evening with* (a person who hurt me in the past)*? The loneliness of living by myself? A new memory starting? Or simply another January for me? Loss—I feel loss. I miss my mother. I find myself wondering if her health is okay. She looked bad.* (A girlfriend of mine) *is leaving—that's scary. I thought it would be better after the holidays. But the pain is enormous tonight. Who is hurting? What's happening inside? We are really scared about handling the office and the dramatically increased hours. Loss of flexibility. Sadness and loss because we didn't get to stay at mom's house. We didn't get to have a visit with her. We didn't get to give her a special Christmas present.*

Not spending part of Christmas with my mom brought a mixture of feelings, including loss and fear, fear that I would never have a happy Christmas with her again. However, the girls and I did have a brief visit after the holiday.

January 2 (cont.): Marianne: *It felt like a goodbye. Like maybe we would never see her* (Mom) *again. Like maybe she would die. Fear of losing our kids, our house, our cats, our things.*

Brenda: *You know it's awfully hard doing all this living stuff all on our own. It's not like there's anyone here helping us.*

Judith Ann: *I'm sorry if I gave you the impression we were almost out of the woods. It feels like your expectations were dashed again.*

Getting through the holidays was like holding our breath under water, just trying to make it to the other side, hoping everything would get better or at least easier when the holidays were over. It took so much energy just to survive. But then we did get to the end of them, nothing was better. In fact, the pain was worse because another memory began to surface.

January 3: *Well, I think we need to keep working. Choking pain tonight. That's not good. Where is it coming from? We wanted to go back to bed this morning. We would have if we hadn't committed to going into work. Why do we want to hole up in bed? Why did we run all evening? What's happening?*

Brenda: *Our heart is still breaking.*

Why did it feel like the pain was choking me tonight? Like the loss is taking the very life out of me and I'm going to die. We have always hated our birthday, so it's hard to know if this is any different. There is a lot of hormone, female stuff, pains, cramps, sensitivity at an odd time of month. All those bruises showed up on our right knee. Could be memories coming up. I feel a mass welling up in my abdomen. Memories of loss—where are they? What are they? Children (who are badly hurt)—*screaming and screaming—the threat of losing my family. I'll be all alone. I'll lose everything.*

As always, the body memories and emotional pain arrived before the knowledge of the event. I would now be stuck in limbo with the pain until I could go back to Denver and process the memory. And the next visit to see Faith was still ten days away.

Different parts began adding pieces to the puzzle, but I didn't always know who was sharing.

January 4: *Five nights now—excruciating pain—hard to focus—to move—to do anything—what's happening? I can't quite get a fix on this. It's not exactly grief. It's in me. Nightmares. I don't look forward to sleep 'cause the nights are so full of nightmares. You know what it is—you just don't want to admit it. You're afraid to even say the word. You know, it's not like you haven't been here before. Maybe it's just grief.*

January 5: *Okay, we've got to get at this before it does us in. We have a good start on it. We know something besides the grief is happening. We know it's very deep and painful. We need to make an appropriate decision about how to proceed and that requires more information. We know it's a memory. Don't think you were just watching 'cause you weren't. I would really like to know who you are. You obviously hold some important keys to getting to the bottom of this—to the truth.*

As my parts talked to each other, calling each other out on things that happened, I often didn't know what they were talking about. They were trying hard to let me know what happened, but I didn't want to hear it.

Void of Identity

January 7: *Who am I really? And what am I doing? And what am I supposed to be doing? Am I really alive? Or did the real me die a long time ago? And so I'm doomed to play out this role until my body dies. I'm so afraid and uncomfortable in groups. I never used to be. I felt in charge and in control most times—self-assured and confident. Why is it so painful now? Bible study, small group, office dinners—I don't know who I am anymore, so I don't know how to act or what to say.*

I'm afraid of people. I just want to isolate. I don't want to be faced with that pain and struggle. It does nothing for my loneliness. I feel just as isolated at Bible study as I do at home. The evenings are so quiet and empty. My life feels empty. I feel that I am a void. Where am I? Who am I? Am I an outgoing, energetic, chatty, hardworking, involved person? Or am I a shy, introspective loner who wants quiet, simple living, feeling melancholy much of the time? How much of me in the past has been an act, a role, a response to the needs of those around me, seeking out every expectation and killing myself to meet it. Yet, when I try to put all that aside, I cannot find something different trying to emerge.

My gosh, I've spent 3 ½ years of my life trying to sort out my internal and external messes. Nothing is resolved. And I feel like maybe the real me died and can't be resurrected. I thought I had clues. Mountains—music—truth speaker—high energy. But today I was immobilized. I did not want to move from my bed. I've played no music in weeks. And my only mountain experience was driving to and from Denver.

What's inside? What's real? I'm only a mass of killer pain when I'm quiet. Will it ever go away? Will I ever feel good or content? Will I be alone the rest of my life? Where's the proof that I'm really alive? I think I'm dead. We are stripping away the false and diseased layers only to discover nothing. Someone who can't relate to people, has little direction in life and hardly enough energy to get out of bed. Trust—God please give me the truth.

Today I recognize and understand this predictable, transitional place everyone arrives at during their healing journey, but not at the time. As God always does in each story, he was stripping my false self away, but the true image of my identity wasn't yet visible. All I felt was a void, a void so empty it seemed like maybe I was dead inside.

And my perspective wasn't completely off. At the beginning of my journey, God told me the old self would have to die. He spoke this through John 12:24: "*I tell you the truth, unless a kernel of wheat falls to the ground and dies, it remains only a single seed. But if it dies, it produces many seeds.*" The old me had to die first. And it was! I was right on track; I just couldn't see it.

Lacking hope or perspective, I was floundering. I didn't know who I was anymore, only that I was uncomfortable in every setting, even ones where I had not previously struggled, like in Bible study groups.

During this transition, however, one thing had not changed. I was still impatient! Especially with the process. *Nothing is resolved,* I wrote. That certainly wasn't true; many memories and healing issues were now behind me. And even though I couldn't see it clearly, I did have clues as to my true identity. Yet I was also still in the midst of my healing process and in a lot of pain. With all that going on, I made the mistake of thinking the emotional and physical paralysis was part of my identity. It was not!

And, for goodness sake, I was in the middle of another memory—a bad one, too! I couldn't avoid the mistake of stacking, of laying too many things on top of each other all at once (healing work, new memories, current life-problems, etc.), which just added to my discouragement.

A New Name

January 8: *God please help me. I don't want to go into this memory. I don't want to pursue it. I want to be normal—not a blithering idiot. I don't want to face it. I don't want it to become reality. It's a horrifying feeling inside. I'm fighting to stay in control. Don't let go. Don't let it happen. Grasp the strands of denial for as long as possible. Retreat, isolate. Who needs this world anyway? I don't.*

January 11: *Hard—it's so hard. It's unbearable—the pain—the despair—the hopelessness—the fear—trust God—hold onto him—gale force winds threaten to suck me down into death. It's hard to hold on. Fight the enemy. He is fiercely working to snatch my children away and tempt them to fall.*

January 12: *God, help me. Things are so hard, confusing, foggy. Only one more day to get through. Hang on to God. Trust him. Pray constantly. The light will reveal the truth and the way. Hold on to that. Be patient and obedient.*

The upcoming three-day weekend afforded me an opportunity to dash over to Denver and work on the memory. It wasn't difficult to get it out. I was like a woman in labor, ten centimeters dilated. All Faith had to do was catch the baby, or maybe I should say, catch the monster.

It was a memory of another cult ritual, one including torture. And because the cult's regular pattern was to force everyone to participate—no one simply watched—I was involved. The horror was beyond words, leaving my parts feeling responsible and guilty. My fierce little part, Brenda, was now calling herself "Bad Brenda."

She was devastated.

After getting the memory out, Faith and I did some healing prayer, inviting Jesus to come and minister to Brenda. He was so good to her, so good to everyone.

Before the prayer concluded, Jesus gave Brenda a special gift.

January 15: *It was an awful memory.* (I described the memory.) *They paid money to be there. I wonder how much? Fundraising for Satan's kingdom. The memory came out and left me in the most awful way—convinced I was ultimately guilty for the heinous act. I shouldn't live. I am not wanting to even entertain a differing view. It's bad enough to remember the rapes and violations, incest and terror. But, it's far easier to be a victim than to know I was a perpetrator as well. Granted, I was unwilling, threatened, and really given no choice, but still…*

Jesus unlocked me from my bondage. I felt unworthy to live—a failure—a bad girl—ruining things everywhere I went. Then Jesus met me. He took my hand and led me to sit on the grass beside him. The children (from the memory) *looked so well. So content, whole, at peace. They were concerned about me because I was the one who wasn't free—they were free. They wanted me to be free as well.*

Jesus said twice that he wanted to give me a new identity, and then finally told me that my new name would be "Bold Brenda." Jesus took my guilt and shame and set me free. I was sorry for all I had done. He forgave me and he embraced me with love. I smiled. I was accepted. They were free and I was, too. Once again, God had redeemed what Satan had meant for evil and turned it to good. I know he has a plan. And, Brenda's boldness will be instrumental in bringing hope and healing to many.

Jesus gave her the gift of a new name and identity. She was now, "Bold Brenda." Brenda was one of my most amazing parts. Her strength and self-sacrificing nature saved so many of us. She was finding freedom.

A Desert-Like Abyss

When I returned home, life felt like a vast abyss sprawling before me. The relief of having the memory out and healed was short lived.

January 29: *Weekends are like a dry, hot, barren desert that I have to walk through every five days in order to get to Monday. Then I can distract myself with work until I get to the next weekend. I can be in an environment where people respect me and value me for five days. I feel safe. I contribute. I am part of a team. My mind is challenged with new skills. And then I have to go through the desert again—alone.*

For two and a half days, I thirst for love, respect, relationships, something to look forward to, meaning to my life beyond parenting, which is like encountering cactus and rattlesnakes along the way. I sweat with the emotional pain of being alone, of being alone with a me I don't know. I sweat volumes of fluid from losing family, marriage, identity, comfort zone, naiveté, my confidence. The long walk saps my energy to the point where I believe I won't make it through the desert. But with any step now I will fall in a heap and die of heat exhaustion—and no one will even know for days.

There's only one stopping place through the desert, a gas station. Lots of people stop to fill up there and rest a bit. The owner (God) *is friendly and always treats you as though he has nothing better to do than chat with you. Some folks miss the opportunity altogether, thinking they'd rather not waste the time by stopping. The owner knows the regulars by name. I almost always stop. I can get a big cool drink there and something to eat while I get out of the sun for a bit. But, today, I didn't even stop. I just didn't have the energy to walk the few extra feet to get there. Maybe, next time I'll be able to stop.*

The barrenness is so awesome. It is almost lifeless. It is void of lush vegetation and growth. It is so visually monotonous. I don't even look out much anymore. I just put one foot in front of the other until I finally come to the end of the desert. The deafening silence finally stops each Monday morning when I walk through the office door and hear, "Good morning, Cyndy. How are you?"

Jesus provided the rest stops I needed, whenever I needed them. Anytime I wanted to, I could pull off to the side of the road and gas up, filling up on His Word, finding strength in his company, receiving encouragement to keep going.

Chapter Thirty-Two

1995
February-April

Mediation

Roger and I met with the Christian mediation team for the first time in February. The girls weren't there but each of their therapists were, as well as Faith and three of my friends for support. It wasn't at all what I expected. Roger shared first, saying he wanted a divorce. I couldn't believe it. He hadn't said a word to me about that. I was stunned and completely undone.

Not that I didn't understand his issues with me; I did. I had been shut down since my recovery began. He was as tired of the marital struggles as I was, and resentful of the financial pressures, having to pay for therapy bills for all four of us. It was ugly, for sure.

Although there had never been a hint of resentment toward Faith before, today he said that he believed she had created a dependency role between her and I that rightfully belonged to him, leaving him feeling unnecessary. He saw little hope of things getting better and just wanted out.

When it was my turn, I expressed my biggest concerns, including his rage toward me and Bree, his lying, stealing, and general deceitfulness, as well as the inappropriate relationships he'd had with several women.

And then that was it, session done. The only mediation that took place was to establish a few ground rules regarding the girls. We were told that the emotional and financial issues would have to be addressed with our individual therapists.

It was the most expensive day of my recovery to date, even more than a day in the hospital, having three therapists and the mediators on the clock for several hours.

I felt sideswiped. I thought we were there to try to make our marriage work. In fact, I thought that was the goal of our separation, to give each of us space to work on our issues in hopes the marriage could be put back together. Given the fact he was with another woman during the holidays, however, I had had plenty of clues that he wasn't working on anything except his next affair.

Since Roger was getting more and more resentful about supporting us, I sought a more official arrangement to make sure our various needs were met. With a legal separation, I would know how much money I had to live on. I took the next step.

Finding Cyndy

In the midst of all this, I noticed a subtle change occurring. When it was time for me to start a new journal, I made a different choice. I abandoned the functional steno pads, choosing a colorful floral print journal, instead. No longer were entries written only in perfunctory black or blue ink. I now had entries in turquoise, purple, and fuchsia! For me, color was life. It was like the first spring crocus poking out from the newly thawing earth after a long cold winter.

There wasn't as much journaling this month. There was also less focus on memories and only a few days of therapy. But I did work on my never-ending identity issues. I was starting to figure out who I was, another sign of new life. I found this journal entry particularly interesting. Even rereading it today, I learned a few things about myself I had forgotten.

February 27: *Who am I really? With all masks off, all dirt washed off, all wounds healed, free from every bondage—who am I really? Who do I want to become?*

I am a lover of music. I love to hear it, sing it, play it, direct it. Music is joy for me. I am a lover of the mountains. I love the colors and the smells and the sounds, the trees, water, rocks, the gigantic-ness, the peace, the solitude and the presence of God that I find in the mountains. I am a lover and speaker of the truth. I love to learn the truth, teach the truth, share the truth. I am a high energy person. I love projects, being active, doing several things at once. I love cats, dancing, candy, ice cream, diet Pepsi, frozen yogurt, hot tubs and bubble baths. I am passionate, compassionate, spiritual and serious. I love neatness, balance, beauty, deep colors and order. I love dinner parties with a few friends, fondue, games, puzzles and movies. I love camping in comfort, staying in elegant hotels, warm sand, maid service, seeing new places, mountain cabins, heated swimming pools. I love beautiful colorful clothes. I love romance, being touched, being kissed, being wanted and adored, getting surprise gifts. I love children and care deeply about their well-being. I love Christmas, spring flowers, summer warmth, fresh winter snow. I love apples, bubblegum, and a soft warm robe.

Hmmm…bubblegum? Who knew? (Much of that remains today, certainly loving truth, mountains, and the presence of God. Ice cream and candy, however, are severely rationed now that they instantly turn into unwanted pounds. And I have been awarded a whole new chapter of life with puzzles, games, and movies now that I have grandchildren!) I was finding the real Cyndy.

Diversion in Durango

Even though things were difficult, we were still trying to make things work between us. So Roger and I headed to Durango, the ski and resort town, for a short getaway with the girls, staying in the same motel where we had stayed together years ago.

April 2 (morning): Patty wrote: *We're in Durango today. I like Durango. I have been here lots and lots of times with Roger. Being here makes me sad because this is the motel where we came the very first time we came to Durango. We rode the train, too. I'm sad because I wish it could still be like that. It was nice back then. I'm very sad that it has all gotten so bad that we can't live together. We can hardly talk to each other. I just wish we could be like that again. But we can't. Faith says we can't turn the clock back.*

(Other parts began chiming in) *I don't see any reason why we shouldn't have a really good time this week. Our life is horrible. We can't ever have fun because we always have to be responsible. Well, we don't have to be responsible this week. So, why not break out of the fortress for awhile?*

We NEED it! Why don't all of you come out today and just enjoy Durango and play and be fun and be silly. Let's have a good time with all of you out. Okay?

April 2 (evening): *I'm so sad tonight. I go away—I feel—I go home—I don't feel. It's supposed to be a vacation. I guess it still is. But the pain surges up. Divorces, statistics, families, brokenness, doubts, fears, kids, guilt, confusion, disillusionment, disappointment, dreams dashed, pain, loneliness, singleness, sorrow. God, please help me. I'm scared and sad. I love you, God. And I really need you. You're the only truly certain thing in my life. How can I please you? What would please you?*

So many times now I've given you my life. So many times. Tonight—I give it to you again. I'm all ears, all eyes. Speak, show, reveal, lead, confirm, change, impose—whatever you want. But please be gentle. I feel so battered, so beat up, so fragile, so vulnerable, so needy. Please squeeze me with loving arms tonight. I'm starved for affection, for affirmation, for love.

I know I can always count on you to be Truth. But I can't always count on me to accept Truth. What may seem totally right to me may be totally wrong. And I can listen to trusted advisors, but I can't count on them to speak Truth. So I ask you to get my attention in whatever way you need to. I want to know your Truth. I want to be free and only Truth can set me free. I want life—as you intended it to be. Please take me there. Your loving daughter, Cyndy

We had not gotten very far with the mediation team, when the leader resigned, leaving us in limbo. I felt like another nail was driven into the coffin of Divorce. For the next week, my every thought was centered on what to do about my marriage.

Go? Or Stay?

It is crazy how the collages I continued to create tell a story; how simple magazine clippings reflect such deep realities. My next one was on the theme of marriage. A picture of a broken wedding ring was surrounded with the words, *my husband cheating* and *infidelity.* Below it, a thorny, rose stem wrapped a face, and included the words *Loss* and *Coping with pain.* Tiny words in the corner said, *it's a custody case, your honor.* Another corner depicted a happy family, sitting in the living room. Tinkerbell was added, sprinkling fairy dust along with the words, *once upon a time*. A clipping of a desert included the phrases *lost time* and *expect to be disappointed*. The angry, red, large picture in the middle said, *you're screaming, in the midst of trouble, a blast to the heart*, and *walking a thin line*. The collage certainly captured my emotions about my marriage.

April 24: *I feel like a ball in a pinball machine, being bounced back and forth between reconciling and divorcing. There seems to be no peace either way. I'm not safe with him yet I feel all protection ceases if I divorce. Safety. Of course, it is only in God. Why think about reconciling? He doesn't want me. The once burning house is nothing but a pile of cold ashes. There's nothing there to go back to and nothing new to strive for. Yet, we haven't pursued reconciliation, not really. I'm frightened.*

April 25: *Why can't I make a decision? I'm in agony. Just one step in either direction—some movement. Anything! Something. Why am I paralyzed? What is going on? I've never dithered like this about anything in my life. I can't widen the gap one more notch by separating accounts and credit cards, or by calling an attorney to see what kind of a settlement I could expect. "A heart at peace gives life to the body." (Proverbs 14:30a) I believe it. I want peace. I want freedom from this hell, this daily agony, this miserable life of mine.*

April 26: *Okay, we have a group assignment tonight. Everyone who wants to give input gets to do so. Here it is: What do we think of Cyndy?*

Indecisive, chicken, loser, scary, honest, unrealistic, pretty, old, heavy and plain, godly, mixed-up, lonely, afraid, pathetic, depressed, undesirable, stagnant, has some abilities, no self-confidence, afraid of her shadow, wise, powerful, weak, not taking any risks, no sense of adventure, loves God, prays a lot, loves her kids, is very sad, in agonizing pain, a good friend, hard worker, good with money, afraid of poverty, loves children, angry, tired, impressive to others, compassionate, suffering, lacking direction.

Apparently, the identity list I created on February 27 wasn't the only opinion going on inside me. There were other things in the mix, like fear and insecurity.

The next day we checked in with our parts, trying to get some idea of what we should do. An alter and I began debating whether to stay in the marriage or not.

April 27: (Me) *He* (Roger) *doesn't want to live with someone who doesn't love him. Who could blame him? Yet, how can I become that person he needs and wants? No wonder he is so certain and decisive. Who wants to contribute tonight on this topic? What does everybody think or feel?*

Alter: *Go back to him—are you serious? Why? Tell me one thing good about being with him again—not all the things you'd avoid (like loneliness, poverty, misery).*

Me: *Maybe I would love him this time.*

Alter: *Excuse me but going from hating your perpetrator husband to loving seems like a massive jump. Is he really the man for you? And what about being put in the role of mother and then hated for it? And who's to say that the rage and abuse to both Bree and I won't be back?*

Me: *But, there's so much to lose!*

Alter: *I guess you have to decide what's more important. You can go back to survival in a sick relationship and have the feeling of being safe in a familiar environment. Or, you can choose freedom, a chance to fully realize your gifts and talents, and step into new and unknown territory. You said last night that you wanted to take more risks and develop more of a sense of adventure. If you go back, you're going to stifle and smother your recovery.*

Me: *What if God wants to do a miracle?*

Alter: *Then let him do a miracle. You can't do a miracle. So ask him (*God*) if that's what he wants. That's his department, not yours. You can't go back as things are. We won't let you. Barring a miracle, you've gotta get out and get on.*

Well, that was no help from this cacophony. There was no consensus whatsoever. With the work week winding down, my body repeated its predictable pattern, something I dubbed the "Friday flu."

April 28: *I've got the Friday flu again. Tired, lethargic, diarrhea, withdrawn and so sad. God, I wish you would help me make some sense out of my life. I feel so guilty for even contemplating a divorce. It's like I'm letting you down. I've failed you. I've failed because I can't make myself live with a man I don't love. I can't do it anymore. I can't do it again. I don't have the strength to withstand it day after day.*

I feel I've failed you. I want to hear you say to me that you love me still. And that it doesn't please you to (have me) *suffer in miserable relationships. That you don't think I'm bad. But I feel only how bad I am. And how pathetic my life is. And then I am overwhelmed with the loss of my dreams, my family, my security, my home, my identity. It hurts so bad. I wish there was a pill to make it better.*

We aren't one home anymore. We're two. And Jenny is split between the two. I am so sorry that she has this reality to deal with. My insides scream at me, "Don't go back!" "Don't go back!" "Nothing is worth that!" "We'll give up everything. We can make it." And, then I think— "Just go back, you can do it. You have done it before. Then Jenny won't be split. Then we don't all lose so much." Then I'm a good girl again and not so bad and God won't be mad at me.

What do I deserve? What does God want for me? What do I want? Why don't I ask that question for a change? I want to get over the Friday flu. I want to be in a healthy, right relationship. I want to receive the abundant life God has promised me. Where is it? Will somebody please tell me where it is?

What does Cyndy want? That was a brand-new question.

April 29: *I just don't feel released to divorce. At least not now. Even if there will be no reconciliation, I have many fear issues to work through. I have issues with God to work through about belonging and being abused and safety and security. I have more work to do on myself to be free from things that hold me in internal bondage. If I work through my fears of the future, I'll see more clearly. And if I keep opening myself to anything God wants, I'll know for sure.*

I finally settled into the one position I knew I could trust, a position I've taken each time I'm at a crossroads, needing to make a decision. If I am willing to do whatever God asks me to do, then I know I will hear his voice directing me. I would wait on God.

Chapter Thirty-Three

1995
May

Escaping through Sleep

May 2: *You know it's pretty sad when the high point of your day is when it is finally late enough to go to bed—to sleep for hours and hours—to be unconscious—to not have to fight the powerfully dreadful urge to take a nap—to close my eyes and drift off in an attempt to escape the pain for a little while. There has to be more meaning to my life than this. I don't pray enough. I don't know if I should get involved in something. Church work? There's always a need there—all those summer slots to fill. I feel like a slacker. I feel like I've been on the planet Mars for the past four years and I'm traveling back to earth. I don't know where I belong or even if I belong. I want a life. This is just barely existing. I've chosen to hold off on the divorce decision. That seems to mean postponing recovery, integration.* (Integration is the process of alters rejoining with the host, becoming part of the whole and no longer separate. I wasn't thinking about or really working toward integration, but it occasionally came up in conversation with Faith.) *I have to keep working on the safety and security issues—that is recovery. I belong to myself and to God. I'm under his protection. I must trust his provision even if the numbers don't look good at all. God—what do you want from me? What changes do you want me to make? How do you want me to live my life now? Please show me.*

Even though it wasn't yet time, it was a sign of life returning that I even entertained questions about getting involved in ministry again.

May 3: *Jenny broke my heart today. She ran away from school. Don't ever say it can't get worse. It always can. Jenny is in so much pain and I don't know how to help her. She is so withdrawn and isolated. I feel like I can't reach her anymore. Her pain is so stuffed down inside her, she can't even reach it. She is miserable. And she is afraid. God help us all.*

Of course the girls were reacting. If it isn't hard enough being thirteen, Jenny was also trying to deal with her parent's separation, feeling very different things than her sister. Bree was relieved Roger was out of the house; she didn't have to deal with his constant emotional abuse. Jenny was another story. Because Roger appointed her as the object of his affections, they were close. Jenny was very aligned with Roger, something from which he took great advantage, feeding her frustrations with me and supporting any wild, teenage idea that came into her mind.

Focusing on the Good

May 6: *Today was a nice day. And that is certainly worth noting. No mediation, no work, no therapy, no schedule, and Jenny home for the weekend. We had a nice day, a relaxed day of shopping, a nice drive, no fighting, only moderate pain, company all evening, a good movie, popcorn for dinner. I had a nice day. Maybe more will come. I even got to sleep in. I delivered the promised ice cream. We acted a little silly, too.*

I swam twice this week, that's a good restart.

Not absolutely everything is bad. I have good friends, I have God, my needs are met. Things are hard, but there are things to be thankful for. I also have a roof over my head, a reliable car and food. I have two healthy, gifted daughters. I have good health. I have a good job, a church. And, for the first time, I have petunias growing in my front yard. I don't know about tomorrow, but I'm thankful for today. If there was one good day, then perhaps there could be another—then maybe several. Maybe my life will change.

What's going on inside tonight? (Chattering from my parts) *It was a nice day. I liked the ice cream. I hope it's sunny soon and warm. Will we be okay now? Yes—we are going to be okay. I don't know what it's going to look like, but we are going to be okay.*

More signs of new life were emerging, as I began recognizing there were some good things in my life, finding gratitude, thinking positively, even if it was fleeting. Reentry into normal life after recovery is not a sudden moment of arrival, not at all. It is a gradual change, like healing after major surgery. At the beginning, no day is a good day, everything aches, but then you start to get a little strength back and find you don't hurt all the time. Improvement comes slowly, with fits and starts. And still some bad days.

God Said to Wait a Little Longer

May 8: *I feel desperate and panicked inside. I don't know why. It's getting worse. I had a nightmare…* (I described the dreadful details). *I haven't had such nightmares for awhile. I've had the usual sore throat come and go—just like it always does when there's something I need to tell. I want to run and hide. The anxiety is getting worse. I don't want a divorce. I actually prayed for reconciliation. I can't believe it.*

May 10: *Thank you, God. If* (a girlfriend) *and John hadn't prayed with me tonight, I don't know what I would have done. But they did. It helped.*

Alex wants to be left alone. He wants out of the marriage, clearly. He expressed his fear of Roger's rage and cried when he shared that he thought Roger would kill him. We asked what Jesus wanted me to do about the divorce. He (Jesus) *said that he is still working and doing a lot of things I can't see. And that I just needed to wait a little longer. So, the pressure is not so bad tonight. I feel more at peace but definitely exhausted.*

The push and pull regarding the marriage made it difficult. I didn't have even one part that liked Roger. The only part siding with me to try and make it work was motivated by fear of having no one to take care of us.

May 11: *It's hard to buy Mother's Day cards when you feel anything but loving toward your Mother. I always thought I would be a good mother because I wanted to be. It mattered to me. It's hard to face that I have been so lacking. I pray for God's grace to make up the difference. It still hurts today—a lot. But it seemed as though the craziness was reduced. Jesus is protecting us now. How is everybody inside tonight? The little ones feel safer.* Alex: *We don't have to put up with his behavior any longer. It's bad for us. So stop thinking about going back to the way it was. Because it's not an option.* Judith Ann: *We need to relax in the unknown until the picture is made clear.*

May 13: *I don't know what to say. I don't know what to write. God said to wait. He said he's doing things I can't see and I should just wait awhile longer. I want to be obedient to that. But now Roger wants weekly get-togethers to see this 'magic from God.' I never said God was going to do magic. I only said I didn't want a divorce. That God had not said to me to get a divorce. I'm terrified of him. I'm terrified of sharing anything about myself with him. I don't know what God is up to, but I'm scared. I had to sit there and listen to Roger say horrible things about me* (during a mediation session). *He said he doesn't like who I am, and he thinks he never has liked who I am. I feel like a nobody. I feel worthless. My life is a meaningless blob. God, what are you doing?*

May 14: *The craziness has diminished. I don't know where this will head, but I feel peace about the direction. I have to try this. I have to believe that God said to wait awhile longer because he's doing things I can't see. It's not time for a decision. I must meet with Roger and talk with him. And I must do it several times. But I'm still terrified. How can I feel stronger—that I don't want a divorce—and hate who he is all at the same time? It seems like he will never understand what he does to me and how it affects me. I don't know if he'll ever understand loving and giving. But at least this should make or break it. This will either be the breakthrough we need or clarify that divorce is inevitable.*

I actually had glimpses of a life today. I didn't go back to bed. I weeded one flower bed. I thought about singing. I thought about teaching again. I thought about the message in the kids' program, "O Jonah." And how I've wanted to run from God's plan for me because it's so scary. Maybe he won't call me to anything for a very long time, maybe he'll call tomorrow. Whenever, I'll say, "yes."

May 14 (cont.): Alex and Marissa expressed how unhappy they were that we were meeting with Roger every week. Me: *Alex, talking doesn't mean reconciliation. Your feelings are important. Remember God has a future for us that is good. You're still needed. Marisa, please don't jump ahead and make assumptions. We are only testing the waters. Please be patient. No, it's true, he doesn't understand how to relate to the inside parts, and he doesn't know how wounding he is to everybody. Let's see if he can learn.*

May 15: *I liked what* (a girlfriend) *said to me last week.* (When her marriage was struggling) *she decided that if her marriage was going to fail, then she wasn't going to be the reason.*

How are things inside tonight? Please share whatever you want to share. Little Cindy: *He was very mean, and he said he doesn't like us and never has liked us. He's a terrible man. He's very, very mean and I don't like him. He scares me. He's never going to be nice to us. I don't like him, and I don't want to talk to him 'cause he's so mean.* Me: *Remember, Little Cindy, that Jesus is inside with us and has promised to protect us. So stay close to Jesus and nothing bad will happen to you.*

May 17: *My life seems so meaningless. My days are empty. My heart is empty. The days are an endless cycle. God, save me from despair. These days are too hard.*

I was tired of everything. I was tired of going to Denver, tired of therapy, tired of living in a wasteland, tired of being in limbo with my marriage. Just plain worn out.

May 18: *I dread the trip tomorrow. I dread getting up early, packing, preparing to be gone. My mind is mush. I didn't even think to get gas or money until tonight. I just want to check out mentally and emotionally—sleep—avoid.*

One more trip—one of the countless numbers. When will it end? What am I doing? I'm so scared of Roger. What are these weekly meetings going to do? They terrify me. Will I ever have a life? Is something worthwhile going to come of my life? Will I ever be kissed again? Will I ever be caressed? Will my heart ever beat rapidly in the arms of another man? What is there to look forward to?

Over the weekend, I had made another mad dash to Denver for three days of therapy. Mostly Faith and I were trying to help the parts deal with their reactions to the weekly meetings with Roger, along with the ongoing stress with the girls. But there was also another cult memory to process. And then there was an interesting comment my mom made during a phone conversation, one that sent everyone to the moon: *I would appreciate it if you told me what I did wrong. Nobody appreciates what I do.*

Really, mom? Where do I start?

Accepting the Pain

May 19: *Accept the suffering. That's what* (Faith) *said today. Isn't that an incredible thing to say? To just accept it—accept it is God's plan for my life today, but not forever. Like going through the refiner's fire. It's a totally different mindset than where I have been—and am. To ask what God has for me in it each day—to learn from it—to yield to the suffering. I have never thought of it in such a light. I am used to God asking me to lead a program or start a group or help a person. I am now used to God asking me to face my past, to walk through my memories and do the hard work. I am not used to God asking me to yield to pain, to not do anything but let it be, accept it, live through it, not resent it, not fight it, not succumb to self-pity. She said I'm going through the fire.*

It may sound silly, but these three words made a big difference: *Accept the suffering.* Changing my perspective improved my tolerance. Just choosing to see it as God's plan rather than something bad or wrong helped me cope better.

May 20: *The day ticks by. Accepting the suffering as God's plan for me now—I'm still thinking about that. I guess if I find peace in it, I'll know I'm on the right track.*

Inside people are looking for ways to dissociate from the pain. The loneliness and rejection are killing us. Can we endure the pain with no breaks? No dissociation or diversions through work or busyness or drinking are allowed. All our exit modes are cut off—that is unless I choose to retreat into one of them again.

Or shall I take my weakness instead to God—give up on the idea that I can make the pain and suffering stop—accept my lot—look for the lessons? Were he to ask me to go to someone and help them and pray with them, I would. Were he to ask me to give money somewhere, I would. Were he to ask me to move, I would. Or start a new ministry, I would not deny him. I just never thought he would ask me to suffer so much, so long.

Obviously, my healing is not complete, and I never imagined such a phase to be gone through. His ways are higher than my ways. So why am I continually surprised at what he chooses to do? Why at this point do I have any preconceived notions about recovery? It has unfolded each step of the way such that I am blind as I walk forward. I don't know the mysteries of God's plan for this wasteland time. Maybe, as I accept and stop resisting my eyes will be open to the mysteries. Temptation rides high now. I will need to be dependent on him in my weakness.

May 21: *I survived another therapy marathon. I have assignments—letters to write. Anger that needs to be expressed. I have to go home and face my life again. It does seem like it will be easier to live with the pain now that I see it as a necessary recovery phase. And there's really nothing I can do to diminish it or shorten its duration. Hopefully, I will hear God's voice now that I'm not resenting and rebelling against it. Alex is very angry about the upcoming lunch visits. I need to let him write to Roger and to me. And I need to reassert my needs for honesty and boundaries with my mother. I need to respect the suffering and the amount of time it will go on—unknown time. And I need to get back on track with self-nurturing.*

After Roger and I met for another lunchr, I journaled my thoughts.

May 26: *Fighting for my marriage? Am I nuts? Prolonging this limbo state—am I procrastinating the inevitable? Is God happy? Are we going the right way? Can the kids take it? Can I take it physically and emotionally? All I know is that it seems like the appropriate steps now. Trust God. Wait for him. It's all I know for now. I'm so tired. I work so hard. And I come home so tired. Will I get well? How much longer? Isn't 4 years enough? Apparently not.*

Jesus wants me. He loves and adores and protects me. I need only be dependent on him. Fill the deep holes, Jesus. Heal the yet unhealed places.

All I could do was lean into Jesus and Truth.

May 29: *What's there to say. The day from hell. I am ready to give up. I don't want to live like this anymore. I can't. The pain is unbearable. Where do I get off? Drinking, pills, suicide? They are all destructive, obviously. I've held on to Jesus and ridden it out until I sleep. But tomorrow I work. Where is this pain coming from? Why is it here? I want to know. How are you doing inside? Who needs to talk? My daddy was a very bad man and he is running away and won't face what he did. Sometimes it seems less real and I try to forget. But tonight it is all back in living color. And my mommy turned her back on me when I desperately needed her help. And Roger blames me for everything. And I hate myself.*

That was the day I received a letter from my sister.

Chapter Thirty-Four

1995
June

Family Responses

Relationships with family members had been complicated since remembering the abuse. Except for the common reaction that no one believed me, no two family members responded the same.

Dad ended communication with me. Mom was still in the picture, but only marginally, with the relationship hanging by a thread.

I had had minimal contact with my half-brother, Scott, over the decades, seeing him only once during those years, which was before remembering anything about our dad. He didn't support me, even in the little I did know at that time. Despite his own hurtful relationship with our father, Scott thought I was nuts. Except for one family gathering on my dad's eightieth birthday, I haven't seen him again.

My younger brother's response was the least painful. He never judged me or rejected me, which I greatly appreciated. He never said he believed me, only that he didn't know what to think about it all. At least he didn't pull away from me. He was the only family member with whom there was no interruption.

Then there was my sister.

Losing my Sister

My sister and I were always close. From the time she was born, since I was twenty months older, it was important to me that I look out for her. I sewed clothes for her, helped her with her hair, and showed her how to wear makeup. She wasn't particularly appreciative of my lesson on how to shave her legs; I forgot to mention how to tighten the blade down and she drew blood all the way up her shin. (The old-style razors had a knob at the bottom to secure the drop-in blades.)

Now that she and I were living in different states, a thousand miles apart, in the days before email and social media, we frequently wrote long letters to each other. Once she wrote, *It's always so special receiving your letters. I really appreciate that you are committed to keeping in touch. You probably don't realize just how important that is to me.* I felt the same.

In January of 1994, I told her a little bit about what was going on with me. She replied with tender words: *"I'm praying for you and your family a lot these days. My heart is heavy for you. I know that I need to release it all to the Lord but in my weakness, I continue to worry.*

"I feel like a child sitting in my Father's lap. I'm crying because one of my most precious dolls has been stolen by a mean neighbor girl. Whenever I spot the girl, she is dragging the doll along. The doll is getting more and more tattered. I can even see that her arm is partly torn off and her dress is tattered. My Father is telling me that I can do nothing about the situation, but that he has already taken care of it.

"My Father is God and you are the doll. I really don't know what to say and yet my heart aches to be in communication with you. I was horrified at what you said to me on the phone when we last talked. I love you and am fervently praying about all of this."

Two months later, she said, *"I was so encouraged to hear that you are surrounded by so much love and support right now. I still agonize about whether I can help in any way but know that the miles between us are the main hurdle. I'm so thankful that the Lord is translating my prayers into the direct involvement of your own friends who live near you."* She went on to ask me twenty-eight questions, trying to understand everything about this crazy world where I found myself living.

Just two weeks later, a letter added what she remembered about the sitter, the one Dad said never existed. *"I vaguely remember the babysitter we had and that she was a harsh sort of person."* She also suggested I investigate old police records and newspapers to try and substantiate my memories. Good luck with that.

There is no way to substantiate memories of abuse. The cult exists in the shadows. They leave no trace. Nothing is ever investigated. And a five-year-old doesn't know who these people are, how to find them, or anyone's real name. Even non-cult abuse normally can't be substantiated. When someone slips into your bedroom and rapes you, there are only two stories. Unfortunately, most of the time the perpetrator is believed, and the victim is discredited. Victims are rarely believed or receive help.

When I wrote back, I mentioned none of that, but I did attempt to answer her twenty-eight questions. I also sent some reading materials, at her request, to help her understand dissociation and repressed memories.

In June 1994, another letter arrived from my sister, adding this information about an event from 1975: *I can vividly remember my visit to Texas with Uncle Dan after your wedding. There is something about that trip that disturbs me greatly now that didn't then, due to lack of knowledge of Mom's history. In later years I learned of Dan's abuse of Mom. In yet a later time, Mom had occasion to ask me if Dan had abused me on that trip. He hadn't. As I look back on it now, one question dominates: why had Mom allowed me to go alone with Dan or not at least warned me? This indicates to me that Mom either chose not to or was not able to keep her children out of harm's way. For me, that revelation sheds some light on your experiences."*

It was the same question I had asked myself a million times. Where was Mom while all this abuse was going on? Why wasn't she protecting me? She told me once that she was terrified of her father-in-law (my dad's father) and didn't trust him. She said she feared he might do something to her, although she didn't say what. If that was the case, why was I alone with him so often?

Since the confrontation with my dad the previous fall, he and I no longer had contact. However, he did communicate with my siblings. I only knew this because my sister copied a recent letter from him and included it with her own.

In Dad's letter to my sister, he said, *"he was appalled at your* (my sister's) *inability to understand the impact of those words* (my sister's statement that she didn't know what happened) *on an innocent father. I have never felt such pain in my life."* Later in the letter he said, *"Why aren't you now saying, 'Dad, I know there is no way you ever would have taken the little baby you loved so much to a satanic orgy and passed her around to be raped by her grandfather and anyone else who wanted her.' That is what I must hear before we will be able to resume our relationship."*

Dad's letter, threatening to end their relationship if she didn't take his side and declare his innocence, left my sister reeling. She was scrambling to sort out what she should do. She didn't want to disrespect me or harm our relationship, but she didn't know what to say to our dad, either. So, in her letter to me, arriving June 1st, she asked for photographs of scars and records that would prove my story. I had no way to produce either.

Her letter echoed my sentiments. *I frankly cannot ever in my life remember missing Dad or being close to Dad. Whether he is involved in my life or not doesn't really matter to me. What I mean is that time with him is not important to me, but being on speaking terms is. I want to continue to express God's love to him.*

I, too, dreaded the thought of being estranged from my family. It was bad enough having so little support. To never hear from them again was more than I could handle. I didn't need *more* pain and suffering.

It wasn't immediately evident, but the foundation of my relationship with my sister was beginning to crumble.

Love, Denial, and Self-Protection

The family's varied responses pushed all the bad buttons in me. I had had enough difficulty walking forward, fighting my own denial, forever questioning whether any of it was true. I didn't need their help doubting my reality.

No one wanted this to all be a bunch of hooey more than I did. I would have done anything to stop this, to change things, to negate everything, but I couldn't. Not that I didn't try. Plenty of times I tried to walk away. *Forget it! Who needs this!*

In my deepest recesses, however, I knew it was true. Was every detail of every memory accurate? Probably not. I was a little girl. I didn't have the capability to process everything that happened. But, even if *half* my memories weren't true, then half *were* true. That is still horrific.

As I said before, it might be possible for someone to invent wild stories, but the gripping terror and painful body memories? Not a chance. I did not go looking for this, it came and found me.

The one irrefutable piece for me, the piece that always grounded me when denial tried to once again smother me, was how this whole thing got started. God started it. Through all that crazy Holy Spirit stuff, through the dreams, through many other people, through his Word, and straight into my heart and mind, God told me there was some hard stuff that we needed to deal with in order for me to live as the woman he made me to be. And then he led me into dozens of memories of abuse. I did not do that.

I wanted to tell my family, *If you don't believe me, then take it up with God, because he's the one who started it and led my steps.* Instead, I said nothing. In fact, I stopped sharing anything about my recovery with my family. There was no point, it only led to more hurt for me.

In spite of all this, there was love expressed in other directions. I knew my family loved me then and I know they love me now. And I feel the same about them. It might be tempting to say *it isn't loving to reject someone, or insinuate they are lying, or withhold support.* Believe me, that is exactly how I felt at the time. But my perspective today is different.

Our walls of self-protection are fierce. My dad lied because admitting the truth would have broken down the walls he had created to keep himself from his own truth. To choose to believe me meant the family would have had to enter the same hell I was in, losing their perceptions and memories of being the model family, as my dad liked to call us.

No one wants to believe their parents are liars and have done evil things.

I hated their choice, but I understood the risk was unacceptable for each family member, should they have chosen to believe me. Letting me be the scapegoat was the easier option.

While they agreed with each other that my story was nonsense, no one agreed on who was to blame. My sister chose the version that I was influenced by Satan, that I was taken captive by him, and my memories were from him. Dad blamed it on Roger, that he had somehow twisted my mind. My mom blamed Faith. She was convinced Faith planted the memories in my mind. I confronted Mom on that once, telling her that my memories started coming back before I met Faith. But my mom stuck to her guns—it was Faith's fault. If I'd learned anything, I'd learned that if you don't want to see the truth, you won't.

The one thing of which no one ever accused me, surprisingly, was lying. They all upheld my honesty and integrity. Go figure. I'm not sure how that all lines up.

Part of me is glad they didn't accept the truth, as surprising as that may sound. I never wished for my family to go through the pain I had to. But, at the same time, I knew they were in bondage, too. And only by dealing with the truth, and following God's plan for healing and redemption, can we experience the life he's planned for us. And that is something I do want for them.

During all this back and forth communication between her and I, my sister diligently tried to get answers from our parents, but they responded with lies at every turn. When she asked Mom about giving me Phenobarbital, my mom told her it was cough syrup. When she talked to dad, in her words, *"...he was very convincing, he really believes that he is totally innocent."*

But, then again, my father was a salesman and a practiced liar. He could sell an air conditioner to a native Alaskan. And what did she expect? A full confession? As the decades passed, the lies got more outrageous.

A Generational Issue

I, too, think Dad had convinced himself he was innocent. Early in my recovery, before Dad ended our relationship, he randomly called me one day. Unusual. He hated phone calls. He went on to tell me this story about an old friend who had flown into town and had had dinner with him the night before. In the midst of their dinner conversation, she shared that she was diagnosed with multiple personality disorder (MPD or DID, Dissociative Identity Disorder, as it's known today), resulting from abuse in her childhood. He said it was a horrible story.

Then he said to me, *"It made me wonder about what you are going through, and whether you were also multiple."* His words just about stopped my heart. I had been diagnosed by then, but I had not told him. I confirmed his suspicion, to which he responded, *I am so sorry, honey*. He did not, however, ask me why I was multiple.

That got me thinking. For my entire life, my dad had referred to what was going on in his head as 'The Committee.' He frequently mentioned how difficult it was to deal with all the voices inside. I began to wonder if he was multiple. It would certainly explain a lot of things, like having twelve years of his childhood blocked out in his memory, and being able to live in a false reality, believing he had never abused me.

It would also explain the reason behind the weird call. I was pretty sure my dad was lying about the woman from out of town, making up the story as a way of broaching the subject with me. My best guess is that he was aware of MPD because he, too, had been diagnosed at some point. But revealing a diagnosis to me would have made it hard to maintain his innocence, so Dad made up a cover story.

My father was just as much a victim of my grandfather and the cult as I was. I do not say that to excuse or condone his actions. Everyone is responsible for their actions, whether they are a multiple or a "mono-brain." (Mono-brain is my made-up term for everyone outside the MPD/DID world.) However, this was a generational issue in my family. These things, this culture of abuse, doesn't just drop out of the sky. It is passed down.

Both my parents were victims of significant abuse and never received any healing. They muddled through life the best way they knew how, trying to make it work. But because my dad had no relationship with Jesus, and my mom didn't allow Jesus into those damaged places, they continued to perpetrate damage and destruction on the next generation, to me and my siblings.

That is always how it goes. Either Jesus sets us free, or then we, in turn, become offenders to others.

Self-Nurture; Good or Bad?

June 1: *Boy, it comes in waves. To deal with Roger, Mom, Dad, and* (my sister) *all in a few days. No wonder I'm ready to go off the deep end. What was I searching for? What am I waiting for? Why do I feel so angry at the church? Why can't I get past that? Should I expect nothing? What on earth does God want from me now? Should I buck up—stop whining and get on with my life? Ignore the pain? Should I give into what Roger and Bree and Faith all want—divorce? Is waiting the right decision? Can I do something about this pathetic life of mine? Is there some reward for waiting? Or am I simply postponing the inevitable? Where am I? Should I stop expecting anything from anybody?*

The subject of self-nurture, taking care of myself, came up constantly, each time creating an inner struggle. When I decided to journal about it, my wise part (she didn't identify herself) was kind enough to respond.

June 2: Me: *What I want to know is this—is self-nurturing a biblical concept?*

Wise part: *So, what are you suggesting? Maybe a sackcloth and ashes lifestyle—if so, you're getting close.*

(I detected more than a little sarcasm.)

Me: *I thought Scripture promoted pleasing God—not pleasing self.*

Wise part: *So, doesn't embracing life, celebrating, dancing, joy, abundant life please God? Where does it say being miserable pleases God?*

Me: *But it just seems so selfish. Doesn't he want self-sacrificing? Pick-up-your-cross-daily-and-follow-me stuff?*

Wise part: *Not even Jesus got nailed to the cross every day. He enjoyed parties, people, fellowship, solitude, close friendships. And everything he did pleased God.*

Me: *Then why can't I enjoy anything?*

Wise part: *Because you're bitter and angry and depressed.*

Me: *But I feel so let down.*

Wise part: *Stop looking to people for your worth, look to God. And stop trying to please Faith—please God.*

Me: *So, I need to let God fill my dance card. I guess Jesus was let down—by his closest friends—and he forgave.*

Wise part: *Food for prayer.*

I was a hard case to crack. Change wasn't easy and I fought myself all the way. My church upbringing and knowledge of Scripture gave me the impression I shouldn't do nice things for myself. Fortunately, somewhere inside me was a more balanced view, that even Jesus knew how to have a good time.

Dwindling Support

June 4: *The mysteries of God. I've known him personally for 27 years and yet his ways are still mysterious to me. I feel all alone tonight, but I know he's here. I feel so confused about what I am doing or should be doing or shouldn't be doing. But he's not confused. He knows exactly the way I'm to go. I feel my life is worthless. But I'm the daughter of the King.*

I feel as though the numbers of loving, caring people are pitifully small. But now I am beginning to see that this is a reality that most human beings are experiencing. Christ himself experienced it—the abandonment of his closest friends. Yet he forgave them and asked his father to forgive them. God is sufficient to meet my needs. Yet I feel pathetically needy. I want to be carried, I want to be ministered to, I want someone to cry with me, I want to be listened to, to be held, to be visited, to be loved. What am I? What is happening? When does the pain end? When does my life come out of the pit? I feel the powerful words come up from deep inside me. (This was a precursor, revealing a glimpse of God's future plans for me.) *Why? What are they for? Can I do this another day, another week? I'm worn out, crushed, spent, empty, lonely.*

By now, my support group was shrinking. One couple left when Roger and I separated, saying they could not support that decision. Others just created a little distance. I don't blame them for falling away. My recovery had gone on a long time and there seemed to be no improvement and no end in sight. No one on my support team had any reference to or understanding of the things I was dealing with, even when I shared details with them. It was difficult for anyone to understand.

Most people were afraid of getting too close to my pain, like maybe it was contagious or something. Some wanted to help but didn't know what to do, thinking they needed to be proficient in dissociation or sexual abuse to be supportive. The reality, though, was that the most helpful thing someone could do was be willing to sit with me and let me talk if I needed to talk, to just listen and care. No person could fix me or the circumstances of my life. Besides, God had that base covered, using Faith and John and my intercessory prayer team.

Social support for me was one of the most powerful recovery agents, helping me maintain my equilibrium during my season of healing. Having people (not professionals) around me who spent time with me, tracking with my life was grounding. When I was grounded, I was less likely to become overwhelmed and veer into suicidal ideation.

It also needs to be said that survivors can, at times, be highly resistant to support. We can be our own worst enemy, rebuffing offers of help. Sometimes we first need to discover the support person is serious, trustworthy, and safe. So there is often testing involved. Some survivors would rather have no friends than risk being rejected or abandoned by one more person.

It helps when people are willing to help without taking responsibility for the survivor, setting clear guidelines on what they can do and are willing to do. And then follow through! Support people must have the freedom to say no to occasional requests for help or they won't be able to go the distance. If survivors can't accept that reality, the support person will likely get burnt out.

For me, my friends who stayed involved no matter what, not buckling under my rebuffs, gently and persistently (but respectfully) offering company, these were the ones who were effective and greatly appreciated.

Even though my recovery was complicated, what I needed from friends was not complicated. I just needed a friend to give me an occasional hug. Sometimes I was lonely and afraid and just needed someone to be with me. I'm grateful God provided a few friends who did that for me. It helped tremendously. I knew I was fortunate to even have the support of a couple people because so many survivors have no one.

June 5: *What will God now do with this crushed person? God help me. Please help me wait but keep healing. Please help me communicate in loving ways to my family. Please complete your plan. I need to cry. Please help me cry. Please hold me and protect me. Please guide my every footstep. I love you so much God. I wish I could permanently hide under your wing. The world is so scary.*

When I could do nothing else, I turned to God. I collapsed into his comforting presence and he received me every time.

June 8: *Zest for living—now that's an inconceivable idea. I want this tiredness to go away. I want my life in order. I want the waiting to be over. I either want a love relationship with Roger or a divorce. I want to know if I am going to keep my house or move. I want my kids to be whole, healthy. I want to desire to live. I want to want things in my life—friends, projects, trips, ministries. I want the lethargy to be gone. I want to spring out of bed, not drag. I want to be done with bitterness and anger.*

Healing was starting to appear, although not recognizable to me yet. I was able to forgive my family, even though we had not reconciled, which reduced my bitterness. I had a little more acceptance for my journey, even though it was still not finished. And, I longed for better days.

June 10: *Steps. I guess that's what's happening now. One step after another—a letter to Roger, a letter to Mom, a letter to* (my sister)*—a revelation that the lack of support from church is truly not personal. It's not about me or rejection of me. It's hard to feel movement or progress but Faith says she sees it. I do feel a bond with Roger that can't be explained by my feelings for him or by his nonexistent demonstration of change. It's not logical or rational but it's real. I can only pray.*

I would be lying if I didn't say I was disappointed with my church. I wanted them to care about me and at least offer a modicum of support. There were individuals within the church who did that, but not the leadership per se. I don't think they knew what to do with me. I was an enigma.

The Christian church, in general, does not acknowledge the reality of Satanic ritual abuse, DID, sexual abuse or incest. There are a few churches who do acknowledge this sinister world of evil, but even those who do are often ill-equipped to help. Some of this is due to a lack of understanding and information. But there is a tremendous amount of fear, too. No one wants to think these things go on right under their nose, let alone meet someone who experienced it. Blatant evil, and long-lasting pain scares people.

The same paradox exists within each church as within each person. No church and no person are entirely good and entirely bad. The Church belongs to God, it is his institution for good. That doesn't mean sin doesn't occur within its walls or that God isn't angry with the Church sometimes. The fact that the Church sometimes falls short, however, doesn't negate its value and the good it does.

While others might make a different decision, staying connected with my church was more positive than negative for me. God used many people there to help in my healing.

Chapter Thirty-Five

1995
July

Latent Adolescence

July was eerily quiet, my journal going silent. It was the calm before the storm. Literally.

Late in the month, I woke up one morning with an idea and called my friend. *Hey, Sandi, want to run away to Lake Powell for a few days and have a little fun?*

Being spontaneous was never a character trait of mine, so the idea of just taking off gave me an exhilarating sense of freedom. *How soon can you be here?* She immediately packed a bag and had the five-hour drive over the mountains behind her by dinner time. We gathered a few supplies and left the next day.

Frankly, I was looking for trouble, hoping to meet some cute guys. I definitely found trouble, although it arrived from a direction I hadn't anticipated.

Because the recovery efforts were working, I was changing and healing. New areas of my identity were emerging as I discovered who I was (and wasn't). In some respects, I never had a normal adolescence. I skipped the rebellion stages, including smoking, drinking, and listening to music my parents would have hated. For goodness sake, my favorite artists were Beethoven and Bach! My identity was too bound up with being a rule-follower and a good girl to take risks and break away from adult expectations. Besides, if I lost control, who would take care of my mother and siblings? Someone had to hold it together and be the responsible adult.

Better Late than Never was my motto that summer. It didn't matter that I was twenty years post-teen. I was finally ready to be an adolescent. I wanted to go into dangerous places, like bars, late at night. I wanted to flirt with strange men, and drink (a little, anyway). I wanted to be bad, to know what that was like, to know that I was free to choose, whatever it was that I chose. I needed to prove to myself that my choices were mine, no one else's.

For all these reasons, now at thirty-nine, it was important to me to know whether I lived the way I did because that is what I wanted, or because that is what everyone expected of me. Getting that answer required a short experiment in rebellion and Lake Powell seemed like the perfect place.

Lake Powell

Sandi and I packed little more than some clothes and our sleeping bags, stopping for groceries along the way. Five hours later, we arrived at Bullfrog marina. We picked out a little patch of sand and laid out our sleeping bags. This approach was far different from my previous visits, when I had rented a houseboat. Even if we could have afforded it, there were very few places to stay at such late notice and no houseboats available.

Straddling the borders of Utah and Arizona, Lake Powell, the second largest man-made reservoir, boasts nearly two thousand miles of shore. Even though the very narrow lake is 186 miles long, there are only four marinas giving you access to the water. Without a boat, there is little to see.

Roger and I and the girls had been going to Lake Powell for years, vacationing with friends. Getting a houseboat was a convenient way to transport the group and our gear deep into the reservoir where we would dock for the week. We'd use a ski boat to explore the lake and waterski. It had always been a blast.

On those trips, those who didn't sleep on shore, slept on top of the boat, hoping for a breeze to cool down the hot, summer nights. We were lucky if the 100+ degree days would drop even fifteen degrees at night. Unless we were making meals or using the bathroom, no one wanted to be in the houseboat—it was too hot. The best relief was found in the water, our hang out for hours every day. Ah… wonderful memories.

An Unforgettable Boat Ride

Neither Sandi nor I had much money. So, all we could afford was a sixteen-foot, fishing skiff with an outboard motor. Before Roger and I sold our water-skiing boat, I had driven it many times, giving me confidence I could make the transition to the small, metal boat we rented.

After a three-minute lesson from the boat rental guy, we headed out onto the lake, southbound. I was eager to show Sandi the breath-taking beauty. The ever-changing canyon was a visual delight, featuring 50-foot vertical walls around one bend which then suddenly opens up into red-rock arches. There was nothing like it back home in Australia and my photographer friend was captivated.

We explored the fingerlets, touring the lake until we were ready to stop to eat our lunch. We pulled the boat up onto the shore and climbed up to a flat spot on the rocks for our picnic. We were deep in conversation when I realized I hadn't glanced out at the lake for a while. When I did, the sky toward the north was an ominous black.

I shouted at Sandi to grab everything and run to the boat. Within seconds, we were zooming back toward Bullfrog Marina.

Summer storms were nothing to mess with, particularly on the water. The intense summer heat frequently combines with moisture in the upper air streams, producing epic storms. I prayed we could get back before it let loose.

It didn't take me long to realize I had probably been the only one in the area not paying attention to the weather. No one else was on the lake. I pressed on, keeping my hand on the tiller and my eyes on the lake ahead. As the wind picked up and the waves got choppier, I needed more strength to control the boat.

Soon the waves were coming up and over the side, into our skiff, frightening me and Sandi, who was now silent and huddled up in a ball at the bow. I did my best to keep my voice calm, reassuring her that we'd make it as I tried to believe my own words.

It felt like we were never going to get back as the lake endlessly stretched out before us. Multiple times my hopes were dashed as I rounded a bend, expecting to see the marina. The waves kept getting more violent, now washing over us completely. It was hard to see with water constantly splashing in my face. Suddenly I spotted another boat, a huge touring vessel, hoping they would come to our rescue. They had to have seen us, the only other boat out there, but they never veered our direction. Despair set in.

It was now pouring rain, making it even harder to see, but there was nothing I could do except to keep going, with no place to ride out the storm or stop. My arms and shoulders were starting to seize up, but I couldn't let go of the tiller. No matter what, I had to keep the boat pointing straight into the waves. If I allowed the boat to get turned sideways, we'd capsize for sure. Twice, the engine stopped, and I had to pull the cord over and over to get it to restart, my heart pounding as I prayed to God to save us.

After an interminably long time, we entered a section that created an optical illusion, a large circular, bowl-like area, carved out of the steep canyon walls, with no visual exit. My panic rose as I realized I had no idea where to point my boat. I knew there was an exit somewhere, but I couldn't see it. I cried out to God to send us his angels to guide me toward the way out, and minutes later, the small opening appeared in front of me. What a relief! As we passed through the rocks, we saw our destination ahead.

Several marina employees realized our plight and rushed to shore to meet us, helping us out of the boat, swinging blankets over our shoulders as they led us inside the building. Sandi was nonverbal, but I was still in survival mode, asking for calls to be made, answering their questions, sorting out our next steps. I had long since dissociated and my survivor parts were handling the details. In fact, as I later learned, Brenda had been the one to bring the boat in. Once again, my hero.

Aftermath

I don't remember the hours or days after the storm ended. I can't recall where Sandi and I slept that night or the drive home. From a physical standpoint, it appeared we were unscathed by the frightening ordeal. While it was true we were safe, we were not unharmed, not by a long shot.

After returning home, I created my last collage. In the midst of clippings of water, boats, and red rocks were these phrases: *the cruel sea, the unsinkable, dangerous, dire straits, I had a tough time going the distance, intense, women's work is never done, when's the last time you actually looked forward to a great vacation—sorry I missed that, next rest stop 40 miles, big weather, fighting and switching, deep disaster.* Certainly, apt descriptions.

I'm not sure who felt worse—me, for nearly getting Sandi killed, for dragging her into my harebrained scheme, for making so many poor decisions, or Sandi, who later expressed remorse for not helping me in the crisis. But I knew she couldn't help because she had dissociated, too.

Being unaware of the fresh trauma now living in my body and brain, I simply carried on with my normal life. Or tried to. I was well-practiced at keeping it all together after disasters. I knew exactly how to do that: compartmentalize all thoughts and feelings and pretend nothing happened. But, for some reason, my past strategy wasn't working this time.

I ended up having to take a leave from my job and was home for six weeks trying to recover. I couldn't sleep at all. My anxiety was through the roof. My doctor prescribed hydrochloride for sleep, six pills a night, enough to put an elephant to sleep. Even with that, sleep was hit and miss.

Angry thoughts and feelings were coming up, seemingly unrelated to my near-death experience. I was angry with God.

July 30: *Okay, God, please explain to me why you let me be (*born*) to my parents so that I would be unwanted, cruelly abused, tortured, and fragmented. Only to grow up in this messed-up life, with two horrendous marriages, with men who didn't want me either. Only to remember and* *relive all the past garbage as if once wasn't enough. Relive them for years, with no light at the end of the tunnel, no end to the suffering, no point to my life other than to hold the place of "mother." What's the point? Why have you picked out this special hell for me? It doesn't matter if I do what I'm told. It doesn't get better. I am unwanted by my parents, husband and children. I am a failure. There's no point. There's not even a guarantee that there'll be a decent life for me if I finish the therapy routine. I have never felt so lethally suicidal.*

I blamed God for everything. I was no longer able to keep a lid on my uglier thoughts and feelings. What I did not understand at the time, was that there was no more room in my brain or body to hold this new trauma. If I was a hospital, then the patient beds were already at capacity. This meant my system for coping was melting down.

July 31: *I am on a journey and I do not know where it leads. It is like walking in the Kalahari Desert. After finally reaching the top of the sand dune, parched, heat exhausted, feet aching, you then get to view a sea of dunes yet to cross. And there's no water in sight, only sand. And you are told you must keep walking and never stop believing that this journey will bring you life, that the daily hell you live in will be over. Recovery will no longer dominate your life but all you see is sand. And you haven't had a drink of water for the longest time, so your physical, emotional, and mental reserves are gone. You know God has not yet failed you and that he somehow has a plan. But it doesn't ease the parchedness of your throat. You don't even know if you are walking the shortest or best route. You are just walking. Every day is the same, the pain. Your feet carry you further into the desert and you have no idea how many more days until you have crossed the desert.*

I was sinking into hopelessness.

Chapter Thirty-Six

1995
August

A Vacation from My Vacation

I recorded nothing for ten days after the boating incident. For some reason, I could never journal when I was in the midst of the really hard stuff.

Neither Sandi nor I were doing well, so her therapist suggested we go to a condo in the mountains to get some rest. We brought my girls with us.

August 6: *My how time flies when you're having a good time. As usual the unwritten days tell the greatest stories. Gee whiz—my great boat story, my nervous breakdown, my rages, my letters—no mention. So why write?*

I'm up at Silver Creek having a vacation. Only problem is that I slept until 7 pm. I have 2 days at this place and I slept one away. I missed it. Then woke up in a rage. We weren't a family. Bree was watching TV. Jenny was on her bed listening to music. And I am totally pissed off that my mother allowed these things to happen to me. How could she?

I was exhausted, barely coping, trying to insist I was fine. After all, I made it safely back to the marina; I didn't get injured. What's the big deal? But I wasn't fine. Rage was emerging, rage I tried to pin on my girls who were stuck in a vacation home with an emotionally unstable mother, doing the only things they could do.

When our weekend was up, we went over to the Front Range. I dropped the girls off at my mom's house and returned to Boulder with Sandi.

I had therapy sessions four days in a row. Inside me were many disrupted parts needing to process the event at Lake Powell. One of my parts told Faith, *I was laying on the wooden bench, waiting for you to call. The waves were washing over us.* It was no surprise to learn Brenda was the one who saved the day. Now, two weeks later, she was trying to deal with the trauma. This is what she told Faith:

I was going to be killed. It was too hard. Why won't anyone help me? I can't do this. If I make a mistake, we'll die. I can't keep the boat straight. It will turn over and we'll die in the cold water. Everything hurt. It was freezing cold and we were soaked. Every time we hit a wave I'd bash into the seat. I couldn't let go but I could hardly hang on to the motor. We'd die if I let go. I didn't cry in the boat. Sandi cried. I didn't think we'd live. The waves were bigger than the boat.

Not having anyone help was a major trigger for me. The boat in the storm was a reenactment of my childhood, being on my own in a life-threatening situation. So it wasn't surprising that talking to Faith about our experience in the boat triggered more cult memories of sexual abuse and rituals, including some with Native American elements. The Native American stuff never made much sense to me.

Just like in so many memories before, after it was out, Jesus healed my hurting parts. He rescued the little girl, as he dealt justice to the bad guys.

Emerging Sexuality

I didn't learn much from the trip to Utah, apparently, because I still thought an adolescent-like rebellion was a good idea. So one night, Sandi and I went to a bar. My parts were freaking out.

August 15: *I'm free writing because I don't have any thoughts really, just intense feelings. There is one thought: I'm coming apart. I'm not going to make it.*

Let's just go to sleep. We were very bad and did too much and we're very tired.

We should not have done those things in Boulder. That was a bad place—bad music—you know we should always look good to the public—evil nightclubs don't qualify.

So what? So what if we do bad things? It makes no difference. We're bad if we think about it and we think about it all the time. So we might as well do it.

Fortunately, nothing happened that night, nothing except scaring several little parts inside. But, clearly, I was conflicted within myself.

Change is always messy. I didn't like that reality. For so many years, I had been locked up in an inner hell, one that paralyzed my identity, emotions, and sexuality. My sexuality was the most vulnerable part of myself, living in the core of my being. So when the childhood trauma occurred, my core area shut down as a protection. Without healing, sex and promiscuity were options I could consider, but a true offering of intimacy with someone else was not.

With all the healing I had been experiencing, my core self, including my sexuality, were thawing, they were coming back to life, lunging back at me with unfamiliar and intense feelings and longings. But because I was a married woman, one who was separated, there was no place to go with those feelings, well… no healthy place.

August 15 (cont.): (Even though I don't know who is talking, the following chatter offers important clues about how we were doing on the inside.)

You're really going to get us in deep trouble.

Well, that would actually be a pleasant change from this boring life of ours—we don't even have a decent sex addict's story to tell at a 12-step meeting.

I'm not going to any meeting!

Where are the feelings and the up and coming panic attack?

I think they're gone—so we're all done—let's go watch our movie.

No, let's wait a moment and see what's really going on in there.

We're getting an eating disorder you know—we're eating fattening food every time we have these feelings—we're a pig and we're going to get fat.

You know we can't do this—what little bit we're doing pushed us over the edge—so this new stuff—the deeper feelings—the rage—the sexual feelings—the abandonment from our father and mother—and who knows what else—will never come without us dying—we'll die without a Mom and Dad. Who knows who else might have abandoned us! There could still be some fun surprises.

Why do you laugh about this?

Why do you pretend? Why do you act like you're just fine?

Nobody wants to keep hearing it's bad, it's horrible.

Well, I'm disappointed because I thought we were going to stop being a fake person.

And do this pain? Are you nuts? I'd like to know who agreed to it. I sure didn't.

Well, we're in it—no turning back. We're getting well if it kills us.

Very funny.

We're not invincible, in case you haven't noticed—we can't do everything—we aren't super-client anymore—we're pathetic wimpy client now—we can fail—some of those waves out there are bigger than we are—and there are no guarantees we will be able to get help when they hit. I hate being out of control and I don't know what's going to happen. And I don't know what it is going to be like or if I can handle it. I'm big time afraid I won't be able to handle it.

My parts were giving me a status report, but I wasn't listening. *I'm coming apart. I'm not going to make it.* I should have listened to them.

Light through Flowers

While staying at the condo in Silver Creek, I was able to connect with God. But it took me awhile to get around to writing it down.

August 18: *Some things need to be recorded because they are so important. First of all, I have a goal to live an expansive life. To live without barriers and walls, useless walls. Secondly, God spoke to me while staying at Silver Creek. And I don't want to forget what he told me. He said my father's decision to toss me out of his life last fall validates his ability to treat me the way he did 30 years ago. His self is all he cares about right now—and back then. God said, "It's true Dad threw me out—but he threw out a precious gem—not trash."*

Then, in prayer ministry last night, God healed the wounded and false image of myself. What John saw was a black coil binding me. The coil came loose and fell to the floor and slithered away. I saw myself blocked from God. I was a large piece of clear glass with many beautiful flowers pressed inside the glass. And I was blocking the passage. Jesus simply took the beautiful piece of glass and hung it where the light could shine through it. There were hundreds of beautiful flowers in the pieces of glass. I also saw myself having fun discovering my identity. And I saw myself in the future, feeling and expressing outrageously excited feelings about some idea or project. John also saw the poison and sting being sucked out of all the memories—remembered and not yet remembered. I left feeling peace. Thank God.

The prayer vision was a light shining in a dark place, a hopeful moment when I desperately needed one. Although I had no idea what the references to projects might be, seeing God's light shine through images of beautiful, colorful flowers was exciting and hopeful.

I Wanted to be Wanted

God uses many things to speak to us and get our attention, movies included. This wasn't the first time he reached my heart through a movie.

August 19: *It's raining outside and I'm home all alone and feeling very strange. I just saw* (a movie) *and I'm glad I did. The desire to have an affair has been so strong for months. And to see tonight her pain* (the main character) *and the sacrifice she had to make her whole life was heart-wrenching. I certainly don't need heart-wrenching in my life. I thank God he has protected me from opportunities because many, many, many times I would have fallen to the temptation. I want so much to be free to express all of who I am, whoever that may be.*

So what have I learned about myself today and tonight? And why did I choose to once again distract myself from my pain? I learned that I want a passionate relationship, but one that will be sustained—no rejection or abandonment. I'm a one-woman/one-man person. I don't want the pain of an affair. I want the fullness of a lasting relationship.

Tonight, I feel very sad. I'm sad for the hollow, sad foundations that create doubt and dislike. The loneliness pulsates. The uncertainty of my marriage mystifies me and creates confusion and impatience. I can't cry at home, but tears well up inside. I tried to be a want-able child and (my parents') *own sicknesses were too powerful to protect me and love me and nurture me. God have mercy on them.*

Whenever I was home with the girls, I tried hard to hold my tears back and hide the pain. I felt like they had enough to deal with on their own, without me adding more pain.

Processing in my journal naturally led me down to the bedrock issue, the driving force behind my perceived need for a man, for a sexual relationship: I just wanted someone to want me. *I tried to be a want-able child.* But nothing I did satisfied my need to be wanted.

As the hot August days passed, I became more depressed. There were too many issues going on inside me. And now, with the fresh trauma from the boating incident, I was not able to deal with any of it.

The ongoing marital issues didn't help, either; they were inescapable.

August 20: *For some reason, I can't get Roger off my mind. Everybody says put the marriage out of my mind so I can focus on this stage of therapy. Our 13th anniversary is coming up. What will our 14th year bring? Will I be forced to let it go or will I finally want to let it go? Or will God turn water into wine and save it. It's hard to put it out of my mind. It's in my face all the time. Dare I hope for a sudden and soon healing?*

Is that what Linda's dream meant? I can't count on that of course. What am I supposed to do now? How do I let the pain out? I never cry at home.

Linda's Dream

After returning from Lake Powell, unbeknownst to me, a woman had a dream about me, a compelling dream that she knew was from God. When Linda called to talk to me about it, she was quite concerned, saying she had been praying for me every day. I thought this was strange. Yes, I'd known Linda through church for years, but, until then, she had had nothing to do with my recovery work. Yet I'd always known her as someone who was wise and humble, and much more spiritually attuned than I was.

In Linda's unsettling dream, God told her to go and get our pastor and to pray for me because my life was in danger, and then, still in the dream, she held me close in her arms for the rest of the night. Over the phone, she said she strongly felt that I needed prayer, so much so that she called our pastor and asked him to set something up. I wasn't sure what to think about the call or the dream.

As more days passed, I fell into hopelessness and gave up. Even after Linda's warning, I lost my desire to fight and let the darkness swallow me up.

Late in August, after seeing the girls off to school one Monday morning, I decided I was done. I gathered up all the pills from the unused antidepressant prescriptions I'd accumulated over the years.

Chapter Thirty-Seven

1995
September

Darkness Closing In

I emptied the bottles onto the couch and stared at the pills; as I wrote letters to my daughters, family, and friends, I was debating whether to swallow them.

Since returning from Lake Powell, I had been sinking deeper and deeper into a black abyss. This was different from the countless hard moments I'd endured over the past years. It was like the atmosphere had changed, becoming suffocating, yet calm. As I felt the darkness closing in around me, I retreated inside a bubble of isolation and let the world fade away.

It was the enemy, no doubt. In some bizarre way related to my fresh trauma, Satan broke in and sunk his talons into me, preying on my weakness. He's such an opportunist. He saw his chance for victory and gave it his best shot.

I had been sitting on the couch with the pills for seven hours, void of any desire to live, ready to end it all, strangely calm and peaceful, anticipating the struggle soon being over, when the phone rang. A friend had felt compelled to call and check on me. She talked me through the moment and encouraged me to not give up. Later, I felt somewhat miffed because I was left not knowing whether I wanted to live or not. I wasn't sure.

The crisis seemed to pass, briefly. It was the fiercest spiritual battle I had experienced to date, and it wasn't over.

Over Labor Day weekend, my pastor called to set up a meeting with me and Linda (who had the dream) and John B., another therapist I had seen a couple times. We agreed to meet on September 13.

The ensuing days were filled with difficulties. I had been sick for a week and unable to get over it, probably because another memory was pushing.

Worse than the flu-like symptoms, though, was the darkness I felt every day. It was on me and around me. It had nearly destroyed me just days earlier and wasn't letting up. My nights were filled with dark dreams. Linda's warning seemed to be playing out, just as she feared. I was in a battle for my life.

September 3: *I don't want to do it. I don't want to face it. I don't want to ask the questions because I'm not sure what the answers will be and what those answers will do to my life. But I've got to work. I've got to find out what's going on. So let's get to work. Why is there someone wanting to die? I want to hear from you. I can't help what I don't know. Is there anything to know or find out about years 8 to 14? If so, it's time to spill the beans. And the sexual fantasies—where are they coming from? Who holds the keys to our feelings about Daddy? It's time to spill all the beans. Let's do it.*

September 6: *Actually, it's Wednesday because it's 12:47 am. I can't sleep, might as well work. No meds. It's been a long time—19 months—since we went to bed without drugs. There must be another way to die, slit wrists seems simple enough, but what a mess for someone to find—especially if it were the girls. I don't want them to go through that. I have to live so I don't mess up their lives even more. I'm afraid I'm going to lose my job. I've missed work on review days twice—what a way to get a good review. I'm not stable or dependable. I'm scared. It's been a long time since I have experienced this level of internal bedlam or horror or chaotic madness—whatever you want to call it. It occurs during that state before falling asleep. It's awful. No one could fall asleep with that going on. Not even the peace of Jesus would stop it. Will I be alive after this phase? Don't talk or die! Those are your choices. This keeps going off in my head. I know it's not true, but I'm whacked out anyway. God help me.*

I wasn't the only one who wanted to die, so did my alter, Patty. She held so much of the sexual abuse, including the incest with my dad, and she was also giving up, as expressed in her poem.

September 7: *Patty's poem: There's nobody left for me to belong to, so somebody tell me, how can I live? For all of my life, somebody's been there to hold me, and touch me, and call me their own. Many have taken me; sometimes it hurts. But I don't mind 'cause I'm their special one. I can't be alone; I can't not belong. So somebody tell me, how can I live?*

I had no answers for Patty.

Filling in the Missing Years

September 8: *Back in Denver. Back with Faith. Back in therapy. Trying hard. Maybe too hard. Maybe letting go a little would help here. Relax a little. Let God have more control. Let the day flow a little better. Stop pushing. Just listen—respond. Patty, what do you think about Faith's question? How about a little exploring? So, belonging brings touching, and holding which brings pleasure and feels good. The opposite of feeling good is feeling bad. Do you think the fantasies might be a distraction from pain or a diversion from pain? Is its effectiveness addicting? Are we trying to recapture some pleasure—some good feelings? What do you think, Patty?*

Patty: *I hate Roger. I want him to go away. I don't think I belong to him anymore. So, I don't know where to take my* (need for) *belonging. Belonging to myself doesn't sink in. I can't make it get in there because it doesn't seem like belonging. I tried to make a bridge reach over from my longings and desperations to my sexual and sensual passions using my fantasies. Every time, I am left feeling frustrated beyond belief. My fantasies didn't work. So, without them I am left with pain, pleasure withdrawal, having to work out a new plan. Sexual satisfaction I guess is not in my near future plans. Pain is, I guess. Sounds like I have to deal with the absence of pleasure in my life and the pain that is causing me. Yes, I believe fantasies mask pain.*

The return of our sexuality, we were told, was a good and healthy sign of healing. But, honestly, it was causing us nothing but trouble. It seemed like a no-win. Maybe Faith could help.

I was back in Denver for my monthly weekend of therapy. Our work went a different direction than the recent post-trauma fallout from the boating incident. This time it was about Dad. Memories of physical abuse surfaced as I recalled how Dad would take off his belt, fold it half, and whip me several times whenever I misbehaved. The pain was unbearable, motivating me to never cross him.

As painful as the beatings were, remembering that was preferable to remembering the incest. My mind went back to the smell of alcohol and the oily feel of his skin as I recalled the details of the abuse.

The game-changing aspect of this memory was that it happened when we lived in Sacramento. Those were years eight to twelve. All my other memories were earlier, when we were still in southern California. This meant there could be more memories of incest, up until he left when I was fourteen.

The new revelation leveled me. Filling in this gap meant there was no time in my life when I wasn't being abused or living in an abusive relationship. I felt as though my entire forty years had been nothing but wreckage.

This accounted for why the suicide danger was so high. With the memories of incest emerging in a powerful way, dying seemed preferable to facing the inescapable truth that I was incested by my father for my entire home life with him.

As I did whenever I was on the Front Range for therapy, I was staying with Sandi. And this weekend we had a big falling out—the first and only fight we ever had. I got scared, gathered up all my belongings and flew out of her condo. Because Sandi and I were both still an emotional mess after Lake Powell, her therapist and Faith decided to set up a meeting with the four of us to try and straighten out the situation. It did not go well. It was not only unsuccessful at helping neither of us, it was deeply wounding. I left wondering if I'd ever have contact with any of them.

After the meeting, as I was driving back over the mountains, I vowed to shut my heart forever. It was just too painful to love people. For the next two days, I contemplated giving up—on therapy and on life. Had the prayer session not been prearranged, I'm honestly not sure what might have happened.

When the day arrived, John B., Linda, and I met in my pastor's office. I had no idea what to expect, except that we were going to pray. Twelve days later, my journal recorded the details.

The Miracle

September 25: *Some things need to be recorded. Actually, this is an assignment from John. It was September 13. I didn't want to go* (to the prayer session) *and had really bottomed out again.*

When I arrived, the four of us talked. Linda shared something else about the night of the dream that she hadn't felt comfortable sharing before. While she was holding me in her dream-sleep, she had feared I would commit suicide. I, then shared some of the events of the past months, including the attempt at suicide. We agreed to pray, the four of us together. I was trying not to expect anything, so I wouldn't risk being disappointed. I only hoped that somehow things would get a little easier.

I think my pastor started by doing some basic praying for protection, the Holy Spirit's power to come and lead us, my healing, etc. And then he said the most bizarre thing to me (so it seemed at the time). He said that God wanted to integrate me. And my response was certainly less than enthusiastic. I really loved my parts (most of them) and had come to appreciate all they had done and were doing for me. Many had saved my life. We were a team. I really didn't want them to not be there. I knew they would be with me always. But I also knew integration changed everything. I cried.

Then John suggested doing some healing prayer. But before that Linda held me really close—probably like she had in her dream. But I don't remember what she said.

John prayed that the pain and suffering that had plagued me for so long would come up and out of my body. And then I began to see the dark icky rope-like thing come out of my mouth. And I remembered that this had been a recurrent dream of mine. And, just like in my dreams, it kept coming and coming. It came all the way from my fingertips and my toes, from everywhere. It was almost a physical feeling but there was no pain. And finally, it was done. And we gave thanks.

The next thing I remember is asking to rest a moment. I was reeling from the reality of what had just happened. All that pain was gone. And it was gone. And I hadn't been pain-free in many months, maybe even a couple years. It was a miracle. And now, 12 days later, I'm still free of that pain.

And as I rested, I saw my safe place—the cabin in the mountains. And all my parts had gathered in the main room with the fireplace. And Jesus was in his usual rocking chair. And there was no anger or fear in the room.

Then I remember my pastor asking me if I was willing to let God integrate me. About that time, God was speaking to my heart. He said that he was doing this in such a fashion that I had no control over these events or the healing. That, other than being willing to show up and trust him, the whole show was in his hands. Funny how God has a way of instantly getting to the root of the problem.

Well, then I remembered my promise to God which was this: If God ever made known to me something he wanted me to do, I would never say no. So, like many times on this journey, I gave God a green light. I felt some sadness, but mostly I was glad as I watched each alter (each part inside) *approach Jesus and be embraced by him until he simply enfolded them into himself. I could see the little ones* (sitting) *on his lap. I laughed when I saw Brenda leap into his lap and meld with Jesus. Jesus stood up for some of the awkward boys and embraced them. One by one they came to him. There was no fireworks or grandiose activity. It was quiet and peaceful and natural.*

And when it was over, John prayed that any alters who hadn't come forward, names I had forgotten or not yet mentioned or even met, would also be enfolded into Jesus. And there I was, all integrated.

I was the most surprised person in the room. I didn't ask for integration or plan for it or work toward it. Nothing in my thoughts or expectations before the prayer session included even a hint about integration. It was probably the last thing on my mind. I just wanted to be free of the darkness and the desire to die. I wanted to feel better. But God knew what I didn't. For me, my path out of the darkness was deep, supernatural healing and miraculous integration.

Integration isn't the end of recovery. It is an important milestone, but there remains more healing to do afterward. So it was a difficult adjustment to becoming a "mono-brain." The grieving for my parts, no longer separately accessible, was painful. I missed them so much. I understood they were still part of me—but it wasn't the same, not at all.

It would be awhile before I had perspective on what life was like without my parts.

September 25 (cont.): *I think it was at that point I remembered the name God had given me about a year ago. Even today I have a hard time saying it because I feel so unworthy. But Jesus wanted me to fully receive the name, "Golden One," as a part of the healing that had just occurred.*

Then I began to recall Scripture promises God had given to me over the years of recovery. I remembered Ezekiel 17:22-24, Psalm 70:20-21, Jeremiah 12:5 and others. My pastor said I would be a warrior against evil. And somewhere during the time, we had talked about needing to re-grow through the stages of life and needing time for myself to regain my strength. It was as if I was a baby needing care and had to be dependent.

As we finished up, my mind became flooded with questions. Particularly, "What do I do now? I don't know how to live as a mono-brain." So, now I'm learning to live without alters. It's hard and I miss them. I tire easily because there is no backup during the day. I have to do it all myself. I also feel all the feelings myself which has been very overwhelming at times. My auditory senses are very sensitive and easily overstimulated. That's because my head is quiet, but the world is just as noisy.

My hope for recovery has been restored. The need to belong to a man feels like it is completely gone. The desire (to indulge in) *fantasies is gone.*

As far as the session itself, I still have not absorbed all that God did. I ask myself, why? Part of it is accepting that he would do that for me. It's humbling when he is doing it to/for you in real life, in the here and now. I believe God saved my life—again. I believe it is strongly possible that I would have killed myself within a matter of days had he not intervened. It is boggling that he set in motion the events to save me months before I even got to such a place. I'm always in awe that others go out of their way to help me.

I pretty much feel confused all day. Nothing about my outside life has changed. But everything inside is different. Each daily event and situation requires some kind of a response. But my responses aren't automatic at this point. Each one requires thought and new decision making and questions about myself.

God is just so surprising and as unpredictable as he is faithful and loving.

I had no idea that day of integration what would happen. But God did. These final weeks of this phase of my recovery were known to him and known to the spiritual realm, which is why there was a ferocious fight for my life. God was bringing me into new life and Satan was battling hard to destroy me before it could happen. God won.

Chapter Thirty-Eight

1995
October-December

Adjusting to the New Me

As the seasons were changing, so was I. Adjusting to integration was a struggle every day, sorting out how to do life without help from my alters. The extra energy it took left me tired all the time. I was challenged to figure out how to respond to friends, family, and employers with the new me present for every little thing.

On top of that, I was grieving the loss of my parts. I didn't want to hear anyone remind me that they hadn't left; they were simply working in unity rather than individually. That didn't help me one bit. I wanted to feel Brenda, and Alex, and Patty, and hear from them. I wanted to be able to talk to them, but I couldn't. There would never again be any communication with them.

Sometimes, doing everything myself, without their help, left me resentful and angry. In fact, it was hard to find anything to celebrate about integration. Many of my parts had been characterized by strong opinions and brash words. Now I had those strong opinions and brash words. I was forever trying to hold my tongue or clean up my mess if I didn't.

In a way, it was like those time-travel shows where the actor drops into a new body, in a new life, and they have to figure out how they should act and react without anyone catching on to the truth. Reentry meant relearning and the constant question was, *What is the appropriate response here?* It was such an effort to sort everything out.

Feelings were particularly difficult. I felt my emotions like I had never felt them before, and they were *large*! I was constantly scrambling to rein in big reactions. Whether it was excitement or anger, sadness, or embarrassment, they were turned up, full volume. In spite of it all, though, it was delightful to finally be a fully alive human being.

Over time, all of this became easier to manage. But, even today, my emotions feel strong to me. Today I can easily recognize and appreciate the Alex and Brenda aspects of my personality. Like Alex, I can acknowledge injustice with righteous indignation and personal anger. I accept my anger without judgment. And I'm great in a crisis, just like Brenda. I'm strong and level-headed. I will fall apart after the fact, but when the moment calls for strength, I have it. I have another reminder of Brenda, too—her favorite color, purple, is now mine.

It was awhile before I realized something else had changed. The drawings, paintings, and collage work stopped. The dreams were slowing down. Even the journaling changed, becoming sporadic. Those tools were there to help me connect to my story. Now that the whole story was out, the need for those expressions diminished.

I was still seeing Faith to help me adjust to this new way of living. I also continued to process the incest memories. Of everything I remembered and endured, that was the worst. The level of violation and betrayal surpasses words.

Lots of Letters

It turned out that October was a month for letters. Very unlike me, at least the old me, I wrote and delivered a letter to the owner of a gas station convenience store. Being close to my house, it was a frequent stop for gas and drinks. Recently, the rack of pornography magazines caught my attention. Not that I'd never noticed magazines in a store before, but this time I had a strong reaction. No longer was this *No big deal, everybody sells them.* I knew too much; I'd suffered too much. I was a victim of pornography—as a child and as a wife, twice. I knew what it meant to have pictures like that published. Someone was used and taken advantage of in order to create that magazine. It wasn't innocent.

In my letter, I respectfully informed him that I couldn't patronize his store if he continued to sell pornography and asked him to consider removing it. I never got a response, but it was a victory, nonetheless. I had found my voice and was using it in a healthy, God-honoring way.

I also wrote several of what I call "Let it Rip" letters to express my feelings of anger, betrayal, and disappointment, but not letters to be mailed. My hurt feelings had to go somewhere; writing them out was a great help. As I released my rage toward Roger and my parents, it became easier to move toward forgiveness.

And finally, at my pastor's request, I wrote a letter describing the events of the last four and a half years, culminating with my miraculous healing in September, and shared it with the congregation. I wanted to help remove the stigma surrounding people who are dealing with trauma, abuse, and emotional suffering, and hoped my story would move hearts toward compassion. I knew I was opening myself up to judgment and rejection, but I was willing to accept the risk. For the most part, people were loving.

However, I was not out of the woods, yet. November was ridiculous.

Not a Lot to be Thankful For

I was struggling at the dental office. I was reacting to my boss in ways I never had previously, finding it difficult to be a submissive employee. I began looking into other employment options.

On November 8, I received a letter from my sister. I think she really did her best to be loving toward me, acknowledging the failings and shortcomings of our parents. However, her concluding statement saying, *"I have finally come to the place where I realize that I do not believe your memories,"* was like a dagger to my heart.

I do not judge her. I know the ordeal was hard for her, too. I only wish she would have asked to hear my story before coming to this conclusion. But I never got the chance.

It had been a year since I'd had contact with my father, and now this letter from my sister began a five-year silence with her. She didn't end the relationship. Neither did I. It just stopped of its own accord, creating a cavern of distance between us that was too great to traverse. The loss broke my heart.

This was a hard time for the girls, too. Jenny disappeared one day, freaking me out, my thoughts jumping to horrible conclusions. It felt like she was slipping away from me and I didn't know what to do. And there was this constant question plaguing my mind as to whether my father sexually abused my girls, a question that never could find an answer.

The Shoe Finally Drops

On November 18, Roger called. He told me he wanted a divorce. Fear of the future set in immediately.

The marriage was on life-support anyway, but integration may have been what pushed Roger to that final decision. He didn't want the new me. I was definitely a force with which to be reckoned. I didn't take guff from anyone. No longer did his desperate need to dominate others work with me. I think I intimidated him, causing him to lose any interest in trying.

It was hard for me to find a reason to fight or to find tears to shed. I was full of shame, feeling like a failure—a loser twice over.

I didn't know what to do next. I wasn't sure if I should get a lawyer or hold off for awhile. Changing jobs now seemed foolish, even though my job was getting harder to tolerate. With Thanksgiving and Christmas approaching, I wondered if I'd ever have a happy holiday again.

November 25: *Well, God, it's after Thanksgiving now. I survived another one. But the real question today is will I survive now? I have to tell the girls that Roger is getting a divorce. I guess I am getting a divorce, too. I guess we are all getting a divorce. And I want to die. I'm thinking about getting drunk. And there's always those pills in the bathroom. I don't want to go through this.*

The current situation threw me into a tailspin, triggering my memories and feelings at fourteen when my father walked out. The end of my first marriage was back in my thoughts, as well. Those events were different because they ended suddenly, with no warning. When my father and my first husband left, I woke up one day thinking everything was fine, but by bedtime it was over. They were gone.

This marriage had been a slow death, an incremental severing over a three-year period. I'd been hanging on, always hoping Roger would deal with his healing issues, too. And now the final thread was broken.

November 25 (cont.): *I don't want a divorce. My kids have been through so much. I don't want to tell them tomorrow. I've never lived alone, completely responsible for myself. I want an intact family, but I can't have it. They aren't going to be surprised.*

I feel like I've failed the girls. I made two bad choices, twenty years of miserable, destructive marriages. I'm just as bad as my parents. It's over. I have to face it now. I have to move on.

I told the girls the next day. They didn't say much, but I was concerned how this was going to worsen their already difficult lives and the pain they carried. This was adding more trauma, and they already had had so much.

November 26: *I need a new job. A new start. Something that feels positive and challenging. Please, God, lead me in wisdom and provide for the needs of my family.*

God, your power and privilege and invitation to intervene is ever present. I confess my pride. Please make sin clear to me. The line between wisdom, self-protection, common sense, and then laying oneself out in humility for another go of it, seems fine, indeed. If I have erred, make it clear to me, I pray. My feelings of loss over my marriage and family are enormous. So much to trod through, sort out, and process. Please show me the way of wisdom. Let me not lose my human kindness through the process. God, protect me every day so Satan won't get a foothold. And protect my girls. Wisdom, I need wisdom to parent them. Help me with my big, big feelings and my big, big pain.

Smiling at the Storm

And then, somehow, hope appeared on the horizon. After muddling through another Christmas, the landscape changed again, and I began to see a new perspective on life.

December 27: *I wasn't going to write in this journal anymore. Once I was integrated, I felt as though a chapter was over and a new one begun. And therefore, a new start with a new journal was in order. But it wasn't really like that. It's as if I've been on a journey down a river—the same river for 4 ½ years. I've been through rapids and storms and flash floods, but always on the same river. There have been places where the river flowed gently, and I could have chosen to leave the river and stop the journey. And then there were the places where all things were out of my control and my only choice was to hang on and pray it would be over soon.*

Integration was like passing through a waterfall. It was beautiful and gentle and scary because I couldn't see beyond the falls—it obliterated my vision. It changed me, but every adventure on the river has changed me. The scenery has changed many times. I've seen the glorious, lush, and breathtaking, as well as the dry, dark, and austere. I've experienced the freezing cold dampness that seeps through to the bone, such that I felt I would never know warmth ever again. But, in time, it passed. The sun's warmth thawed me out eventually.

I'm still traveling the river and don't know where its twists and turns will take me tomorrow. But, Jesus, my river guide is ever with me, holding my boat steady. As he promised, I haven't drowned. I must complete my journey. I need to follow the river to its end. I have lessons to learn around each bend. I have scenery yet to see, storms yet to go through. I know where I've come from and I am clueless as to where I'm headed. But the little children's song says it well: "With Jesus in the boat we can smile at the storm, smile at the storm. With Jesus in the boat we can smile at the storm, as we go sailing on."

December 29: *God is surprising me and I sense his delight in doing so. God seems to have my life well in hand and I'm interested in finding out what he has planned for Saturday and Sunday. My run in with* (a girlfriend who is single) *today gave me the much-needed opportunity to dump some pain and tears. And then* (another single friend) *and I connected—both with a desperate need to have a single friend. And we are trying to work out something fun for New Year's Eve. There are roadblocks—but I just want to get out of the way of God and see him work. I feel stronger and more hopeful even though I have not a single answer to my 1,000's of questions. He has every day of 1996 all planned out. I want to listen. I want more surprises—God-surprises. God, remind me of this when I hit rock bottom next time. Help me with my fear. Help me with my kids and job and original family. Pour upon me wisdom.*

For the first time in many years I had at least a somewhat positive outlook on a new year's start.

Chapter Thirty-Nine

1996
January-October

Serendipitous Surprises

The beginning of the year brought no new changes; however, before 1996 was finished, nothing would be the same.

Work at the dental office continued, so did monthly trips to Denver. I was relieved that I hadn't had a new memory since September. Most of my current therapy centered around adjusting to being a mono-brain and learning how to handle life in general, while still coping with my impending divorce.

I no longer remember what I hoped would happen during the holidays, but the plans didn't materialize, inviting fear that I might succumb to old patterns of anxiety and despair.

January 1: *I learned a lot of things over these 11 days of vacation. I was terrified when all plans fell through. Terrified of surviving on my own, all alone, no one in the house, no job, no plans, no appointments, no therapy. What would I do? Would I become suicidal? Bedridden? Despondent? But what really happened was that I was surprised. Surprised by God. And I learned a few things—not necessarily new things.*

I am not alone.

God can handle any situation.

The serendipity of his surprises is delightful:

- *Going to the Ouray* (hot springs) *pool with* (friends)
- *Free dinner with* (friends) *at Bon Ton*

- *Chance meeting with* (a friend) *to dump and cry and receive support*
- *A renewed friendship*
- *Companionship on New Year's Eve*
- *A stranger to shovel my snow*
- *An answer to prayer about the strange events of cash pouring in with the organ selling*
- *Another chance encounter with* (a friend) *to dump more pain*

I need to go to God with the longings of my heart; he's the only one who can satisfy them.

My normal pattern of finding a man to satisfy my need to be needed must stop.

I need to be single now.

He's going to take care of me.

He cares about my desires.

I can survive.

I can be alone and make it.

Healing was bearing fruit and I was growing stronger. I was steadily learning to trust God, not other people. My foundation was now significant enough to help me go forward with at least a small amount of confidence, even if I didn't always make the right decisions, as demonstrated with the sale of my organ.

I still had one of the three organs I grew up with, a Hammond B3; I started lessons on it before I could reach the pedals. But strapped for money, I decided to sell it. It was a highly prized item, sought after by musicians and bands for its unique sound. I had no trouble finding a buyer, but I still miss it today.

All was not lost, because I used a small portion to purchase a keyboard. My interest in playing was renewed, as I pulled out my old music and dusted off my skills. Playing music again was pure joy. God was good to me in many ways.

Throughout the previous two years, Sandi and I remained close, even after our one and only falling out. She frequently came over the mountains to stay with me, becoming an important person in my girls' lives, too. Unfortunately for Sandi, soon after we left the psych hospital, her husband had an affair and left her. Feeling guilt over his actions, he told Sandi to pick anywhere she'd like to go, and he would pay for it. I was lucky enough to be included in the offer.

She decided Mexico would be our destination, a country too inconvenient to visit when she was back home in Australia. In my wildest dreams, I never expected to be able to take a vacation in my current situation let alone visit another country! I continually experienced God's love and power to provide for me, even when circumstances seemed impossible.

We booked a place in Puerto Vallarta and flew down during Spring Break, while my girls were with their dad. It was fun in the sun, including margaritas on the beach. Mexico instantly drew me in and I decided I would find a way to come back. It was a fabulous break from our difficult worlds back home.

Trials and A Trial

Life was still a mixed bag; I wasn't quite finished dealing with healing issues.

April 30: *The deep, black pain overwhelming my emotions and insides were my first clue. The familiarity was disconcerting. Why was this back? The black pain persisted. Then came the body memories, sexual pain, sore throat, diarrhea. The sore throat really made me suspicious that a memory was coming. Then this morning all my nerves felt hypersensitive. Last night I lay in bed feeling as though someone were abusing me while my wrists and ankles were shackled, and I couldn't move. The panic—the fear—the helplessness—I can't move—I'm trapped—will they kill me—cut me—abuse me. What will they do to me? I don't know and I'm scared to death. I can see that I'm on a hill, outside at night. There's a bright moon and it's easy to see everything—the altar, the people, my dad.*

Another ritual memory had surfaced. It was painful to process and deal with, for sure; nevertheless, life was so much better since memories weren't coming constantly.

About the same time, I made an appointment for a routine physical, a visit that revealed terrifying news. I had a breast lump. A wave of self-pity washed over me as I scheduled surgery. I thought I had been through enough. *Really? Now this?* It was fast growing, which the doctor said was encouraging. It freaked me out, though.

I was told it would be done with local anesthesia; however, I wouldn't feel anything. And if I did start to feel uncomfortable, I was to let the doctor know. Well, I did feel it. The pain was horrendous! I kept saying over and over, *It hurts, it hurts.* But I guess there was just enough anesthesia in me that the doctor couldn't hear my voice because he said he had no idea I was in pain.

The lab report brought good news—the tumor was benign. What a relief! I was glad this wouldn't be hanging over my head while I was preparing for the divorce trial.

Early in the year, I realized I needed to find an attorney. This reality hit me in the face when Roger emptied the checking account, leaving me broke. I checked out a few referrals and made my decision.

After six months of letters and documents and meetings, a trial was set for August. The litigation centered around our money and assets. Roger never asked for custody, fortunately, not even joint custody. Faith was among the witnesses called during the two-day trial. She fought hard for me, hoping to buy me more time to complete my healing before I was forced to support myself.

I anxiously awaited the judge's orders as four weeks went by. When they arrived, I wept. I would have been better off going into the trial alone, no representation, no defense, falling upon the court's mercy. At least then I wouldn't have had the $13,000 legal bill.

The judge awarded everything Roger asked for, plus more. Roger never asked for the house; he was agreeable to let me and the girls stay there. The judge, however, ordered it sold within eighteen months, and the proceeds divided. He also cut my support by seventy percent. And the kicker was that he made the new child support orders retroactive, so I had to pay money back to Roger. Also there would be no more money for therapy.

I was devastated. How could things go so terribly wrong? How could God let this happen to me? I didn't want to believe what I'd been told—that it was a good-ol-boy's club in these small towns. More than once, Roger had been an expert witness in this judge's courtroom. Who really knows why the judge showed me no mercy? I was fighting back the bitterness, but not very successfully.

From Bad to Worse

A week later, still reeling from the judge's orders, my boss announced to the staff that he had hired a consulting firm to help with the dental practice and we were required to attend the training in Texas. I didn't think anything of it until I read the extensive bio on the consultant. There were enough clues to lead me to believe he was into cult rituals. I told my boss that I would be happy to support any and all changes he wanted to make in the dental office, but I wasn't able to be in the private residence of someone who I suspected was engaging in occultic practices.

Because I was still healing, I didn't want to be in the consultant's home. I was afraid of inadvertently placing myself in a vulnerable position, being re-traumatized. And with that, I was fired.

I don't blame my employer, although I was angry at the time. He put up with a lot during the three and a half years I worked for him. He let me work when I could and didn't complain when I couldn't. That was a gift, a big one.

After the staff returned from Texas, my good friend and co-worker, Debby, told me the whole thing was creepy. She did not believe in God; even so, she said something was off with this guy, describing suspicious items in his residence, strange late-night meetings with the staff, and an unexplained darkness. She said, *"Cyndy, you made the right decision."*

Right decision or not, now I was really in a pickle. I was flat broke with no job.

My boss graciously gave me time to find another job, so I quickly began applying for anything I could, which wasn't much in a town with a population of 12,000. The jobs I did find paid only $8-$10 an hour. There was no way I could live on that now.

I was going to have to expand my search. Not knowing what else to do, I went to the library, pulling phone books off the shelf. (The internet was still in its infant stages at this point.) I grabbed the Denver phone book, first. *No, Denver is too big.* Then Pueblo. *No, I don't like Pueblo.* Ft. Collins? *Absolutely not; my mother lives there.* That left just one phone book: Colorado Springs. And with that, my decision was made. I would look for a job in the Springs.

Not sure what I wanted to apply for, I wrote down phone numbers and addresses for dental practices, ministries (there are dozens of those in Colorado Springs), throwing in one financial business, just as a back-up option.

A four-day weekend was coming up, so I called a friend living in the area and asked if I could stay with her. I left early on a Thursday morning, stopping at a gas station on the corner of Highway 24 and Eighth Street to change into business clothes. I launched out with not a single appointment.

I arrived at each business with my well-practiced speech: *I need a job. Do you have one?* I heard a lot of, *"Leave your resume and I'll have someone get back to you."* By the second day, with little hope my efforts were working, I decided to swing by the financial company.

I noticed two men talking as I approached the receptionist with my well-practiced speech, *I need a job. Do you have one?* It turned out that the men were the two CEOs of the company. They looked my way and said, *"We'll give you twenty minutes to convince us why we should hire you."* Then they walked me back to their office. An hour later I was on my way with nothing but a promise they would get back to me. That was Friday.

On Monday, they called. *If you can be here in three weeks, you have a job.* And they offered a livable salary.

Three weeks! I've been living here nearly twenty years and have a house full of stuff! I have kids in school; one is a senior. How on earth can I settle everything here and be living in another city in three weeks?

Without other prospects, I took the job, having no idea how I would pull it off.

Parting of the Sea

Fortunately, I'd taken in a renter/roommate, a new hygienist at the dental office, and she was willing to stay in the house until I could make arrangements to get it sold. I was still working full time at the dental office, needing every penny I could earn, so I spent my evenings and weekends preparing to move.

My friend in the Springs knew someone who was willing to rent their furnished basement to me and the girls, allowing me to move with just enough personal items to get me through until Christmas.

Because Jenny was only fifteen, she needed to go with me, regardless of her opinions on the matter, which were hostile, to say the least. I gave Bree a choice, though. She was eighteen, and it was her senior year. I knew moving would ruin her final year. She'd been in school with these same kids for twelve years and was involved in many activities. It had to be her choice.

In hindsight, though, it was a no-win for her. Staying meant living with an emotionally abusive stepfather, or moving in with friends; dear friends, nevertheless in homes that were not hers. Moving meant just going through the motions to get a diploma, losing her dreams for a fun senior year.

She chose to move with us, a great relief to me. I don't know what I would have done, being separated from her. I wish I could say it all worked out great, but it didn't. It was worse for her than either of us could have imagined.

Behind the scenes, Jenny had been talking to her dad, asking him to stop me from taking her to the Springs. Neither she nor Roger spoke a word of it to me. He agreed to do everything possible, filing an emergency injunction, asserting that I was endangering her life; a claim that failed to impress the judge, fortunately.

I began to feel like Moses, trying to flee Egypt, narrowly escaping the clutches of Pharaoh. The fact that I'd turned forty that year lent weight to my feelings. I had been in the wilderness for forty years, and a new life in the Promised Land was in front of me, if I could only get there.

Friday, October 25 was my last day of work. I crammed everything I possibly could into my Ford Taurus and headed over the mountains on Sunday, as I had so many times before, but this time it was for good. Bree stayed back to finish her first quarter, joining us a week later.

As Jenny and I headed east, I could see we would be running into some weather. It worsened as I headed over Monarch Pass, turning into a blizzard at the top. My relief as I crested the summit was short lived when a car with Texas license plates and bald tires began sliding. I was the fourth car in the slow-motion, eight-car pile-up. I knew seconds beforehand what was about to happen but could do nothing about it. The road was pure ice.

No one was injured, praise God, and damage was minimal. Nevertheless, Jenny and I were shaken. Somehow, we got through the remaining two hours, thankful we'd made it as we pulled into Wendy's for dinner.

When I arrived in Colorado Springs, I had $20 in my wallet and $200 in the bank.

I registered Jenny in her new high school, the next morning, before walking through the door for my first day of work at the mortgage company.

Chapter Forty

1996
November-December

Finding Friends and Fun

In a way, it seemed like I was going backward, working at a financial company. That's where I started twenty years earlier, as a loan officer at a bank. I quickly realized, though, I wasn't ready to go back into ministry. Working on mortgage loans was a gift, mindless work: put in your day and go home. And, besides that, it paid better than ministry.

Now that I was somewhat settled, I began looking for a church. I decided to try First Presbyterian, since that was my background. I'm not exaggerating when I say their attendance was greater than the entire town of Delta, where my kids were born. While there, I visited the Sunday school class for singles. Its attendance was two hundred, complete with their own worship band! Holy Moly! This small-town girl was feeling a little out of her element.

Folks were friendly and I met several people, including the drummer of the band, a guy named Bryan. After that first visit, I decided on a different church for this season in my life. This other church was just as big, but I was so raw from the events of the year—my surgery, the trial, being fired, and the sudden move—that it felt good to just sit and absorb worship without having any responsibilities. I wanted to hide. And rest.

While I wanted to be an unknown at the church, I did want to make some Christian friends. So I decided to check out the Sunday school class for singles, where several people invited me to join them at a place called Cowboys. With country-music playing, the dance floor and restaurant were teeming with people. After only one night, I was hooked.

Listening to country music had been a new thing for me when the office manager at the dental office insisted on playing it every day. But I liked it! And at Cowboys, the evening started with dance lessons, so I was learning the two-step, three-step, and the waltz.

I couldn't wait for Sundays to roll around so I could dance the evening away with my new friends. Dancing three or four hours an evening each week was the norm, getting me in better physical condition than I'd been in for years. I had entered a joyful world that I had not known existed.

Initial Challenges

The transition to the Springs was harder for the girls. They were both upset with me—Jenny, because I'd divorced her stepfather and taken her away from him; Bree, because I'd waited so long to leave, forcing her to remain in misery.

Growing up in a small town, the girls had never started over in a new school before, particularly a school many times larger than the one they just left. Jenny was traumatized just trying to make her way through the hallways, telling me she couldn't focus in her classes with all the craziness going on.

17: Jenny (age 15), Bree (age 18), and Me (age 40)

Bree had always found school easier than Jenny, being more social. But after transferring at the beginning of the second quarter, she fell into depression. She slept a lot, rarely making it to school on time, if at all. She did make a few good friends, and was accepted into the show choir, but it wasn't enough to pull her out of her darkness.

The school year became a test of survival. Can the girls just make it to the end?

I was running on financial fumes by the time my first paycheck arrived. It would take a while to get on top of all my bills, but at least I was working.

It wasn't long before my landlady began stressing me out. After moving in, I noticed she had a photography studio in a spare room for the purpose of taking "aura pictures" of people. I'd never heard of that but could see it was something like palm reading. She would take pictures of people with this special camera and *read* their aura. I have to say, I found this a little creepy.

After a few weeks, she began calling me at work with various concerns. She said we were using too much toilet paper and that needed to change. Then she said my car dripped oil on her driveway and I needed to clean it. But the issue that brought everything to a head was her granddaughter. The young girl told her grandma that I was rude to her whenever I called, an absurd claim. I can only surmise that she did not like having anyone living in her grandma's house. Whatever the real problem, it didn't matter. The landlady told me I had three weeks to leave.

Last Christmas in Montrose

The Sunday school class I had joined was sponsoring a city-wide Christian single's Christmas dinner and dance at the Broadmoor Hotel. It sounded like fun.

Many years earlier, the bank I worked at in Ft. Collins sent me to a credit conference at The Broadmoor. It was quite the experience. The world-renowned resort is more like a small city, sporting multiple lodging buildings, restaurants, pools, and its own lake. It was the fanciest place I'd ever seen, and I couldn't wait to go back.

There was only one problem—what would I wear? Coming from a small town, there was never a need for dressy clothes. However, I knew someone who might be able to help. I called my friend, the hygienist, who was renting my house in Montrose. Having never been married or had children, she had the wardrobe to die for. When she moved in, just her shoe boxes took up half of her closet. I had never seen so many clothes and shoes. And, as luck would have it, we were the same size.

"Hey, Sandy, I need a fancy dress to wear to The Broadmoor? Do you have anything I might borrow for the occasion?"

"Definitely!" she said.

I made a quick trip over the mountains to pick up the dress, barely making it back to town in time to change and drive over to the resort. As I walked into the ballroom in my black sequined, halter gown, I felt like Cinderella. The night was magical.

I joined a couple girls from the class at their round table for eight. Across from me were two couples, one I recognized from First Presbyterian. Later, I stepped out for a moment, and when I returned, I found the guy I had recognized, waiting for me at the door.

"I don't know if you remember me. We met at church last month. My name is Bryan Sherwood."

I did remember him. We visited for a while on the ballroom floor, discovering we both had teenagers, and each of us had a daughter named, Bree Anna. He told me the woman he was sitting with was a friend, but they weren't dating. Soon after, he left with her and I remained to dance a little longer. It wasn't the last time I would need that dress.

The next Friday, I returned to work after my lunch break, only to discover flowers and a letter waiting for me. I asked the receptionist, Annette, where they came from. All she knew was that a man had called earlier to find out when I took my lunch, then, while I was gone, someone (not the same person) dropped the flowers off.

I quickly opened the envelope, discovering a love poem and an anonymous letter. The only clue to the sender's identity was that it was someone who had been at the dinner at the Broadmoor. The sender said he was a secret admirer and would reveal his identity to me after Christmas.

My curiosity was certainly piqued, but what could I do? I had met and danced with several guys that night. Besides, I had plenty of other things to think about, finding a new place to live and preparing to move. After a brief search, I found a condo fairly close to work and to the girls' school.

The girls and I returned to Montrose to have Christmas in our own home and pack up our belongings. The task was daunting. Everything had to go somewhere; if not to Colorado Springs, then to the Goodwill. The house also needed some painting and minor repairs so it could be sold.

On New Year's Day, friends helped me get my belongings over the Rocky Mountains. And, once again, the weather was not favorable. Déjà vu. Taking the rental truck over Monarch Pass was too risky in a snowstorm, so we ended up taking a longer route. What a relief when we safely arrived at our new home.

And with that, my life on the Western Slope was officially over. I sorely missed my home and friends, a life I'd known for eighteen years.

Once the boxes were unpacked and we began settling in, I realized I hadn't heard anything from my secret admirer. Hmmm....

Chapter Forty-One

1997
January-April

Dissociating Again

I thought it was ironic that at the very time I moved closer to my therapist, my recovery began to wrap up. I was only an hour away from Faith, but I was now in more of a maintenance phase of healing, only seeing her as needed.

However, there was one bump in the road; I began dissociating again. *How can I have parts again? I'm past that! I've integrated!*

It was cause for me to review my understanding of Dissociative Identity Disorder Class 101. DID is a coping mechanism designed to survive overwhelming circumstances. Well, 1996 was certainly overwhelming with the trial, losing my job, the move, and breast cancer scare. Was it the same level of dissociation as previously, though? No.

I'd known from the beginning that dissociation is a natural human phenomenon; every person dissociates. Everyone has been in a conversation when they suddenly realize they haven't heard anything the other person said for a few minutes. That's because they have dissociated. Daydreaming is a form of dissociation. When we go into a room, looking for something, and then can't remember why we walked in there, we've dissociated.

However, none of those things mean we have created alters to help survive traumatic events. Dissociation is a continuum. At the normal end is the behavior of mentally checking out once in a while. At the extreme, opposite end is full blown DID, with distinguishable parts who have identities and specific roles in the system. That's where I was for nearly forty years.

During this new phase of my healing, I was experiencing the vast middle area of the DID continuum, where it is more than checking out of a conversation, but not to the extent that I had parts with names, ages, and long histories. I heard someone call this *loose ego states*, and that fits with my experience. I was changing my affect and behavior in different situations.

Honestly, though, even with this logical explanation, I found it alarming. I did not want to go backward in my healing. I'd fought too hard for wholeness. Faith helped me calm down and realize this was a normal part of my healing process. She was right when she said my current dissociative episodes were not the same as before.

As time went on, I came to recognize that dissociating was now a choice for me. It hadn't been before. Now I could choose to stay present or choose to checkout and dissociate. Whenever I was afraid or hurting emotionally, I was strongly tempted to dissociate. Like a recovering alcoholic craving a drink, I wanted to leave. But I knew, at this point, doing that was a prideful choice. To choose dissociation meant I did not believe God was sufficient to help me. I was being my own protector and power source and not relying on God.

The battle with dissociation lasted several years. Even today, I know that the option to dissociate is close by, and I can choose to slip into it. I know that will always be true, but resisting the temptation is much easier today.

These new *ego states,* that showed up when I transitioned to a new life in Colorado Springs, dissipated relatively quickly, in a matter of months, and without ceremony.

Good Work, Good Job

I was happy at my new job. Being assigned to the Quality Control department meant it was my responsibility to make sure the loan packages were complete and ready to go on to the next department. The work was a good fit, since I had an eye for detail.

When my three-month probation period came to an end, I was awarded Employee of the Month, and given a raise. I was grateful, but the raise wasn't what I had negotiated with the two owners back in October, when they promised that if I proved myself, I could have my asked-for salary. It was time to use my voice and speak up for my needs, something that was still scary. I brought up the issue to the office manager, who clearly had no intention of honoring the agreement. But the owners stepped in and made it right.

Yes! I would now be able to cover all my living expenses. Victory!

The Anonymous Suitor

But there still was the matter of the love letter. My suitor had said he would reveal his identity after Christmas. It was now the third week of January—*where was he?* I checked back with Annette. Being the excellent receptionist she was, she had a log of every call. She checked back to the page for that Friday before Christmas and, indeed, had recorded the anonymous giver's pager number, but no name. I called and left my number. (Pagers preceded cell phones as a way to contact people and leave your number.)

About seven o'clock that night, thinking he was returning a call related to his construction business, he called back.

"Hello, this is Bryan Sherwood. I'm not sure who called me, but this number was left on my pager."

"Bryan Sherwood," I said, "You've been caught."

He immediately connected the dots and realized who I was—and why I was calling. After a bit of stuttering and stammering, trying to get his bearings, Bryan explained his month of silence. It turned out that God had gotten a hold of him during the holidays with a message: *I don't want you to date anyone right now. I want you to spend this time with me. I am preparing you.*

Not wanting to interfere with anything God might be doing, I accepted his response. *I guess that's the end of that.*

I continued dancing with the other singles from my church, joining them for other activities, too. One night they asked if I wanted to attend a murder mystery party, a popular group activity in the nineties. Having lived a sheltered life in a small town, however, I didn't know what that was.

To set up the murder, my friends explained, several people were asked ahead of time to play a role, dressing up as a character in the murder and then given knowledge of certain facts. The other guests at the party would engage with the characters, asking questions to try and solve the mystery. It sounded like fun.

Arriving at the home by myself, another guest, not the host, let me in. Feeling overwhelmed by the house full of people, I quickly stepped into the dining room, pretending to look at the knick-knacks. *Whose house was this, anyway?* A few minutes later, Bryan walked down the stairs, dressed as a priest.

Our eyes locked. Neither one of us knew what to say. Suddenly the house seemed empty of anyone but the two of us. Not wanting to be rude (or let on what was happening between us), we engaged with the other guests, waiting for the party to finally be over so we could talk.

Our connection was immediately intense, drawing us each into a space we had neither the desire nor strength to vacate. We did not want to go against God's directive, but we could find no way to sever the relationship.

After that night, I entered what I call, "the endless interview." Bryan and I didn't go on any dates. But we did talk, every day, for hours and hours. I thought Bryan would never get to the end of his questions.

Bryan's Backstory

Because Bryan had been badly burned in his first marriage, he was determined not to make any mistakes the second time. He and Sue started dating in high school, something her mother didn't approve of. So, after graduation, Sue's mother moved her daughter far away from Longmont, Colorado, to southern California.

Undaunted, Bryan simply followed them. They soon discovered Sue was pregnant and got married. A year after their first son was born, they had their second son. It was a wake-up call to Bryan, in many ways.

Feeling the weight of responsibility, he needed to find a way to provide for his family of four. It was a job at a cabinet-making shop that turned the tide for Bryan, revealing his creative gift for working with wood and a knack for handling tools. He was soon working in other facets of construction, with one referral leading to another. His success was extraordinary.

Being a husband and father of two boys at such a young age, with a daughter arriving a few years later, also made Bryan keenly aware of his need for God. It was no longer enough that he had become a Christian in high school, now he needed God's help, a real relationship with him.

The family joined a church and Bryan's relationship with God took center-stage. He learned who God truly was, becoming well-versed in the Bible, making the choice to tithe, and even leading the boy's club at his church. His wife, however, didn't share his enthusiasm.

Eventually, Bryan grew tired of Los Angeles. He hated the smog, crowds, and traffic, so he decided to move his family back to Colorado. He bought a home in Colorado Springs and settled his family in a pretty neighborhood at the base of the Rocky Mountains.

Construction is not a business that you can move to another location, so Bryan had to start over, building a whole new client base. But as soon as Bryan got his foot in the door, the work rarely stopped.

About a year later, when Bryan returned home from a backpacking trip, Sue confronted him with a choice to either get a separation or a divorce. Bryan was stunned. The issue had never previously come up between them. From his perspective, they were not having probems in their relationship; he had been thinking everything was fine.

Bryan soon discovered Sue was having an affair, a devastating realization. After trying therapy and a separation, they were divorced. The arrangement for their parental roles wasn't typical, though; it was Bryan who stayed in the house with the kids while Sue moved in with her boyfriend. Bryan suddenly found himself a single father, raising two teenage boys and an eight-year-old daughter. It was rough.

Over the next few years, Bryan dated several women, but moved on each time after discovering they didn't share the same level of relationship with God. Meanwhile, he taught himself to play drums and joined the band for the single's Sunday school class at his church, where we were first introduced. All the while, his thriving construction business continued.

The Three-Week Interview

I hadn't met anyone like Bryan before. He was interested in finding out who I was as a woman, as a person. No one had done that before. He wanted to know my thoughts and opinions on everything from God to Scripture, to marriage, to parenting, to money, to camping in the mountains. With every question, more of his character was revealed to me and my interest grew.

Observing the relationships with his parents and kids, I could tell Bryan was loving and caring, always wanting to give whatever he could give. I could see these commendable qualities in his friendships with other women, too. He was kind and respectful. All new to me. He was looking more and more like a good man.

My hard work toward restoration was paying off. Before, it never caught my attention whether a guy was narcissistic or considerate and respectful. Now, I could recognize signs of a healthy relationship before making a commitment. That was HUGE!

Bryan made it clear from the beginning that he had a firm plan for preparing to marry. Determined not to make another marital mistake, he insisted that he would date his potential partner for a full year, followed by a second year for the engagement. I wasn't sure I liked the plan but understood where he was coming from.

The endless interview had been going on for several weeks, when Bryan went out one night to pick up dinner at his favorite Mexican place. While driving, he and God talked. Bryan didn't know what to do about our relationship. We were getting serious fast, but he had his long-term plan. That's when he heard God speak, *"Hey, you do want you want to do. You can marry her now or marry her in two years; that's up to you. But this is the woman I was preparing you to marry. She is my gift to you."*

At that point, Bryan relinquished his plan, realizing his strategy was more about self-protection than following God. None of this was known to me at the time.

I was having my own private struggle, meanwhile, freaking out because I was falling in love with this guy and didn't trust myself. I had been a marital train wreck for twenty years. Bryan wasn't the only one praying; I was on my knees, too.

I decided I needed the opinion of someone I could trust. I made an appointment with Faith so she could meet Bryan.

A Romantic Moment at Arby's

The night before we were to see Faith, Bryan was up all night; the man who rarely stayed awake past nine o'clock, couldn't sleep a wink. His mind was thrashing around as he wondered whether he should propose or not. After deciding he would ask me to marry him, his thoughts moved on to everything he needed to do to get ready. He began mentally planning how he would complete the unfinished basement, adding two more bedrooms and a bath to accommodate my family. By dawn, he had it all figured out.

That morning, we drove to Denver. After a thorough interrogation, Faith gave us her blessing and said our relationship was a good match. However, she also warned us about further healing that needed to be done in both of us. A romantic relationship would test the solidity of my beliefs about myself, compelling me to learn how to be a healthy partner. And Bryan would need healing for his abandonment issues from Sue.

After the appointment, we stopped for a quick lunch at Arby's in downtown Denver before driving back to the Springs. Over a roast beef sandwich, Bryan popped the question. *"Would you marry me?"* I was ecstatic. And, even though we still had not had a proper date, we were engaged.

We told all five kids over Easter dinner, barely containing our excitement, along with Bryan's parents. His mother cried, so happy for her son; his dad welcomed me into the family. The kids were in shock, not knowing what to say. I was oblivious to the turmoil this caused for the kids, but it wouldn't be long before I knew exactly how they felt about our plans. At that time, the kids were fifteen, sixteen, seventeen, eighteen, with our caboose being almost twelve.

We picked out rings and Bryan went to work adding rooms to his basement.

As much as I loved the impulsive part of our story when he proposed at Arby's, Bryan hated it. He is Mister Romantic: "I have a plan; I am going to do it right." Blurting out the question at a fast food restaurant was none of those things, which is exactly what I loved about the proposal—he wanted me to be his wife so much he couldn't contain himself.

Wanting to redeem himself from his hasty proposal, he planned a romantic dinner. I called my old roommate back and asked if I could borrow the black sequined halter gown one more time, retrieving it in time for our one and only official date prior to the wedding. That night Bryan gave me the engagement ring, a purple tanzanite, surrounded by diamonds, in a gold setting. He was happy to see the dress again (and me in it!), and I was happy to see the ring.

We had not necessarily been in a hurry to plan the wedding, but Bree was about to head off to the Philippines for a discipleship training program with YWAM, lasting six months. Not wanting to exclude her, my choice was to either get married in May or December. I chose May.

Chapter Forty-Two

1997
May-December

Blending Battles

Two months after Bryan proposed at Arby's, we were married. We had a small ceremony at Bryan's church, followed by a backyard celebration at his house, my new home.

Until now, I had been estranged from everyone in my family except my younger brother and was so happy he and his daughter were willing to attend my wedding. The event was also an opportunity to extend an invitation as a peace offering to my mother. Her attendance was healing for both of us. Four of our five kids were there, too, but one chose to abstain, which broke our hearts.

18: Me (age 41) and Bryan

A weekend getaway in the mountains marked the occasion until it was time for our official honeymoon in Puerto Vallarta the following month.

Mexico became our happy place. The honeymoon there was a memory we shared together, one that represented our new life and a new chance for a fulfilling relationship. We committed to return every year, frequently bringing the colors of Mexico and its bright colored pottery back with us, decorating our home with Talavera tile.

19: Faith with her husband and daughter at the wedding.

Once we were back home, settling into everyday life while blending a family of five teenagers was interesting.

No, actually, it was terrible.

Even though we attended a conference to prepare us for combining households with existing children, it wasn't nearly enough to help us navigate our new circumstances. If parenting was challenging, then step-parenting was ridiculously hard.

What I didn't understand at the time was that I started with a negative bank account with my step kids, as did Bryan. They did not want a relationship. It was their mission, and understandably so, to rebel and reject each stepparent. All five were hurting and we were woefully inadequate to parent them through this crisis and their feelings.

Bryan's kids resented me, and my kids resented him. Interestingly, though, the kids seemed to get along with each other. In fact, the two Breannas forged a deep bond, the seven-year spread creating a little-sister, big-sister relationship they both enjoyed.

Having survived my own personal recovery, I thought I could handle anything. However, as I entered the challenges of our blended family, I was beginning to question that. The girls were mouthy and disrespectful. The boys found it funny to steal my things. There was zero desire to cooperate or work together to make this new family work.

I was so naïve. I thought, by coming into their lives with a clean slate, I could win them over simply by being kind and caring, being interested in their lives, attempting to support them. But I was wrong. No one had a clean slate. Their abandonment and rejection issues existed before I was on the scene. Besides that, my step kids had a mother. From their perspective, they did not need or want a second one. They just wanted me out of their lives.

Adjustments

When I moved into Bryan's house, I had certain expectations about how to run the home. But Bryan's family was raised with a different set of expectations—ones vastly different from mine.

During those early months, I was able to form a mental picture of what their life was like, hearing tidbits from people who had been in the home. When Bryan's ex-wife left, it was three men and a little girl. There was a lot of Domino's pizza. Kleenex and napkins were forgotten commodities that I soon reintroduced. The dining room table was the permanent clean laundry location, the contents of the dryer being emptied there and abandoned. Because Bryan was still trying to run a construction business, it was every man for himself and survival was the mission of the day.

I couldn't wait to restore order. In retrospect, I probably moved too quickly. What I didn't realize was that my sheer presence in the home was an affront to Bryan's kids. This was their mother's home. My moving in felt like a violation to them. With every change, it was another small death to them. They were given no time to adjust.

Bryan and I did everything we could think of to improve the situation. We worked hard to help them feel comfortable. When he finished remodeling the basement, all five kids had their own bedroom, newly decorated to their tastes, and their own linens. We included everyone when making plans and adjustments.

My girls were used to cooking the family dinner once a week, a foreign concept to Bryan's kids. When we expanded this protocol to include everyone, we had some pretty strange dinners. My favorite was coming home from work to find instant mashed potatoes doused with Campbell's cream of mushroom soup being served. *Hey, it was a start!*

With five teens, there were also multiple crises going on simultaneously. We dealt with so many things those first years, including drugs, alcohol, criminal activity, running away, unplanned pregnancy, dropping out of school, homelessness, and custody issues.

Neither of our exes were interested in custody until Bryan and I got married, then suddenly they wanted the existing arrangements changed. Between custody battles and the criminal activities, we were in and out of courtrooms and lawyers' offices for years. With all this drama going on, it wasn't long before the census in our home changed.

Our first Thanksgiving together was interesting. We had made the two-hour drive north to have dinner with Bryan's parents. The kids were with their other parents, or so we thought. In the middle of dinner, we got a call that someone had broken into our home, so we made a beeline back; unfortunately, a blizzard had descended. It took us three hours. When we finally arrived home, the boys were having a party and the house was full of kids. Bryan stormed through the back door, yelling, as kids scattered everywhere. He was so upset.

The worst moment that year, however, was a day I was home by myself, when one of the boys came in, under the influence of who-knows-what, threatening me to get out and never come back. *"No one wants you here,"* he kept screaming. I locked myself in the bathroom and called Bryan. Because he was thirty minutes away, he called 911 before heading home. The next thing I knew, an ambulance and fire trucks were in front of the house and several men in various uniforms were in my bedroom. I was completely traumatized by the entire event. *So much for making a good impression on the neighbors.*

There was nothing else I could do to build relationships with Bryan's boys. Within months they decided they did not want to be there. So, at seventeen and eighteen, they were on their own and making their way. This was so hard for Bryan. Never did he imagine that marrying me would mean losing them.

(The boys' unresolved grief over their parents' divorce derailed their lives for many years. Fortunately, things are better today. They finally found their footing, got married, and are raising their own families.)

The younger Breanna stayed with us, but the elder was gone for the rest of the year. Having graduated from high school, Bree began training at the YWAM discipleship school in Hawaii before flying to the Philippines. When she returned, she lived with us for a year or so, before getting a job that could support her rent for a nearby apartment. Jenny, however, my kid who hated change, had three years to go and missed her old home in Montrose. She remained with us, but we arranged frequent visits with Roger.

Out of the Office and into the Classroom

To help Jenny cope better, at her request I agreed to homeschool her for the rest of her high school years, quitting my job in order to make the necessary time. Attending the large city schools did not work for her.

It was a little challenging, dusting off my algebra skills after twenty-five years, but I eventually adjusted to the steep learning curve. Jenny and I initially had weekly battles. She fired me from my teaching position more than once, but we ultimately found a friendly rhythm and homeschooling evolved into a blessing for our relationship.

With the older kids gone, only Jenny and our younger Breanna were living at home. Being just twelve, we had the furthest to go with Breanna. After a long custody battle, including a trial and home visits by a social worker, we were awarded custody, with her mother able to have some visitation. While we were thrilled to have her with us and to know Breanna's needs would be adequately cared for, the court order did nothing to improve her hostility toward me.

Slowly, though, Breanna began to warm up to me. She liked having a stable routine, a home cooked dinner every night and someone who noticed and bought her the things she needed. There was a predictability that gave her a sense of safety. School, however, was not her scene at all. She had been failing core subjects for years. Breanna had no shortage of smarts, but the trauma of her parent's divorce, which started in grade school, left her unable to focus in the classroom.

We gave her an ultimatum: If she didn't start passing her classes, a change would be made at the semester break. It would be her choice, either to attend a private school, or join me and Jenny homeschooling, but a new school arrangement would be made. When the report card arrived, there had been no change in her grades.

20: Breanna (age 13)

After we received the news, Breanna, being the gregarious, demonstrative child she was, began thrashing around, yelling, begging, and threatening, before locking herself in her bedroom. Bryan and I stood silently by, watching the storm blow through, when suddenly she emerged from her room and said, *"Fine, I'll do homeschooling,"* before quickly retreating to her room and slamming the door. I was shocked, certain she'd pick private school over being stuck with me every day.

And then, Breanna thrived. Homeschooling was just the ticket to get her caught up in reading, comprehension, and math skills. She loved it. Someone was there to explain everything she didn't understand. And it didn't hurt our cause that she got to do school in her pajamas and finished up in three or four hours each day.

Her mom, however, was not happy with the arrangement, arguing with Breanna over the phone that she needed to be back in real school. When I heard Breanna's response to her, I knew we were on the right track, *"But mom, this is the first time I have ever understood math."* Breanna wanted to succeed; she just needed someone to help her.

It was a marvelous semester. Every Friday, the girls and I would go out for lunch and a field trip, sometimes with an educational purpose and sometimes just for fun. Sadly, though, when we resumed in the fall, Breanna's mother came over to the house to pick her up one day with an ultimatum. She made it clear there would be no more home-schooling and then she deposited Breanna into another school. It was a terrible environment where kids sat alone in cubicles all day, filling out workbooks on their own while a classroom monitor babysat them.

My heart broke. Breanna had been doing so well, quickly catching up to grade level work, loving learning. And she and I were growing closer.

Bryan and I just couldn't stomach any more attorney's fees and courtrooms and decided not to fight it. We had enough problems going on with other issues.

More Counseling

By now, the stress on our marriage was unbelievable. The court drama and kids' issues were an incredible backdrop to our new marriage, trying to have a fresh beginning and find our bearings. Neither Bryan nor I had any experience being in a healthy marriage and we were floundering as a couple.

It was so hard, trying to resist the temptation to defend our own kids and take sides against each other. Our home was a pressure cooker, ready to explode at any given moment. I was frequently dissociating, feeling paralyzed and hopeless.

Besides constant prayer, Bryan and I did the only thing we knew to do—we got into counseling.

As Faith had forecasted, Bryan needed healing regarding the issues surrounding the loss of his first marriage, and I needed to learn how to relate to a man from a healthy identity, things you can't just read about in a book. It would only be learned by walking it out in a relationship.

We were seeing a male therapist, someone with whom Bryan could relate well, and beginning to work on our issues. Bryan had a lot of anger to work through and the stress of the kids was just adding to the problem. And I needed to learn how to stop reacting to everything.

It was tough work, for both of us. We struggled as much as any married couple can struggle, coming to the edge of failure more than once. One day our therapist suggested we separate for a while, to hopefully cool things down a little.

And that flipped some kind of inner switch for both of us and we quit therapy. *Nope! There's no way we're separating. We both did that in our last marriages, and it was the beginning of the end; for us, separation was divorce practice.* We had no idea how we were going to make it, but whatever we did, we were going to do it together. We stayed together out of sheer commitment. Or stubbornness. Or stupidity. I'm not sure, because it didn't get easier for a long time.

Chapter Forty-Three

1998
January-December

Walking Out My New Life

January 1: *I cannot be encouraged too often to relinquish all to my heavenly father. Today is a good day—in fact the best day to do this again. There are many weighty matters in my life now and I do not wish to foolishly go through these days without his wisdom. And the wisdom comes when I'm listening. And I can only hear when I am connected to him. I can only be connected when I am obedient. Then I receive fully all his love has to offer me.*

January 3: *So many things I'd like to add and subtract—add more positive thinking, more charity toward those hard-to-love people in my life—subtract the absorption with physical circumstances, less burden bearing. I want to pass my heavy yoke over to my Lord. I want to live joyfully. I want to receive more help from the Lord and do less striving under my own power. Today is a good day to begin. I receive this day as the gift that it is.*

January 5: *I have come to the end of myself many times with awful circumstances surrounding my life. Today is different. I choose to be at the end of myself so that God can fulfill his plan for me today. Praise God that my circumstances are no longer so dire and desperate. I rejoice in his many gifts of new life and healing. I truly want to live this day by his strength and wisdom. Anything less will end in another disappointing day.*

Journaling had become sporadic over the last few years; so had my time with God. Honestly, I think after I began emerging from recovery, I needed a break from everything that smacked of healing. I didn't want to record dreams, or write down thoughts and feelings, or do therapy, or artwork. I wanted to live like a normal person, whatever that was.

Unfortunately, somehow God got lumped in with all of that and I wasn't spending time with him like I had been while I was healing. With a new year beginning, I decided to get back to my daily quiet time. It lasted only a few weeks, though. Fits and starts would describe my spiritual connection for the next two years.

Trying to walk in the newness of God's redemption of my past was not an instant process. Challenges were ongoing, forcing me to continually have to choose a new perspective when something hard or painful happened. *Yes, something hard might be reminding me of the past, but that was then, and this is now. I don't have to dissociate. I know I am inherently valuable, regardless of how others see me or treat me.* This was my new work: To stand firm on the truth, to invite others to work through things with me in a healthy manner, and to forgive and accept those who chose not to do that.

I had plenty of opportunities to practice, since I was surrounded by unhealthy people. No one in my world had yet received any healing. This was easier to handle intellectually than emotionally because I was still having panic attacks, lots of them.

Trauma Brain

February 1: *Anemia. Panic disorder. The first is a bit more socially acceptable. The second is embarrassing. Why? Because I don't really understand it? I know it wasn't my doing that brought it on. More medications. Disappointment. More waiting, trial and error, unproductive days, being patient. Keep my attitude positive. Not very good at that. Where is God in this? What is his plan? His desire? A good day to ask questions. He is there/here. I really want to be with him right now.*

The memory work may have been completed, but the effects of the trauma were still with me in some respects. It would be years before I understood what I now call my "trauma brain," but I was living with the reality every day.

Trauma is stored in a different part of the brain than where the information of the event is stored. It is stored at the base of the brain, very deep below the rational part of the brain, a place where it never dissipates or disappears. This is the same area of the brain that regulates our hormones, digestion, heartbeat, and breathing. This is why our heart beats too fast, our breathing becomes shallow, and our stomach hurts when a threat is perceived.

Trauma survivors are scanning the horizon for threats, twenty-four hours a day, listening to every sound, watching every face, noting every movement. That hypervigilance didn't end for me just because I was on the other side of my healing. I was still on high alert for danger, all night and all day. And because the trauma storage area is out of reach, I could not change it with rational thinking. Its responses were ingrained, automatic.

For these reasons, I was still having panic attacks. It took very little to send me into one, which I hated. I was still carrying Xanax everywhere I went. The good news was that the trauma responses were getting fewer and further in between. But coping with stress was still hard.

Only a year into our marriage, my first camping trip with Bryan's family was especially stressful, when I'd noticed innocent garden snakes slithering through the grass. Because I was abused with snakes, they were a major trigger for me. But no one in Bryan's family knew about my past, and I certainly didn't want to dump that story out the first time we went camping together. So, I spent a lot of time in my tent, trying to calm down, while evoking judgment from the family, but it was the best I could do in the moment. I felt like I would never measure up or be accepted.

Even normal activities would cause painful stress reactions, like having a full day of things to do and then have something unexpected happen. I was having responses that would be appropriate if the house was on fire or someone was holding a gun on me. Just a simple thing like packing for a trip sent my stress through the roof. If my work was piling up, same thing, major stress response. No amount of self-talk helped.

I had to learn to manage my life in such a way as to avoid those tipping points, becoming ultra-organized, planning every step of every activity or job. It was the only way I could avoid the extreme stress reaction. And even these methods didn't stop it, only minimized it.

What I know now that I didn't know then is that trauma recalibrates the brain's alarm system, causing it to secrete abnormal amounts of stress hormones. *(Oh, how I wish someone had explained this to me back then!)* So life is a constant sensory overload, triggering disproportionate physical reactions. And you can't simply talk yourself out of it. And when people try to tell you there's no need to react that way, it makes it worse because then you feel unheard and discounted—another reenactment from the past.

21: (Front) Breanna, Bree, Jenny (Middle) Bryan, Me (Back) Chad, Shane

With the blended family issues, there were plenty of stress triggers in my life that were taking a physical toll as well as an emotional one. I became chronically anemic, home-schooling from bed many days. The anemia led me to fall further behind in the stuff I needed to do, which escalated the stress responses. It was a vicious cycle. In spite of these challenges, life was also getting better in other ways.

New Beginnings

When Bree returned from the Philippines, the kid-census in our home was up to three. I was so happy to have her home again. She landed a great job, working as a server at the world-renowned Broadmoor Resort, just up the street from our house. By four o'clock each afternoon, she was gone, returning in the middle of the night. This pattern continued for about a year until she got her own place.

It was probably good that Bree's work hours were opposite from Bryan's. Her yet-to-be healed father issues made it difficult for her to accept Bryan. They eventually did become closer, however, after some healing occurred.

The homeschool support group I had joined became a place of new friendships, great support, and social events. One mom taught me how to quilt, giving me a new hobby and creative outlet. The church where Bryan and I established ourselves also became a source for friends and connections, out of which we started a small group in our home. We even had the opportunity to play music occasionally for casual events, with Bryan on the drums and me on the keyboard. New life was springing up.

I had been supporting several missionary friends for years and I began introducing them to Bryan whenever they were in Colorado. Andy, a friend from my old church who was now serving with his family in Chile, flew into the Springs for a needed eye surgery and stayed with us.

After dinner, Bryan and Andy got in the hot tub and began talking. Hours later, a life-long bond had been forged and Bryan announced that we were going to Chile to build a kitchen for their family. I use the word "we" liberally since I couldn't hit a nail straight on with a hammer if my life depended on it.

It was decided we would go in May and take Jenny with us. The other girls stayed with family or friends, but Jenny was in a vulnerable place, so we felt it wasn't safe to leave her. I had recently intercepted a letter indicating her plans to run away with a guy who was several years older. We just didn't want to take a chance she'd disappear while we were gone.

Chilly in Chile

We flew down in May, arriving at the beginning of the cold and wet season. We were accustomed to dry Colorado, where it is fairly comfortable anytime the temperature is above forty. Not in Chile! I'm not sure how they live without central heating, because we were freezing in their forty-five-degree days due to the humidity. We wore every warm thing we had packed, even while we slept!

What the days lacked in warmth was vastly exceeded by the love experienced during our two weeks with Andy and his wife, Tabi, and their four kids. While Bryan was over at the new house, building a kitchen for them, chatting with Andy, I was with Tabi, helping cook meals for the nine of us, experiencing the different markets and new foods.

One day, Bryan and I, making a heroic effort to learn some Spanish, launched out to the market alone, armed only with our battery-operated translator. Among other things, we were supposed to be buying yeast to make bread but struggling to find it. We asked the young woman whose job it was to stand in the aisle all day and assist shoppers, *"Donde està la lavadora?" ("Where is the yeast?")* or so we thought. She looked confused, so we repeated ourselves, which then made her giggle. So we typed the question into our translator and she quickly located the yeast for us.

When we got home, I asked Tabi why the girl laughed at us. Tabi said we were asking her for a washing machine. Yeast is *levadura.* It was one of many moments when we entertained the locals with our gringo Spanish.

Once back in Colorado, Bryan began planning how he could arrange his construction work to accommodate regular short-term mission trips. It became his new passion to use his skills to help missionaries.

Babies, Puppies, and Kittens

While Bryan was discovering new passions, my old passions began resurfacing. I was ready to run with the horses and wanted to be back in ministry, giving to others again. This growing desire came out in my dreams at night and in my thoughts during the day.

For two years, I had dreams of puppies, kittens, and babies. If it wasn't a dog having multiple liters, then I was having babies, dozens of them. I also had dreams of having milk, but no baby to nurse. It happened so often that Bryan began asking over breakfast how many babies were born during the night.

Passions emerged during the daytime, too. A message of truth and hope would just spontaneously erupt inside me, words about healing filling my mind. These thoughts and dreams reflected my deep longing to minister to others. I prayed, asking God over and over to once again open the doors for ministry, but the answer was *No, not yet*. He said I had to wait a little while longer.

Chapter Forty-Four

1999-2000

Autumn Changes

As the seasons changed in the fall of 'Ninety-nine, so did my life. Sandi had been living in the States for five years when she decided it was time to move back to Australia. Since then, she's been back to visit several times. A couple years after she returned to Sydney, I had the trip of a lifetime, visiting her for two weeks. Although the opportunities to be together have been few, our hearts remain knit together even today.

I couldn't spend time with my friend Sandi anymore, but I did begin to see my family. The past estrangement changed, little by little. After a two-year void, I reconnected with my mom at my wedding. I hadn't seen my sister, however, for five years, even though there had been letters between us. I know the agony over the loss of relationship was equal on both sides, and the long gap was more about me, than her. But I just couldn't face any of my family members who blatantly said they did not believe anything in my story, particularly when they didn't know the story and wouldn't give me a chance to share my reality.

I wish they knew how many times I had retraced my steps, trying to figure out how I had arrived at my predicament, trying to find some other explanation, seeking a way to deny everything that had happened. But when I did, it always led me to the same conclusion: God started this journey, led this journey, and worked in this journey to restore me to wholeness. I didn't do any of that. I knew in the depths of my soul that I had neither authored nor propelled what had come about.

Even today, the ache in my heart for my family to see me and believe me never leaves. My prayers for the truth to be known never cease. But these things are out of my control. All I can do is choose to love to the degree that God gives me grace.

That same fall, my mom let me know my sister and her family were coming to Ft. Collins for a visit. I really missed my sister and the kids and wanted to have a relationship again, even if it was superficial. After a stressful day or two thinking about it, I made a spontaneous decision to make the two-hour drive to Mom's, first stopping at the store to buy presents for my six nieces and nephews.

As mom answered the door, my sister glanced my way and burst into tears, fleeing the room for several minutes—not a good start. She was livid that I would show up unannounced. I could see her point. Being caught off guard in an emotionally charged situation wasn't good. But I also knew it took all my courage to take the step, and I was terrified of seeing her. I felt my best chance for reconciliation was a face-to-face meeting.

We limped through the visit, but it did the trick. It broke the ice, allowing us a new beginning. Did it fix everything? No. In fact, it fixed very little. The elephant in the room—my memories of abuse—was never addressed. But things were better for both of us because we were able to resume visits with each other and exchange friendly letters. General details of each other's lives could be known. We would attend weddings and important occasions together. And that was better. The pain of estrangement is horrible.

Two Down, One to Go

By now it had been seven years since I'd seen my dad, and six since he told me to never contact him again. I wondered if he might be ready to change his mind. I sent a Christmas gift and a note saying I would like to see him next time he made the trip out our way. He let me know he was glad to hear from me and would put me back on the circuit the next time he made the road trip to see all four of his kids.

Bryan had not yet met my dad, and, knowing what he did about my past, wasn't too keen on the idea of having him in our home. But ever the gracious host, Bryan agreed to a visit. There isn't much to say about how it went other than, as with my sister, it broke the ice, making a way for future contact.

People have wondered how I could forgive my father and why I would even want to see him again. The *why* is easier to answer than the *how*. Honestly, I did it for me. I did it because I had come to loathe the pain of estrangement. Estrangement wasn't freedom and wholeness; it was bondage. I didn't want to be in bondage anymore. I wanted to be free to make the choice to see him or not. I had received enough healing by now that I wasn't his victim or anybody else's. I could say what I wanted to say and do what I wanted to do. And I had come to realize that I wanted to be able to occasionally see him.

How I got to this place is more involved. I could never have arrived at a place of true forgiveness had I not faced the abuse and received God's healing. That had to happen first, and that took years. When the healing was finished, I discovered God had made good on his promise in Ezekiel 11:19, *"I will give them an undivided heart and put a new spirit in them; I will remove from them their heart of stone and give them a heart of flesh."* My old heart of stone was gone, the one filled with anger, hatred, fear, and bitterness. It was no longer in me, I felt differently now.

Healing had cut the cords of bondage, making me ready to release my dad to my heavenly Father. I did not want that burden anymore.

By forgiving my dad, I wasn't saying that what he did to me was okay (it wasn't) or that it didn't matter (it did) or that it wasn't immensely devastating to my life (it cost me nearly everything). Forgiveness was not condoning his actions or minimizing my pain, it was setting me free. It was for my benefit.

By forgiving, I was saying I valued myself enough to no longer be shackled to his offenses against me, that I was worth being set free.

I now understood that God's hands were trustworthy and capable, much more than mine. Nothing would ever change the facts of what happened to me, but God could change the effects of those facts, of the abuse. And when he did, the abuse no longer impacted my life. God could do more with my dad, reaching him with truth, than I ever could. So I forgave my dad, allowing God to cut me free from the effects of my dad's abuse.

For ten years, Dad and I continued to have visits, sometimes in Colorado, and sometimes at his condo in San Diego, until the situation changed again. During those years he never brought up the abuse. I did write to him, however, asking him to please tell the truth while there was still time, for his sake and the sake of my siblings.

Instead, he spent those years running from one woman to the next, constantly getting on and off cruise ships, never happy and never at peace. One time he said to me, *"I know I'm running, but I don't know what I'm running from."* I tried to bring up Jesus a few times, but his response was always the same, *"My God and I are just fine, thank you."* In other words, *I don't want to hear it.*

My relationship with God was also changing again; he asked me to agree to stop guarding my heart. Oy vey! That was a hard one. I well remember that wrestling match. In the midst, God gave me a visual of a well-defended castle, complete with moat and drawbridge, surrounded by sentries. (Think, Camelot, except this wasn't a fairytale.) I was anxious about God's request, irrationally fearing the loss of my self-protecting ways. In the process of working through this, I realized my ability to protect myself had been an illusion. Not at any point had I truly protected myself from pain or loss. Self-protection was the fairytale. As the truth broke through, I realized my guarded heart was blocking me from giving and receiving love. It was also keeping God out.

So I laid myself out before the Lord, as I had done so many times before. I lowered the drawbridge, dismissed the sentries, and invited God all the way in. It was a beautiful moment I will treasure forever and the beginning of sweet intimacy that has remained ever since.

The trust invitations just kept coming, one right after another. He had taught me a lot in the wilderness; now he wanted me to apply it. For so much of my wilderness experience, he had carried me like a babe in arms. He was now putting me down and teaching me to walk. He was asking me to grow up into spiritual maturity. Trust meant opening my heart again. And that meant risking again. And that meant believing he was enough to care for me in all circumstances.

There was also a shift in the pattern of my days that fall. Home-schooling was winding down. Jenny was taking a couple classes at the local college while finishing up her last few high school subjects with me at home. There wasn't a lot for me to do at this point, so I began looking for something else.

Little did I know that would be the last time my life would include idle time.

A Door Opens Toward Ministry

I set up an interview with the coordinator of volunteers at my church. After listening to my experiences and interests, she mentioned a program called "Renewing and Rebuilding" (R&R). But she quickly discouraged me from getting mixed up with those people, mentioning that strange things went on in their group. She was certain I didn't want to work with such an intense group. I wondered what was so strange about it.

At the end of the interview, she decided that typing the weekly church prayer letter would be the best fit. Not being one to complain, I accepted the task. After several weeks, I knew it was not what I had in mind. Not that I minded typing or working with the people in the Pastoral Care office, but I was looking for something a little meatier. Nothing was wasted, however; God used it as a stepping-stone to get me where he wanted me.

One day Brent, a pastor working in that department, and a very kind and compassionate soul, stepped into the little room where I was typing. He was curious who I was and wanted to get acquainted. *"Wow!"* he said, when I was done. *"That's quite a story. I have someone I'd like you to meet, Cheryl. She runs a class called, Renewing and Rebuilding. I think it would be a good fit for you."*

I laughed (to myself). I had a suspicion "those strange people" were probably my kindreds. Brent arranged for me to visit their class. The visit was delayed several weeks because Bryan and I were headed back to Temuco, Chile, this time with our son, Shane. On this second trip, Bryan had additional building projects planned for our friends, Andy and Tabi.

As we did on all our international trips, we added a couple days to enjoy the surrounding area. The lakes and trees of Chile were reminiscent of Colorado, but the volcanic mountains with their pointed summits and black soil were novel. After a day of hiking, we soaked in the hot springs pool of a beautiful resort called Termas de Puyehue.

By the time we got back to Colorado, it was February, and the "R&R" class was far into their year, having begun in August. Cheryl had me jump right in, leading a small group. I'll never forget watching her teach for the first time, filling this gigantic white board with thoughts and ideas about healing. Being the itty, bitty woman she was, she could barely reach the upper part as she busily scribbled notes over every square inch.

It took me several minutes to take it all in, but I realized her notes were rich with healing concepts. As the weeks passed, my eyes began to open to the possibility of helping people heal through a class setting, an idea that was attractive to me because I'd been teaching classes since I was a teen.

Cheryl had been through an intense healing process of her own, and, like me, had learned the steps of healing with God as her teacher. Her interest in healing led her to enroll in a university program where she was on the road to becoming a therapist.

Being one of the most talented group processors I've known, I learned a lot from Cheryl. I had led hundreds of small groups, myself, but they were either church small groups, Bible studies, or Sunday school classes. This processing was different. She was demonstrating how to help people bring out and work through their healing issues—very different from, *So, what did you write for question number four?* I was soaking it up.

Cheryl was an intuitive person. She didn't have lesson plans. She simply arrived at class with something on her mind that she wanted to share with the class. After we'd been working together for a few months, she said there were Scripture passages she thought would dovetail nicely with the class, but she didn't feel comfortable teaching them. Since she knew I had a background in teaching Scripture, she asked if I would consider doing these lessons. I agreed.

We became close friends, working together that summer in a weekly training she led for those of us assisting with the class. In a matter of months, I had gone from typing a prayer letter to co-teaching a class on healing. When God decides it's time to move, he wastes no time.

I wrote and taught a handful of lessons which Cheryl incorporated into the class in the late summer, when the next R&R class began. Being involved in the next class from start to finish helped me see even more clearly how powerful this classroom process could be, when effective teaching was combined with small group processing. My wheels were turning.

Life and Death

After finishing high school, I gave Jenny her graduation gift, a trip of her choice. She had always felt cheated of the family trip to Washington D.C., seven years earlier, after getting sick and missing some of the sight-seeing. So she asked to go back there. I gave her a tour book and let her plan the itinerary. We had a fantastic week together.

While sitting at the Dulles airport, waiting to catch our flight home, Bryan called to tell me his father had died that morning. Three weeks earlier, Don had contracted streptococcal meningitis and had been in the hospital ever since. Bryan and I had gone to see him, taking turns sitting with him and praying over him. After the first week, Don had turned the corner and was doing well. In fact, the little board outside his room said, *"Going home."*

Apparently, the stress of the infection was too much for his body because he had a heart attack and died within minutes. I struggled to digest what Bryan was telling me. Nevertheless, I was glad I would be home in a few hours, a God-ordained *coincidence.*

We joined Bryan's mother, helping with the funeral arrangements and the family coming in. It was a time for the family to gather together, but that posed a unique challenge because one of our kids was in prison on drug related charges. Bryan called the prison to see if there was some way he could be released with an escort in order to attend the service. The prison agreed to do this if we paid the related expenses.

It was an impactful picture no one would ever forget, seeing our son, wearing an orange jumpsuit, wrists cuffed and ankles shackled, as he shuffled toward the front of the church to say goodbye to his grandpa at the foot of the altar. There wasn't a dry eye, such a visible metaphor of our dependency upon Jesus to release each of us from our captivity.

Bryan's descent into depression wasn't immediate, but within weeks he was nearly paralyzed with grief. It wasn't merely the loss of his father's life. Don had not been someone with whom anyone had a close relationship, including Bryan. But with his father's passing, the door for a real relationship closed forever, a reality that had a more profound impact on him than the death itself.

The month before Don died, during my morning time with God, I had pulled the book of Ruth out of my Bible Reading Box. The box was an approach to Scripture reading I had devised to get me reading the whole Bible, not just my favorite books. It was sort of a lottery system. While reading Ruth, I clearly heard God speak to my heart, *"I want you to be a Ruth to your mother-in-law."*

I wasn't sure what God meant, at the time. With Don's passing, though, God's directive was evident. Wanda had never written a check or paid a bill in her life, having gone from living on a farm directly to married life with a banker. She now needed many things, including help with her finances and legal matters. But mostly, she needed someone to just be there, something that was difficult for her three kids to do with their full-time jobs.

For the next year, I went up each week, helping my mother-in-law make the transition to widowhood while teaching her how to manage her finances. It was my joy to be able to use my financial skills to help someone I loved.

One October day, I headed up to Longmont with some hard news. I told Wanda that Bryan and I were going to be grandparents, bittersweet news when none of your kids are married. It was a horrible situation, involving drugs and drug dealers, and serious safety concerns. Since finding out, I had cried buckets, enduring countless sleepless nights.

Because the father was a drug addict, and his family dangerous, we were supportive of the decision to move toward adoption. I was immensely relieved that abortion was not a consideration and later enraged at the doctor who pushed for it anyway.

We made the decisions together, as a family, Bryan and I attending meetings at the adoption agency. We were given family notebooks to review, supplied by parents who were hoping to adopt. I got teary each time I looked through one of the notebooks, fairly certain they were Holy Spirit tears, so I was not at all surprised when everyone agreed on the same family. After making our choice, we met the couple who would be adopting my grandchild, feeling optimistic about who would be the new parents. They had already adopted another boy, who was two, so our grandson would have a brother. And the greatest news was that this family loved Jesus.

When the big week arrived and labor began, I found myself in the operating room. After many hours of unproductive labor, a Caesarian section had been ordered. Even surgically, I could tell that mother and child did not want to be separated, as I watched the surgeon wrestle the baby out of her womb. When finally out, my grandson was purple and distressed. He had punctured his lung with his first breaths, necessitating he be in NICU. This limited our opportunities to hold him, unfortunately. Cheryl was the one friend I brought to the hospital to see my grandson.

Five days later, we watched our daughter place him in another mother's arms. Everyone in the room was sobbing. I could not hold it together, but I didn't care. I knew it was the right decision, but every cell in my body wanted to grab my grandson and run out of the hospital.

God had continually made his favor and grace known to us. *After* choosing the family, we were told they lived only an hour away and were requesting an open adoption. Highly unusual even for an open adoption, this family wanted us to remain in their son's life, which we did all the way into adulthood, continuing on today. Knowing my grandson was well and being raised in a Christian home brought peace to my heart.

Only weeks later, I found myself holding my grandson for hours, as we began our routine visits every four months. I would be lying, though, if I didn't say our hearts ached every time we drove home.

Chapter Forty-Five

2001

The Promise

As the R&R (Renewing & Rebuilding) class continued, I began having ideas for bringing more Scripture lessons into the program, feeling a fire in my spirit for how powerful this could be. About the time Cheryl and I started talking about this, the church decided to put the R&R class on hold for a year. It didn't have anything to do with us. In their words, the national counseling board was on a witch hunt, shutting down any church program they felt was offering healing without a license to do so. (I wonder if God knows you need to have a license to offer his healing.) Wanting to protect R&R, the church felt it was best to lay low until the pressure was off.

By then, Bryan and I had moved to another church, one closer to our house. So I suggested to Cheryl that we move the class to my church. We both felt it was important to continue the ministry. It was a seamless transition, one obviously led by God.

God had a lot to say to me these days. At the beginning of 2001, God kept taking me back to Second Thessalonians. Two verses kept popping out:

With this in mind, we constantly pray for you, that our God may count you worthy of his calling, and that by his power he may fulfill every good purpose of yours and every act prompted by your faith. We pray this so that the name of our Lord Jesus may be glorified in you, and you in him, according to the grace of our God and the Lord Jesus Christ. (2 Thessalonians 1:11-12)

Speaking through this verse, God made it abundantly clear that he had called me to this healing ministry, still in its infancy. And also that, if I was acting in faith, meaning that I was seeking God's will and asking him to lead me, and then acting, to the best of my ability, upon what was in my heart and mind…okay, here comes the mind-blowing part…that he would fulfill my plans. He promised he would make it happen—every needed resource, every dollar, every door opened—whatever needed to happen, he would do it.

I just couldn't believe it at first, that God would think so much of me to tell me these things too wonderful to imagine. I think that's why I camped out on this scripture month after month. I needed convincing I had heard correctly. Yet, no matter how many times I returned, God reiterated the same powerful message.

Going forward in this promise didn't prevent my knees from trembling at times, but it did calm me whenever I returned to this passage.

Retreats

Besides talking to me in my morning quiet time, God often spoke when I went away for a personal retreat, a practice I started in my thirties. I had recently discovered a place in the mountains called the "Christian Prayer Retreat House." I found their initials, CPR, fitting. God often resuscitated my heart and soul while staying there. The sparsely furnished rooms and silent mealtimes were conducive to spiritual reflection.

During one visit, I wrote a poem, of sorts.

July 24, 2001:

We read a book written by someone who shares personal insights regarding the nature of God and living a successful Christian life…and this is good and even essential.

We listen to a sermon, given by someone who shares from the depth of their relationship with God and vast knowledge of the scriptures studied for years…and this is good, and even essential.

We pray to God, listing the circumstances of our life, of which he is already totally aware, and sharing our needs, which he understands far better than we ever will…and this is good, and even essential.

We read the Scriptures, seeking our own insights into God's character and the path that he has called us to walk upon...and this is good, and even essential.

We join a class or attend a conference in hopes of improving our walk with the Lord or understanding him better...and this is good and even essential.

But there is truly nothing sweeter in this life than being enveloped in God's presence, in being completely overwhelmed with his light and his truth and his joy, tingling with his grace and flooded with his love. Nothing reveals his nature so much as this nor directs my life more effectively...and this is the best and worth dying for.

This is why I love going away with God, I feel the sweetness of his presence all around me and often hear his voice.

Behind the CPR house were walking paths winding through the forest. Along the way were benches where guests could stop and breathe in the mountain beauty while exhaling God's praises. I was sitting on one of the benches when God began speaking to my heart.

July 25, 2001:

I walked to the Meadow Bench today—the furthest from the lodge on the long hike. And I sat and waited to hear the Lord's voice or know his presence. I wasn't sure I would at first. Not because I wasn't sure he could or would show—I knew he was there with me.

But I hadn't heard him last night, as I settled in, read a little and prayed. Nor did I hear him this morning as I focused on praise and confession and read my daily devotional and Scriptures. Nothing happened on my short walk before lunch or my reading afterward. So I didn't know what to expect as I quietly sat on the bench and listened.

I focused on him, quickly dispelling distracting thoughts and images. After many minutes, I noticed something unusual. My spirit was quiet. It was at peace. Then I noticed my whole being was quiet and content. I truly realized I was absent of pain, anxiety, anguish, agony, turmoil, fear, longing, bitterness, and hurt. Not that my life was suddenly void of problems, unresolved issues and hardships. But I was at peace. And my mind, emotions, body, and spirit were congruent. There was no clamoring inside of me and I was content.

And so, I thanked God over and over and over and over for bringing me to a moment of sheer peace. And as I thanked him, joy rose up inside and I literally sensed my spirit soaring free. I declared my newfound sense of freedom repeatedly because it seemed to increase the exhilaration in my spirit.

It has been a very long and hard journey, one that began exactly ten years ago. But it was all worth it because God has healed the past, made me whole, and given me a new life. Today, I am free to serve him unabashedly and wholeheartedly because of his grace and mercy poured so liberally into my life and my being. He is so good. I love him so much. I really, really, look forward to this part of the journey. The FRUIT! Finally!

This was the moment, my moment, when I realized the healing of my past was finished. God would continue to grow my faith, and there would be new wounds to my life, wounds that would need healing, but the work God began in 1991 was now finished. God had given me his blessing to move forward.

This journal entry was incorporated into a lesson I later wrote, a lesson about being a congruent person. What I didn't know at the time was that God was handing me the beginnings of my ministry. My future material just kept arriving, unexpectedly, at every turn. He brought another future lesson that summer. Here is an excerpt from a journal entry I wrote after reading Luke, chapter seven, an excerpt I included, almost verbatim.

August 28, 2001:

A woman with nothing, disrespected by everyone, full of shame. No doubt she grew up a victim. She never had the privilege of a protective, secure, loving home. No one arranged a marriage for her. She had few options and probably turned to prostitution to survive.

And then she encounters the living Christ. She can't read and knows nothing of Scripture. But she does know God is sending a Messiah. She probably can't articulate a biblical truth to save her soul, she never attended Sunday school or a woman's Bible study. But she has met Jesus. And the truth in Jesus penetrates her hardened shell, her bitterness, her anger, her cynicism. She may know nothing of prophecy fulfilled by Jesus—but she knows he is her hope!

His truth penetrates her soul and she is transparent, honest and vulnerable in his presence. And all she can do is weep.

She purchases the most valuable thing she can afford—perfume. She is invisible in the gathering—on the floor—behind Jesus—at his feet. Her tears flow all over his feet, mixed with the beautiful fragrance from the perfume.

Jesus knows exactly what is happening. He SEES her. No one has even seen her. She has been used, taken advantage of, abused, but never SEEN for who she is and what she needs. She asks for nothing. But he knows her true need and he gives it to her—forgiveness—salvation—eternal life! She didn't even know to ask for it, or she felt too unworthy to speak a request.

He saw her as a princess of the Most High King and brought her into his father's kingdom. And then—he doesn't stop there—he affirms her salvation and gives her peace. And at that moment she felt God rain down upon her tortured soul, rivers of mercy and grace. God put out her pain and for the first time in her life, her soul rests and she is at peace. She goes home a changed woman.

The woman who anointed Jesus' feet wasn't the only one changed in that story. God changed me as I read it that day. Somehow, as he let me know how he felt about her, his complete acceptance of her, void of any judgment, just pure love spilt upon her, he conveyed the same message to me. I couldn't wait to share this good news with other women.

Healing Journey is Born

Cheryl and I advertised the class and ten women signed up. We split them between us, each leading one group.

With this move to my church, Cheryl released all the teaching to me, and I began writing weekly lessons. Because the class was changing, we decided to give it a new name, "Hope for Healing." Our first Monday night class will be etched in my mind forever, September 10, 2001, because we woke up to 9-11 the next morning. It was obvious what the subject matter should be for Week Two: Grieving.

Each Tuesday morning, I gathered my Bibles, reference books, and legal pad and went to work, seeking the next lesson God wanted me to teach. As I began writing lessons, Deuteronomy 32:2 became my regular prayer: *Let my teaching fall like rain and my words descend as dew, like showers on new grass, like abundant rain on tender plants.*

For seven months, I wrote weekly lessons until suddenly I knew I had come to the end. It was finished. People often ask me why my class is twenty-nine weeks. All I can say is that that is the number of lessons God gave me.

When we started, I had no idea how it would go. R&R had been an eleven-month program. I knew that seemed overly long, but I didn't know how many weeks Hope for Healing should be. So, every week, I told the class that if they would come back the next Monday, I was confident God would give me another lesson. And he did.

And then there was another class, and then another and another.

Chapter Forty-Six

2002

A Spirit of Wisdom and Revelation

Wanting to get the new year off to a good start, I committed to a day of prayer, one that yielded a bumper crop.

For years, I had been captivated by the author, Oswald Chambers, reading his classic, My Utmost for His Highest, many times. His January 1 devotional hit home:

"We shall all feel very much ashamed if we do not yield to Jesus on the point He has asked us to yield to Him. Paul says—"My determination is to be my utmost for his Highest." To get there is a question of will, not of debate nor of reasoning, but a surrender of will, an absolute and irrevocable surrender on that point. An over-weaning consideration for ourselves is the thing that keeps us from that decision, though we put it that we are considering others."

My journal entry continued: *AMEN! That is the whole of it—surrender of will. I have to put my selfish desires down, put my will to death. I resist and hide behind consideration of others—but it really is self-centeredness, thinly veiled. God have mercy. Forgive me of my wickedness.*

After reading Ephesians, I added this: *"I keep asking that the God of our Lord Jesus Christ, the glorious Father, may give you the Spirit of wisdom and revelation, so that you may know him better. I pray also that the eyes of your heart may be enlightened in order that you may know the hope to which he has called you, the riches of his glorious inheritance in the saints, and his incomparably great power for us who believe." (Ephesians 1:17-19a.) I am overwhelmed with humility and gratitude at this moment. God is so good. I am so undeserving—but he gives me this gift anyway. He is so amazing—so generous. Thank you, God. I receive your gift—the spirit of wisdom and revelation so that I may know YOU better. There is nothing I want more this year.*

This passage became my verse for the year. I truly believe it was God's Spirit of wisdom and revelation that enabled me to write the new lessons for my class. Ephesians 1:17-19 was the passage that launched my writing.

A few months later, another Chambers/Scripture combo hit me hard again.

June 18: *"Be reckless immediately, fling it all out on Him."* My Utmost for His Highest, June 18. *"Oh LORD, God of Israel, there is no God like you in heaven or on earth—you who keep your covenant of love with your servants who continue wholeheartedly in your way." (2 Chronicles 6:14) In my mind today, I heard a voice that I believe was God's. The voice said, "Learn, Cyndy, learn." God, I hear you. I believe you are asking for my whole heart today. I believe you are asking me to follow you with reckless abandon—as I read in My Utmost for His Highest today. Like Peter, you want me to walk out on the waves, keeping my gaze on you—not on the turbulent waters. "My whole heart." I feel fear and anxiety at the thought, but I have promised to obey any request you make of me, so what can I do but grant your request today. After all you have done for me, it really is the least I can do. My whole heart—today it is yours. Father, I transfer authority and control from me to you. I resign and pass you the baton. I yield to you and your greater wisdom, power and authority. I praise you God. I love you!*

Surrender. It happened over and over, and it is still happening today. Every day, I have to surrender again.

Round Two

The first Hope for Healing class was winding down and I was looking forward to its conclusion. I was happy to have been given the opportunity to share my heart for healing issues with these ladies and not particularly thinking about next steps.

However, while this class was still underway, I noted that someone asked me if I could give them materials to share with their sister in another state. *No, I don't think so. It's just a live teaching. Sorry! All I have are some points scribbled on a legal pad.*

I didn't think much more about it until that April, when I began having a strange emotional reaction whenever I drove by a big yellow house, down the hill from where I live. I was familiar with the ministry there, Family Life Services, a transitional housing facility for single mothers and their children. Bryan, having a tender heart for women raising kids alone, had been supporting them for years before we got married.

Each time I drove by, I would tear up, as compassion gripped my heart. This went on for weeks, when I finally asked God, *So what is up with this? Why do I cry whenever I drive by this house?* He shot right back, *"Because I want you to teach the class to these women."* Oh! That had not occurred to me, so I called and made an appointment to meet with the director.

Ron Bennett didn't know me or anything about the Hope for Healing class, nevertheless, he looked it over and then invited me to teach it to the four moms currently residing there. Every Thursday evening, starting in June, Valerie, Mari, Novella, Shirley, and I met in the dining room of the large Victorian house while I taught the twenty-nine lessons again. Kari, a woman from the last R&R class, sat in, as well.

By now, Cheryl's church had decided that the coast was clear to resume her class, so she and I parted ways. She returned to lead Renewing & Rebuilding at her church, and I continued teaching Hope for Healing. We didn't lead together again, but I am forever grateful for all that she taught me.

I have never been a visionary. I am simply a teacher. Give me a white board and a dozen students and I am a happy camper. But God sent visionaries, first Cheryl, then Kari, to walk by my side, so I could get where he wanted me to go, something I was clueless about at this point.

When R&R concluded, a year earlier, Kari had asked if I would be her mentor. I agreed, although I wasn't sure what a mentor was supposed to do. Mostly, I just became a resource for her. The conversations and time together led to a beautiful friendship and partnership with this new class.

Because I had never repeated a teaching, even though I'd written tons of curriculum in my B.H. (Before Healing) years, this was a new experience for me. With the outline of the lessons done, during this second pass through I was able to think more deeply about the concepts while making revisions.

The first time I taught the class, while I was simultaneously writing the lessons, I never knew what was coming next. Now I could see themes connecting the lessons that I hadn't noticed before. Like a third-party observer, I was beginning to see how the curriculum fit together as whole. Getting clues of the impact it could have excited me even more.

Novella

Week after week, I drew closer to my four sweet ladies as I brought the lessons to them, but to one in a much greater way. Novella was an utter disaster when we met, having been homeless with her toddler son, and into many destructive things. She came in each week with a big smile, a joyful spirit, and every excuse in the book why she couldn't do her homework. Before long, she had latched onto me with invitations for connection that I readily accepted.

Novella let me speak truth to her, something of which I took shameless advantage while we ate pancakes together at IHOP. She wanted Jesus and wanted to do the right thing, even though she could never quite extricate herself from bad influences in her life. Nevertheless we prayed many prayers of healing together as she soaked up the lessons.

I still have a letter from Novella.

Dear Cindy: You have made me feel things I thought I'd never feel agin (sic). *Some good and some hurt. And the one's that hurt I'm running from. That's what I know best. I wish I could be with you every day when you hug me. I feel God—love—and trust in you and it's so good and pure and I can't get past my way of thinking I'm not good enough and I will always be just*

Novella. Your class is strong and I tryed (sic) *so hard to be ready to* (sic) *because my soul is an old soul and everything in me wanted to run agin* (sic). *I truly don't want to loss* (sic) *everything, Lucas* (her toddler son). *But I feel it coming and my old ways and friends are all just showing up. Every were* (sic) *I go. Last night I went out and the place was full of evil and evil people. Some came over and was* (sic) *talking to me and just talking to um* (sic) *felt like death was right next to me. I'm having a hard time and I know what to do. I just can't. Thank you for the B-day card. I'll keep it forever. I love you. Novella*

Even after Novella left Family Life Services, we stayed in touch. Later, when her mother went for surgery to remove a cancerous tumor from her face, we sat together at the hospital all day.

Time passed and one day I opened the paper and read an article about a young woman who had been in a terrible accident. My heart stopped when I read Novella's name. She had been car surfing with friends when she fell off the roof and was hit by a car coming up behind them. Her friends left her for dead by the side of the road, fearing arrest if they called the police. But she wasn't dead.

I called hospitals until I found her in an ICU. I was relentless, trying to see Novella, visiting the hospital, calling, leaving the family notes, all to no avail. Because I wasn't family, the hospital wouldn't let me in, and the family wouldn't respond to my requests for permission to see her. I never had a further word about her, except that she was eventually released. I grieve even now, wondering how she is doing.

After our class was over, I didn't see Shirley again, but Mari joined my class two years later. When Valerie, a mother of four teenage girls, finished the class, she touched my heart, saying, *"Thank you. Because of this class, I am a better mother."* My suspicions were confirmed—this class would impact people. I hadn't seen the last of Valerie, not by a long shot. And it also was not the last time I would have my heart broken by the love I felt for the class participants.

Round Three

In August, a group of ladies from church approached me. *We heard about the Hope for Healing class you did last year. We were wondering if you would teach it again.* Well, holy cow, I wasn't even close to finishing the class at Family Life. Teach two classes at the same time? I had never considered such a thing.

Why not? I thought. More people, more healing. And if there was anything in the world I wanted to do, it was to help others find God's healing. Just before starting, a woman named Judi approached me after church one Sunday to say she was signing up for the class. Then she added, *"This had better work. I've tried everything and nothing has helped me. If your class doesn't work, I'm throwing in the towel. I'm giving up."*

Oh wow! No pressure there! I started to panic about what she might do if she didn't get the results she was expecting. But I turned it over to the Lord, by saying, *God I can't fix Judi, but I can teach these lessons. So I'll do my part and let you do yours.* Praise God she did get healing—tons of it!

Something else happened with that third class that I'd never seen before but would now see in every class going forward. I had a student, Susan, return to do it again. Hmmm… I wondered, why would she want to take it again? Susan said nothing had ever brought this much healing to her life, so she thought if she took it again, she might get even more healing. And she did! So much so, she asked me to train her to be a small group leader. She, too, wanted to help more women find healing.

This third class started in September. In January, my class at Family Life finally concluded, and I began a fourth one at my church in March. Kari helped me this time, leading the other small group. This set up a challenging pattern I repeated for four years, starting a new class every Spring and Fall. The requests for the class just kept coming.

And with each new class, I got the same question. *"How can I get these materials? There is nothing like this out there."* It wasn't just from my students; people from other places and even from foreign countries were requesting the materials too! Word travels fast. Still, I had nothing to give anyone.

I also felt no need to solve the problem, mostly because I didn't know how. I had no thoughts, plans, or ideas for doing anything other than continuing to teach my live classes.

Spiritual Lessons

God continued to use Oswald Chambers' devotional to teach me the deeper things of faith. Three of his teachings were particularly transforming.

August 31, 2002: *"The joy of Jesus was the absolute self-surrender and self-sacrifice of Himself to His father.... The full flood of my life is... in the perfect understanding of God, and in the communion with Him that Jesus Himself had.... He wants to get us to the place where we will be His witnesses and proclaim who Jesus is."* My Utmost for His Highest, August 31. *I feel this call upon my life. This is the place where God has me today—I am here. I am tempted to be terrified for I know I am called to teach these "Hope" classes without holding back, to let it rip. I feel so vulnerable in doing so—so open to attack and hurt. I guess this is taking me to a new level of letting God be my protector.*

September 7, 2002: *"Keep at the Source, guard well your belief in Jesus Christ and your relationship to Him, and there will be a steady flow for other lives, no dryness and no deadness."* My Utmost for His Highest, September 7.

This became my guiding belief, embedded into the marrow of my bones. I knew I had to remain attached to Jesus, continually in the Word, seeking his voice, intimately connected, or I would not be able to do what he was asking of me. Time with him was no longer optional.

November 1, 2002: *"There is no such thing as a private life—'a world within the world'–for a man or woman who is brought into fellowship with Jesus Christ's suffering. God breaks up the private life of His saints, and makes it a thoroughfare for the world on the one hand, and for Himself on the other."* My Utmost for His Highest, November 1. *This is so incredibly profound! The timing is amazing! This is exactly the thing I am struggling with and exactly the thing he wants from me. If I choose to deny him this—I am certain his purpose for my life will not be fulfilled. If I die to myself, then all things are possible—his will definitely will be accomplished. He is calling me to be a thoroughfare and I want to be a cul-de-sac. Another level of faith is before me. And, even as I write—even as I struggle—even as I feel grief and loss and sadness at the thought of losing privacy and safety and instead risk attack, criticism, and judgment—even as I struggle, I know I will deny myself because I truly want to deny him nothing. As I have finally begun an intimate relationship with my heavenly father—although certain a vast terrain of intimacy remains unexplored—there is nothing I want more than to know him better and be on HIS road—not mine. His peace will be with me no matter what happens. His protection will guard me against anything outside his will. His power will make it all happen.*

A thoroughfare, that was a frightening idea. *Really, God? You want me to allow just any ol' person to traipse through the middle of my life?* Yep, that's what he was asking. More trust steps. I would have to believe that he was trustworthy and capable of caring for my heart, or I would not be able to do this work he was giving to me.

More than a Class

One day, I decided to drive over to the popular tourist area where I live, Garden of the Gods. With summer over, there wouldn't be as many people, making it less distracting to spend the day in prayer and reflection and enjoy the breathtaking views. It was a pleasant day. My time with God was gentle and quiet, nothing noteworthy until 2:30, just as I was getting ready to leave.

November 22, 2002: *"Though the fig tree does not bud and there are no grapes on the vines, though the olive crop fails and the fields produce no food, though there are no sheep in the pen and no cattle in the stalls, yet I will rejoice in the Lord, I will be joyful in God my Savior. The Sovereign Lord is my strength; he makes my feet like the feet of a deer, he enables me to go on the heights." (Habakkuk 3:17-19) I don't know what it is—but whatever it is and whatever happens—even fruitlessness—barrenness—failure—poverty—I willing go. I am yours. Lord, you know my heart—I have never sought out any big deals for myself—my life. I want only you. I am content—satisfied. The simple and quiet and small is fine by me. You are telling me it will be different. I sense it will be different soon. A healing retreat—God wants me to do a women's retreat for the purpose of healing—in the power of the Holy Spirit—powerful—praying—weeping—release from bondage. The Healing Light. I will be working in the Spirit, not in my head—it will take courage and faith. It will be different from what I've done before, but very powerful. Healing Light Ministries—I keep hearing this in my head.*

It is going to change me—new power in my classes. It's time to unleash the gifts and set them free to bless and minister—the healing gifts. "I am pleased with you." He said this to me. Thank you, God—your goodness overwhelms me. You are so faithful, so generous, too wonderful. Thank you for opening this next door. I knew you would—but I certainly didn't expect it today—so soon. Please prepare me. Pour into me your truth—show me the way. Take me there, Lord—I rely on you—I look forward to your purposes being revealed. I see that you desire to pour out an anointing of your healing blessing upon these women that you have chosen—I see brokenness and weeping—very powerful—Come, Lord Jesus!

As God inaudibly began speaking to my heart, I wrote as quickly as I could, trying to capture his words. *Cyndy, this isn't simply a class, this is a ministry, and the name is His Healing Light Ministries.* Okay, then, I'd better write it down if that was going to be the name. *Ministry? What does he mean by ministry?*

This fit together with what Kari had been saying for some time, that we needed to find a way to get this out to more people. She kept saying that everyone needed to hear this message of healing.

Later, I told Kari what God told me, and she jumped right on it. Her brother, a trademark attorney, helped her get our name registered. We then formed a board, asking Susan and Diane, our other small group leaders, if they wanted to band together with us. Our first board meeting was April 12, 2003, the official start of His Healing Light Ministries.

Chapter Forty-Seven

2003

A River Runs Through It

A few months after our first official board meeting, the ministry received a check in the mail for one hundred dollars from someone Bryan and I had recently met. For many reasons, I thought this was odd. Not only had the sender not taken our class, but she was living in another state. And this on top of the fact that we hadn't asked anyone for money. All the donor said was that God had prompted her to send the check.

I went back to the Lord. *What is this money for? What should I do with it?* This was another day I was glad I was using my Bible Reading Box, the lottery system that circumvented my limited wisdom, relying on God's instead. God took me to Second Kings. When I got to the third chapter, the battle of the three kings against Moab, he answered my question.

July 12, 2003: *"This is what the Lord says: Make this valley full of ditches. For this is what the Lord says: You will see neither wind nor rain, yet this valley will be filled with water, and you, your cattle and your other animals will drink. This is an easy thing in the eyes of the Lord." (2 Kings 3:16-18a) He reminds me today that it is no problem for him to provide for our needs—we just need to have faith and do what he says to do.*

The tri-army alliance had run out of water and were poised to lose the battle against Moab the next day, so they prayed to God, asking for his help. That's when God told them to dig ditches because he was going to supernaturally fill them up with water, and he did just that. The next day, water flowed from the hills of Edom and they won the battle.

Okay, Lord, so what does that have to do with this $100 check? God said he would let me know later what the money was for, but for now, I was to open a checking account and deposit it. He said there would be more money arriving. And there was. In fact, to date, the funds have flowed liberally into our ministry without stopping, without fail. God has met our every need.

We have remained what I call a 'loaves and fishes' ministry, a small ministry with a small budget. Yet God uses our modest ministry to change the world as he impacts individual lives in miraculous ways. And he prompts hearts to give, providing for our needs.

As our new ministry board began meeting, we weren't sure how to get this whole thing launched, so we did the only thing we could think of. We combined our Christmas card lists and mailed a letter inviting them to become the first to receive a quarterly newsletter with updates from our new ministry. (This was back in the ancient days when people still mailed Christmas cards and letters to their family and friends.)

A hundred people responded affirmatively, and we were off and running.

More Journal Entries

August 17, 2003: *I heard God say, "We're going to soar." God was showing me the future of the ministry. I could sense women's hearts were broken everywhere. They had heard God's message of hope and his plan for healing them and they had heard the truth and let God into their wounded places and were being healed. God said thousands of women would hear the truth and be set free.*

His words were so encouraging. A couple weeks later, he asked for more steps of obedience.

September 2, 2003: *"'Let me inherit a double portion of your spirit,' Elisha replied." (2 Kings 2:9b) As I read this, I felt the presence of the Spirit of God. It was fairly strong. I heard his voice in my head, telling me to ask for this. I asked God if this was why he brought me back here for the third time* (to

2 Kings). *I heard, "Yes." I heard the voice again. "Ask for it now." The Lord said I don't ask for enough. There is more available to me. I should ask for more. The presence of the Spirit was strong. I felt fear. It was hard. I tried to question God's choice about this and realized my error and sin. It's not my place to question—only obey. I tried to ask God what would happen as a result of the request, but quickly realized that error, as well. It is faith. I must trust in God—he knows what he's doing—what he is doing is good—he will never leave me for a moment. So, in obedience and belief, I prayed for a double portion of God's Spirit. I prayed it 3 times. Don't ask me why—it seemed like I should. I have no idea what this was all about, but time will tell.*

This was a year of beginnings and big steps of faith. Not only did we have our first board begin meeting, but I also began writing this book. Even though I didn't finish it at the time, I'm grateful I captured as much as I did because I was much closer to my healing years than I am now. Those nearly 70,000 words written then were immensely helpful in piecing the story together today.

October 12, 2003: *I am trying to operate from God's standpoint in his ministry, writing—especially the book. But I do feel lost and discouraged. I feel hugely ambivalent about writing my story and haven't worked on it for about 3 months. I have no intention of writing a book about abuse. It's a book about healing and I want to write about how God did it in my life. Why would anyone want to read it? I really don't know. I'm not a writer—I knew that before I started. I have absolutely no idea who would ever want to publish this book. I'm just trying to be obedient to what God called me to do and that is very hard. I feel lost and insecure.*

I'd been asked to write my story many times and made a pass at getting that accomplished in 2003. But I'd been conflicted from the start. While I accept God's stamp of approval on me as a writer today, I did not accept it then. In fact, I was full of doubt about writing anything, certain I was not qualified.

But that wasn't the main issue that left me drowning in doubt. The content of the book was the hardest obstacle. I didn't want to write about my past and couldn't imagine anyone wanting to read about it. All I could do was grit it out every day, by sheer obedience. When I stopped, I filed it away and forgot about it.

Building a Bible College

Family matters were finally calming down a bit. My nest was now completely empty. The boys were on their own, working in construction and landscaping. Chad met someone special and was engaged. Jenny got married and made her home with her new husband in Montrose. Bree, the oldest, was still working at the Broadmoor Hotel, now as a sommelier (a wine expert) at their five-star restaurant. Our younger Breanna was going back and forth between her mother's house and ours while attending an alternative school. We were hoping this would be the environment she needed to graduate.

Taking our kids along with us on our foreign construction projects had been a joy for Bryan and I, now having had experiences with four of our five kids. Jenny and Shane had both been to Chile. In between their trips, we had done a building project for missionary friends in Spain, taking Chad and Breanna along with us, stopping over in London for a couple days of sightseeing. Then in 2002, Andy and Tabi, our missionary friends in Chile, began talking to us about repurposing an old building into a much-needed Bible college to train pastors. We decided to head back to Temuco and check it out, taking Bree with us, the last of our tribe to join us.

The building was certainly nothing to look at with its rusted front garage door and dirt floor. Other than four exterior walls and a roof, there was nothing useful in its existing state. Undaunted, Bryan took measurements and created a functional design, agreeing to return the next year to do the construction.

While in the area, we popped over to Argentina, having a beautiful adventure through the rugged mountain terrain, enjoying their famous barbeque, and experiencing the chocolate capital of the world (so they say)—San Carlos de Bariloche. We stuffed our bags with as much chocolate as we could carry home.

Because this next project was more than Bryan could handle alone, we gathered a small team, including those who would help him with the construction, and others to help me with the cooking. We went down in February, the height of the Chilean summer. Bryan arrived ahead of the team so he could line up all the building materials and the rest of us flew down the next week. Hard work had never been so much fun. Miriam, the local pastor's wife, taught us how to make empanadas, Chilean style, adding deliciously to the hearty food we made every day. Two weeks later, we handed over the keys to a move-in-ready, Bible college. The pastors were ecstatic, astonished at the miraculous amount of work accomplished in only fourteen days.

Bryan and I stayed on a few more days for a much-needed rest, visiting our favorite hot springs, Termas de Puyehue, before facing the big projects waiting for us at home, or so we thought.

Eight-Month Drought

In the construction world, spring is typically the time when projects begin gearing up. Bryan had several large ones scheduled, owners just waiting for him to get back from Chile. However, world events changed the plans for all of them. When the war broke out in Iraq, fear and anxiety took over, and the owners got cold feet. So the construction projects were put on hold.

Suddenly, we had no income. When I married Bryan and began experiencing the construction trade, I realized we were always one paycheck away from unemployment. Fortunately, trusting God's provision was an area where Bryan and I were in agreement. We honored God, obeying his Word, and he took care of us.

But these new circumstances would put our beliefs to a test that we had not yet experienced. Bryan hadn't had a gap in work since he began construction twenty years earlier. I thought about looking for a job, myself, but felt no peace about going in that direction. God had clearly told me to get started on the writing projects. A full-time job would kill those prospects. We decided the only obedient path was to sit still and trust God to provide.

I did a little calculating, noting our savings and tallying our expenses. Five months. That's how long we could hold out without something changing.

A couple months into the drought, I melted down, freaking out about circling the drain financially.

June 1, 2003: *"He who walks righteously and speaks what is right.... His bread will be supplied, and water will not fail them."* (Isaiah 33:15, 16) *Today is a hard day and the Lord encourages me in these verses. In about 5-6 weeks our money will be gone. Without income at that point, we will be forced to sell off our assets to pay bills and live. Yesterday I had a horrible bout with fear and struggle. It wasn't fear of being poor or of change but of the pain of losing my home and physical life here. It is hard. I don't know what he has planned. I know he will provide but I don't know what that will look like.*

June 3, 2003: *"Then he went up to the temple of the Lord and spread it out before the Lord. And Hezekiah prayed to the Lord."* (Isaiah 37:14b-15) *God responded to Hezekiah's prayer—our prayers matter to God—they are effective. Today is better. After 2 hours of prayer with Bryan on Sunday, I am again back in his peace. He told me—"I am going to provide for you guys." We are in his will and on his path. The journey is not easy, but fruit will come from it. He very well may take us down to nothing before something shifts—that's okay.*

June came and went, so did July and August. And that's when I learned something: God does funny math. Circumstances that don't look like they add up to me, do add up when God is in charge. He prevents expenses from occurring, while sending money from sources you didn't expect. How it all worked, I'm still not sure. But in September, God turned the faucet back on, and not with one job, but with five! God kept his promise and provided for us every day through our eight-month ordeal.

If You Build It...

Before I went to Chile, I was having lunch with friends, Carol and Susan, when they said to me, *"You need to get this written down. This teaching God has given you needs to be put in a book."* Not being a writer, nor having had any such aspirations, I tried to shrug off their comments. But like honey on my fingers, I couldn't shake their words. God was pressing in, too. I remember one sarcastic prayer, in particular: *So what is this, God, like in the movie Field of Dreams, "If you build it, they will come"? So if I start writing, the words will just suddenly come to me? Is that it? Is that what you're saying? Because I have no idea how to write or what to say. Do you expect me to put my fingers on a keyboard and just start typing?* Well, it turned out that was exactly what God wanted. He had something he wanted said, and he wanted me to be his stenographer.

Right after I returned from Chile, I began writing. I'm not sure why, but when I started, I began two manuscripts at the same time. The first was my story and the second was Road Map to Healing. With requests continuing for my materials, I thought that perhaps putting my teaching in a nonfiction book might assuage the need. Both remained unfinished, however, for years. Road Map wouldn't be published for another six, and it would be eighteen years until I finished my story.

Bryan may have had no work, but the opposite was true for me. Besides writing and launching a new board of directors, I had two classes underway. Added to that was the first healing retreat, following up on God's directive the previous fall. I had a strong sense the retreat would bring accelerated and profound healing to my graduating students. I was not disappointed.

It was a busy spring! The crocus continued to bud, peeking out from under a spring snow as signs of life were emerging.

The 3 P's Lesson

Now that our ministry had a new name, His Healing Light Ministries, we decided that the class should, as well. Starting that fall, it became the Healing Light Class. I was still writing new lessons for this fifth class, as the curriculum continued to develop.

October 26, 2003: *God's word was true. "Up! Leave my people, you and the Israelites! Go, worship the Lord as you have requested." (Exodus 12:31) God's power released the people from bondage. "…they had been driven out…" (Exodus 12:39) "The LORD had made the Egyptians favorably disposed toward the people, and they gave them what they asked for; so they plundered the Egyptians." (Exodus 12:36) It was like a war only no one was fighting except God and Pharaoh. And to the victor went the spoils—the*

Israelites not only gained their freedom but took the wealth of Egypt with them. They had so much to learn. "It would have been better for us to serve the Egyptians than to die in the desert." (Exodus 14:12) God had just delivered them from bondage and they still had no faith. "And when the Israelites saw the great power the LORD displayed against the Egyptians, the people feared the LORD and put their trust in him and in Moses his servant." (Exodus 14:31)

The ideas for the lessons I wrote for my Bible studies (and, later, for the devotionals in my books), were birthed in my morning times with God. He would take me to a passage and begin showing me another teaching for the class. I was reading in Exodus when God gave me the beginnings of a lesson that would be called, "The Three Ps: Power, Protection, and Provision." This wasn't in the original class, but after this journal entry was written, I added it.

Only Trust Me

A few days later, I went up to the Christian Prayer Retreat House for a personal retreat, wanting one last visit before they sold the property. While there, I heard God speak. This doesn't happen to me often, but God occasionally dictates words and letters to me. I hear it in my head and just start writing as fast as I can, not wanting to lose a single word. When it happens, I am not thinking about the words, only hearing them. Today, he had a lot to say.

October 31, 2003: *Dear Cyndy, you are my precious child and I am pleased with you. Please stop beating yourself up.* (A woman in my class who was criticizing me) *is my child and my responsibility—not yours. I have never asked you to be a perfect teacher. I am so pleased that you are willing to risk and do what I ask. That is enough. Please continue on. I am with you. We are doing this together.*

Even Moses didn't always say or do what I wanted him to. I accept you. I lead you. You are mine and I love you. Please continue on. I will lead you. I hear the agony of your heart. I haven't forgotten you in your writing. I know it is so hard for you. You are doing what I asked. I promise—I promise—I will take this project to completion. Please do not fret. This is my work not yours. It will be an absolutely beautiful work when it is completed. I can hardly wait for the day.

Pace yourself, Cyndy. You do not need to rush. I appreciate your diligence. You are obedient to my word and I never ask for one thing more than that. You are my precious child. I know what you need even before you ask. I am going to provide everything that is needed. Only trust me. I am so pleased with your seeking heart. You are putting me first and going behind me. I see this.

I am going to bless you immeasurably. You can't imagine what I am going to do in you and through you. I know you don't want to know and that's okay because you aren't ready. I will do this—not you. Only trust me. You will be uncomfortable. Only trust me. My inspiration will be upon your words—spoken and written. Only trust me. This is just the beginning. I am showing you the truth.

Yes, it is my voice revealing to you the truth about your undisputed memory in the auditorium. Your parents did not protect you or care for you. Your father did nothing. Your mother did nothing to help you. Can you see the truth in this? It was no different when you were little. They did nothing to help you then, either.

It broke my heart to see you, my precious little girl so victimized, and all the people I placed in your life to protect you failed. This is truth. I know you struggle with what really took place in those early years. Only trust me. Cyndy—would I have taken you through years of healing and recovery for nothing? Cyndy—the memories are true. Don't look at your family for truth—no truth resides there. Don't look at the fact that you stand alone. Trust me—I am truth. Your life is not a sham. There will come a day when all the darkness will be brought into the light and you will see clearly as will your family. Only trust me.

Cyndy, you must go forward boldly with your testimony. I am with you. It is truth. It must be shared. Don't be afraid. Rest in me, Cyndy. Rest. You must rest, Cyndy. You hear my voice—truly you do. Remember our day together by the river on Independence Pass, August 1991, I told you that you were pretty good at hearing my voice when I shouted, but you needed to learn to hear me when I whisper. Well, you are hearing my whispers. You recognize my voice now. Please trust this. We are dancing together. You are my beloved daughter. Thank you for the dance. It gives me joy. I love dancing with you. We will dance for all eternity. You are going to love the music. Oh, the joy to come.

I was doubting my memories again. So many times, I had come to the place where I was sure I would never doubt them again, but then I did. As I got a little distance from my healing years, and all that I went through began to fade, doubt returned. God, however, was ready for it. He met me in a convincing way.

The sexual abuse at school, on my fifteenth birthday, was never a repressed memory, nor were there any alters holding that information, at least not that I was aware of. Like the red medicine given to me for stomach aches, I was always conscious of this, which is why God said, "undisputed memory." Referring to that abuse helped me see how my parents didn't respond any differently, any better, than they did to everything else I remembered. If my parents had responded as normal parents, they would have lost their minds when they found out what the boys did to me in the auditorium. There would have been significant follow up and repercussions for those involved. My parents would have sought help and support for me. Instead, nothing was done.

The comfort, love, and affirmation I felt from the Lord's letter that day exceeded words. He so faithfully came and shored me up, once again, when I was floundering. He was there when I needed him.

The spiritual journey never stops, thankfully. As I continued with him, he taught me more and more.

December 18, 2003: *"The idea is not that we do work for God, but that we are so loyal to Him that He can do His work through us—'I reckon on you for extreme service, with no complaining on your part and no explanation on Mine.' God wants to use us as He used His own Son."* My Utmost for His Highest, December 18.

Chambers never stopped shocking me with his view of the Christian life. Being raised in the age of 'it's all about me' left me with the impression that God was here to serve me, not the other way around. *Extreme service… no complaining…* no one in my world taught me those things. The only message I heard was, *Take care of yourself first.* I soon realized that wasn't in the Bible.

Like climbing stairs, certain spiritual steps must be traversed before later ones. I had to first learn my inherent value and begin treating myself with love and respect, before I would be ready to take the next steps, to follow Christ's mandate to take up my cross daily.

December 28, 2003: *"For with much wisdom comes much sorrow; the more knowledge, the more grief." (Ecclesiastes 1:18) This impacts me in a profound way this morning. Solomon seems to have stumbled onto a truth that explains a reality in my life. So much healing and growth has occurred for me—God has generously revealed more and more of who he is and the mysteries of his word—I see more and hear better—yet I am filled with grief and sorrow frequently. I now realize I had a wrong expectation—that somehow as I grew in the Lord these things would diminish—but they don't. My heart is heavy this week to the point of breaking. This way is far superior—Solomon saw this too. "I saw that wisdom is better than folly, just as light is better than darkness." (Ecclesiastes 2:13) So wisdom and light are better—but sorrow and grief increase.*

This was a paradigm changer for me. My assumption had been that my heart would become lighter and happier as my wisdom grew. But that wasn't happening. My heart was growing heavier. As I better understood the reality of how people were living, what they were doing to themselves, how they were rejecting God, and what was at stake for them, I was overwhelmed with sorrow. This knowledge made me sad.

Then I realized this is what God feels every day. I began to see God better. My respect for him grew, realizing his love and faithfulness remains, no matter the choices we make. The cliché has merit: Ignorance is bliss. Knowledge and wisdom, however, is not.

Chapter Forty-Eight

2004
January-August

I Could Have Chosen Anyone

The classes were growing larger and would no longer fit in the small church building where I attended, so I asked a nearby church if they would allow us to hold our fifth class on their campus. The new pastor's response blessed me: *This clearly fits with our church's goal to be an outreach to our community. Please come aboard; we have plenty of unused space and would like you to use it.*

The ministry kept expanding and with it came opportunities for me to grow in character and spiritual wisdom.

February 14: *"Now he gives you the gift of humiliation which brings the softness of heart that will always listen to God now." My Utmost for His Highest, February 14.*

With healing, my spiritual vision improved. Humility never would have seemed like a gift to me before, but now it did. It was a treasured gift. Without it, I would never be able to know God's voice and follow it.

One battle I fought was being willing to put myself out there and take risks with people. Besides being an introvert, I still had scars from previous attempts to share myself. Each time the challenge presented itself, I had to stand on truth and step forward, pushing through my reluctance.

February 26: *"Beware of the pious fraud in you which says—I have no misgivings about Jesus, only about myself."* My Utmost for His Highest,

February 26. *This is a profound thought to me for I say this very thing. But he's right, to have doubts about myself is to doubt his ability to do all things.*

Chambers helped me see that to doubt myself was to doubt God, if, indeed, I believed God was the one working through me. It was a fine line to walk. On the one hand, I had to be confident God would accomplish his plans for me, but at the same time, never forgetting for a moment it was his accomplishment, not mine.

I learned a lesson when God spoke a profound and direct word to me, one I never forgot. *"I could have chosen anyone."* These words have been a gift of incalculable value. I have heard many words of flattery and appreciation. Materials, classes, and events have succeeded. Lives have been changed. I could have easily said, *Look at what an amazing person I am and all that I've done.* Had I succumbed to such prideful thoughts, my career would have ended a long time ago.

God made sure I understood, from the beginning, where all of this was coming from. I wasn't the author and none of it was my idea. The words and principles are his and his alone. God did not *need* me to be able to accomplish this ministry. *He could have chosen anyone.* Yet he did choose me. I'll never know why I was given the great privilege of being the one, I only know that God put me in this role, something for which I will be eternally grateful.

If there is wisdom in my words, God put it there. If a class or event is changing someone's life, it is because of God's power. If a large project succeeds, God gets the credit. I am merely the conduit, God's pass-through vessel to bring redemption and restoration to anyone who will come and receive it.

Why was this clarifying moment critical? Because the moment I begin to take credit is the moment I would no longer be able to hear God's voice. And if I couldn't hear him, it would be like a faucet turning off; nothing more would flow in and through me. Game over.

Not even the ability to write or teach is mine to claim. God made me and God put those things in me when he did. I'm simply exercising those gifts. There is only one thing for which I can take credit: I was willing to be used by him. I allowed myself to be a thoroughfare for God's pleasure.

March 25: *"This is what the Sovereign LORD says: I myself will take a shoot from the very top of a cedar and plant it; I will break off a tender sprig from its topmost shoots and plant it on a high and lofty mountain. On the mountain heights of Israel I will plant it; it will produce branches and bear fruit and become a splendid cedar. Birds of every kind will nest in it; they will find shelter in the shade of its branches. All the trees of the forest will know that I the LORD bring down the tall tree and make the low tree grow tall. I dry up the green tree and make the dry tree flourish. 'I the LORD have spoken, and I will do it.'" (Ezekiel 17:22-24) I still remember the day when I was impressed that the Lord was speaking these words to me. It was 15 years ago, 6-4-89. I was camping by the Little Cimarron River with my family. We were using somebody's cabin, but I don't remember whose. I was sitting in a lawn chair by the river reading my Bible when I read this passage. I remember wishing it was warmer. The clouds kept covering the sun making the air feel chilly. When my eyes fell on this passage in particular, I felt very disrupted and personally impacted. I was quite unsettled. I remember it vividly. And even though the passage is a prophecy about Christ primarily—I had no doubt God was saying that it applied to my life. I was like the little dry tree that God would make flourish. It has greatly encouraged me over the years—particularly during the hard years of recovery. My favorite part is about the birds. I think the fulfillment is beginning to be realized now in my ministry.*

This was one of my own 'Joseph moments,' God telling me the end of the story while I was still at the beginning. My original experience with the Ezekiel passage occurred in 1989, three years before my healing journey began, thirteen years before I taught the first class on healing, and twenty years before I had an inkling about its impact. I marked the date in my Bible, and never forgot the humbling moment.

That was about the same time I began praying for something, recording it inside the cover of my Bible: *Lord, help me become a woman who is pure, wise, and obedient.* Praying for wisdom has been a life-long request.

May 8: *"But the LORD said to Moses and Aaron, 'Because you did not trust in me enough to honor me as holy in the sight of the Israelites, you will not bring this community into the land I give them.'" (Numbers 20:12) "...honor me as holy..." Moses represented the truth of God to the people—he was their example, their shepherd—his problem came from a lack of trust—a tall order for Moses—and for me, too. I am humbled by this story and feeling reverent fear—Oh Lord, God, I implore you to guide me with a firm and steady hand. I feel the weight of responsibility to reveal you accurately and truthfully to all the women you entrust to me. In no way do I ever want to misrepresent you or ever diminish your holiness one iota. Please cement your truth—eternal truth—into every fiber of my being. Equip me perfectly to be an instrument of your truth.*

As a Bible teacher, representing God's Word was a responsibility I never took lightly. I am keenly aware of the fact I am a clay pot, set apart for God's holy purposes, forever dependent upon him to guide me in the truth.

Again, I cannot say enough about the Bible Reading Box (my lottery system for reading Scripture), and what it has done for me spiritually. On a day in May, I pulled out Habakkuk. Who just automatically chooses to read that book? But that's what I pulled out this particular morning, and I'm glad I did, because God began talking to me after I read it.

May 27: *"For the revelation awaits an appointed time; it speaks of the end and will not prove false. Though it lingers, wait for it; it will certainly come and will not delay." (Habakkuk 2:3)* God's voice to me: *"Cyndy, I have things well in hand. Stay the course. Do not be anxious. Only trust me. We are headed in a direction I have chosen, and we are on course. Only trust me. Keep writing. It is not time for the appointed revelation. Things are not yet in place. Enjoy this time. I am with you. I love you and will sustain you. Only trust me."*

I noticed that God often said things more than once when he was telling me something. Whenever he repeated phrases, I tried to pay close attention.

June 19: *"If I am devoted to the cause of humanity only, I will soon be exhausted and come to the place where my love will falter; but if I love Jesus Christ personally and passionately, I can serve humanity though men treat me as a doormat."* My Utmost for His Highest, June 19.

The concept of being a doormat causes most people to recoil. *I will NEVER be someone's doormat. I'm worth more than that.* If Jesus took that stance, there would be no salvation for us. It is only because he went to the cross, allowing us to trample his rights and dignity, that we are able to have life today. Jesus was the ultimate doormat. Yet his identity was never compromised, nor his worth. He was God's precious Son the day before he died, and the day after he rose.

I teach this concept in Healing Journey and get pushback every time. I feel sad about this. As long as we insist on our rights, we'll never be fully available to serve Christ. Believe me, I get the level of personal struggle this brings. Humility is a battle fought daily.

I took another personal retreat on June 24 and recorded this: *I hear Him speaking to me. "Will you speak for me?" I heard this several times. I answered, "Yes! I will speak for you."*

Transitions with Kids

Breanna, our youngest, was now nineteen and graduating from high school after five difficult years. It is still an emotional memory for me, when I recall her walking across the stage to receive her diploma, something we weren't sure would ever happen. That July, we threw a huge backyard party, so proud of her for sticking it out and finishing school. We were all there together, including Bryan's ex-wife, Sue, and her family, celebrating together—a rare and beautiful moment.

That spring, Breanna artfully designed a Mother's Day card and wrote a letter inside.

Happy Mother's Day, Cyndy. Good and bad I've spent almost half my life with you and I seldomly come to the full realization of how lucky our family is to have you in it and I'm sorry. It's not that in the back of my head that I don't know it, it's just so hard sometimes to show it and I should and I will. So with one last thought and one last breath, if I had no time left, I'd say you're one of the reasons why I live, live to give, give to be, for you to be so pleased with me! Your opinion is honestly worth the world to me. With more love than you'll ever know, your littlest daughter, Breanna.

It took seven years for she and I to arrive at this place, but it was worth the wait. Her words were *honestly worth the world to me,* too, her card a treasure beyond words.

The older kids were pairing up during this season. Bree began dating someone while working at the Broadmoor Hotel, a young law student named Kris. Shane moved in with his girlfriend, Beverly, and later they married. A year after Jenny and Steve were married, they found out they were pregnant. And Chad and his fiancé were pregnant when they got engaged and now planning their wedding. The two grandbabies were due three weeks apart.

Our Lives Forever Changed

Within months of Chad and Jen's engagement, their relationship went south, eventually breaking down. So much so, when it came time for the baby to be born, Jen had Chad barred from the hospital. He wasn't allowed in to see his child born.

Despite the busy season of life, on Wednesday, August 18, Bryan did what he had been doing since he was fourteen and headed up to the Flattop Wilderness area in Colorado to go backpacking with his family and friends.

Before he arrived at the turnoff, the place where he would lose cell phone reception, Breanna called Bryan. She recently had had a falling out with a girlfriend and Bryan had encouraged her to extend forgiveness. Breanna had taken her dad's advice and wanted him to know. At the end of the short conversation, she signed off, saying, *"I love you, Dad."*

The next day, August 19, Sydney Claire was born, Bryan's first grandchild. But it was a few days before the news trickled back to us. No one from our family was present for the birth.

Bryan and his friends returned on Saturday, spending the rest of the weekend with us before heading home. Bushed from the long day, packing out and driving home, they had a leisurely soak in the hot tub after dinner, and turned in for the night.

Jenny and Steve were also visiting because Saturday was her birthday, August 21, and we had a tradition of going to the state fair and attending a country music concert there to mark the occasion. Her baby was due in three weeks. Sunday afternoon, Jenny, Steve, and I headed to the fair with Bree and Kris, stopping for dinner before entering the fairgrounds. Bryan stayed home with our other houseguests.

As our salads were being served, Bryan called. *Breanna is dead.* I could find no way to comprehend his words. *What? What are you talking about?* He then added, *"I just found her body."* In the crowded restaurant dining room, Bree screamed just before bursting into tears. Everyone else was paralyzed. After a hasty exit amid dozens of staring guests, we made our way back to Colorado Springs.

I'm not sure what I would have done if Kris hadn't been there to drive. I couldn't understand what was going on. I didn't know what was happening. Nothing made sense. We couldn't get back fast enough; the forty-five-minute drive seemed like hours.

As we arrived at the park where Bryan said to meet him, I noticed that many family and friends were already there, along with the police and a coroner. I searched for Bryan, spotting him a short distance away, up a small embankment. As I walked in his direction, he quickly intercepted me and said, *"Don't go up there."*

All Bryan knew was that Breanna had bolted from her mother's house, just blocks from the park, about ten o'clock the night before, angry after a fight with her mom. Breanna had been drinking. Sue heard a gunshot and immediately began searching the neighborhood, trying to find her. Having no luck, Sue called Shane and several others to help look for Breanna. They combed the area, including the park, before finally giving up.

Bryan didn't get a call about any of this until late Sunday afternoon, after Breanna failed to show up for work. He met Sue at the police department. After many questions, trying to catch up with the story, Bryan headed over to the park, alone. He walked straight to her body.

He will tell you, this was God's gift to him in the worst moment of his life, to allow him to be the one who found her and be alone with her for thirty minutes before everyone else began arriving. To me, it is something only a father can understand. I would not have wanted to be there alone, but he was grateful. God hid Breanna's body until Bryan could get there, almost twenty-four hours later, allowing him a moment with his daughter, a moment to see her and say good-bye with no other person intruding.

Somehow, we made it back to the house. Our pastor followed, staying with us until the middle of the night. As I stood in the kitchen, all of a sudden, my body began shuddering and I collapsed. I sat on the sofa, dazed, not knowing what I was supposed to do with myself. Everything in Bryan and I began shutting down; all we could do was breathe, but just barely.

When we were finally alone, I remained on the sofa, eventually getting some moments of fitful sleep. While I was sleeping, I saw Breanna. She was alive and beautiful, larger than life, in the living room with me. I could see her long, golden brown hair draped over a flowing gown. The dream was a gift I will treasure until I see her again, a special touch from God, letting me know Breanna was now with him. Even though we were not fine, and wouldn't be for a very long time, she was fine. Later, Bryan had a similar experience, seeing his daughter in heaven, riding a horse.

Monday morning, the friends who had been backpacking with Bryan left. Jenny stayed. Calls had to be made to let remaining family members know. Arrangements needed to be made for the funeral details. Soon many friends and family were coming into town, several staying with us.

The next days were a blur, just going through the motions. The viewing was Wednesday evening. Sue chose a pine coffin with a writable surface. I wasn't sure what I thought about that until I took my turn to write my good-bye: *Breanna, you will always be my sparkle.* It was a moving and healing moment for all who wrote their good-byes.

Thursday was the graveside funeral for family and close friends, followed by a memorial service at our church. Hundreds turned out, so many teenagers, it was standing room only. I spoke at the service, followed by our pastor. We wanted the salvation invitation extended as part of the service. Six people, that we know of, accepted the Lord that day, including our future son-in-law, Kris. Life from death.

I couldn't believe it had only been a month since we were all in our backyard, celebrating Breanna's graduation. How did we get here just weeks later?

Whatever supernatural grace I had to walk through those first days quickly expired after Thursday. But we still had a couple dozen out-of-town friends and family, gathering for meals in our home every day. The pressure inside me continued to build, until I thought I was going to implode. I needed to be alone. I needed everyone out of my house. Slowly, the numbers dropped as each one caught their flights home. On Monday, the last few were still there, intending to leave after lunch. I left for a few hours, deliberately missing the goodbyes. I had nothing left.

The outpouring of love and gifts and meals those first days and weeks was overwhelming. So many gestures of kindness and support that will never be forgotten.

Afterward, Bryan and I settled into an endless nightmare, years of suffering and questions, much worse for him being her father, but horrible for me, nonetheless. It appears we will never know why Breanna took her life. We later learned about a few of her struggles, but nothing that would explain why she did what she did.

"Here my prayer, O LORD, listen to my cry for help, be not deaf to my weeping." (Psalm 39:12a)

For a very long time, it seemed as though joy would never return.

Chapter Forty-Nine

2004
August-December

Lessons from Suicide

It was years before I had a good perspective on the suffering I experienced when Breanna died. The first weeks of shock soon wore off, then the real pain began setting in. As horrible as it was those first days, that was a picnic compared to how I felt after the funeral was over, after the people had left, after the casseroles were gone. Functioning was beyond consideration; clear thinking, out of the question. I couldn't handle grocery stores or people or pointless chit chat or loud noise or commotion.

August 28: *How can I write? I'm not ready to write the words. I can hardly move today. I love her so much. I miss my beautiful sparkle. My mind is mush—my body is weak—my heart is throbbing. I can't really write yet.*

September 14: *"Then the dragon was enraged at the woman and went off to wage war against the rest of her offspring—those who obey God's commandments and hold to the testimony of Jesus." (Revelation 12:17) Satan destroyed Breanna—she was in his camp and she knew it. She wrote about it. I hate what he did. I hate that he came to her in her weakness and her suffering and he stepped on her. She gave up—her burden too heavy to bear—not in truth, but in the lies Satan spoke to her. God can handle all of our burdens. But I also believe Satan made such an assault upon her as a way to get to me. He is making war against HHLM* (His Healing Light Ministries) *and me. God told us "expect opposition." I must engage my weapons and fight, but I feel weak—I don't want to do anything—God help me.*

While not the most important aspect to me while my grief was so fresh, nevertheless, it was a good reminder as to who was behind Breanna's choice.

On November 16, I went away for a retreat and wrote a letter to God: *Lord, God, I seek you tonight. Please come to me. Oh, my Shepherd and Overseer of my soul. You are the one I desire—you are the one I want. Nothing satisfies the yearnings of my soul like you do. I seek you, Father. You promise to be found by all who seek you. Come to me. Oh, Lord, reveal yourself to me. I long to know you more.*

Me: *Father God, where are we going?*

God: *Ezekiel 17:22-24*

Me: *Oh, Lord, I know—but I don't know. You gave this to me 15 years ago. At the time it made no sense at all. And now, like Elijah, I see some clouds on the far horizon. Lord, it has been such a bittersweet journey, but I am grateful for all you have done and for how you have restored my heart and set me free from my bondage. I truly desire for your purposes for my life to be fully accomplished.*

The picture looks so large and overwhelming. It seems like it will take forever to finish even the portion of the project I can see and have started. The book needs so much work. I wonder if the lessons need an overhaul—which of course, means a revision of the curriculum—all to be completed before we can get a publisher and that before videotaping. And, then what about other materials, a men's curriculum, a 2nd level class—and who knows what? I know you not only have it all figured out—you see it completed! You even have the needed resources waiting in the wings. By your breath you bring life into existence. You speak a word and all creation leaps to attention and obeys. This is truly not a matter of concern for you. Calm my anxious heart—Oh Lord. Please set my course. Am I on track or floundering? I don't even know. There is so much to be accomplished. What do you want me to do?

God: *Follow me. Trust me. I will show you the way. We will work more. There is more to come. A season to write will come. It won't take as long as you think. I'm sorry you have lost Breanna. I am sorry for your unrealized dreams. I want you to finish healing from this, Cyndy. It will all come together sooner that you think. Don't make the mistake of framing this in your limited power. Remember, I can do immeasurably more that you can imagine.*

Me: *Lord, it is so weird. I can't wait for it to be fully realized and at the same time I dread what's coming—and I don't really know what's coming! What a mixed-up mess I am. I am anxious to start writing again—but I don't want to work on the book. God—please straighten me out!*

God: *You'll know when you are ready to start writing. I will make it clear. Just like before, you will not be able to contain it. It will pop out of you. And it will be your joy. It will be a very fruitful season. We will be collaborating. Don't worry.*

Me: *Lord, why did Breanna have to leave us? She was so young. Why is she gone? Why does Bryan have to suffer so much? Chad, Bree—all of us? Our lives have been forever altered. And, so many lives—been forever altered. She affected so many people. I just feel sad, Lord. We had a complicated relationship and I hadn't processed through all the pain and problems before she was gone. I have regrets and remorse. Lord, I cared about her and constantly walked a fine line between encouraging her toward righteous living—healthy choices—wisdom—successful paths—and yet trying to respect her need to make her own way—her own choices—discover for herself what would work and not work in her life. Lord God, I could have done more. I let her down. And now she is gone. And, Lord, we all feel our family is incomplete. Come, Lord, heal my empty, hurting heart.*

God: *I will.*

Me: *I miss her.*

God: *I know.*

Me: *Such a sad waste, Lord.*

God: *I feel the same way.*

The Hard Work of Grieving

With the third and fourth His Healing Light classes, it became apparent the workbook I had been using for the homework portion of the class was not fitting well with my lessons. The Hope for Healing workbook was one Cheryl had written to go with the "Renewing & Rebuilding" class. As I continued to revise my lessons, I got further and further away from the original content of her class.

It became clear that I needed to write a new curriculum to accompany the lessons, a project I had begun earlier in 2004. But that writing came to a halt when Breanna died.

It was months before I could write again. Leveled by grief, I was operating at a place of mere survival. That area in my brain that spawned creative thoughts was shut down. I wouldn't be able to write until I dealt with the upheaval occurring in every particle of my being. And one aspect of my grieving was guilt at not being a better stepmother, recalling sharp and regretful words spoken to her, my moments of impatience and frustration.

When suicide is the cause, the grief process has similarities to losing loved ones under other circumstances, for instance because of a disease or car accident. You feel unbearable pain and sadness, as with any loss. But suicide brings other things like confusion and guilt.

For so long, Bryan and I were scrambling to try to understand why she would take her life. *What did we miss? What did we do wrong? How did we let her down?* But there were never enough clues to answer our questions.

Trailing right behind guilt and confusion was anger toward God for not stopping her, for allowing it to happen. I was speaking to a group, one time, about Breanna's death, and someone asked me why God didn't intervene and save her. I was so stunned that someone would ask me that question, my mind went blank. I had no idea how to respond.

In time, though, God showed me the truth. He *was* there. He was there fighting for Breanna in the days leading up to the event and in the moment of crisis. He *was* there, hand extended, eyes pleading for her trust, but she chose not to look his way and receive his help. Breanna was responsible for her decision to reject God and his help. That was a choice she made, but God did fight for her.

Once I had worked through my anger toward God, realizing he was not responsible for her decision, then I was angry with Breanna. *How could she be so selfish as to inflict this pain on all of us? How could she leave us?*

This wasn't the first time I had lost family members to suicide. Years earlier, my dad's brother and mother had taken their lives, too. But because my relationships with them were fairly distant, the impact was minimal. With Breanna's death, the impact lasted years.

Nevertheless, by applying what I'd learned during my healing years, my heart began to mend. I had to reject the lies and believe the truth. *This was a choice Breanna made, and no one else is responsible, not me, or God, or anyone else.*

It was when the first year without her was finally over, after we'd endured all the firsts (first birthday, Thanksgiving, Christmas, etc.), that I discovered the second year was even worse. That was the point when the finality of her passing knocked me over. *She's never coming back. This is my reality for the rest of my life.*

Throughout the process, I had to actively and intentionally grieve her loss, talking to friends (many times), writing about it, visiting her grave site, wrangling with God at every stage. And then, after many years, it was necessary that I forgive Breanna herself in order to find peace again. My healing process wasn't something that could be worked through quickly. It was a process of many steps, taken over time.

The grieving work eventually paid off. Joy returned and I could think about Breanna, revisiting memories of her with a smile, instead of searing hurt. I could leave the door open to her bedroom without choking on pain when I walked by. I could mention her in conversation without steeling myself against tears.

Somewhere along the way, as I walked through this horrible event—this deadly explosion that intruded and sent destruction into my life—I realized something profound. God did not change. The safety net of his faithfulness and comfort had held me.

I never imagined having to test God's character to this depth, but when I did, I experienced his sufficiency at a whole new level. I can now say with confidence, there is nothing I can go through that will cause me to doubt his love and sufficiency. God is enough for anything and everything, even losing a child to suicide. I can't handle these things, but he can. His arms are strong enough to carry me through anything. His love holds.

Chapter Fifty

2005

Long Enough on this Mountain

January 1: *"The LORD God said to us at Horeb, 'You have stayed long enough at this mountain.'" (Deuteronomy 1:6)* (Then I heard God say this to me.) *"It is time to move into the new territory—the Promised Land. You have done what you are doing long enough. It is nearly ready. Continue to fine tune the lessons through this current class and then stop. I will guide you. We will make the final revisions together. This is the year it will start. I will give you everything you need. Go my way, Cyndy. I will help you. Never be afraid. It will be different this year. Trust me to lead you. I am pleased, Cyndy. You are my daughter and a joy to work with. Your heart is right. It is time to go in. We will finish the project together. I will give you the remaining words."*

This became a pivotal word for me. Because I'm not a visionary, nor a girl who seeks out the big deals, I was quite content teaching my live class twice a year. Nevertheless, I heard what he was saying. *Long, enough, Cyndy! We're moving forward.* But, as always, he did it in a gentle and loving way, encouraging me at the same time.

The next day, Chambers' words reinforced what I already felt. *"You do not know what you are going to do; the only thing you know is that God knows what He is doing."* My Utmost for His Highest, January 2. There was certainly no argument from me on that one. I was clueless.

God kept reiterating his word to me. January 4: *"For the Lord your God is bringing you into a good land…" (Deuteronomy 8:7a) Our wilderness time is coming to an end. God says it is time to go into the Promised Land.*

On January 20, I was reading the first few chapters of 2 Chronicles, noting the magnificent temple Solomon made, when God began explaining to me: *He oversaw the work—he didn't actually make anything. He had the vision I gave him and followed through. He carried out my directions. This you will do, as well. Cyndy, don't ever forget this is my work—not yours. Never place too much importance in your own abilities. Just obey what I tell you to do and stop worrying about the rest. I will give you wisdom and honor and riches, as well. I promised you this at the beginning of your recovery. Your financial drought is over. I have been testing you and Bryan—sifting you for my work. We are ready to go forward now. It will be a different year. I love you, Cyndy—never forget that. I will never abandon you even for a moment. I love you, dear one. Go forward now in peace and confidence. Enjoy this work. It will be an exciting time.*

I need to say, this was an unusual time in my life. It was a season when God spoke to me clearly and often. While he still speaks to me today, I don't experience this nearly with the same frequency.

The reference to the drought lifting went back to 2003, when we returned from building the Bible college in Chile and Bryan had no work. Even with no income for months, God provided for us. When Bryan's work returned, God did, indeed, bring financial recovery. In fact, 2005 was Bryan's highest earning year.

Over and over, God's message was the same: we're going into the new land now; get ready.

June 14: *"See, I have placed before you an open door that no one can shut." (Revelation 3:8b) He did it again. I felt the Lord all over me. He told me these words today. He is encouraging me that I am in his will—where he wants me to be—heading where he wants me to head and he is doing it all. He has chosen this; therefore, no one can interfere.*

And all along, he kept promising me that nothing would stop his will from being done. He would do it and I could count on that. His promise to me in Revelation 3:8 is one I have clung to ever since. Almighty God was behind this work.

Temptation and Baptism

Going into the Promised Land came with a cost. I had to give up things I loved doing. This was one of the strongest temptations, testing my faith. I would have these urges to teach Sunday school again, or regular Bible studies, or financial management classes. I still cared about these other parts of the Christian life. I loved teaching, and that included teaching on many different topics, for a variety of ages. (Even today, I still get urges to volunteer to teach four-year-olds about Jesus!)

I also wanted to serve on the Elder board and to direct the women's ministry. The temptations never let up. But I knew these temptations were not coming from God. He told me in no uncertain terms to stay the course—his course! It was hard giving up these other things, even knowing God's judgment was right. I could never do what he wanted me to do if I took on other ministries.

As it was, I was constantly giving my board of directors heart failure just doing the ministry projects God did give me to do! They once put me on a 'diet,' holding me to no more than two projects a year. I laughed. *Have you asked God about that?* The books, Bible studies, retreats, events, and filming just kept coming. But I'm getting ahead of my own story.

Along with all this, something had been bothering me for a few years. My memory of the satanic baptism disturbed me, even though I was a preschooler and forced to do it, and even though I was sprinkled in a Christian baptism a couple years after that. Still… it didn't set well with me. So I arranged for a proper dunking with my pastor and several friends as witnesses, a baptism of my choice with my will fully engaged. I just felt the need to cleanse that event from my history.

Bryan did the honors in our hot tub in the backyard, followed by a potluck celebration. Afterward, I not only felt victorious, I felt vindicated. God would have the last word in my life in all things.

Sydney

It was fun having two grandbabies, the same age, ones I could play with on a regular basis, Jenny's son, Joey, and Chad's daughter, Sydney. A couple months after Sydney was born, Chad and Jen made up and began making wedding plans again. Bryan and I were closely involved. With her own father not in her life, Jen even asked Bryan to go with her to pick out a wedding dress.

One Sunday, Jen and I spent the afternoon together, talking about colors and flowers, when just days later, she called the wedding off. We were confused and heartbroken. *What about Sydney? What would this mean for us, as grandparents?* After being a regular part of Sydney's life for six months, suddenly we were not allowed to see her again. It was an abrupt and complete end.

Grandchildren brought the greatest joy and the greatest sorrow to my life. Sydney would not be the only grandchild I lost.

Cameras and Teaching

That fall, my ministry board sensed God was leading us in the direction of filming the class. The idea wasn't a new one. For years, people had been asking me to film the lessons so women in other locations could take the class, but I didn't know how to make that happen.

Filming was a problem for me for many reasons, not the least being the fact that I knew nothing about it. The biggest obstacle turned out not to be my ignorance—it was my past. It is funny how God has a way of bringing to the forefront things that still need healing. As soon as we started talking about the project, I could feel fierce resistance rising up in me. Having been used in child pornography, something that involved cameras, I could not imagine teaching while being filmed. The notion was unthinkable.

Choosing the least likely person is God's trademark, but he kept his word, providing what I needed. In this case, it was a person. Deb Leach joined my class in the fall of 2004, having a background in videography. Only weeks into the class, she asked, *"Have you ever thought about videotaping your lessons?"*

She already knew my story, so after I told her my dilemma, she proposed an idea. Before launching the official project, she offered to plant her camera in front of me every week while I taught the lessons, helping me get comfortable with it. The idea worked. These small steps, combined with some healing prayer over those old memories, cleared the way for filming.

Kyle'ea

Deb wasn't the only interesting person God brought to the class. In the fall of 2005, a woman in her late thirties also joined. Kyle'ea was not like any student I'd had before, but like myself in many respects. She was a delight and a consternation, all at the same time. Never had a woman wiggled her way so deeply into my heart while at the same time vexing me at every turn.

22: Kyle'ea

We were early in the class year, when it came time to share our stories with each other. When I began telling my story, Kyle'ea bolted from the room, ending up in the hospital with anxiety. I found out she was pregnant, about five months along.

I didn't know what else was going on with her, but I sensed her fragility. Even when she returned, she wasn't able to share her story. Nevertheless, I knew she needed to be there. Speaking as few words as possible, one day she whispered that she was a multiple. Knowing I had been multiple gave her a sense of safety, enough that she continued coming.

Kyle'ea struggled with the class every week, finding victory if she could just show up and sit through it. It was unthinkable she might share her thoughts, or process through something in her life. In November, she went into labor, three months too early. Ryland Kyle Aslan was born, 16 ½ ounces and 10 ½ inches. Her son was alive, but in the NICU, struggling for survival, just like his mom. He would be there for six months.

I later learned Ryland was the result of a gang rape, which explained why Kyle'ea could never tell me who the father was. She didn't know.

For the next four years, she signed up for the class every fall, making progress each time. As I began to piece her story together, I learned she had been ritually abused in a Satanic cult throughout her life.

My five years with Kyle'ea were filled with equal amounts of laughter and crises. The suicide threats and attempts were ongoing. Even so, she learned who Jesus was and became his child, soaking up Scripture, learning the process that would heal her. I helped to build a team of people around her who would support her through her multi-year process.

In one of her many notes to me, with a bright purple marker, she wrote, "*Thank you for not giving up on me and our connection. Thank you for your gentle pushes (I can say this afterwards—ha ha) as I tend to be a bit stubborn especially during difficult times. Thank you ALWAYS for your* honesty. As you are aware, trusting others is a huge issue for me but your *honesty helps build the foundation of trust between us. Thank you for loving me even when I push you away during my fight/flight moments. This may be something helpful to work on reducing, do you think? Ha, ha. I thank God that He used the pain that you experienced to help women like me. You may not have a degree in counseling but your life experiences allow you to identify with others and allow others like myself to know that I am not alone; and that there is healing through this type of unspeakable pain. I love you, Kyle'ea*

Kyle'ea was terrified her family members would find out she was talking about her life. So it was quite a dance we did together, helping her go forward, while navigating her alters and family situation.

And it wasn't just emotional crises; it was physical, too. It was hard to keep track of all the things wrong with her body: stage four breast cancer and kidney failure, heart problems, and lung disease. I knew she would not live a long time; I just didn't know which disease would bring the end.

Publishing

With filming on the horizon and the Healing Journey Student Manual taking shape, we decided to look for a publisher. I also wanted to get my book, Road Map to Healing, published. I had an agent who represented me for a time. A couple of publishing houses were interested, but they felt the scope of the project was too large. They could get my nonfiction book into print but couldn't handle the filming or curriculum.

Communication with publishers was another stepping-stone God used to direct me. One of the acquisition editors encouraged me to self-publish, something I hadn't considered. *"Because you have a platform, an established ministry, you should consider handling this yourself,"* she said.

I could see her point, but, honestly, I had hoped someone would hold my hand through the process. *What did I know about getting these materials published?* I had no idea what to do so I went on another retreat, seeking God's voice.

December 3: *Thank you, Lord, for taking me back to Nehemiah. You know the deep searching of my heart right now for direction on the publishing. Two roads stand before me. Neither may be the right road—but they definitely aren't both right. But today you are reminding me of your unmatchable power to accomplish even the most daunting tasks using the most unlikely vessels. If perfume makers, merchants and goldsmiths can tackle a giant building project* (Nehemiah 3)*—so you can get this curriculum published, written by a housewife. You have put it in my heart to do this project and you will see it to conclusion. Just like Nehemiah—my job is to remain in constant prayer and uninterrupted faith. I know you are fighting for us. I choose to keep my eyes on you all the way. Thank you, Lord.*

December 5: *"They were all trying to frighten us, thinking, 'Their hands will get too weak for the work, and it will not be completed.' But I prayed, 'Now strengthen my hands.'" (Nehemiah 6:9) Lord, I implore you to pour into me strength, wisdom, discernment and every needed resource to see this project to completion. Lord, have mercy on those who are suffering alone and without hope or help. Lord, your Word heals and brings freedom and now you have created a class, a book, and a curriculum as a ready vehicle for rescuing wounded women. Please do not delay in taking us through to the finish line. Many thought this an unlikely if not impossible project for publication. How unlikely a choice was Nehemiah? A slave hundreds of miles from the job site. Why would God choose him? Why would God choose me? "I could have chosen anyone!" Thank you, God, for those words last Spring. It constantly keeps me grounded and properly focused. Yes, amazing things are happening in the lives of women through these lessons that are delivered from my lips. But that is as far as I can go taking any credit. I obediently show up and do my part. And then the door is open for God's amazing love to transform lives. "So the wall was completed..." (Nehemiah 6:15a) And so will the publishing be completed.*

Nehemiah and I were buddies. Few Bible characters helped me more than Nehemiah did. His circumstances made him the unlikeliest candidate for this important and daunting task. Yet I knew that if God could rebuild the Jerusalem wall using him, he could complete the production of Healing Journey using me.

Chapter Fifty-One

2006

Filming Comes to Fruition

Deciding I needed to bring myself up to speed on publishing options, I attended a writer's conference. I also met with author friends who encouraged me to self-publish, informing me on how much the traditional publishing world was changing. Their advice confirmed what I was sensing. Now that I knew I would publish this 'in house,' I set that aside to focus on filming, the more pressing part of the project. Deb Leach agreed to be our videographer.

Our focus that spring was on filming. Because I was still teaching live classes September through April, the filming needed to be completed in the summer, which was only a few months away. I finally knew what the money was for, the money people kept randomly donating. By now, we had about five thousand dollars saved, not terribly impressive when the filming budget came in at seventy thousand dollars. *God, where are we going to get all that money?* One thing was for sure, I wasn't doing bake sales.

When it came to fundraising, God put me on a short leash. He spoke a clear word to me while reading George Mueller's diary, the man who trusted God to put food on the table for thousands of orphans in the mid-eighteen hundreds simply by praying and asking God to meet their needs. I knew what God wanted me to do: make the needs known but go no further. No slick campaigns or fundraising dinners allowed, just tell folks what we needed.

This would be another test of my faith in God's provision. In fact, this project would test my faith in every conceivable direction.

April 16: *"Moses said to the LORD, 'O, Lord, I have never been eloquent, neither in the past nor since you have spoken to your servant. I am slow of speech and tongue.'" (Exodus 4:10) Moses is struggling with the very thing I am. How can I speak well enough?*

God and I talked about this passage a lot. Even though I didn't stutter like Moses, I was plenty insecure about my capabilities to teach well enough for filming. *Why does God always choose the most unlikely candidate?* This does seem to be a theme with him. I had no filming experience, no teaching credentials, and no letters behind my name proving I was qualified. It didn't help that certain people regularly reminded me of that. This was a huge step toward believing God was enough to do this through me.

April 20: *"Have we been slandering God by daring to worry?"* My Utmost for His Highest, April 20. *Lord, I feel deep remorse and sadness because I have been worrying. Will the money come in time? Will we find a location? Will I be able to deliver the lessons well enough? Lord God, I repent of my sin. I have slandered you, my precious Lord—the only one who has never let me down. I am worrying that you won't come through. Forgive me, Lord. I know the truth. No man or event is capable of blocking you from accomplishing what you purpose to do. If there is anything in this project that is not of you, it should be sifted out. Lord God, your will be done. Lord, I have nothing to offer this picture except what you put in me. But with you, I can do all things. This is your ministry, your healing truth, and it is your project. None of it is mine. I am here to serve you.*

Our preparation window narrowed to six weeks and I still didn't have a location. I was busy buying the wardrobe, lining up someone to do the hair and makeup, recruiting an audience for each session, and getting the set designed. At the eleventh hour, a friend with a large home agreed to let us use her living room. Phew! I had all but one base covered, but it was a doozy. I still hadn't converted my notes into filming scripts.

May 13: *"The LORD is my shepherd, I shall lack nothing." (Psalm 23:1) In my most honest place with you, I am terrified of the prospect of both preparing the lessons for filming and delivering them.*

Until now, I had taught from an outline. I wasn't willing to take a chance, though, on what might come out of my mouth, if I chose to wing it while the cameras were rolling. The responsibility was too great. I wanted to get it right, but also make every word count, packing as much truth as possible into the lessons. Every lesson needed to be written out.

May 16: *"I sought the LORD and he answered me; he delivered me from all my fears." (Psalm 34:4) Lord, this is pretty relevant in my life now. I can hardly imagine—in fact I can't imagine—being ready and able to deliver these lessons for videotaping, 2 a week for 4 months. Lord—you told me to stand back and be amazed and already I am amazed. What you have already 'pumped' into HHLM* (His Healing Light Ministries) *financially is incredible. People have been so generous, and you are amazing. How you pulled together all the elements for the practice production blew me away last week. But this little detail of me preparing and delivering the lessons on schedule is causing great anxiety. Please deliver me from my fears.*

The week before we started filming, I went away on a retreat, hoping to get some of the lesson scripts ready. The evening before I left, Kyle'ea's son died. We were so disappointed; he'd fought so hard. I was honored to sit with her in the hospital as she held her son for the last time. Walking through Ryland's death together, deepened our relationship even more.

May 23: *Lord, I have troubling thoughts and feel distraught. The enemy is on the war path to cause me great suffering. Holding tiny Ryland in my arms last night—dead—a dead, precious baby—watching Kyle'ea say goodbye to her infant son—whom she never even got to bring home 1 day—I can hardly stand it—it broke my heart.*

May 24: *Lord, I am needy today. I am fearful and overwhelmed. I am tired of people putting their straws in my cup. There is nothing in my cup—it is empty—drained to the dregs. Please fill my cup.*

May 28: *"Though you have made me see troubles, many and bitter, you will restore my life again; from the depths of the earth you will again bring me up. You will increase my honor and comfort me once again." (Psalm 71:20-21) Lord, you blow me away. You knew I would need your promises today and you took me back to the promise that sustained me for 5 years during the depth of my recovery. You have been fulfilling this all along—but I also know that Tuesday will be an even greater fulfillment. Thank you, Lord for your sovereign power to heal and restore. You are my comfort and rock today.*

I managed to get four filming scripts written on my retreat. It was a start, but I still had twenty-four to do. The day before our first filming shoot, I had a meltdown. *God, there is no way I can do this! I don't know what I'm doing! For the next four months, I have two days of filming each week, plus writing the lessons and practicing them. This is the craziest thing I've ever done. I can't do it!*

After I was done ranting to God, I called Faith. She talked me down off the emotional ledge and my panic receded, slightly. Although success seemed ludicrous, I showed up to the set the next day.

May 30: *"My flesh and my heart may fail, but God is the strength of my heart and my portion forever." (Psalm 73:26) Lord God, I look to you today for strength to deliver this 1st lesson to the camera. Lord, I am so far out of my realm of experience here. I am completely dependent upon you. I am nervous, Lord. It is hard to even write. Please come and fill me with every needed thing. I love you, Lord, and pray that everything that happens this morning will be to your glory.*

I did a terrible job on the filming of the first one. No, really; I'm not being modest. Deb was kind enough to not tell me until much later. She waited until the end before letting me know we needed to re-film the first lesson.

Wedding Bells

June 3: *"Open wide your mouth and I will fill it." (Psalm 81:10b) Lord, I come to you this morning a mess. My circuits are fried. I am vulnerable and on the very edge of sanity. The tank dried up months ago, yet people are still trying to suck me even drier. I need you, Lord. You are the Spring of Living Water and I need a BIG drink this weekend. My mouth is open.*

We had only filmed two lessons, and I was wiped out. I spent my first Sunday, sitting in my backyard for hours, doing absolutely nothing except resting and trying to find some kind of emotional equilibrium.

June 16: *Lord, the attacks this week have been so fierce—particularly Kyle'ea's suicide attempt. I praise you that you intervened. You preserved her life and had mercy on me, sparing me from another devastating wound.*

As always, life didn't stop just because there was a big ministry project happening. Kyle'ea had one of her closest calls that week, with a well thought out suicide plan. When I suspected something was up, I called the police and went to the hospital with her. She was physically fine but choosing to live each day was an ongoing battle for her.

June 20: *Lord, you alone know the incredible stress and anxiety within me these past 4 months. It has about swamped my boat. I haven't had such anxiety for many years—since my recovery. But, Lord, you have sustained me. Here I am now—four days from my precious daughter's wedding—the joy of my life—one of the happiest moments and greatest privileges of my life to see her walk down the aisle. Lord God—I ask of you this one very important request—that these four days would be filled with your peace and joy.*

Life wasn't all difficult, not by any means. Bree and Kris had gotten engaged and were planning their wedding. So I built into the filming schedule a couple weeks off to enjoy and be part of the festivities, including hosting the rehearsal dinner at our house.

Back in April, before the project started, Bree and I had a fabulous mother-daughter trip to Manhattan, staying in a friend's loft apartment. Never seriously thinking we might find and afford a wedding dress in the Garment District, we still thought it would be fun to look. What a fun surprise, when we stopped in a bridal gown outlet and found the perfect dress thirty minutes later. My journal entry that week said, *"Four wonderful, magical days in Manhattan with Bree."*

The wedding was beautiful, including a delightfully fun evening with music and dancing. It says a lot for the healing that had occurred in our family that Bree asked Bryan to walk her down the aisle, and a testament to how far their relationship had come. With his own daughter now gone, it would be his only opportunity to give a daughter away, something that meant the world to him.

Back to Work

In terms of work, it was the hardest summer of my life, putting in around a hundred hours a week. I was so tired, starting my days before dawn, often staring at my notes for an hour before I could make enough sense of them to start practicing.

July 8: *It is hard—very few understand—I look like a lunatic the way I live. I value different things—few understand—most judge. I want to serve God—I want others to be set free by knowing the truth. Amusement is pointless to me—it leads nowhere. But seeing the light of God come on in a woman's heart—that is worth all the sacrifice and striving.*

"I will give you every place where you set your foot…" (Joshua 1:3a) I sense God is telling me, we (HHLM) are now crossing the Jordan River. God is presently doing an amazing miracle as he accomplishes this taping project. It is the event/passage that will take us into the new land.

"Keep the message going that, God is alive. Keep the message going, spread it far and wide. God is alive. God is alive. God is alive today." I haven't sung this song in more than 30 years. Lord, why do you bring it to my mind today?

God: *I want you to keep telling women the truth that I am alive in their lives today. Just like with Hagar—I see their misery and I have come to release them from their misery. I am the God Who Sees. I see them. They have not been forgotten. Tell them how much I care."*

Me: *Lord, I will, I promise. It is not a struggle for me to promise this to you because my heart desires it as much as yours.*

God: *You are going to go to some new places. I have prepared the steps and have waited a long time for this to come. It is almost ready.*

Me: *Lord, it will be my joy to do this for you. Lord, did you bring this song back for another reason?*

God: *Yes, you will go all over the earth. There will be people from every color and belief* (who) *hear you speak. This is a global ministry.*

Me: *Is there anything else? I cherish your words.*

God: *Watch out. Watch out for the devil. He seeks to destroy you.*

Me: *Lord, I know that. But that is too hard for me. I must ask you to watch over me and fight for me. I don't want to work the way Nehemiah did—with his weapon in 1 hand and tool in the other. Lord, please fight for me. Please battle your enemy on my behalf. My suffering has already been vast. Please spare me further harm at the hand of Satan.*

God: *I will. I honor your request. You are my daughter and I will protect you as your loving Father.*

God always met me in my need and encouraged me.

August 23: *"If you have raced with men on foot and they have worn you out, how can you compete with horses?" (Jeremiah 12:5a) Lord, this verse pulled me through many years of healing. I did not want to be worn out by men on foot. I wanted to run with the horses, and now I am. It is amazing. You have restored me. You have put in me your strength. I am running with the horses.*

My long-standing dream to run with the horses was being fulfilled.

September 30: I recorded another quote in my journal: *"You have been shaped by your experiences in life, most which were beyond your control. God allowed them for his purpose of molding you.... It is* (painful experiences) *that God uses the most to prepare you for ministry. In fact, your greatest ministry will most likely come out of your greatest hurt." Why would God choose someone to teach these recorded lessons who was abused via camera and is terrified of being filmed? Few will ever know the miracle God provided,* (and) *the power* (he used) *to create this video project.*

I recorded a helpful quote in my journal: *Mastered by Christ, you can handle anything.* I needed to remember that. No one was more aware of the extraordinary accomplishment God had pulled off that summer than me. He provided every dollar of the seventy thousand needed entirely through donations!

With the filming finished, it was time to begin the hard work of editing the footage and testing the videos in our fall classes, a process that took a year. It was a mammoth undertaking, with over twenty-four hours of teaching.

Eighty women had taken turns sitting in our audience over the summer, exposing a whole new group to our ministry. As a result, we had more than seventy new women join our classes in the fall. So many that I was scrambling to find small group leaders for all of them. It was a far cry from the classes of ten we were running just a few years earlier.

During this time, I was busy making the final changes to the curriculum. We changed the name of the class one last time to Healing Journey, a step that left some of our early people forever confused. One dear friend still refers to it as the "Healing Light Journey Class."

I began looking to the future and how we would launch the materials. Putting the class in the hands of strangers had me concerned.

November 9: *"Don't be afraid; just believe…" (Luke 8:50b) Lord, I realize this morning that I am afraid. I am afraid for the women who will take this class in the future in our satellite classes that they won't be led with wisdom and integrity and women will be harmed. The small group process scares me. Lord, please protect us—protect every woman in the class through the entire future of this class and ministry. I pray for an anointing of wisdom upon every small group leader, both in my classes and in every class to come.*

I realized it didn't do me any good to worry about it. All I could do was put it in God's hands and let him protect the integrity of the class and each person who took it.

November 16: *"If you are rightly devoted to the Lord Jesus, you have reached the sublime height where no one ever thinks of noticing you, all that is noticed is that the power of God comes through you all the time."* My Utmost for His Highest, November 16.

This has been my constant prayer, whether speaking in a prison, teaching a Bible lesson, or leading a healing event, I want participants to see Jesus, not me. Looking at me will do them no good. Looking at Jesus changes everything.

Mom Multiple

It was a fitting end to 2006, such an intense year, to take our family down to Puerto Vallarta for a week just before Christmas. This fulfilled a longing Bryan and I had had since beginning our annual trek after our own wedding. All four kids were going, along with Bryan's sister and our grandson, Joey.

We included our mothers, knowing it was difficult for them to travel alone anymore. But our plans changed the first weekend of December.

My mom was trying to scale down her life, and so had purchased a smaller condo in 2005. Since then, she had been sorting and passing things on to kids and grandkids. But she needed help for some of the sorting, particularly the garage, which not only had no room for a car, a person couldn't even walk through it. My brother and two of his adult kids joined Bryan and I for a weekend of sorting and heavy lifting, or so we thought.

When we all arrived in town, mom sat us down and read the list of what she wanted done. *Oh, good, a plan of attack.* My optimism was soon squashed when I discovered all she wanted us to do was move a few items and get her Christmas decorations down, about thirty minutes of work for one person. We were not happy.

It was my first clue at what would become a repeated pattern of resistance with Mom. She often used this ruse to get people to visit her. Rather than just inviting someone to come see her, she would make up a story about needing help, but then not allow them to do anything when they arrived. It was fine that she wanted some company, but five adults just cleared a weekend to help her move. And she did need help, lots of it, if she was ever going to move into the new place.

Saturday morning, we decided to make a go at sorting some things anyway. I was working inside the house, trying to go through the kitchen and closets, throwing away old food and decades old make-up and toiletries. It was hard to see how my mother was living; I was realizing she had become a hoarder.

My brother and Bryan took on the garage. Having rented a U-Haul for the supposed move, they began loading the contents into the truck, planning to take it to the local Goodwill. This was the stuff Mom hadn't seen or used in ten years, if not fifty, like faded plastic flowers from the sixties and broken appliances.

Mom became agitated, watching her things being loaded into the truck. She then started screaming at Steve. He tried to calm her down, pulling the things back off the truck she wanted to keep (which was everything). Finally, she wound herself up to deliver her best swing at Steve's face. Having missed her target, she fell over from her own momentum onto the concrete floor, giving herself a bloody nose.

Mom rushed into the house, screaming, *"Steve hit me!"* I couldn't believe how quickly she bent the truth. After plugging her nose with a tissue, she sat down. I tried to talk to her, but she didn't seem to hear anything I said. I returned to my work in the kitchen while keeping an eye on her.

Minutes later, I looked over to see her sitting on the floor in her living room, playing with her dolls. Her affect was that of a very young girl. Mom had completely dissociated from what had just happened in the garage, switching to a different personality. (Dolls had been her safe and happy place her entire life, propelling her to become a collector. She easily owned a hundred or more dolls.)

When the stress of the move had become too much, Mom dissociated from the present moment and returned to an inner world where she felt in control again.

I'd known my dad had Dissociative Identity Disorder for years. And I now saw the evidence my mom was DID, too. I wasn't terribly surprised she was multiple, she was also a trauma survivor, but I found it overwhelming to see her switch right in front of me, and not in a subtle way.

My mother's behavior that weekend left me emotionally traumatized. Witnessing the depth of her deranged thinking, the manipulation and lies, her rage, and the hoarding was too much. No one wants to see their own mother acting like a maniac. It took me months to even begin to get over it.

Later, Mom not only stuck to her story, telling everyone that Steve hit her and gave her a bloody nose, she added to it, saying she got a concussion, which is why she wasn't well enough to go to Mexico with us.

It was probably just as well she didn't go. The remaining thirteen of us went ahead without her, enjoying a tremendously fun week at the resort.

Chapter Fifty-Two

2007

New Seasons

The new year brought a new season. Bree and Kris moved to Sacramento while he finished his last couple years of law school. And this meant my girls were both living away from me for the first time. I reacted with the same grief as I had when Jenny moved back to Montrose, four years earlier, journaling about my sadness for many weeks.

It's not that I wasn't glad Bree and Kris were starting their new life together, but I was having a hard time making my heart feel happy about it. So, as quickly as I could break away, I flew out for a visit.

Being back in Sacramento was interesting, seeing again where I'd spent my grade school years. We visited the neighborhoods where I had lived while I reminisced about my childhood. When the trip was over, I felt a lot better. Being back in Sacramento without experiencing a setback or feeling uncomfortable was another victorious moment, affirming my healing.

The filming of Healing Journey had been finished for six months, but we were far from finished with all the production details. After I recovered from the insanity of the previous summer, I turned my sights toward getting the curriculum produced and on the shelf to sell, something that would take a full year.

In a way, this part of the project was harder than the filming. There were many tedious hours checking footage, making corrections, and adding power points. Plus, we still had a thousand details to figure out, each one brand new for me.

March 1: (I wrote this after reading about building the tabernacle in Exodus chapters 23-26.) *Lord, we are trying to produce the class materials, where women will come in and commune with you. We believe this has also come from you. We will lack nothing. You will fulfill these acts prompted by our faith. Lord, I see your ways—you were so specific—planning every detail* (of the tabernacle) - *size, quantity, materials, design, function—you chose only quality materials. It wasn't just functional—it was beautiful. Lord, please pour into the team the wisdom—the detail—the design—the people and the finances. Please flow your knowledge and vision and power through me to accomplish this work. Holy God, I praise you and thank you. I worship you and honor you for you are the one true God.*

Whatever phase of the project I was working on, God gave me what I needed.

Sometimes, God would give me a strong spiritual sense in my prayer time, and I would know it was him talking to me, but wouldn't know what it was about, at least for a time. This is what happened on May 19 while I was reading Luke, chapter one.

May 19: *I have no idea what this means, but I felt the presence of the Lord—quite strongly—while reading this passage. Something spiritual is going on, but I don't know what.*

As I continued my reading in Luke that month, these thoughts came to me while I was reading chapters fourteen to sixteen.

May 29:

1. *Humble yourself—put yourself last.*
2. *Make sure nothing has a place before God.*
3. *Willingly give up everything God asks you to give up.*
4. *It is the delight of God's heart to see one life changed.*
5. *He cares about every lost life and rejoices when they are found.*
6. *Be devoted to nothing and put no one above God.*
7. *Avoid the traps of the world and pursue only God.*
8. *Current comfort has no eternal value.*

These were continual themes in my spiritual journey, reinforced countless times until they became guiding principles.

Pilot Classes

I wanted to test the curriculum with a small number of classes before we made it available to everyone. So I recruited five churches and trained pilot leaders to be our guinea pigs.

My great fear was that someone leading Healing Journey would not treat their students in a safe manner, but instead, do harm. I knew all too well how vulnerable people were when they were working on their healing issues. With their hearts exposed, a misguided leader could do some damage.

I also knew that I had no control over this. Once I released it, that was it. Anyone could do whatever they wanted. For this reason, I applied ample prayer all the way through.

The one thing I could do, and did do, was empty everything out from my personal tool bag, everything I'd learned in leading a dozen classes, spelling out the best leadership and processing techniques possible. In addition to offering Boot Camps for training, I wrote a guide for leaders and facilitators, and filmed a training DVD, giving leaders a way to watch what effective group processing looks like.

Nine women gathered with me for that first Boot Camp, staying in the beautiful home of one of my board members, who happened to be on vacation at the time. It was here that I began pouring out everything God had shown me over the years about how to effectively lead processing groups.

As a group leader, it wasn't enough for me to simply sit with ladies for an hour and listen to them talk about their pain and problems. I wanted them to heal. I wanted them to experience the same powerful redemption from God that I had experienced. I wanted their lives to change.

I had intuitively learned how that happens in groups, but now I had to figure out how to explain that to other leaders. The nine women graciously hung out with me for four days while I made my first attempt. We had a great time, being pampered by friends who brought in our meals, sleeping in luxury, laughing and crying together while God changed each of us from the inside out. They were ready to go.

With fear and trepidation, I launched the pilot classes. Two months later, holding my breath in anticipation, I visited each class.

I discovered my worry had been for naught. God had done a miracle, creating a curriculum that could safely be transferred into the hands of new leaders and churches. What a relief! Tears of joy expressed my delight. It was happening, exceeding any expectations I'd harbored.

Always remembering God's words, that he could have chosen anyone, I was grateful he had chosen me. What a privilege to watch all this unfold.

We also launched our first website that fall with exactly three products for sale: The Healing Journey DVDs, Student Manual, and a Meditation Verse Pack. It would continue to grow, surpassing fifty products in the next several years.

Lessons from Luke

September 21: *"For the Lord your God will bless you in all your harvest and in all the work of your hands, and your joy will be complete." (Deuteronomy 16:15b) The harvest is a death that brings life. This is harvest season now—both in physical crops and in spiritual crops in my ministry. I feel a death occurring inside me, but I don't understand it. Pain grips me unlike anything I have felt in many years. Lord, you have blessed the work of my hands. Thank you.*

"I tell you the truth, unless a kernel of wheat falls to the ground and dies, it remains only a single seed. But if it dies, it produces many seeds." (John 12:24) Lord, I'm dying. This is what I feel inside me. I know this is of you. I feel held by you. I feel led by you. I sense you are finally opening my eyes this morning to (at least a portion of) the mystery of what is happening to me. A death is occurring in me, but I don't know any more than that. Show me, Lord what you want me to see and understand. Harvest. Death. Life.

God was moving in me, moving me toward something, but I didn't know what.

September 23: *"Separate yourselves from the peoples around you..." (Ezra 10:11b) Lord, I hear you say to me, "separate yourself." I am not sure what that means, but I am listening.*

After finishing the book of Ezra, I was ready to pull a new book out of my Bible Reading Box. I pulled Luke. Pretty surprising since I had already drawn it three times in less than a year. This next entry clarified for me what was happening on May 19, when I previously read Luke.

September 25: *Lord, reading these words evoked uncontrolled weeping. I could not stop sobbing. I could not even read the words. Even now—45 m. later—I can hardly look at them—my chest is heavy, and it is hard to breath. There was more, but I don't want to write the words.*

It started when I read Luke 1:45, "Blessed is she who has believed that what the Lord has said to her will be accomplished!" I began weeping right there. All I can sort out here—though I may be wrong—is that the Lord was speaking directly to me to say he has noticed my beliefs and confidence in him to accomplish the ministry project.

I read in verse 64, "Immediately his mouth was opened and his tongue was loosed, and he began to speak, praising God." I began to think about whether this would happen to me. Yes, I have already spoken—several times. But I feel something larger, still inside me, still unfulfilled, still to come. I thought about John—being filled with the Holy Spirit from birth—he was compelled to speak out.

Then I read verses 74-75, "...and to enable us to serve him without fear in holiness and righteousness before him all our days." I know that I have fear. It is so bizarre because both a passion to speak and a great fear coexist in me. And I asked the question, "But John was a prophet—of course he could do this. I know I am a princess of the Most High God, but I am insignificant in the kingdom, in the big picture. Who am I to do this?" WHAM! That's when I totally lost it.

The next words I read were in verse 76. "And you, my child, will be called a prophet of the Most High..." Surely this is not true. There is no way. I am not worthy in any way, shape or form. I am undone. I am reeling. I am overwhelmed. I do not understand what is happening this morning. It makes no sense. But I cannot deny what is happening here. I can only give testimony to what I saw and heard and felt.

God will have to reveal the meaning to me in his perfect timing. But, I'm not sure I want to know any more. Something is happening, but I don't know what it is. Lord God, I praise you for reaching into my little life and speaking to me today. You are doing something in me today and I yield to your will and your wisdom although I do not understand. I love you and I am your girl.

The power of the Holy Spirit overwhelmed me while God told me he was calling me to speak for him. I cannot expound on that or even comment. All I can say is that for all eternity, I will never forget September 25, 2007.

When it was over, I called my friend and mentor, Keeta, and asked if she could meet me right away. I had to talk to someone about it, someone I could trust implicitly, someone who understood things like this better than I did. She told me there was nothing I could do except walk this out with God and let him show me what I needed to know and understand. I think I knew that already, but I felt better after hearing Keeta say it.

23: Me and Keeta

While I was dazed by my encounter with God, one part of it was not confusing. God said he wanted me with him every single morning. Oy vey! That meant changes.

Every Day, No Excuses

Up to this point, I had a neat and tidy schedule each morning. On Sunday, Tuesday, Thursday, and Saturday, I would get up and have my time with God. Monday, Wednesday, and Friday mornings were reserved for the gym. I felt quite pleased with myself, finding a way to fit both into my schedule. Heck! God was getting the larger portion—four out of seven!

God's thoughts on the subject, however, were different than mine. He wanted time with me every morning.

If I did that, how would I exercise? If I did both, I wouldn't be ready to start work until after ten! That wouldn't work. I had too much going on in the ministry. The only reasonable solution seemed to be to give up the gym. Besides, I was pretty sure it was only temporary, just extreme measures while I was trying to get to the end of our production project.

Wrong. When the project was done, I tried to go back to my tidy four days on, three days off routine, but the conviction of God landed on me with significant weight. It took me about a year, but I finally worked it all out by changing my sleep schedule. Instead of going to bed around ten or eleven at night, I retired at nine. That allowed me to get up at five-thirty which gave me time to add a workout back into my schedule, while sticking with my everyday appointment with God. It worked well.

October 14: *Lord God, I was so confused as to why you picked Luke again—5 times in less than a year and now two times right in a row, but now I see. As you said, "I missed an important piece." I'm sorry I am so slow. Thank you for opening my eyes. "Then an angel of the Lord appeared to him, standing at the right side of the altar of incense." (Luke 1: 11) The altar of incense was in the Holy Place in the tabernacle and represented the prayers of the saints. It was only 18" square, covered with gold and used only for incense, once a year, for the atonement of sins.*

Lord, you have called me to a time of prayer—to come meet with you in the Holy Place—where my prayers create a holy fragrance for you. This was the event that preceded the birth of the prophet, John. It began in the Holy Place at the altar of incense. That is where you spoke to Zechariah and that is where you are speaking to me. Zechariah was alone and so you have called me to be separated unto you for a season—alone in darkness and solitude.

"But the angel said to him: 'Do not be afraid, Zechariah; your prayer has been heard…'" (Luke 1:13) "He will be a joy and delight to you…"

(Luke 1:14) Lord, I give you my fear and ask for your comfort and strength. I'm not afraid for this season of being buried with you—that is the greatest, most wonderful thing—it is safe and satisfying. No—I fear the time when you give birth in my life to whatever is coming. That is too fearful for me to even try to imagine—so I don't. But at the same time, I know you are right—it will be a joy and delight to me for I am deeply, deeply grieved for the state of all mankind. It truly would be my joy and delight.

So, today I have another piece of the puzzle. Birth will follow our time together in the Holy Place. You are meeting me here at the altar of incense to prepare me for the coming birth. Lord God, my prayer today is that you would enable me to serve you without fear in holiness and righteousness before you all my days.

What sweet words! Who can resist such a request? God wanted to be with me.

It was a time of spiritual electricity that I hadn't known since the beginning of my healing journey, sixteen years earlier. God was preparing me.

Most of the filming Deb and I did together for the Healing Journey class was for the actual lessons. But one of the videos we filmed was my personal story, which I share during the course of the class. It was important for students to know what God had brought me through during my own journey. It was hard enough, sharing my story in person; producing it on a DVD was more than I could handle.

October 18: *Lord God, I am in agony about* (putting) *my story on DVD. How can I expose myself to unknown people everywhere? I want to be unknown—NOT known—unseen—NOT seen. I can't do this! I am in agony. The pain is too much. Lord, do I need healing? What is the source of the turmoil? I certainly have no peace about it.*

Then you answered my questions, "Yes, there is something wrong. You are in pride." Crushed at my own sin, I laid my pride at your feet. Then I heard you again, "Will you give me your story on DVD?" Ugh—the pain and resistance—my chest was burning—this was too hard—too much to bear. But, really, there was no other choice that would lead to peace. So, I laid the DVD on the altar of sacrifice. I gave it up. He received it. It is no longer mine. By faith I know in time, God will replace my agony with peace.

If I was going to go where God was going, then I had to put my will to death. I had to surrender everything to him, and that meant my privacy, too. I was still learning how to be a thoroughfare instead of a cul-de-sac.

My morning time with God had been plenty eventful lately; I wasn't looking for any more big deals. But God had one more word for me.

October 26: *Lord, I hear your voice again. "I took you from the pasture and from following the flock to be ruler over my people Israel." (2 Samuel 7:8b) And Lord—you have taken me from lowly things and places. I am no one. "I have been with you wherever you have gone." (2 Samuel 9:8b) So have you been with me, Lord. "Who am I, O Sovereign Lord, and what is my family that you have brought me this far?" (2 Samuel 7:18b)*

Father God, I am weeping again and filled with the presence of your Spirit. For I am no one. I am not worthy of this honor. You have been too good to me—too generous. I don't know why. "For the sake of your word and according to your will, you have done this great thing and made it known to your servant." (2 Samuel 7:21) You have done a very great thing, O Lord. You have formed your truth into this curriculum. You have done it. Lord, it is yours.

Lord God, I know I have received your anointing, although I don't know completely where this is going. Like David, I say, 'Who am I?' But I know the answer—I am your precious daughter and your willing servant. It took many years for David to get from the pasture to the palace in Jerusalem and it has taken many years to get me ready (ready for what?) We, too, have traveled a long road together. I hear your voice today. It's time to go to Jerusalem.

Chapter Fifty-Three

2008

Connecting the Dots

We were on the cusp of launching Healing Journey—so close. Every week we were getting nearer to the end, finishing the various aspects. I knew it wouldn't be long now.

Anticipating our launch, I was amazed at how far I had come. Not at any point in my journey with God had I imagined this ministry that was unfolding. But he imagined it and sent me on all the right paths to prepare me for this moment.

I reflected back to the eighth grade, when I taught my first Bible lesson, and later my first Sunday School class of fourth graders. I thought about my nineteen years working in Christian Education, teaching, writing curriculum, training teachers—all in preparation for this moment. But that was only half of the equation.

My skills may have been honed, but my heart was still hardened with pain and suffering. I had to *become* the person for the job and that meant removing what had marred God's original design, a process called healing. My wounds were walls, blocking my true heart from flowing out to others.

As I thought back to my hopes in 1996, something else was evident to me. All I wanted then was to stay in Montrose and keep my house. Losing both was an opportunity for bitterness and judgment against God. *Was that too much to ask? After all I've been through, God, can't I at least keep these two things that are dear to me?* But if God had granted my request, I'm convinced there would be no His Healing Light Ministries today, or, at the very least, not one that included me. I'm reminded of the country song lyrics: *I thank God for unanswered prayers.*

A small town never would have released me from my past and the messiness of my healing years, nor allowed me to grow and live as the woman I had now become, my true and authentic self, no longer tainted by my past wounds.

I had a new perspective on everything: the unfavorable outcome of the trial, losing my job the same month, the crazy circumstances of finding a job in Colorado Springs, escaping legal clutches when Roger filed a motion, claiming I was endangering Jenny's life. It was like a violent storm, coming against me from every direction. But instead of destroying me, God used those awful circumstances to get me out of Montrose to begin the new life he had planned for me.

I was now running with the horses and I needed a new field in which to do so.

When God makes a move, nothing can come against him to prevent his will from being done. And now, here I was, eleven years later, doing what God created me to do, pinching myself every day.

Enlarge the Place of Your Tent

April 12: *"…that God may open a door for our message…" (Colossians 4:3b) Lord, I confess doubt that anyone would be interested in buying this curriculum kit, now that it is almost finished. But that is the foolishness of my flesh. Forgive my pride. Throw open the doors, Lord. Let your will be done. We're almost done!*

Finishing the curriculum had been a battle from Day One. Nothing about it was ever easy, especially our relationship with the guy printing the Healing Journey Student Manual. Although another ministry recommended him to us, I hadn't met him. We asked him to print three hundred books, something that should take a few weeks. He, however, took many months, breaking countless promises, demanding more money, claiming the order had *"ruined his life."* It got so bad, Bryan had me step away and let him handle it. He was concerned what this guy might say or do to me.

He finally delivered the books, in small batches over several months, but it was a nightmare to the end.

That wasn't the only challenge. On May seventh, close enough to see the finish line, I got a call from a different person working on the project, saying there would be another delay. When I hung up, I melted down. It had been two years of solid work and the curriculum kit was just about finished, but now unforeseen problems would push it back again.

I couldn't take it and called my board, ranting and raving. (Like that was going to help something?) My patience had run out; my good nature expired. Emotionally and mentally, I needed to be done.

One of my board members swung into action, quickly arriving at my house to pick me up. She took me out for ice cream, knowing my comfort food go-to, and listened while I dumped my emotional load. It made a difference. Such a simple act of kindness, but I'll never forget it.

God came to my rescue the next morning: *"Enlarge the place of your tent, stretch your tent curtains wide, do not hold back; lengthen your cords, strengthen your stakes. For you will spread out to the right and to the left." (Isaiah 54:2-3a)* God gave my heart courage to go forward, promising me he would get this thing done, and, in fact, would spread this ministry out far and wide. He had it all under control. From that day forward, I have prayed this passage repeatedly.

I finally received the video masters and the next day I was on a beach in Puerto Vallarta, recovering from an exhaustion that went to the marrow of my bones. Sand, sun, and warm air were my recipe for recuperation.

The first week of June, the curriculum kit was finished and made available to the world. But it had about finished me in the process. I was so glad to be done. I never wanted to do another filming project again! It had wiped me out.

Once it was done, I had a hard time imagining that many people would be interested in buying it. After all, we were a small ministry, known by very few people, and we weren't advertising it. Who would buy it? Who would even know about it?

Then one day, I was in my kitchen, getting ready to head out the door, when the phone rang. It was a woman in Arkansas who I'd never heard of. *A friend told me about the Healing Journey class. I was wondering if I could purchase the curriculum kit.*

Oh, wow! *So sorry, God. Why did I doubt you? I get it now. You want me to do my part and leave everything else to you. Got it.*

Later that summer, I was sitting in my hair stylist's chair chatting about it all. Having done the hair and makeup for the filming, Gayle had been integrally involved in our project. I conveyed my intentions to never do anything like that again. Her response left me speechless. *"You have more studies in you, more to teach, and more to film."* I tried my best to brush off her words, but they resonated in my soul.

Grandchildren

Meanwhile, our children's families were growing up. Joey, Jenny's son, was now four and exhibiting behavior that was hard to understand. His tolerance level for frustration was painfully low. He wouldn't wear anything that was the slightest bit stiff or binding. Epic meltdowns were common. And all this was causing stress between Jenny and Steve, trying to agree on how to handle it. It was suggested they get some comprehensive testing done for Joey.

Several months later, we learned Joey had Asperger's, a condition on the autism spectrum. The encouraging news was that kids with Asperger's are very intelligent and high functioning. He wouldn't have any trouble digesting information, but his learning environment would always be an issue. Homeschooling solved that. And most of the accompanying sensory issues could be managed.

The harder part of this diagnosis was the fact that no one knew Joey had Asperger's when they met him, imposing inappropriate or unrealistic expectations on him. Tantrums were a regular part of life, and punishment or scolding made everything worse. Extreme patience was required to help him navigate his world. Jenny became an expert and championed Joey's cause through each new challenge.

Sydney was also four, but we hadn't seen her since she was six months old. Bryan sought help from the courts to see if we could get grandparent rights for visitation. It was a long shot. Sometimes the courts would grant this, but not always. While in the middle of those legal dealings, paperwork was filed to try and get Chad's parental rights enforced, too, since he wasn't seeing her either. That was what ended up working for all of us. Once Chad's rights were court mandated, we also had access to see Sydney again.

Before we were cleared, however, we had to endure monitored visits for several months, visits where we were babysat by social workers, but it was worth it. We were elated to have Sydney back in our lives.

With graduation from law school approaching, Bree and Kris were eager to start their own family. How exciting to hear the news she was pregnant, knowing she had talked about being a mom and raising a family since junior high.

Several months before her due date, I booked a flight to Sacramento, keeping my fingers crossed that the dates would coincide with the baby's birth.

Bree called on a Sunday night, worried she would never have the baby and be pregnant forever. I assured her every mother before her had felt the same way, promising her that she would indeed give birth.

The next night, she went into labor. *Oh good! The baby will be born on Tuesday and I'll be there on Wednesday. Perfect! I can use the entire two weeks to help her with the baby.*

Later that night, they went to the hospital, but were sent home because Bree hadn't dilated enough. Very discouraged, she returned home to another twenty-four hours of labor. Finally, Tuesday night, they went to the hospital again, and Kris, in his most authoritative voice said, *"We're staying. Admit her."*

Before catching my flight the next morning, I checked in with Kris. He let me know things were finally moving along with the birth and that they had arranged for a coworker to pick me up at the airport and drive me to the hospital. I made the pensive flight west, thinking, *My granddaughter is being born right now. I can't wait to meet her!*

After landing at the small airport, I pulled my two large suitcases, one with personal items and the other full of things for the baby, outside and waited for my ride. I called Kris to let him know I had arrived but hadn't connected with his coworker, but there was no answer. Forty-five minutes later, still waiting at the airport, Kris called back.

"Sorry, I didn't call back. Bree's having the baby right now. I don't know what happened to your ride."

"No problem. What hospital are you at?"

"Kaiser."

"Great. I'll get there as quickly as I can."

Having only a flip phone and no internet, I called Bryan and asked him to locate the Kaiser hospital. Pulling up the list, he told me there were ten. *Ten! Holy cow! Start calling each one until you find her.* Praise God he located her on the third call.

I hailed a cab.

"Where are you headed, ma'am?"

"Kaiser Hospital. My daughter is having a baby right this minute!"

"No problem, ma'am, I'll do my best to get you there as quickly as I can."

The kind driver entered my drama, making it his mission to get me there in time for the birth. I was doubtful I'd make it, given the fact we were still a half hour away. Nevertheless, he sped along as safely as he could. Approaching the hospital, I was dismayed, seeing construction in the way, everywhere. The driver was already swiping my credit card as we pulled into the parking area.

"Now don't you worry, ma'am. I'm going to get you right to the door. Go down the hall and up the elevator to the second floor." Tires still rolling, *"Here, sign the slip."*

After thanking the driver for all his help, I dashed away, looking like a mad woman as I ran through the hospital with all my luggage. I quickly located Labor and Delivery. I pushed the intercom outside the locked door. I'll never know why the nurse let such a crazed person in the door, but I wasted no time finding Bree's room number.

There it is! As I timidly poked my head in the door, my granddaughter was born.

Only God could have arranged a plane ticket, months in advance, orchestrating my life to be there at such a precise moment. And for my entire two-week stay I was available to help my daughter during those first sacred days.

It was interesting, recalling how I also went into labor on a Monday evening, and gave birth to Bree on a Wednesday afternoon. Who can explain such things?

Getting Back on the Horse

Soon after returning home, Gayle's words did indeed prove prophetic. God let me know he had another study for me to write. Funny how quickly my attitude changed when I heard God's voice. When he told me the subject matter, I couldn't wait to get started.

Chapter Fifty-Four

2009

The Banquet Hall

After writing lessons for several months, I pulled a class together so I could test out the new material for my Running with Horses Bible study, repeating the class in the fall. Teaching on humility and servitude was a joy since this was the territory where I was now living.

Studying the sacrificial life isn't everyone's cup of tea, but it is definitely mine. I hate waste, waste of any kind, but none more than a wasted life. Having gone to the depths of hell and back, my perspectives on just about everything had changed. No longer was I interested in following the rules, for the sake of the rules. I'd been the good little Christian girl for forty years, going to church and reading my Bible, showing up for every event.

Now I have found true life. After taking God's hand, I traveled to a place I never knew existed, a land beyond simply playing the Christian game. Life isn't about rules, it is about Relationship.

It was when I was down in the depths of hell, that I saw the true heart of God. He was real, not just a figurehead. I was with him, just as intimately as I ever was with another human being—no, in fact, far beyond my most intimate moment with any person. All those words about him being a God of justice, mercy, power, grace, and love were *real*. I could feel the embodiment of them when I was with him.

But I never could have gotten there, or been there, or witnessed that, or felt that truth had God not stripped every bit of my former life away. I had to first be emptied. I wouldn't have seen it otherwise. It was precisely when I was in the deepest pit imaginable, nothing left to lean on but him, when all the lights came on.

He is real! God is everything He says He is in his Word. He is the Creator and God of the universe, the One who holds all power, the only Sovereign Authority. And why did that matter to me? *I need never fear another person or circumstance, no matter how painful or tragic, no matter the loss involved. I need never fear following Him or serving Him, no matter how difficult, no matter whether I have any idea what I am doing, no matter if I have any idea how it will be accomplished. God is trustworthy, faithful, and true.*

But that was just the beginning of my new perspectives. *He knows me! An insignificant ant in a vast universe, living but a brief moment in time—yet He knows me! He has planned daily steps for my life, steps leading to wild success, steps leading to satisfaction and contentment in my soul. He is living in my life with me, following the minutiae, caring about the details, guarding me from destruction through His Truth. Because my life has value to Him, it is now valuable to me. I no longer see myself as pond scum, but as a precious daughter of the King. I am royalty and my life matters.*

It was when those two statements of faith merged, understanding God's character and my identity, that the power of God was ignited in my life: *Because He is the Sovereign Authority, and because my life is significant, He will pour all His resources into and through my life, using it to fulfill His purposes, which for me, personally, is to bring the message of healing and freedom to all who will hear.*

When God took my stony heart and replaced it with a heart of flesh, with his heart, it was like I went from seeing in black and white to seeing in color. The beauty, the magnificence of his plan—it was incredible. When the lights came on, my motivation for everything changed. I was interested in only one thing: helping people see the truth about God along with his power and desire to redeem their life from hell, and free them from the torment of their wounds.

Anything else was a waste of my time. And time is life. And I only have one life to give. So I'm giving it to Jesus.

To see God pour life and truth and redemption through me, using me as a simple conduit, fulfills things far surpassing any temporal satisfactions. Money is an unsatisfying lover, to say the least; so is achievement, material possessions, recreation, or anything else. My desire and intentions were pointed toward Jesus.

February 28: *"First, we form a concept of that which we shall do.... Second, we feel that we want to do it, or must do it. Third, we determine that we will do it. Desire and intention are the most dynamic of our faculties; they do work. The determined fixing of our will upon God and pressing toward him steadily and without deflection; this is the very center and the act of prayer."* (Excerpt by Evelyn Underhill from Devotional Classics.)

God and I are doing life together, (although not perfectly on my side of things), and that is what matters to me. The fact that God wants to do life with me is pure joy.

In my vision so many years ago, after leaving my little, white cell and being in the hallway (where God told me, *"Cyndy, it's time to unpack the boxes"),* he let me peek into the future, briefly opening the door. As I peered inside, I saw a banquet hall, a richly ornamented hall, roomy and spacious, featuring a glorious spread of delectable delights, teeming with joyful people who were serving God.

He showed me this picture before we even started my healing journey, offering me hope that one day I would go into the banquet hall and serve him. And he was right. Now that I was here, there was a lot to be done. The banquet hall was a busy place.

A Published Author—Who Knew?

The next thing on God's list for me was finishing my nonfiction book. I had roughed out the first draft of Road Map to Healing six years earlier. But when the magnitude of filming and producing Healing Journey eclipsed the book, I set it aside.

It was now time to dust off the manuscript. As I re-read it, I was glad I didn't put it out there originally, because it needed revising. My writing skills improved every time I exercised them, so I was eager to bring up the quality.

When it was done, I was faced with the same dilemma I'd encountered so many times. *Here I am again, doing something I've never done before, and I don't know where to start.* So, like the Israelite priests in the book of Joshua, I put my toe in the water and trusted God to part the river and get me to the other side.

Now that the Healing Journey lessons were recorded and the curriculum was on the shelf, being sold through our website, I was even more grateful for the publisher's advice to retain control of the materials and do it ourselves. Since that had proved to be a good decision, my courage was bolstered to self-publish Road Map to Healing. I dove into the project, trusting God to teach me to swim in these waters, too.

After consulting with my author friends, I hired a professional editor, and then began researching how to self-publish a book. There was a bit of work involved, but nothing compared to what I'd already done. Writing was the hard work, publishing was not. I've frequently said that raising children was easier than writing a book!

In October, I had the thrill of holding my first book; such a moment of wonder and victory. I couldn't believe it was finally finished. I immediately had the same thought I always did, (which I'm embarrassed to admit) ... *Who on earth is ever going to buy this book? No one will ever read it.* I was wrong. Gratefully wrong.

Filling in the Gap

In the midst of finishing my book and teaching Running with Horses, my dearest friend, Keeta, pointed out a glaring problem. *Healing Journey students are not ready for Running with Horses after they complete that first class. There is a gap between the two curriculums.*

Hmmm... I hadn't noticed. I was discouraged, feeling defeated, worried I'd made a wrong turn somewhere.

It was cause for me to ponder what was missing, to ask myself what is the process that takes someone from their own healing journey to living the great adventure in the Promised Land? So I sat with the Lord and asked him to show me the way. *Lord, what is the bridge from the one to the other?*

Then it hit me, the Relationship! Before we allow God to heal our wounds and our offenses against him, we don't have the ears to hear him or the eyes to see him. Our senses are diminished, obscured by our pain and the lies we believe about ourselves and God. That clears up with healing. Healing allows us to see and know Truth.

When we saddle up our horse and ride into the Promised Land, we've got to have a solid, trusting relationship with the Lord or we will get slaughtered. The Promised Land is not Disneyland. It is a land of giants and fortified cities. It is a place of challenges and enemies and battles.

My thoughts took me back to the book of Numbers. The freshly released captives arrived at the edge of the new land, just months after leaving Egypt. But, instead of charging into the Promised Land, they cowered in fear and doubt. They weren't ready. Their faith wasn't strong enough, they still didn't know their God. And that was what the next forty years were about, learning to know God and trust him. Until the relationship piece was in place, they would not be ready to go in.

I knew what was missing. I hadn't previously considered the process of rebuilding (or building for the first time) our relationship with the Lord before we could take on the giants. Once I could see that, writing Resting in Jesus, my next Bible study, wasn't difficult.

One More Chick

It was in the midst of writing these new lessons that I got a tearful phone call from my friend, Heather.

Heather joined my Healing Journey class in the same fall as Kyle'ea, but quickly dropped out after moving back to Amarillo, Texas. With her husband deployed to Afghanistan, and being pregnant with her second child, she wanted to be closer to her family.

In the weeks before Heather left, we became acquainted while driving to church from the nearby army base, where I picked her up for class with her toddler, Natalia.

The next fall Heather returned to Colorado Springs, at the same point in the class where she'd left during the previous year. I didn't usually let students into the class so late but felt I should make an exception for Heather. Kyle'ea was in the class again too, and they quickly became friends.

Life was messy for Heather and had been since she was born. I often say it was like she was raised in the forest by wolves. No one taught her anything or helped her grow up. Her dad was an alcoholic and mom a drug addict. Heather scrapped for survival every day. By the time I met her, she had a heap of wounds.

Heather was faithfully attending the class and doing the work, dealing with her issues, when she melted down one day. Her descriptive picture is indelibly etched in my mind of the overwhelmed, young mom, sitting on the kitchen floor, paralyzed, surrounded by Cheerios split everywhere, and two screaming babies. I reached through the phone line with the most gentle and supportive words I could muster.

After she regained composure, I continued to be a resource to Heather while she completed her healing. When she learned her husband was being transferred to Fort Knox, Kentucky, as soon as his deployment was over, she went on to train to be a leader so she could take the class with her. She, too, wanted to help other women find the same healing she had experienced.

While Heather was preparing to move her family for the umpteenth time, she discovered she was pregnant again. In her fifth month, she got a call from Amarillo, learning her mother had been put in hospice. She made plans to head there immediately. Kyle'ea went with her for support.

And that's where Heather was when I got her tearful call that day. She was watching her mother drown in her own lung fluid, while still going outside for regular smoke breaks. It was a brutal way to die and an awful thing for Heather to witness. The army let her husband return for the funeral. As soon as he left, she lost the baby she had been carrying. And because the army wouldn't grant him another leave so soon, Heather was alone. Grieving the double deaths was a long and difficult process.

Heather often remarked how much I looked like her mom, and we were the same age, too. With all that we'd gone through together, I guess becoming Heather's surrogate mother was a natural progression. Like a duckling spotting its mother across the pond, we have been connected since that moment. Another bond forged in grief.

At the time, I was dealing with my own grief, having just received news that my stepfather had died. I hadn't seen Jim in over fifteen years, not since the time we met at a Fort Collins restaurant, early in my recovery. Sadly, he had developed Alzheimer's in his later years. His son, my stepbrother, spoke at his funeral, attended by a number of family members and fellow colleagues from the university where he taught for decades. Attending the funeral was good closure for me, and an opportunity for a final round of grieving.

Later on, after Heather's family settled in Kentucky, she became pregnant again. We cried tears of joy together, that is until she called on another day, evoking tears for a different reason. There were problems with the pregnancy, and the doctor told Heather to expect to miscarry her baby. He suggested she have an abortion.

That was not going to happen, Heather decided. I was so proud of her for making her own decision on the matter. She told me on the phone that God had created this child and given it to her, and he would be the one to decide what her life looked like. We prayed fervently for the next months.

The week Heather was due, Kyle'ea decided to fly out to Kentucky to be with her. Only a day or so into the visit, Kyle'ea ended up in the hospital. On Monday morning, July 19, 2010, Heather called me to say that Kyle'ea had died in the hospital.

July 20: *"Now is your time of grief." (John 16:22b) O God my Father, have mercy on me. My heart is weighed down with grief and sadness. My friend, Kyle'ea has died. I need you, Lord. Help me grieve and grieve well.*

July 21: *Father, this soul desperately seeks to be alone with you this morning. Come to me, O Comforter in Sorrow, for the weight of my heart is unbearable. My friend has died. While I rejoice that she is released from her suffering and is now with you in Paradise, I am deeply grieved for my loss.*

In spite of being high maintenance, Kyle'ea was a joy, one of the most giving and generous people I've known. She had great artistic talent and loved giving gifts, showering me with presents many times, even though she had no money.

Just before she died, after years of fighting for it, her government disability finally came through. She received a check for $5000 and immediately booked a Disney cruise for herself and her sister's family. I was upset with her for blowing all her money. But Kyle'ea was right. I think she knew she didn't have much time left and wanted to give this gift to her niece and nephews. Three month later, she was gone. Her loved ones would carry the memory of that vacation forever, and I would never forget our friendship.

24: Heather, Natalia, Me with Cynthia, Matthew

Four days after Kyle'ea died, July 23, Heather gave birth to Cynthia, my namesake. It was such a strange week, life and death colliding. Joy and sadness together. Circumstances that are hard to understand even today. Today Cynthia is a healthy youngster, precocious and thriving.

Men, Really?

Breanna had been gone five years and Bryan's grief was still significant. His garbage piles were deep, including earlier wounds from when his wife left him and the kids, and when his dad died, closing the door on that relationship. It was hard for me to sit by and watch him suffering. Here I was leading a national ministry for healing, yet unable to help someone I loved so much.

I suggested he try going through the material on his own, since there were no classes for men. (Not that I hadn't been asked to do this! I had, in fact, been asked countless times to, please, start a similar healing ministry for men. My consistent response was, *"Sorry, but I am not a man, so I can't. If there is ever to be a men's ministry, it will have to be done by men, for men."*)

Bryan accepted the challenge, watching the lessons and doing the processing steps on his own. He loved it. Right away, he began feeling hope again, that is until he tried writing his story. When he got to the part about Breanna's passing, he couldn't do it. Paralysis took over again, derailing his healing for two more years until several men began pestering him about doing it with them.

Would you consider starting a Healing Journey class for men? After several requests, Bryan agreed. He began the first men's group in the fall of 2009. It was just the ticket. Having the accountability and support of other men allowed Bryan the environment he needed to heal. His heart began to mend.

Expanding our Horizons

Bryan wasn't the only man who wanted to start the ministry. Gary Short, a marriage and family counselor in New York state, was also eager to get hold of the curriculum.

Gary had stumbled upon the materials while attending a conference in Colorado Springs. During his visit, he and his wife stayed in the home of Bob and Verna Smith, dear friends of mine. In fact, Verna was one of my small group leaders, which is why the Healing Journey Student Manual was on her kitchen counter.

While perusing the materials, Gary asked, *"Where did you get this and how can I get my hands on it? I've been looking for something like this for twenty-five years."* Verna connected us, and Gary took the materials back home to the ministry center where he worked, to Family Life Network.

He started a women's group immediately. Sensing its impact, he called and ordered another twenty student kits. Before long, he was leading groups for men, too.

As Gary and I got acquainted, I suggested he and other potential leaders take advantage of our Boot Camp training. It made more sense to fly me to New York for this than for a group to come to Colorado, so we scheduled our first New York Boot Camp. Gary, being the charismatic guy he is, managed to get over twenty people to attend. The New York Boot Camp began something that became nothing short of a phenomenon, as it quickly spread beyond New York into Pennsylvania.

For years, the joke has been to be careful about getting too close to Gary Short; anyone coming within ten feet will be recruited for Boot Camp or enrolled in a Healing Journey class! He is a fan, to say the least, and an encouragement to us.

Chapter Fifty-Five

2010

Laying Down My Isaac

Living in the new territory of the Promised Land was not without testing, as I soon found out. God led me through my own "Isaac trial" for two years. He wanted to make sure my priorities were in the right order. This struck at the core of my being, as he and I began examining my relationships with my beloved daughters and grandchildren. He could not have confronted anything more costly. I cried many tears as he and I wrangled over this month after month.

God wanted to be first in my life, even above my family. It boiled down to an issue of whether I trusted God to be in charge of these relationships, or whether I would continue to stand in his place, deluded that I had control over my family. Would I believe his love and goodness were sufficient to even care for my most beloved?

I didn't know the cost I would bear if I agreed. *Would he ask me to move somewhere that I wouldn't see them? Or not often? Would I travel so much that visits would be limited?* I simply didn't know what it would mean, what I would have to give this up.

January 11: *Father God, I surrender all I have and all I am to you. I know that it will be extremely painful to turn my back on my family—they are the dearest thing to me, save you. However, I believe you—the only way to save my life is to lose my life. If I don't give up everything then you don't have free reign in my life. What I want most is for my life to be made completely accessible to you.*

Like Abraham, I didn't have the full understanding of what God was doing at the time. Even though it felt like God was asking me to turn my back on my family, that wasn't the case. But I wouldn't know that until I surrendered and walked this road with him.

After significant anguish, I decided to make my peace with God on this issue.

January 27: *"Now I know that you fear God because you have not withheld from me your son, your only son." (Genesis 22:12) Lord God, I now see how this test is part of everyone's journey with you, not just Abraham's. We must give up everything to receive the life you've planned. My sacrifice still hurts my heart so much. I want so much to be with my daughters and grandchildren. But I choose to put nothing before you. I can have nothing blocking the way you have planned.*

February 22: *God finally has the highest priority, but it was a painful two-year battle for me and I am grieving now—however, I am grateful to the Lord for moving in my life and bringing me to my Genesis 22 crisis—one every follower must encounter if he is going to serve God.*

February 27: *Father God, I see myself at the train station. I am sitting on the platform, a single bag beside me, alone and waiting. I know the train is arriving soon. You are on the train, the conductor, and coming soon to pick me up. I don't know where we're going or what I'll be doing exactly. Although I do know I am the Lord's mouthpiece. Wherever and whatever—I will be sharing the truth of your Word. Lord, I am peaceful and feel no anxiety about this because I know you are good and everything you have planned is good.*

Once again, the way was clear for God to direct my life.

Going to Prison

It turned out that God wasn't done using my friend Verna. I found myself visiting in my living room with Mel and Annie Goebel, after Verna suggested we meet. Mel had served with Prison Fellowship for two decades before he and Annie caught the vision that the same outreach needed to be offered to incarcerated women, and then began a ministry called "Daughters of Destiny." (Later, Daughters of Destiny would become part of the Prison Fellowship ministry.)

I shared a little about my ministry and Mel asked to see the materials. Sixty seconds later, he said, *"This is what I've been looking for. I want to get this curriculum into women's prisons. And I would like you to consider becoming one of our circuit speakers."* Mel was, no doubt, a visionary.

Why don't you take it home and look it over? I suggested. Mel didn't think that was necessary; he'd seen enough to know he wanted it.

I loved the idea of bringing my message of healing to ladies in prison. Ever since I taught the class at the transitional housing facility, eight years earlier, I was eager to help the most vulnerable populations of women. My board and I prayed through this new opportunity and discerned that God was giving us a green light.

With another filming project coming up, I couldn't start working in the prisons right away, but agreed to begin the next year.

Never Say Never

Now that Healing Journey was off and running, we were able to turn our sights to our next project, filming Resting in Jesus. And so, four years after my first filming experience, I found myself back in front of the camera. Gayle was right; I would write and film more studies.

The second time around wasn't quite as intimidating. I went to work, lining up all the resources for hair and makeup, wardrobe, set design, and a location to film. Wanting to catch the nice summer weather for the intro and outro filming, we decided to film the short beginning and ending spots first. We were ready to roll when life brought a significant disruption.

Earlier that summer, I had fainted in the middle of class one evening after my foot started hurting, resulting in a very expensive ambulance ride to the hospital. When I got there, the foot pain was excruciating, yet a diagnosis eluded the doctor. No one in the ER could figure out the connection between my foot pain and fainting.

When the foot pain persisted, I was sent to a foot specialist. He said he was certain I had stress fractures in my foot, so certain that he felt an MRI wasn't necessary. *I want you to be non-weight bearing for six weeks and wear a boot.* Six weeks! I was filming for the next six weeks!

Postponing it would mean waiting until the following summer, a year-long delay. Not ones to be easily derailed, Deb Leach and I came up with a plan to film anyway. *Hey, the theme is resting, right? We'll just film you sitting in a chair!* It was a pretty hysterical sight, seeing me roll around on a knee scooter in the Rocky Mountains, filming the different segments. But we got it done.

(When I finally got a correct diagnosis two years later and found out the real reason for the fainting and foot pain, I was annoyed I had to go through all that. It turned out the fainting was due to a rapid drop in blood pressure. And, since it was the first time it happened, it flooded the veins in my foot, causing them to expand suddenly, something that was very painful for months afterward. My foot was never broken!)

Trusting God was required in every circumstance. God gave me a verse to help me remember this, another verse I began praying weekly, *"Yet he did not waver through unbelief regarding the promise of God, but was strengthened in his faith and gave glory to God, being fully persuaded that God had power to do what he had promised." (Romans 4:20-21)* No matter what obstacles came my way, no matter how difficult the circumstances, God let me know that my job was to stand in faith and believe him. Never waiver.

November 1: *"God breaks up the private life of his saints, and makes it a thoroughfare for the world on one hand and for Himself on the other." Father God, I remember when you spoke these words to me years ago and what a shock it was to me that it was not okay with you that I live a quiet, private life and keep to myself. No! You wanted me to live outside, in the crowd, among your created ones, and give my life to them for your sake. How hard this was for me! "No human being can stand that unless he is identified with Jesus Christ. We are not sanctified for ourselves…. Let Him have His way with you." Come, Lord Jesus, and help me! This is still hard to do. "He comes with the grip of the pierced hand of His Son, and says—'Enter into fellowship with Me; arise and shine.'"* (The three quotes are from My Utmost for His Highest, November 1). *What else can I do, Father, except come to you each morning and give you myself all over again and pray for your mercy and strength. My life is not my own; it belongs to you, Lord. I know you have sent me and that this is your work. Nothing in this ministry originated from me, it is all yours.*

Validation

As my dad's health began to decline, he wasn't able to make the drive to Colorado anymore, so Bryan and I committed to go out to San Diego every year or two. It had already been eighteen months since our family gathered to celebrate his eightieth birthday, so we booked a flight out for a few days.

25:Dad's 80th Birthday (Front) Dad and Me (Back) Steve and Scott

After spending a day at SeaWorld, Dad took us out in his Mustang convertible, top down, to tour the city. He had grown up in San Diego, so he had lots of memories here. Driving to the crest of one of the many hills, he stopped in front of a church and began describing the years when he'd served here as an altar boy. Then he shared about a recent event when he had gone inside this same church to hear a musical performance. As soon as he sat down, he had a panic attack and fled the church. It was unusual that my dad brought up this experience since he was normally tight lipped about painful past issues.

All he mentioned was a vague reference to the evil that was done in that church when he was a boy. I'd always suspected he had been abused by a priest. As an adult, he would not attend a church, never specifying what his issue was exactly, but he had previously told me there was sexual abuse in his past. Dad didn't spell out the abuse that day we were touring, but I'd had enough panic attacks myself to know some form of trauma had occurred in that building.

As the tour continued, Dad began sharing random stories, including one I'd hadn't remembered hearing before, about living on an Indian reservation. Apparently, my grandpa had been a missionary to a Native American tribe before World War II, when my dad was a little boy. And they had lived on the reservation for two years.

As I sat in the back of the convertible, I thought my heart was going to stop, my mind going back to the one memory that always seemed out of place from the others, the Native American ritual on the hillside, the one where I danced with the scarves. My grandfather was part of that ritual, too. Now I knew where the Native American ceremony had come from, how that had become part of their life. Like the final piece to finish a puzzle, that memory suddenly had context.

I desperately wanted to talk to Bryan, but I couldn't say anything for many hours. When we were finally alone, I sobbed as I shared the incredible connections to my story, randomly made by my father.

April 9: *I have a hard time being around my dad. I want him to care about my life, but he doesn't. There is no interest in anything I do. I want him to respect my opinions and thoughts, but he doesn't. He pontificates constantly. It is painful and tedious to spend large amounts of time with him.*

Lord, I thank you for the father you have given me, because he is your choice. Many good things have come out of the struggles in this relationship—mostly my relationship with you and my dependence on you for all the love and nurturing I need. Even though my dad has never met my needs, you have always met my needs. You are loving and faithful in all your ways. Thank you for being my true Father.

Yes, I know God's grace is sufficient for everything, even my relationship with my dad. I can better demonstrate my beliefs by accepting his way of being and acting and worst of all, his talking. More importantly, I can choose to keep loving him and sharing myself with him.

Father God, I totally need your love, strength and grace to be poured into my heart and mind so that I can be an ambassador for Christ even with my dad. Lord, I just want my dad to be saved. It is really all I care about here in this relationship. I yield myself to you as your vessel. Please come and do what I cannot—save my dad. You are my father's only hope.

It was God's grace that day, allowing me to receive more validation for my memories, validation from the only person who could give the information, my dad. God knew what I didn't, that this would be the last time I would ever see my dad.

Chapter Fifty-Six

2011-2012

Maximum Security

Travel was rapidly becoming a regular part of my schedule. The leaders´ Boot Camps were expanding to other areas, including states in the South, and now I was adding trips to women's prisons, typically five or six each year.

Annie Goebel was kind enough to ease me into the prison world by accompanying me to my first event in March 2011. I was glad for her company and guidance because I was feeling a little nervous about the whole thing.

I spent six weeks honing my material, having been asked to provide two hours of teaching for the four-hour event. Forty-eight hours before I was to fly out to Illinois, I got a call. *By the way, signups have exceeded our capacity for the room. We're dividing them into two groups. So you will need to cut your material in half and teach it twice.*

What? You're kidding, right? It doesn't work that way. That's like asking someone to tear off the front of a house or the back. It all goes together! Don't they understand? I kept my thoughts to myself as I scrambled to modify my message. *Maybe I can talk fast.*

I quickly learned that prisons are chaotic places as far as communication, administration, and organization. What you were told would be happening is often not true when you arrive. So the name of the game is flexibility.

We landed at O'Hare airport and headed south about three hours to Dwight, Illinois. Prisons are typically in remote areas, so getting there often requires various modes of transportation, including lots of time and expense.

As we pulled up to the prison, it began to dawn on me what I was about to do. I turned and asked Annie, *"Is this a minimum or maximum security prison?" "Maximum,"* she answered. I began considering the implications of this. *Hmmm...probably didn't ask enough questions before I got myself into this.*

Annie had warned me how many crazy things can happen when you go through the security processing. She wasn't kidding. By the time I finally cleared the machine I had taken off my jacket, shoes, belt, necklace and earrings. I was glad nothing else needed to come off. The next step would have been embarrassing.

Because I was getting over a cold, I had a slight cough and was blowing my nose a little and was continually thirsty. I had brought a cough drop with me. *"Can I take that in?" "No,"* I was told. Cough drops were considered drugs. The officer said they would unlock a bathroom, so I could get toilet paper if I needed to blow my nose. You were not allowed to bring anything inside the prison except an unopened bottle of water. *Note to self: bring water next time.*

I prayed under my breath, *Lord, get me through these next four hours.* We waited for the heavy doors to open so we could proceed into the prison. I lost count of how many times we were buzzed through different security doors.

The first room we passed through was the cafeteria and visitation room. Since it was Saturday, there were many inmates sitting at tables with family, friends, and children—mostly women. My heart was immediately sad. There was no laughter or lively conversation. The room was strangely somber, considering how many people were there. I noticed a lot of fidgeting children and people staring at the floor. One group was silently building a puzzle.

As we crossed the compound toward the chapel, I kept thinking, *Maximum Security... what's this going to be like?* I was anxious and a little afraid as we arrived at the dome-shaped building. The chapel had paneling around the inside, surprisingly nice. But it did seem warm. *Is there any way to control the temperature?* Nope. No air conditioning. *You could try opening the window.* Right. The window was about a foot wide; probably wouldn't do a whole lot.

I learned prisons are not comfortable places. They do not fix things, nor is the comfort of the inmates a priority. So the temperature is usually not comfortable. It is either too hot or too cold. I've spoken to women huddled together wearing sweatshirts and coats, and others desperately fanning themselves, trying to cool off.

This should be interesting, I thought to myself, since heat is one of the things that causes my blood pressure to drop, making me faint. Better pray again: *Lord, keep me upright.* At security, they handed me a small Styrofoam cup in case I needed to get a drink from the bathroom faucet. I decided to use it while I was waiting. *Yum. Tastes like rust.*

Still, my excitement began to grow as we prepared the room, passing out the handouts. I walked over to the entry area to wait for the ladies. *I wonder what they will be like. Will they say anything?* Soon they filed in, chatting away. *"I'm really excited to hear what you have to say to us today. We've been praying for you all week. Bless you, sister, for coming here today."*

Wow! That was not what I expected. I was here to minister to them, yet they were ministering to me! I realized many of these women knew Jesus. They loved Jesus. They wanted Jesus. They were excited for the Word of God. These were my sisters in Christ. *This is going to be fun!*

As soon as the ladies were seated, the officer began barking orders. *Keep your mouth shut. I have no interest in hearing anything from you. Sit down and don't move. No one is allowed to stand up. Raise your hand if you need to get up. If you cause any trouble, I will remove you immediately.*

The officer seemed to be on a power trip, relishing his authority over the women. He was demeaning and disrespectful. For the second time that day, my heart broke. *How would these ladies ever discover their true value and how much God loved them in an environment like this?*

I was angry with the officer. Fortunately, I can honestly say I never encountered an officer quite as bad at other prisons.

Annie got our program started, leading the ladies in several worship songs. Even though they weren't allowed to stand, their voices rose to a great and joyful noise to the Lord. They loved singing to Jesus, especially this song called "Trading my Sorrows": *I'm trading my sorrows. I'm trading my shame. I'm laying them down, for the joy of the Lord.* These ladies were ready to trade their shame for the redemption of Jesus.

I launched into my story, sharing how God took the brokenness of my past and healed me, how I learned my true value and worth to him, and how he redeemed my life and turned it around for good. When I was done, many ladies came forward to thank me, saying how God had encouraged their hearts through my story. I desperately wanted to hug the ladies, but it is prohibited. (It is entirely possible, however, that I broke the rules a few times.) We repeated the event with the second group, experiencing the same great response.

When it was over, I was hooked! What a tremendous privilege to be able to speak into the lives of these precious souls. Leaving, I realized, I had had no fear or anxiety. God himself had created this holy moment in time and ushered us into his very presence.

Since that day, I have been in prisons all over the country, from Connecticut to New Mexico, Mississippi to California, and many other states. There is no end to the opportunities and no end to my joy in serving incarcerated women.

Retreating and Regrouping

Like every year since launching the ministry, 2011 was a busy one. In just ninety days that spring, I had led a Healing Journey retreat, Boot Camps in three states, flown to Houston for a nephew's wedding, spent a weekend with my mother-in-law at her cabin, and camped with the family. Phew! I needed a break!

I decided to give myself a personal spiritual retreat at Glen Eyrie. I began as I always do, laying myself out before the Lord and inviting him to do anything he wanted to do.

July 5, 2011: *"When through charity and an upright intention, a person offers himself in all his works and in his entire life to the glory and praise of God, and when he seeks rest in God above all things, then he should humbly and patiently, with self-surrender and fine confidence, await new riches and gifts—but always without anxiety as to whether God will bestow them or not."* (Excerpt by John Ruusbroec, from Spiritual Classics) *Father God, I desire to press my will into yours in order to more fully become part of you. I want to more fully leave my prideful and very selfish ways, to empty myself (only by the power of your Holy Spirit) of all that is not of you. I seek to rest in you these two days above all things in order to await new riches and gifts—although I only want more of you and more of what you intend my life to be. Come, Father God, and meet with me as I begin this over-needed prayer retreat with you. I grant you full access into any area of my life or part of my being where you wish to enter and do business. I agree to do any type of spiritual work you choose to do. I surrender it all to you. I am here to do your bidding and give glory to you. Please nourish my exhausted and depleted soul so that I may re-enter the race and continue on for your glory.*

These spiritual breaks were so good for me, helping me stay in the battle and fight the good fight. With another filming project right around the corner, I needed some restorative time to be ready.

The Last Letter

I had long ago given up trying to send a newsy Christmas letter out in December, opting to do it instead in a less busy month. My last family letter went out in August 2011. My dad's birthday was soon after, so I followed it up with a call, wishing him a happy birthday and letting him know I was considering a trip out to see him in January.

On the phone, he didn't sound like himself, being vague when I brought up the visit. As soon as I finished the brief call, there was a knock at my front door. It was my neighbor, delivering a large envelope, saying, *"The mailman accidently put this in our box, and I wanted to make sure you got it."*

It was from my dad. *That's odd. I wonder why he didn't mention it when we talked a few minutes ago.* In the envelope was a letter, plus a copy of every correspondence that had transpired between us during my healing years. He wanted me to read it, as if I'd forgotten something. Most assuredly, I hadn't.

He was writing in response to my annual "not-at-Christmas" letter. It had dawned on him that my ministry was birthed out of my painful past. Why this realization occurred now and not ten years earlier, I don't know.

It is clear to me that you think I am the villain who engendered your ministry. I can't take it anymore. I have felt this pain too long. In the past years, repressed memory has been debunked. The psychologists I know will not go near it for fear of litigation. During the Korean War when our P.O.W.s returned home, they had been so effectively brainwashed, that they were radical Communists. I believe you have been so brainwashed by Roger, Faith, and later by those grad students at Colorado University, that you truly believe your memory to be the truth. I don't have a lot of time left, honey. I have a lot of medical issues, and a great deal of pain. I try on a daily basis to have peace and serenity in my life. I am very close to my god and ask him daily to intervene and restore our relationship as a father and daughter should be. I do love you and always will and I forgive you because I truly believe you are a victim.

I was beginning to see what my dad had done over the years. He had to find some way to explain my memories other than accusing me of lying or being crazy. So he began making up stories in his own head about how it happened. And I think, over time, he convinced himself that his fantasies were true. More than once, he referred to a non-existent brainwashing program at the state university in Boulder. I can't imagine where he came up with that; I've never even stepped onto that campus.

It was the same thing I'd gotten from my family at the beginning. They all knew I was truthful. So they had to find some other way to explain it all away. Dad blamed it on Roger early in my healing journey, but this brainwashing angle was a surprise to me. It seemed so bizarre.

September 13, 2011: *Father God, what am I to do today except to fall down before you, seeking your comfort and strength. Lord, I am feeling greatly disrupted. But I am reminded that "All this also comes from the* L*ORD*

Almighty, wonderful in counsel and magnificent in wisdom." (Isaiah 28:29) *I need your counsel and wisdom. Please come to me. You have been my Shepherd all my life. Even though the attack has come again, help me remain steady and walk in the center of your path, not veering to the right or left. You have used the tragedy and sin of my past for good and truly are saving many lives through it all. I believe that today I am in the protection of your arms and that you will save me from all harm.*

I couldn't control the circumstances (my father's letter was a done deal), but I could go to my Source for comfort and strength.

September 18, 2011: *Lord, I am overwhelmed at the thought of responding to my dad's horrible letter. You are comforting me. Just yesterday your Spirit affirmed me when I heard, "Cyndy's voice will not be silenced." You are God and will have the final say. May your will be done and my all be to your glory.*

My letter in response to my father was very long, reiterating all the things he'd said over the years that supported my memories and refuted his. A large part of the letter was encouraging him to accept Christ as his Savior, something he'd never done. His religion was one he fashioned for himself, one that was based on nothing except what he wanted it to be.

I then addressed the ministry issues that he had brought up:

You believe that I think you are a villain and that you engendered my ministry. I don't believe you are a villain. I believe you were victimized, likely by many people and sources, certainly by your father and the church. I believe you came by your pain and struggles honestly, just as I did. You didn't go looking for it—they found you.

The ministry has been birthed by God alone, no one else. It was his idea. And everything that has come from the ministry is to his credit. He is the power and wisdom behind it all. Yes, I went through a very painful healing journey before the ministry began, but what I teach is God's healing principles found in Scripture. The healing journey I experienced involved many, many different events and people. Yes, you were a big part of it, but so were many others.

I have no trouble believing your story about the POW's, but I wasn't in a war, nor was I captured or tortured. It doesn't have any relevance for my life. No one brainwashed me. You will have to let this one go. There was no one from C.U., no grad students, and Faith didn't become my counselor until my memory had already returned. Roger wasn't involved at any level with my healing process. He never said a word. In fact, he had no interest in what I was going through and certainly nothing to say.

To the bitter end, I kept inviting him to tell the truth.

Before I mailed it, I asked Jenny and Bree to pray over the letter with me. More than anything, I wanted my dad to be saved. I sensed this was a "make it or break it" moment.

Weeks later I received his response. Fortunately, Bryan had the foresight to read it first and then destroyed the letter. My dad had made it clear he never wanted to see me again. Bryan said, *" I don't ever want you to read such vile and hurtful words."* I am grateful he did. I'm glad those words aren't spinning in my head, tormenting my heart. There would not be another letter or visit or word spoken between us again.

Time to Saddle Up

The day after we finished the Resting in Jesus project, we began getting ready to film Running with Horses. I knew just where I wanted to film it.

Boasting many tourist attractions, Colorado Springs has a lot to offer people coming for a visit, including the Flying W Ranch. Russ Wolfe and his wife had built the sprawling ranch and its numerous outbuildings over a period of sixty years, serving the famous chuckwagon dinner and Western sing-along show since 1953. Their many western-themed buildings would be the perfect setting for the Bible study filming.

On a warm, September afternoon, Bree and I moseyed on up to the ranch to take a gander. (I was thrilled to have Bree now on staff, working in the ministry with me.) Never able to find the manager with whom we made the appointment, we decided to look around. Moments later, Russ Wolfe came straight toward us and struck up a conversation. Being retired and in his later eighties, there was nothing he enjoyed more than sharing the history of the ranch. We couldn't have had a better tour guide.

He eventually got around to asking us why we were there, since the ranch was closed during the day. When I shared our desire to film my Bible study on the property, he didn't hesitate. *This place has always been dedicated to the Lord. I would be honored to have you film your Bible study here, and I won't charge you a thing.*

Hot-diggity-dog! I hit pay dirt! I later talked to the manager and he was not only shocked that I'd talked to the owner, but more than miffed that Mr. Wolfe had given us the approval to film. The manager obviously saw us as an inconvenience, although we assured him that we would do our best to minimize the intrusion.

I never saw Russ again, but will be eternally grateful for his generosity.

A Wild Month and a Wild Fire

April was a rough month. I learned that Tim's mother, Donna, my first mother-in-law and my girls' grandmother, had died suddenly. She stepped out of bed one morning and crumpled in a heap on the floor due to an aneurism. The girls and I made the trip together to Ft. Collins for the viewing and funeral. Tim was there, providing the girls a rare visit with their father, and the last one they would ever have.

Three days after the funeral, I got a call that my mom had been found unresponsive, laying on the bathroom floor. She was taken by ambulance to the hospital, staying there several days.

It is hard to put all the pieces together, but when Donna died, it triggered unresolved emotional pain in my mom, and she stopped taking care of herself. When her body got totally depleted, she collapsed. Mom had always been enmeshed with my life, including the chapters with Tim and his mother, so the recent event with Donna's death sent her into a tailspin.

While these events were occurring, I was still wrapping up the Running with Horses filming project, doing the outdoor shots for the beginning and ending segments, and also preparing for the first of four Boot Camps that spring. One day, after leaving the Flying W Ranch, I began to feel achy and feverish. The stress of everything had caught up with me and I had the flu. I knew I had to clear the next several days to rest and heal or I would not be able to make it to Tucson for the Arizona Boot Camp.

The death and funeral, mom's hospitalization, flu, and final filming all occurred in a two-week period.

A few days later, I was on a plane to Tucson, then on to New York in mid-May, and finally back and closer to home for the Colorado Boot Camp in early June. Among the names of men and women on the Colorado roster was someone near and dear to my heart, my friend Valerie who had been in my second class ten years earlier. What a joy to see her join our leadership team, becoming a small group leader.

The Boot Camp season finally wrapped up in New Orleans, later that month. While I was there, Bree called, quite concerned. She had seen a cloud of smoke roll over the foothills above her home a few hours earlier. A fire had broken out in Queen's Canyon.

Our team went to prayer immediately; wildfire in the wooded neighborhoods of the west side of our city had the potential to cause terrible destruction. While praying, Bryan saw a vision of the main boulevard, Centennial, three blocks west of Bree's house. The Flying W Ranch was on the other side of Centennial. As he prayed, Bryan could see the fire coming down the ridge, stopping at the west edge of Centennial. We weren't sure what to think.

We wrapped up Boot Camp on Monday, talking to Bree frequently and keeping close tabs on what was now being called the "Waldo Canyon Fire." The fire was spreading rapidly but was still contained in the canyons west of the city.

Our flight home wasn't until Wednesday, so we were still in New Orleans on Tuesday when I got a frantic call from Bree. They'd been out when they saw smoke rising over their neighborhood. They dashed home to grab their dog and a few things while police barked orders with a bull horn, ordering immediate evacuation. As Bree's family pulled away in their van, the smoke prevented them from seeing even ten feet in front of them, crawling out of the neighborhood along with hundreds of other vehicles.

As they headed south to my house, the flames were to the right of their van, on the west side of Centennial. Bree's home was on their left. My grandson was only a baby, but my four-year-old granddaughter was screaming, fearful of dying in the blaze. For a full year, every time she got in a car, she asked, *"Are we going toward the fire or away from the fire?"*

My only thought was wishing I was home with my family. It was agony, being so far away. But there was nothing I could do except wait for my flight the next day. They made it safely to our home, one of the fortunate ones. Three hundred fifty homes burned that day, including the Flying W Ranch. It was completely incinerated. Our footage there is likely the last ever taken of the original ranch.

When the fire was finally out, three weeks later, it had stopped right at Centennial Boulevard, just like in Bryan's dream. The thirty thousand homes to the east were spared, including Bree's.

Chapter Fifty-Seven

2013-2014

Broken Glass

It was much safer to visit my mom if I wasn't alone; she was less likely to say hurtful things. So on a hot July day, Bree and I drove up to Ft. Collins with her three kids, ages five, two, and five months.

We arrived at noon, planning to pick her up for lunch, but she didn't respond when we knocked at the door. The small window in her front door allowed me to peer into the entry and living room. That's when I saw Mom peering back at me, but from her patio area. She had locked herself out of the house. I had a house key, but not one for the screen door, which was also locked. I tried to jiggle it open without success.

We walked around the 4-unit building to the grassy common area behind her condo. Talking to her through the six-foot fence, we began brainstorming options. After finding the gate padlocked and nothing to allow us to climb over the fence, we called a locksmith.

Mom was agitated, but we stayed at the fence, trying to keep her calm while waiting. Everyone was hungry, so I made a quick run for food, expecting the locksmith to arrive while I was gone. I was surprised to find the situation unchanged when I returned. We'd been there at least an hour by now.

As the temperature rose, so did my mom's anxiety. We called the locksmith again and found out he was having trouble finding the address but was close. Bree walked out to the corner, hoping to catch his attention while I stayed with mom and watched the kids. When Bree saw him drive past without looking or stopping, we all began getting frustrated.

Mom began screaming, *"Get me out of here!"* terrifying the children. My granddaughter was hiding behind a tree, crying. I looked between the fence slats and saw that my eighty-year-old mother was attempting to pick up a small but heavy yard statue and throw it through the window. As I begged her to stop and wait for the locksmith, I heard glass shattering. She was beating on the window with the statue.

Jagged shards protruded from the window frame toward the center, leaving only a small opening. It looked like the jaws of death. Even so, my mom was determined to climb through the window. She grabbed the shards, trying to loosen them from the frame, cutting her hand in several places.

I was screaming at her to stop when I noticed the locksmith pulling up to the house. Then I heard sirens. Mom had apparently pushed the Lifeline button she wore around her neck. A fire truck, police car, and ambulance pulled up and six large men in uniforms rushed into the house. By then, the door had been unlocked and we had Mom in the living room, sitting in a chair.

I dressed my mother's superficial cuts as I answered questions and filled out forms. The first responders wanted to take her to the hospital, but I declined, signing a waiver. I knew the hospital would offer no help for her real problem, a brain that no longer processed information correctly due to years of earlier unhealed abuse and trauma.

In our remaining time, I located a glass company who cleaned up the mess and sealed the window until a new one could be installed. Mom had nothing to say.

The five of us began the two-hour drive home, totally traumatized by the day. So much for safety in numbers.

Adult Protective Services

The more my mom's mental faculties declined, the more my siblings and I tried to get her to move closer to one of us. The ongoing conversation, however, was always met with resistance.

The recent years had included a number of shocking incidents. Her paranoia was increasingly a problem, always suspicious people were out to harm her or take advantage of her. Eating in restaurants was particularly embarrassing since she believed her food was rarely prepared correctly, giving her free license to give the server a verbal dressing down.

She had a neighbor in her condo complex, a young hothead (my mother's description) named Joe. They were always getting into it over something. One day they got into a fight while standing on the front lawn. I don't mean a verbal one, either, although it started as a shouting match. When she tried to hit him, Joe ducked and then he hit her! An eighty-year-old woman! The police arrived and Adult Protective Services were called in.

Mom was obviously shaken up as she recounted the details to me. I was horrified that someone would hit my mom. Fortunately, her injuries were not severe. I felt relieved that a case worker was assigned to visit her on a regular basis and that there would be someone I could call when I had concerns.

Every few weeks, the case worker and I checked in with each other. Jane and I were on the same page, believing Mom should no longer be living alone. But Jane didn't have any more persuasive power than I did to help Mom see that the charade of pretending she was going to be moving wasn't getting the job done. Jane was also frustrated Mom wouldn't implement her suggestions to help her stay safe and healthy. All Mom was interested in was chit chat, valuable in and of itself, but not addressing her other needs. In spite of the impasse, Mom and Jane became friends.

One day, out of the blue, Mom called me. *I don't want you talking to Jane. You know how it is, when you spend a lot of time talking with someone. You end up sharing things.* Mom was vague. I thought the random request was odd but didn't think much more about it at the time.

The next time I talked to Jane, she informed me that she was bound by my mother's directive to not call her family members. Jane felt it was not wise to leave us in the dark about critical information, so suggested I call her, something my mom didn't have control over.

In October 2013, while making my routine call to Jane, she casually shared something that had come up in an earlier conversation with my mom. *I tried to get your mom to see how inappropriate and alarming it was that she found your father, drunk and naked in bed with you when you were a little girl. But she just brushed it off, saying he didn't know where he was because he had been drinking.*

Jane obviously thought I had already heard this from Mom. She had no way of knowing that this was the first validation I had had from my mother regarding my father's incest. For over twenty years, since I began remembering the abuse, she staunchly stood firm by her version of the story. *The abuse never happened because I was a good mother.*

I died a thousand deaths that day. *So she did know. She did see something. She actually caught him in bed with me but convinced herself it didn't mean anything.* I was reeling. My mom had lied to me and to my siblings. She said there was no abuse because she never saw anything. She let me suffer with this alone, withholding important knowledge, knowledge that, if she'd shared with me at the time when I was going through my healing (let alone if she'd acted on it when I was growing up), would have perhaps prevented the ruin of my relationships with my siblings and with her.

November 9, 2013: *"When I heard these things, I sat down and wept." (Nehemiah 1:4a) Father God, I too have received horrible news. My mother has finally admitted horrible abuse she witnessed by my father to me. Yet I cannot cry. O Lord, please heal and restore me.*

February 25, 2014: *"'Come, let's sell him to the Ishmaelites and not lay our hands on him; after all, he is our brother, our own flesh and blood.' His brothers agreed." (Genesis 37:27) Father God, you know my family has sold me out, too, even though I have been honest and told the truth in all matters. And now, after 22 years, my mother has finally admitted (although not to me, to Jane) she saw my father naked in bed with me. Even so, she, to this day, sees nothing wrong with that. God have mercy on me. Please do not allow the lies and deceit to go unchecked. Be a light in this darkness.*

My mother abandoned me to the abuse when I was five. She abandoned me when I relived it all when I was thirty-five. And now, here she was, once again, abandoning me, willing to tell a stranger, but not her own daughter.

I wanted to call my mom and confront her about it, but I knew how vicious she could be. I had no doubt she would raise a ruckus and get Jane fired from her job, or at least try to do so.

The depth of my pain surprised me. *So it did all happen.* Not that I was living in denial anymore, but the phone call took me back to the reality all over again. My mother had never admitted anything. She'd left me hanging out there alone, casting me as the evil daughter who brought such pain and shame on her family.

I was disappointed to discover the information wouldn't change anything with my brother. After I told him about the phone call, he shrugged it off without a word. I decided not to tell my sister. I couldn't take any more abandonment. Besides, if I'd learned anything in the last decades, it was the lengths a person will go to deny something they didn't want to see. If my family had wanted to know the truth, all they had to do was ask me or look within and ask God. The truth is in each of them, too.

I fought through another round of disappointment and bitterness, but eventually found peace after visiting my place of deep grief once again, being honest about my pain and, eventually, again forgiving my mom. For me, peace is a most valued possession. I may lose it for a while, but not for long. I know it is mine to claim as soon as I am ready to relinquish judgment and ownership to my heavenly Father.

Flying Fishing with God

In August 2011, Bryan took a mental health day, meaning he headed out for a day of fly fishing. Nothing gave him a re-set faster than sloshing up and down a river with a fly rod in hand. Being in the mountains was his best time to talk to and hear from God.

What he heard that day, however, changed his world.

He was so undone and near panicked, he didn't mention anything for three weeks. He told God, *If this really is your voice talking to me, then please confirm what I heard.* And, in God's grace, he did.

While Bryan's experience fly fishing was unknown to me, my wrangling with God about a men's ministry was unknown to Bryan.

August 31, 2011: *Father, there is so much that only you can do. I need your power every day working in my life for your will to be done. Please answer for me today my questions about men taking the Healing Journey Class and how the church will receive a class that men are taking which is taught by a woman. May your will be done.*

September 1, 2011: *Lord, God, I know I am accountable to you for my life and I certainly want to please you in all things. Today I am in great turmoil. I believe in my heart of hearts that you have led my steps to speak, teach, train, and write. And now, by their choice, men are coming under my teaching—yet your word says women shouldn't teach men. We had men at all our events this year. I beg you to direct my steps, O Lord, my God. Much is at stake. If I am out of your will, move me back in line. If I am in your will, give me peace. As always, I bow my life to your authority and seek only to obey you.*

This searching for guidance from God about a men's ministry went on for a few weeks, when the story finally came out and Bryan told me what God had said to him. Bryan was to be the one to film Healing Journey for men and lead the men's ministry, a plan that terrified him.

It made sense, of course. Bryan had been leading groups every year, and now other men were leading, too. The men's side of the ministry was growing! It happened all on its own, without any effort or encouragement from me. The problem was they were using the women's videos and materials. They didn't seem to care, but I knew many churches would not allow men to receive teaching from a woman and would ban the men's classes. Regardless of what anyone thought about that, it was a reality.

Filming the lessons for men was not a problem for God, but certainly presented a challenge for Bryan. Having never filmed or been a Bible teacher, his learning curve was steeper than mine. Nevertheless, we jumped in and went to work.

I translated the women's materials into a language for men and Bryan tested the new lessons in his next classes. I sat in the back corner of the room while Bryan taught, listening and writing down the changes he naturally brought to the material with his own stories and expressions. This helped me bring his voice into the lessons. The process took three years before Bryan was ready to film the lessons.

Our next task was finding a location. Bryan had been doing construction, commercial tenant-finish, for one particular company for years, and they graciously offered a large, unused space to us at no charge. This was the first time we were able to build a filming set to our specifications. Bryan and his crew did the construction and Bree handled the design and decorating. It was fabulous.

We all smiled later when several people came up to us and said they were pretty sure they had stayed at that Colorado lodge. We were pretty sure they hadn't since it was a false set in a commercial building. But it made us feel good they thought it was real. Completing the men's version of Healing Journey and getting it ready to distribute in the fall of 2014 was another great victory.

After that, changes in our ministry were rapid. We expanded our staff, board of directors, and leadership team to include men. We also added men to our Boot Camps and started doing men's Healing Journey retreats. Men's classes were now popping up everywhere.

A Boot Camp for the Records

We continued to train leaders in our Boot Camps, heading east each spring to Bath, New York, in May. We always began the trip with a positive outlook, although the travel never seemed to go smoothly. The 2014 Boot Camp definitely ranks as the most challenging.

We were in trouble right out of the gate. (Or should I say *before the gate?*) We left for the Denver airport at seven o'clock in the morning, just ten minutes before the airline sent an email telling us to reschedule our flight, an email we wouldn't see until we got to the ticket counter at nine o'clock, two hours after most everyone else on our flights started rebooking.

By God's providence, there were three seats left on a flight leaving in five hours, routing us through Atlanta, but getting us into New York at eleven-thirty that night. Not ideal, but at least we'd make it in time to start Boot Camp the next day.

Having asked what the problem was in New York, we learned they were having a one-hundred-year-flood that had closed the Elmira airport where we had hoped to arrive. The whole region was being deluged and it wasn't supposed to let up until the next day. *Oh, great.* I was feeling more than a little uncomfortable about the trip.

On the final flight into Rochester, we began to fear it would be too late to pick up our rental car since it was nearly midnight. What a relief to find they were still open, and our car waiting for us. We grabbed our bags and headed south to our host's home, normally a ninety-minute drive.

The driving rain and nearly nonexistent lights along the country highway made visibility nil. After a while, Bryan said if the rain didn't lighten up, we'd have to stop and get a room. It wasn't safe to push on.

My heart sank. After all we'd been through that day and now, to be only forty-five minutes away and have to stop for the night! We went a few more miles and suddenly the rain turned to a light mist. *Praise God!* We pulled into Gary and Barb Short's home at about two o'clock. Bryan was asleep in thirty minutes, but I only finally fell asleep for an hour at six.

The adrenalin for the day ahead kept me going while we set up and prepared to serve over eighty future leaders. We were almost ready, just ten minutes before show time, when I noticed several large, official looking men coming in the back door and heading toward my podium.

Ma'am, the river is at flood level. (The building we were using was only a few hundred yards from the river.) *If it rises more than a few inches, it will crest the banks, flood the bridge and prevent anyone from being able to leave this building. You should put an evacuation plan in place and locate an alternative venue.*

You know, there are just some moments that are so far beyond the ridiculous that all you can do is laugh. *Alternative venue, right! Yes, we'll just call around and see who is able to receive eighty people with five minutes notice, including ten breakout rooms and meals for four days. Right! No problem!* I kept those thoughts from coming out of my mouth, simply responding with, *"Okay. Got it."*

I mean, what else was I going to do? Every element of this was out of my hands. I actually prefer these kinds of crises. When there is absolutely nothing I can do except pray and let the Lord solve it, it is easier. And that's what I did.

Lord, I'm really busy right now. It's been a heck of a thirty hours. I've slept exactly one hour. Eighty people are sitting in front of me, looking at me to start training them and we are having a flood like no one as seen here for a hundred years. Good luck and let me know what you want me to do.

And with that, I started speaking.

The river didn't rise even another inch and I never saw the large, official looking men again. *Thank you, Jesus!*

I got more sleep Friday night, and after a second night of sleep on Saturday, I was feeling pretty good going into Day Three.

About an hour before we left for the venue, I was in the bathroom doing my hair and makeup. I always had trouble sleeping during these big events, so I set out my over-the-counter sleeping pills to put in my pocket for later tonight. As I finished up in the bathroom, I looked down and noticed the pills were gone. I searched the area thoroughly and could only assume the worst. I had inadvertently swallowed them, drugging myself with sleep aides.

Gee whiz. This is preposterous! Now what am I going to do? Well, there was nothing to do except pray and down as much caffeine as I could. What followed was one of my most painful days of speaking, slurring my words at times, pulling on every ounce of focus that I could in order to stay on track and keep teaching.

Like every other challenging moment I'd been through, I just kept going, knowing the Lord would give me what I needed. And he did.

Letter from God

The following are words I heard in my heart from God, words that illustrate just how much he loves and cares about us.

August 10, 2014: *Cyndy, you want to know how to focus your fall and what you will be doing. You are on the right track. I have things well in hand. I am with you. I am pleased with your obedience this past year. You didn't shirk the work I had for you or shrink from my plan. I know it was hard work, but my grace is sufficient for you. And this will be true for the next 2 years as we continue the work I have for you.*

I love you. I am pleased with you. You are my child. I have much for you to do. You are far from finished. I know others don't understand what I am doing in you and with you. But that's okay. Don't worry about that. My plan is unfolding in you. You are hearing my voice. You are seeing the road I am taking you on. Just follow me.

The work is good and it is exciting. You are going to like where we are going. There's some fun stuff up ahead. Yes, and much hard work. It is true the road I have for you is different. Few will understand. Finish the devotional this fall (I had been working on my devotional book, Healing Words, for about a year). *Start on the revisions right away and get it done. I'll give you the last few devotionals soon. This is going to be a very popular book. It will change things.*

You are moving into the world's light now but don't be afraid. I'll take care of you. Remember always that you are mine. I won't let anything happen to you. I know you are worried about your feet and fainting and the stress of travel. Know that I am always with you and will take care of you. I know you don't like this part. You don't like the travel and you don't like the limelight. It pleases me that you choose to go there with me anyway. I see your obedience. Thank you for trusting me. Thank you for giving up everything else to do this for me.

We are just getting started. There is so much to come, and I am very excited to show you, to take you there. Remember, it is good. I'm sorry it is so hard, at times. The worldly tension you experience is unavoidable and will increase. But I am sufficient. I won't let you go. I won't let you go anywhere or into any situation without my presence and protection. I will guard you. I have a legion of angels surrounding you. You are mine and I take that very seriously.

You are right about filming. We're going to do the Healing Journey class one more time. Don't worry about getting it right. I will help you with that. I'll give you everything. Don't I always? Don't worry so much about the timing right now. Yes—2 years, not 3. It will all flow seamlessly. I have it all figured out. Don't I always? We'll change some things, but not the essence. I'll give it to you when you start writing. Don't worry about it right now. Just focus on the devotional book.

The training DVD will come together more easily than you think. It will get done. Follow me. Enjoy your work. Listen to my voice. This is a fruitful time. Trust me with your body and your health. I love you so much and I see your love for me. It delights me. I enjoy our time together each day. Thank you for giving me that. It is how I shape and mold you. I'll give you the time to write. And I will answer your prayer and give you the gift of words. Actually, you already have it. Enjoy today. Rest. Relax. Play. Your heavenly Father who adores you.

I could not believe we were going to re-film the women's class. Oy vey! We had just finished the men's curriculum—literally, this same week! But we were getting feedback that the first videos looked a bit dated, and after everyone saw the gorgeous men's set, they wanted us to redo the women's filming. And because we were already committed to re-filming the training DVD, adding role plays for men, this meant another busy year.

I was surprised God mentioned my feet. Getting an accurate diagnosis in 2012 was good news and bad news. It was good to know why I fainted and that there was nothing wrong with my feet. And the diagnosis cleared up so many earlier mysteries, like why I felt like I was going to be sick anytime I went in a hot tub and why I felt like I was going to melt on hot days.

The downside of the diagnosis was learning that I had a communication problem between my brain and heart, and would forever have to be careful to avoid anything that encouraged my blood pressure to drop. For most people, when their blood pressure drops, their brain tells their heart to compress their blood vessels, forcing more blood to the brain. Mine does the opposite; it tells my heart to dilate. This causes my blood pressure to drop even more, making me topple over like a fallen tree.

I've always suspected I might have a little brain damage. Now I knew! The really big downside to all this is that traveling, standing, speaking, and being too warm all increase my chances of fainting. When I am home, it is easy to control. All I have to do is eat something, drink water, and put my feet up. Simple. Not so simple when I am on the road, doing a speaking event, particularly one in a prison where I can't control the environment.

Not that any of this is essential information, but it does explain my hesitancy about traveling and speaking. I never know when my blood pressure will drop, and I'll go down—something I don't relish doing in front of an audience.

All this just made my list longer, that list of reasons why I thought I was a ludicrous choice for this job. But, that's just like God—always choosing the least likely person. When he does, it just reveals his amazing love and power, even more.

It meant the world to me that God gave me his reassurance. He would hold me up.

Chapter Fifty-Eight

2015

Women's Filming—Round Two

Once Healing Journey was produced in 2008, it began to take on a life of its own, popping up in new locations all the time. The organization at home began growing, too, adding more staff, and moving the materials into a proper office after we outgrew our basement. As God promised, through it all, the donations never stopped arriving since we received that first check back in 2003.

Each year was full, training leaders at Boot Camps, speaking in women's prisons, leading classes, writing new materials, and preparing for the next filming projects. It was a busy but satisfying rhythm. I felt blessed to be able to do something I loved so much.

I rarely initiated anything in the ministry, still not the visionary, but simply kept running to catch up to whatever God was already doing, like the situation with the men's ministry. It was after God started several men's groups and then told Bryan to film the lessons that I realized we needed to move in that direction. And it absolutely was not my idea to re-film the women's Healing Journey lessons, ten years after the first go-round. But I did agree with the consensus that the original footage was looking dated. And, it was true, we were now able to produce a higher quality project.

When the calendar turned over to 2015, we were knee-deep in plans for filming the revised women's study, planning to shoot the outdoor segments that summer.

My production skills had also grown over the years. The first time around, I was just looking for a pretty scene behind me while we filmed. This time, I wanted the backdrops to tie into my lessons. Since the class has a strong "Egypt" theme and referenced traveling through the wilderness, we took a three-day road trip to the Great Sand Dunes (an amazing phenomenon in the middle of the Colorado Rocky Mountains) to film several segments. For the lesson where Joseph the Patriarch was put in prison, we shot the scene in front of an iconic prison, built in the 1800s. And we located an alley for the lesson about Satan's feeding on the garbage of our life, shooting while I stood next to a dumpster. The result was satisfying.

Falling in Love with Writing

I've always been a simple girl, not looking for big deals. I've never wanted to be rich or famous or powerful. I've never looked for the spotlight, which helps to understand my embarrassment when people come up to me and say silly things like, *"Are you Cyndy Sherwood? I feel like I'm with a movie star!"* I'm not anyone special, at least not anyone more special than any other person on the planet.

My heart's desire is simply to make an impact through books, materials, classes, and events that introduce people to the real God so they can experience his redemption and healing, too. As much as I love speaking truth, I know that writing truth has the potential to reach more people, by far.

With that in mind, an idea began stirring in me after we finished filming Running with Horses in 2013. I wanted to write three devotional books along the subject lines of my Bible studies, one on healing, one on enhancing our relationship with Jesus, and one on living the sacrificial life. This was an enormous undertaking, requiring nearly eleven hundred devotionals. (I'll leave it to others to judge my plans as wisdom or sheer lunacy!) Nonetheless, writing each one was a pleasure.

Like everything else I'd done, I didn't really know how I was going to do this. I just started, noting passages that I came across during my morning time with God, and roughing out some thoughts about what I thought it was saying. A couple years later, after filling three journals with these *starter* devotionals, I created my first devotional book, Healing Words.

This process, starting with a passage of Scripture and allowing the Holy Spirit to reveal its message, is the way I wrote everything, whether a Bible study, speech, or devotional book. Then I would continue to build from there, fleshing out the meaning, adding metaphors, and stories. Seeing the devotionals come to life was exciting.

It was just as much a thrill when I opened the box to see my second book, Healing Words. I started creating Resting Words, right away and later, Running Words, working continuously for six years until the three devotional books were done.

I loved the writing, as much or more than any project I've worked on, providing joy in a year that had very little to offer.

Losing Grandchildren

I often refer to our family as very American, a little of everything. When people ask me how many grandchildren I have, the answer is complicated. My girls have five kids between them, Bryan's boys, four. But then there are Heather's three kids, whom we consider as our grandkids, too, even though there isn't any biology between us. A couple of our grandkids have siblings, so we include them, too.

Some of our grandchildren were not planned, but nevertheless, they are blessed surprises. This was the situation with our granddaughter, Samantha. Little did we know how this would later lead to painful realities.

Even though Samantha's parents were not married, we had been part of her life from the beginning, meeting her in the hospital the day she was born. For five years, we'd celebrated birthdays and Christmases together, including her older brother as well. We'd been together many times throughout the years.

On April 9, 2015, we arranged for Samantha and her brother to come over and play after school. To make it a little more fun, we invited Bree's three kids, too.

The five of us found ourselves waiting for Samantha and her brother to arrive, puzzled, since they lived only ten minutes away. As time passed, I called to see if the kids were still coming. No answer. No response. After an hour and a half, we concluded they weren't coming.

What we didn't know that day was that we would never see those kids again. Bryan and I were heartbroken. I can only try to fill in the blanks, because no explanation was ever given to us, but I am assuming it was simply too painful or difficult to remain part of our family, knowing that marrying the other parent would never be an option.

To try and redeem the day, we took Bree's kids out to dinner before taking them home. While we were eating dinner, I got a phone call. It was Karie.

26: Koby (died 4-09-15)

Karie was Kaleb's adoptive mother, my first grandchild. Because it was an open adoption, we had had a close relationship with her and her husband, Tim, for the previous fourteen years. They had also adopted another son, Koby, who was two years old when Kaleb was born. Like we did with every grandkid, we enfolded Koby into our family, too.

Koby was quite the athlete, "elite" being the term his lacrosse and football coaches used. I had been able to watch his Lacrosse game the previous summer when he was playing in town, going out to dinner with the family afterward.

I was surprised Karie was calling. I had just spoken to Koby two weeks earlier, when he called to thank me for his birthday present and let me know he had gotten his driver's license. He was so excited to be able to drive on his own. Karie got right to the point. *Koby killed himself today.* I felt like my life was sucked out of me in an instant. I could not believe I was getting this phone call, again, eleven years after Breanna had died. How could this be?

April 14: *"I will pour out my Spirit in those days." (Joel 2:29b) Father, my heart is so heavy and sad for this senseless tragedy, for the loss of Koby's life, for the hard road we must now all walk, particularly for Kaleb, Karie, and Tim. Yet your promises and encouragement remain steadfast. I receive whatever you want to say to me or do through me. Pour out your Spirit according to your will. And may your mercy and grace be upon us all.*

Life became a blur, once again. A week later, we were in Denver, sitting with the family at Koby's funeral, hearing story after story about this wonderful young man, stunned he was gone.

Being parents who had also lost a child to suicide created an even deeper connection between us. Unfortunately, we knew the hell they were going through. This common link gave us the opportunity to comfort and support them. Three weeks later, Kaleb turned fourteen, so young, yet his life already shattered.

27: Kaleb (age 18)

More Death

Four days after Koby's funeral, the phone rang again. This time it was Bree telling me that her father, Tim, had died. This set off an explosion of emotions in all of us.

Bree and Jenny both had had occasion to be in California recently, not far from where Tim lived, but had been denied a visit with their father. They knew Tim wasn't well, having been diagnosed with a rogue protein growing in his brain. But his wife had never been able to reconcile the fact that Tim had another family, so she blocked the girls from seeing him.

Not being allowed to say goodbye to their father made his death even more difficult, almost as difficult as the next phone call, requesting we not attend the funeral. I was glad we had already purchased our plane tickets, making it easier to politely decline the request. I couldn't believe the cruelty, telling the girls they were not welcome at their own father's funeral.

Since Tim's remarriage, thirty years earlier, the girls had only seen him a handful of times. They had been robbed of a relationship with their father and then refused the chance to see him before he died. I would not agree to miss his funeral.

When we got to the church, we slipped in quietly, sitting in a pew off to the side. We had no intentions of staying for the reception but felt we should pay our respects to Tim's father and siblings before we left. I hadn't seen the family since Tim's mother died, three years earlier. I was glad she was spared the grief of attending her son's funeral.

There were no words adequate to help my girls unravel the morass of feelings. When they showed the obligatory montage of old photos of Tim's life, there was a noticeable ten-year gap, the ten years during which we dated, were married, and birthed two daughters. It was simply omitted. It was as if the girls and I never existed. When the photo appeared on the screen of Tim, his wife, and three kids visiting Pikes Peak, we realized he had been in town, but never bothered to let his girls know.

During the service, I felt moments of rage rise inside me. I had thoughts of standing up and telling everyone who I was, and that Tim actually had two other daughters they knew nothing about. *Let me introduce all of you to Bree and Jenny.*

For the sake of the girls, I behaved myself. No one likes to see their mother make a scene. But, believe me, I *wanted* to make a scene.

April 28: *Father, there are few times in my life when I have been as low as I am now. I am under the bus, flat and weak. Yet you are God and your power knows no limits. Breathe life back into my soul that I might serve you again and with unquenchable fervor. How can I go on feeling like this? Only by your grace.*

April 29: *"Then he fell on his knees and cried out, 'Lord, do not hold this sin against them.'" (Acts 7:60a) Father God, I forgive* (Tim's wife and family) *for their gross injustices against my girls and against me. May we now heal and know your peace.*

What a month. Koby and Tim were gone, and Bryan and I would never see our granddaughter again.

Buying Real Estate

For ten years, my siblings and I had unsuccessfully tried to get Mom to move near one of us. We were concerned for her safety. I finally told God that if he wanted her to move, he would have to do it. Only Almighty God could make this happen.

Unbeknownst to me, Mom contacted a real estate agent in Colorado Springs and tried to make an offer on a condo. However, with the Springs being one of the hottest markets in the country, it was sold before she could get here.

My mom is a survivor, I've got to give her that. She'd been abused and abandoned herself, over and over. No one ever helped her or supported her, not as a child, a young adult, or later, after being left by two husbands. Yet, in every circumstance, Mom had found her footing, worked hard, and made savvy business decisions. Her ability to recognize a good real estate opportunity had provided a comfortable income. So she knew what she was looking for.

Six months after she lost the first opportunity to buy a condo, the same agent let Mom know a unit like it had just come on the market. She knew she'd have to move quickly, or she'd lose this deal, too. The next day, her offer beat out five others. In less than two days, she had become the owner of property only five minutes away from my house. It looked like God did want Mom to move near me, something that would greatly impact my life. That was April.

Okay, God, that was a very impressive miracle, but we're not out of the woods yet. She still has a townhome to sell, one that is crammed full of stuff. I've watched her drag a move out for years! Who knows if or when she'll ever move down here!

I found Mom's motivation for moving mysterious. *Why not move near my brother or sister?* It was beyond my comprehension why she decided to move near me, buying a place in the Springs. After all that had happened between us, I was worried about how we would navigate life together.

I can honestly say, though, I didn't harbor any bitterness toward her. Mom still vexed me on a regular basis, but I loved her and wanted her to be well and happy.

And the miracles kept coming.

Moving Mom

In June, I encouraged her to get an agent to help her sell the townhome. *Nope, I've bought and sold my own real estate my entire life. I don't need any help.* When she told me that her strategy was to put a for sale sign in her living room window, I was sure nothing would happen. After all, she lived in a cul-de-sac. No one would see it except a few neighbors.

Within days, a couple knocked at the door. *We would like to buy your condo.* Mom told them the asking price and, standing on the front porch, they agreed. That night she decided the price must be too low since they didn't try to counter. The next day she called them and raised the price five thousand dollars. The buyers were undaunted. *No problem, we'll have the contract drawn up.*

Are you kidding me? Really? Miracle number two. *Okay, God, clearly you are moving heaven and earth to facilitate my mother relocating to the Springs. But you've forgotten something. My mother is a hoarder and unwilling to part with anything. Not only is her four-bedroom home full, so is her garage and storage unit. And her new place? Did you not notice it is only half as big?*

With filming and everything going on in the ministry, I didn't have a lot of spare time. I had one open week in July and offered to come up and help Mom get ready to move, still dubious it would ever happen. Thinking back to the last time I tried to help her move, nine years earlier, the day she tried to hit my brother and gave herself a bloody nose, I couldn't imagine accomplishing anything useful. I was anxious about the whole thing, and afraid of being alone with her. I prayed for God's grace as I made the two-hour drive up the interstate.

July 11, that morning, before I left for Mom's: *"Does he not see my ways and count my every step?" (Job 31:4) Father, I am immensely tired and slept very little last night yet I have three terrifically hard days ahead of me. I need your strength and help. May there be peace today.*

I arrived in the afternoon, on a Thursday. On Monday, I was following a moving truck down the interstate with all the furniture Mom intended to use in the new place, even her bed. Miracle number three.

The four days were fraught with tension and meltdowns, and moments of frustration with her inability to make any decisions. But I just kept pressing forward. When she blocked me in one area, I simply moved to another. The fact that she wasn't getting rid of anything yet, just moving some stuff, made things a little easier.

July 14: *"I know that you can do all things; no plan of yours can be thwarted." (Job: 42:2) Father God, I have seen this firsthand. You have decided to move Mom down here; truly a miracle, and nothing can stop you. Thank you for this great demonstration of your power and love. And help her with the final tasks.*

After the moving truck was unloaded in the Springs, Bree and I got everything settled in her new condo. I consciously took note of how clean and cute it looked; aware I would never see it this way after my mom moved in. If she moved in.

Okay, God. You must really want my mom to live down here. Not in a million years did I think we would make that much progress in four days, nor did I think she would allow me to pack up her stuff. But you forgot something, Lord. Mom is still living in Ft. Collins, and her house is still full of junk.

There was one compelling detail, helping motivate her to follow through. Mom was now under contract to be out of her place by November 7. I wasn't sure how that would happen, but clearly God wasn't short on miracles.

I made four more trips to Ft. Collins, the last two with Bryan, bless his heart. Mom hated Bryan, and had no problem making things unduly hard for him. I did as much as I could without him, but there was more stuff than I could manage alone.

Everything was a fight with Mom. Even stacks of old newspapers and magazines had to be negotiated. I must have filled up the back of my car fifty times, running loads down to the drive-through Goodwill, hoping she wouldn't look to see what I was hauling off. I'm sure they questioned why I kept bringing them garbage.

Friday, November 6, Bryan and I headed up to Ft. Collins one last time. The basement hadn't been packed, neither had the storage unit. And the garage was still full. The worst, though, was her bedroom. In all my previous trips, I hadn't been able to gain her cooperation to go through it and clothes and things were piled up in every direction. *Impossible, Lord. There's no way we can be out of here tomorrow night.*

November 6: *"...God has been gracious to me and I have all I need." (Genesis 33:11b) Father, I believe you have and will perfectly provide for all I need this weekend in order to move my mother. I feel like I am staring at the Red Sea—an impossible situation with no human way of getting through. But you are God, and nothing is impossible for you. I know you'll make a way. Please guard our hearts and minds as we go through this.*

After arriving in Ft. Collins, good friends of my mom's stopped by to take her out to dinner, just the break we needed. Before she returned, Bryan and I had the basement packed, and ready to go. Mom had made prior arrangements with a salvage company to come and haul away everything in the garage. The next morning, an old man and his son started loading.

Later, my mom went out to see what they were doing and spotted an antique doll wagon in the back on the truck. *"You can't take that,"* she said. The man told her she could have it back for $40. I thought I was going to lose my mind. *Really, you're going to take advantage of my mother that way?* Yes, he was, and without shame. But before I could lose my mind, my mom lost hers. I thought there was going to be blood. She was screaming and crying.

Just then my nephew arrived from Denver, like a knight in shining armor, to take mom's old station wagon off her hands. *Thank you, Jesus.* I slipped the awful man forty dollars while my mom wasn't looking and grabbed the toy wagon.

Robert was a Godsend. One of mom's favorites, Robert was able to get my mom to sit on the bedroom floor with him and pack everything up. I was beginning to see hope. While Robert had my mom distracted, I took Bryan over to the storage unit. It was mostly full of trash. I was sad thinking how mom had paid storage fees for this for nine years.

At five o'clock, we were finished. Too tired to make the drive home, we got a couple of hotel rooms for the night.

November 8: *"...and gave him success in whatever he did." (Genesis 39:23b) Thank you for accomplishing this miracle. No one besides me knows the extent of this miracle and your amazing power behind it.*

Sunday, November 8, my mom was living in her new home in the Springs. Miracle number four.

And, just in the nick of time. I had a filming project starting in a month.

Unforgettable 36 Hours

Having finished the women's Healing Journey intro and outro filming over the summer, it was time to get ready to film the lessons, and there was a lot to do. We had a full set to build before the dress rehearsal, December 12.

Like with the men's filming project, Bree used her God-given skills to bring to life an empty, commercial space, as Bryan built the set to her specifications. We would have to work fast if we were going to finish it in time.

On a cold, snowy weekend, Bryan left early that Saturday morning to let the crew into the building where we were filming. As I opened my car door, an hour later, I saw that the glove compartment was open and the contents spilled onto the floor. *Hmmm... maybe Bryan was looking for something.* Then I noticed my car key and garage door opener were missing. *Oh no! Someone broke into our garage and got into my car.*

I told Bryan about the break-in as soon as I arrived on the set. Disconcerted, he dashed home to disable the garage door just in case they came back.

It was a long day, setting up the lights and cameras for the first time, making sure everything was just right. The shoot went well. As we drove home, the snow was getting heavier.

We were both anxious that night as we got ready for bed. We kept thinking about someone being in our garage the night before. Bryan got his shotgun out of the safe and slept in the guest room, the room right over the back door to the garage.

Several hours later, he woke me up, shotgun in hand. *Call 911. They're back.* While I was on the phone, Bryan was in the kitchen, debating whether he should open the door to the garage, and go in. Praise God he waited for the police. As soon as they arrived, the intruders fled through the backyard. The police had no trouble tracking their footprints through the deep snow but lost them a few blocks from our house, when they got away by car.

It was a terrifying night, but I have to say, they were the most stupid criminals. Who alerts their victims by burglarizing them and then returns the next night? They weren't even quiet while trying to bash in the door to the garage.

It was four a.m. before the police were gone and we stumbled back into bed.

The next morning, at nine thirty, my dad shot and killed himself.

Chapter Fifty-Nine

2016

Disowned

I couldn't believe I was dealing with another suicide. Five in one family is just too much. While my uncle's and grandmother's deaths were not terribly impactful to my life, Breanna's and Koby's deaths were. Those were direct hits to my heart, changing my life forever. Dad's death impacted me in still a different way.

Trying to digest all that had happened over that infamous December weekend was difficult. The sense of violation coupled with fear and anxiety over the break-in had me quite shaken. Neither Bryan nor I could sleep very well, concerned they might return a third time. (Fortunately, the crime ring of young adult and teen robbers was caught a month later.) Now with Dad's suicide added to that, I plummeted fast and far. I was just days from Christmas and weeks away from filming, but I was in no shape to deal with any of it.

My feelings were complicated. On the one hand I had not seen my dad in more than five years, since the day he informed me that he never wanted to see me again. Thinking about that left me feeling cheated and angry. Added to that was the temptation to gloat and say, *Good riddance,* given our history.

But, as I'd learned over the decades, it wasn't that simple. Every person is born with the need and desire for a satisfying relationship with their parents. The parent-child bond is created by God. We can try throwing gasoline on it and setting it on fire, but the essence of the need for a relationship with your closest loved ones is impervious to flames. To a degree the need will remain, no matter what efforts we make to remove it, even though we may no longer yearn for a relationship with the parents to which we were born. That's why many people find satisfaction in their relationship with God when our earthly parents supplied none.

Even with all that had happened, I couldn't deny the truth; I still loved my dad. And when he died, I felt sad. Sad for him, living such a lost and depraved life, never knowing truth or finding healing, and sad for me, never having the father I wanted and needed. It was sad all the way around.

I grieved immediately, deeply, throwing myself into processing it, talking about it with anyone who would listen, acknowledging the kaleidoscope of emotions and thoughts.

The morning my dad died, God gave me an unforgettable gift. Traumatized from the night's event and not yet knowing my dad's fate, I rose to read my Bible. So ingrained in me now, after submitting to the routine for decades, it was the only thing I knew to do. In the previous weeks, I had been reading Psalms, working my way through it each day, when I naturally came to Psalm 23 that morning.

The Lord is my shepherd, I shall not be in want. He makes me lie down in green pastures, he leads me beside quiet waters, he refreshes my soul. He guides me in the path of righteousness for his name's sake. Even though I walk through the valley of death, I will fear no evil, for you are with me; your rod and your staff, they comfort me. You prepare a table before me in the presence of my enemies. You anoint my head with oil; my cup overflows. Surely goodness and love will follow me all the days of my life, and I will dwell in the house of the Lord forever.

My dad was still alive when I read this. Later I realized, God had found a way to reach into my life and comfort my soul. He knew before I did that I would be entering the valley of death again, and he wanted me to know his comfort and presence were already with me, already holding me, even before the phone rang that afternoon with the news. It was a palpable touch of God's love for me.

December 14: *"Though my father and mother forsake me, the Lord will receive me." (Psalm 27:10) You are my only Father and that has always been true. However, I am reeling, devastated and heartbroken because all hope for my father is lost. Decades of prayer for him appear to have come to nothing. He died unrepentant and wallowing in pride. He rebuffed every attempt we made to share the truth with him. He was an evil man and lived an evil life—just like his father. So why does my heart sear with pain? Why does grief envelope me? It is impossible for a child to erase the love they have for their parents. No matter what they do, no matter how horrible they are, no matter how much abuse there is, no matter how many lies they tell—love remains. I have forgiven my parents. I did that long ago. May God have mercy on their souls.*

I don't remember Christmas, but I'll never forget New Year's Eve. A few of our grandkids were spending the night while their parents went out, and some of our other kids were over, playing games, when I got a call informing me that my father had removed me from his will and requested that I not be at his funeral.

Not again! Unbelievable! I shouldn't have been surprised at people's insensitivity by then, but I was. Bryan was livid that someone should deliver such cruel news to me. So incensed, he grabbed the phone out of my hand and hung up. Of course, his real anger was at my dad for making those decisions. We were in shock and reeling from the news.

This had been such a hard road for Bryan. Knowing what my family had done to me, and kept doing to me, was just more than he could handle sometimes. Every fiber of his being wanted to make things right, but any option conceived in his mind was illegal (ha!). Had there been a murder, he'd have been the first suspect. I was forever pulling him off the ceiling and trying to calm him down. New Year's Eve was particularly bad.

My father's final act toward me was abandonment and rejection. At least I can say he was consistent to the end. The pain I felt, having been removed from his will and banned from his funeral, hurt far worse than the pain of his death. I struggled with this for a long time.

January 3: *"Set a guard over my mouth, O LORD; keep watch over the door of my lips. Let not my heart be drawn to what is evil…" (Psalm 141:3-4a) Father, I truly need your help here for I want to blast my family with the truth. I want to rant and rave and accuse and judge. I want to let them have it for selling me down the river, for lining up with the evil, rapist monster;*

for supporting him, and rejecting me. It is just too much. I can't take it anymore. I can't be silent any longer. My rage is out. My pain is gushing out like an unstoppable river of blood. Help me, O God. I want to honor you. Please carry me to a place of clear obedience.

Back to the Set

Far too soon, it was time to begin filming the women's Healing Journey lessons. People asked me why I didn't cancel the filming, or at the very least, put it off for a while.

I think the issue for me was that I was not willing to let evil win. Satan had stolen far too much from me, inspiring countless people to bring harm to me and my loved ones. Had I laid down and given up, Satan would have won.

Satan authored the burglary, my dad's suicide, and his decision to cut me out of his will. It was a dance perfectly choreographed to coincide with filming. I had no control over the circumstances, but I still had control over my response to them.

If we are devoted to Jesus Christ we have nothing to do with what we meet, whether it is just or unjust. Jesus says—Go steadily on with what I have told you to do and I will guard your life. My Utmost for His Highest, June 27.

God told me all along that it was going to be a rough ride, and he wasn't kidding. I've never done any project, writing, filming, or otherwise, when the gates of hell haven't opened up, firing fiery darts my way. If I'm going to cower before the flames, then I'm never going to accomplish anything God gives me to do. My only option, the only option acceptable to me, is to believe God is sufficient to carry me through the fire.

By now I have a hundred stories I could recount, illnesses on the way to speaking events, derailed flights on the way to prisons, attacks on my kids when launching a writing project. It just never stops. And I don't either, not unless it is God asking me to stop to rest and regroup. I'll stop for him, but that's it. Insane, stubborn, or obedient—I guess that'll be up to God to decide.

While re-filming Healing Journey, I began reflecting on the years since our first filming project, and it struck me that I had either been preparing to film, filming, or in post-production for a solid ten years. I'm glad God never told me what was coming down the road, only what was on the next mile. It would have been too overwhelming.

With five major filming projects now under my belt, and countless smaller ones, I felt like I could write the book: "Filming Bible Studies for Dummies." I was seasoned in film production. What seemed foreign to me ten years ago, now came naturally.

Three months after filming the first lesson for the revised women's Healing Journey class, we wrapped up. It was the day before Easter.

The Busiest Year

Earlier that winter, my staff, including Bree, began talking to me about re-doing the filming for Resting in Jesus. Bree, who had beautifully designed both the set for this project and the men's filming two years earlier, said: *"Mom, you really should consider filming Resting in Jesus again before you tear the set down. It would be much easier and cheaper just to change out a few colors and key pieces and reuse the set."*

Easy for you! I thought to myself, *You're not the one filming!* But I could see she was right. It really did need to be redone. And with the cost of a new set running around ten thousand dollars, there was prudence in it, too. So, forty-eight hours after our party, celebrating the end of filming for Healing Journey, I started preparing to film Resting in Jesus. We finished six weeks later. Boy was I pooped!

If there hadn't been so many other projects in the works, as well, my stress level might have gone down a little. But the ministry was also filming a new introductory DVD, rebranding our ministry logo, and building a new website. And just because we had a triple-header that year with filming didn't mean the regular events stopped! So Bryan and I were still leading Boot Camps in the spring, and I was speaking in women's prisons that fall.

"No desire will ever be placed in you by the Holy Spirit unless he intends to fulfill it. So let your faith rise up and soar away to claim all the land you can discover." Streams in the Desert, March 26. This was my guiding

belief, that if God placed in me the desire, he would supply the provision, including my mental, emotional, and physical strength.

Green Pastures

As we were transitioning to the next filming project, I booked a retreat for a couple days of rest. At the very least, I needed a mini break!

March 30: *Father, thank you for this pastoral and restful setting. Please grant me rest and restoration. This past week really kicked my butt and I certainly haven't recovered, particularly with all this back pain. Coming into a 2nd filming project on Monday was brutal. I was empty, exhausted and in pain. How would I do this? How could I be ready to film again in 12 days? Yet, I am confident you are leading me and so I trust this time to you. "You have been with me wherever I have gone…" (1 Chronicles 17:8a)*

March 31: *"Surely God is my help; the Lord is the one who sustains me." (Psalm 54:4) Father God, our crazy season isn't over yet. However, my confidence is in you. You are my sustaining strength. I know and rely upon the love you have for me. (The Lord then began talking to me.) "Cyndy I need you, too. I am pleased you have come to me. It brings me joy. Know that I love you and will always love you. I am with you. Go to your work now. I will be with you through all of it. Don't worry about anything or be anxious. I've got you. I always have you. You will get through this season. I am with you. I will give you what you need, including the money. I have everything covered. Just trust me. Rest in me and know that I've got you covered. I love you.*

Chapter Sixty

2017-2019

Grandkids to the Rescue

Talking to Bree one day and thinking about the transition parents make every year when their kids get out of school, spawned an idea. It isn't easy for mothers to keep their sanity when kids are home all day, asking what they were going to do every minute. So I offered to take them one afternoon a week.

For eight weeks, I planned field trips to keep my grandkids entertained and give her a few hours off. What started off with unselfish intentions, however, soon evolved into purely selfish ones. I was getting the greatest benefit.

***28**: Elijah, Matthew, Gideon, Amelia, Joey*
Playing at the Great Sand Dunes

We did lots of wet stuff—water parks, pools, and fountain parks, complete with picnics and blankets. Santa's Workshop amusement park in the foothills was a huge hit, as was the petting farm on the plains.

But the coup de gràce was our overnight at a castle. We have a bona fide castle, built in the 1800s, right in our town—the Glen Eyrie--owned by the Navigators. The kids had a blast sleeping in the castle and eating breakfast in the King James Dining Room.

Not willing to break the cardinal rule of grandparenting (Don't disappoint your grandchildren!), I didn't let anything interfere with my weekly interlude. I was having more fun than should be legal for a grandma. And the excursions rescued me from my home office to enjoy the beautiful Colorado summer.

Healing brings many gifts to our life, including fun and satisfying relationships. As we begin living the life God has planned for us, not only do we get to exercise the gifts he's given us, finding our joyful place working alongside God, but he lavishes blessings on our life. That's what makes God happy! Doing life with my grandkids has been one of my favorite things.

The field trips were such a success, we made it a regular summer plan. Bryan missed all the fun that first year, but quickly jumped onboard every summer after that, helping to plan new and exciting adventures with the grandkids. They say grandkids are life's reward for raising kids. I agree. They bring so much joy!

Recording the Library

While sprinting to the finish line of 2016, something new began to stir in me. God had taught me so much about his Word, his true character, his process of redemption and restoration, his heart for relationship with us, the fantastic way he has created each of us, and the life he wishes us to live. I call it the library. God wrote all these different volumes on my heart and mind, and they were now sitting on the shelf in the library, a library inside of me.

Most of the library had been shared in this or that book, or in my various Bible studies. But it was scattered around, not that easy to access all of it. I wanted to find a way to open the whole library, making it easily available to be used by anyone.

My first thought was to write a ton of mini-books, one for every topic. Then I realized there was a better way to share the library: podcasts. So for two years, I wrote podcast after podcast, one on every subject I'd taught, plus even more ideas that came to mind as I went along. I approached them like a balsamic reduction, a common sauce used in cooking, reducing them to a lean and mean message. I wanted to get each one down to its essence. Eighteen minutes was my goal for the length, thinking everyone can find time to listen if I kept it under twenty minutes.

Bryan helped with the mechanics, locating a free recording studio at our public library. We were able to produce these at no cost because he did the recording and editing himself. He loves that kind of stuff and had the time of his life producing the recordings. It was satisfying to produce these messages, and I was happy the library was finally available.

29: Bryan and Cyndy recording podcasts

I didn't know how many podcasts I would end up with, but just like everything else I'd written, I was pretty sure I would know when I was finished. We recorded ninety-eight podcasts over the two years. I still add to the library occasionally, when I get a new idea.

Letter from God

Just before we began recording the podcasts, I sensed I needed some extended time with God, so I headed back to the Glen Eyrie Castle, staying in my favorite room, Dawson Trautman's room (the founder of the Navigator's). While there, God began speaking another letter to my heart.

August 15, 2017: *"Cyndy, I love you. I am for you. I am on your side. I will help you as you go forward here. We will get through everything together. You are mine. I take that very seriously. No one will ever snatch you away from me.*

"We are not done. We yet have great things to do together. I will use you mightily in the days to come. Do not fear. Do not worry. I have you. I always have you. I will never let you down. I know it's been difficult recently. I see your pain and struggle. Relax in me. I won't let you fall. You are mine. My grasp will not be loosened. Remember what you heard me say years ago: a legion of angels surrounds you wherever you go. You cannot be touched. You are my mouthpiece, my spokesman.

"Keep sharing the word I have planted in you. Don't worry about results. Just share. Keep sharing the message. I will guide you. You are mine. My Spirit will always tell you what to say. I will take care of you.

"I will take you to new places. Things are going to change now. But don't worry. I've got you. You are mine. I am pleased with your service and pleased with your heart.

"Thank you for coming to meet with me today. I appreciate it so much. You are dear to me. Enjoy your day. Enjoy recording the podcasts. I'll be there, too, helping you all the way. It's going to be good. I love you more than you can know. Your Loving Heavenly Father."

Right as we were gearing up for two years of podcast recording, still with many more segments to write, God poured into me encouragement and affirmation. As always, I was so humbled by God's words, nearly speechless at his tenderness and care for me.

Back in Prison

My next trip to prison was quick, but eventful. On October 6, 2017, I caught a flight to Sacramento with my friend, Dana, arriving in the early afternoon in good order, in plenty of time for the evening event. Linda, my contact for Folsom Prison, picked us up and took us to her house for dinner. We were joined by two other members of Linda's team, Jackie and Carolyn. Being only minutes from the prison, Linda suggested we leave at 6:00 for the 6:30 event.

By 6:15 we were processing into the prison. Standing in front of the little booth, the officer behind the glass said he could not find the clearances for Dana or me. It wasn't in his book; therefore he wasn't letting us in. Linda, a 6-year veteran serving at this prison, was used to the prison system's administrative chaos and had the foresight to secure a copy of our clearance papers earlier, which she promptly handed to the officer. That seemed to make matters worse.

"You're not supposed to have that!" the guard barked, *"That is for internal use only. Besides, I don't have it in my book, so I'm not letting you in."* Linda was fuming. We were now past our start time. Linda set out to places unknown, talking to anyone she could, calling everyone she knew, trying to get someone to let us in. After all, the prison had cleared us. And she had proof.

Folsom Prison is a massive complex, including five separate prisons within its gates, mostly for men. While we waited in the smaller, women's building, Linda went to the main entry area, only to find the officer she had known for years was off that night, and his replacement was on his first day of work. Linda was trying to explain to him where the book was, the one with all the clearances. No luck there. Apparently, there was more than one book, and nothing was alphabetized. (Because that makes sense? Right! Never look for anything to make sense when you're doing prison work.)

Meanwhile, Dana and I were praying up a storm. As time passed, I got more nervous. I really needed at least ninety minutes, two hours was preferable, to do a decent event for the ladies. For Pete's sake, my story alone is forty-five minutes! Was this even going to work if they ever did let us in?

At some point Dana leaned over and said, *"Oh, by the way, did I tell you God said I would not be doing my testimony tonight?"*

"No! You didn't!" I joked. *"That would have been helpful information to have!"* I had asked Dana to share as part of our event. Apparently, God knew ahead of time (imagine that!) that we would have trouble getting

in. At this point I was just trying to stay calm, as the officer continued to glare at us from his little booth. We kept praying.

We heard over the loudspeaker that our event has been cancelled. *No!* I'd fought many fierce battles trying to get into prisons, but God always made a way. *Would this be the first time it didn't happen?* I didn't want to doubt. But, honestly, I had that question. We'd easily spent $1000 to get there, plus all the prep time. *Would that all be wasted?*

It was now 7:00 p.m. and we were still waiting. No sign of Linda. Our teammates had gone inside, so Dana and I were alone. Finally, Linda returned, discouraged. No one would help her. Sometime after 7:00, we noticed the officer picking up the phone. We couldn't hear the conversation, and we will never know who was on the other end, but when he finished talking, he slowly put the phone down, motioned us to come forward, took our driver's licenses, and buzzed us in. We were inside!

But now what? Most of the ladies had returned to their cells. A faithful few, however, had remained in the cafeteria, our meeting room. They were praying, refusing to give up hope that we'd get in. They raced down the halls, informing everyone we'd been allowed inside and that the event was on.

The ladies returned, some happier than others. A few of the inmates were being required to be there, and they thought they'd escaped the event. No such luck, they had to come back. This small group took the table in the far, rear corner, making sure everyone knew that whatever I was serving, they didn't want any.

It didn't matter how late it was when the prison finally got their act together and let you in, you still had to finish at the scheduled time. And there was only forty-five minutes left. No time for music, no time for Dana's testimony, no time for chit chat. I just dove in with my story.

As soon as I began speaking, it was like God plugged me in and lit me up. I was on fire, sharing my story along with God's hope and love for each of them. In a matter of minutes, the special table in the back had stopped talking. In fact, everyone had stopped talking. Except for me, the room was silent; nobody moved for the remaining time. It was not because I'm the world's best speaker, but because

God had some business to do that night, in that prison, with those ladies, and he would not be deterred.

I poured my heart out, leaving nothing on the table. We concluded with a salvation prayer and a time of healing. Everyone responded, even the ladies in the back corner. As we concluded, we shouted together, "Jesus is Lord!" over and over as the ladies got to their feet. The enemy had thrown his best effort at us, trying to defeat us, but God won. God had the victory.

Several ladies came up to thank us, mentioning how much my story was like theirs. It always breaks my heart to know so many of us have experienced the unspeakable.

The clock ticked 8:15. The ladies left, and so did we. We quickly processed out of the prison and headed to our cars, only to find our host's late model car would not start. The battery was dead. Even though she had just had her car checked out, even though that had never happened before, the ignition wouldn't turn over.

While we're waiting, Jackie began to tell me how excited she was to hear that I had been a Pioneer Girl so many years ago and that I had attended the California camp (a detail of my story). It turned out, Jackie had been a counselor at that camp, and after comparing dates, we realized it was highly likely she was a counselor when I was there, fifty years earlier. She said, "I always wondered whether God used any of that for good. I am greatly encouraged to meet you and see that he did." A small thing. Here we were, doing some current business in a prison, but God touched a dear servant, with an answer to a prayer, spoken long ago. He's always working on many levels, seen and unseen.

Linda called many people before she finally reached her husband. He arrived shortly thereafter, but without jumper cables. He had a portable battery with him, but that wasn't solving the problem. Finally, an employee walked out of the building, someone who did have cables. He pulled his vehicle over to ours and we were on our way in five minutes. Oy vey!

I was unfazed by the inconvenience, however. We had accomplished what God had sent us to do, and even being stuck in a prison parking lot for ninety minutes could not dampen my enthusiasm for what had just happened. God had changed those women, and I got to witness it.

We finally reached our hotel by ten. The next morning, we enjoyed a celebratory breakfast with our dear, California prison team, basking in the Lord's goodness before catching our flight home. While we were waiting to catch our flight back to Colorado, I recorded a podcast recounting the story.

What to do with Teens

For the past twenty years, I've affectionately said our ministry supporters have been the most demanding people, always asking for more, no matter how much we put out there. Their demands, however, fill my heart with satisfaction and gratitude, knowing they are being touched by our ministry. As soon as I started teaching the women's class, they began asking me to create Healing Journey for men. And when that was finished, they wanted me to create a curriculum for high school students.

I can't even use the word 'requests,' because many times their expressed desires came with frustration, bordering on anger. *When are you going to get this done!* But it is good; it encourages me because it tells me what we are doing is having a positive effect on their lives, and that is why they want more.

Even so, I couldn't get to the teen curriculum for a few years because of other projects. Finally, in 2018, I was able to start the teen project, writing a new curriculum to fit their world, testing it out with a pilot class. I was still a long way from finishing this project, when God said he had another assignment for me.

November 21, 2019: *"The LORD will cause His glorious voice to be heard…" (Isaiah 30:30a) Another word comes today—to start writing my story—my next book. I've sensed this was on the horizon for some time, but now I have confirmation. I still have no idea of the purpose, thrust, or focus of the book, but I know I am supposed to begin writing it.*

God told me to get my story written. It had been a long time coming.

Chapter Sixty-One

2020

Family Today

My dad has been gone several years now and my mom is in her last days. She lives a few minutes from my house, and I help her in the limited ways I can. Our relationship is minimal, which is all that is available to me. I accept these terms. I try to bring moments of brightness to her otherwise dismal life—a bouquet of flowers, a lunch out, or a visit with her great-grandkids.

My half-brother Scott still lives in Arizona and we have no contact. Because we haven't had a relationship for fifty years, there isn't anything with which to work. I have an amicable relationship with the twins, usually seeing my brother every year, and my sister on special occasions and when she comes to visit our mother. I'm not sure what will happen with our relationships when Mom is gone. I stay in touch with both, and that makes my heart feel good.

Military life has Heather and her family in Alabama, but we are still very much part of each other's lives, arranging annual visits.

Our sons live minutes away, working in their respective careers, raising their families, gathering with us for family occasions.

It is hard to believe my girls are now approaching middle age, both married and living busy lives. Jenny drives over the mountains for frequent visits with Joey, who will soon launch into adulthood. The Asperger's syndrome will always be part of him and his life, but he is intelligent, learns easily, and functions well independently. I look forward to seeing the path he chooses after high school. Bree lives minutes away and her school–age children are in my home frequently. The summer field trips continue happily for all of us.

Joys Today

Bryan is retiring from construction, allowing him more time to work in the ministry and keep up with our busy lifestyle. I love doing ministry work with him. We thoroughly enjoy doing the live-events and classes together. We are a great team.

30:Bryan and Me

And when we aren't doing ministry, we're usually indulging our other love, playing with the grandkids, taking them places and having them over for spend-the-nights. Our whole family camps together in the Rocky Mountains every summer, and Bryan and I have our own Colorado mountain camping experience, too. We're both content whenever we're in the mountains. It is a good life.

I feel blessed to work with many amazing people around the country, dear friends who champion our cause, bringing God's healing to people everywhere. And I have many fabulous friends, right here in Colorado Springs, who pray for me and support me in this crazy life I live. I am blessed beyond measure.

Struggles Today

Because I am a work-in-progress, there are areas where I still struggle. I try to give myself grace, forgiving my weakness and imperfect efforts, but I don't always succeed. I can be hard on myself. I find it much easier to give grace to others than to myself. But this is only in certain areas. For instance, I easily forgive people when they make mistakes. Watching them waste their life is harder, though, and does evoke judgment at times. And even more so when they are harming others with their life-choices. God and I work on that a lot.

I am not a patient person. I recognize the brevity of life and strive to make every moment count, and this makes me an intense person, as my good friend, Keeta, likes to point out. And so I work intensely, desiring to finish the work God has given me to do.

But this is not the whole story. I am much better at making reasonable choices for myself, acknowledging I am not a young woman, and so need a different rhythm in my sixties than I did in my thirties. And my impatience with wasted lives is born out of a deep love and desire for others to know the joy of running with the horses and living the life God created them to live. Every coin has two sides.

Work Today

While I still direct His Healing Light Ministries, I hope that role will transition to another person in the next few years. I have been actively moving responsibilities off my plate for years, seeking to open up as much time for writing as possible. Writing is my passion, the thing I crave to do with my time.

The amount of travel seems to be slowing down, which is good. While I love ministering face-to-face to people after I arrive, the coming and going part is for the birds. My issues with heat and fainting continue to worsen, so that is hard. I like being home; a great asset for a writer.

I am not sure what lies beyond the writing of this book and producing the new curriculum for teens. But I usually don't know what God is going to have me do after I finish his current list for me. I thought I was done when I finished producing Healing Journey in 2008. So much for what I think! I never know and I never ask. Today is enough for me.

I can say, though, that I don't believe in retirement, at least not from serving God. I view myself as a very young senior citizen. I have a lot of kick left in me. I may not kick as high as I used to, but I'm still kicking. As long as the Lord has work for me to do, I will do it. It remains my joy to serve him.

Epilogue

Reflections on Healing

What Others Meant for Evil

While revisiting my story to write this book, I was surprised by the amount of pain and suffering I have endured. I've never laced everything together as a whole, and so found myself shocked at my own story. *Wow, this is a ghastly story. Who would ever want to read this?*

And that, in and of itself, speaks volumes for the healing process. Because it no longer has an impact on my life, I don't think about that old stuff anymore, so I had forgotten a lot of it once God finished my healing. The redemption process worked.

As I invited God into each painful event and memory, releasing everything to him, he changed my mind. God took the tormenting thoughts away, restoring my mind to peacefulness. The result was a mind free to create books and studies and events that bring new life to others. I continue to enjoy and celebrate these changes.

God changed my heart, too, replacing my stone heart with a heart of flesh like his. The very process that eliminated my feelings of betrayal, abandonment, and rejection, set my heart free to love others, and inspire hope that their life can one day be free, too. God redeemed what was meant for evil and used it for good. Life literally sprang from the ashes of my past, and it happened without any thought or intention from me.

My plan was to simply teach one Bible study about healing to ten women. God, however, wanted the message out there for everyone, so he took that humble study and ran with it. He is a much bigger thinker than I am!

Holding the Paradox

I keep learning and growing. Along the way, I've learned perspectives that I didn't have during my recovery years. A big one is about the paradox of relationships. Every relationship contains a paradox, a contradiction, and if I can't *accept the paradox,* (or *hold the paradox,* as I like to think of it), I have no choice but to end the relationship. My parents contained huge paradoxes.

No one is all good or all evil. Even the vilest human being has value and some goodness in them. We tend to categorize people in black and white terms, either as worthy of a relationship or not worthy of a relationship. But it is not that simple. If we remain in relationship with people for any length of time, they will disappoint us and hurt us, without exception.

If I can't accept that reality, if I can't manage enough grace to accept the imperfections in other people, then I will not be able to have a relationship with anyone. We are all screw-ups at some level. Everyone has bad moments, bad attitudes, and bad responses, at least occasionally.

That is not to say it is always wise to have certain relationships. There are many reasons why we should avoid some people. Safety is a factor to be considered. I've had seasons in my life when I could not be around my parents for my own mental health and safety. But after my healing was finished, I had enough inner strength, combined with an identity now solid enough, that I could entertain a limited relationship. I was healthy enough to say yes or no when I needed to.

Pride is the human condition. We are all born with a prideful disposition and will remain prideful unless something changes us. This is the work Christ does in us, that fancy word the Bible likes to throw out—sanctification. A few choose to cooperate with that important work. The rest remain in pride, unchallenged pride, pride that says, *"I want my way. And if you get in the way of me having my way, I will do things that are hurtful to our relationship."*

I don't have the power to change pride in another person. I don't even have the power to change me, apart from cooperating with the work Jesus is doing in me. My only hope is to surrender myself every day, never forsake the reading of his Word, and stay in constant fellowship with him.

In the context of my history with my mother, it would be understandable to say, *"You are a bad person because you did bad things to me. That means you are unsafe to me. And that means you don't love me because love doesn't hurt others."* That is mostly a lie, though. She is not a bad person; she is a precious creation of God, as I am. And, as I said, every love relationship eventually hurts the other person. For all who love, pride coexists within them, and it is the pride aspect that hurts people.

To say my mother didn't or doesn't love me would mean that I didn't love my children either. But I did and I do! I love them to the moon and back. Even so, I've made many prideful choices that hurt them. My mother has loved me the best she knew how, living as her very messed-up self.

My mother is a trauma survivor, too. But she never received healing, so, like yeast, her wounds continued to grow and grow, until they completely took over her mind and heart. Sadly, today, there is very little resemblance left of the woman God made her to be. She hurts me and others continually.

But that doesn't mean she doesn't love me or her family.

My dad was also a trauma survivor, abused as a child. He perpetrated huge crimes against me. Even so, he also loved me. The best he knew how, as his very messed-up self, he loved me. Does that excuse one thing he did to me? No. Does that make it more palatable? Not one iota. Nevertheless, he was made by God, loved by God, and a man who also had good qualities.

Confusing, isn't it? In our limited wisdom and perspective, it is so difficult to make sense of these things. It is hard to accept the paradox that exists in each person.

The other thing I could never have conceived of being true is that I would ever again want a relationship with my parents. It was unthinkable during the worst of my healing years. But then God healed me. In and of itself, that is a miracle. But there was more to the miracle.

When God replaced my old heart with a new one, my new heart felt differently. The new heart wasn't angry and bitter anymore. The new heart could be with my parents, albeit in limited and superficial ways, yet enjoy a small measure of joy. Was it all I hoped it would be? No. Were they suddenly different people because I was changed? No. They were the same. But this limited contact was satisfying to me and a great improvement over the total estrangement I had experienced for many years.

Feeling God's Pleasure

We are so quick to judge God, blaming him for the bad things that happen to us, or for the good things that don't happen. That perspective, however, will flip redemption on its backside, rendering it impotent.

God is not responsible for the suffering other people cause. People are responsible for that. And, in many situations, no one is responsible, as with natural disasters, accidents, and disease. As long as we hold to the belief that it is God's job to provide an easy, pain-free life for us, we'll never find the joy and freedom he wants to give us.

I would never want to repeat a second of my journey, but neither would I trade it. Even if God came down from heaven today and stepped into my office and said, *"Cyndy, if you'd like, I'll erase your past, all the abuse and trauma and years of recovery. I'll make it as if it never happened. Just say the word,"* I would decline the offer without hesitation.

And that's because I would never be who I am today, or be able to do what I do, had I not gone where I have gone. It is a package deal. It was the trauma and pain that led me to the heart of God, that opened my eyes to see him. I would never exchange that.

It is all worth it because today I get to serve in God's kingdom, doing what I love, what I was created to do. God made me to write and teach; when I do (if I may borrow from Eric Liddell), I feel his pleasure. That is something to which I cannot assign a price; it is worth any amount of suffering I may have endured. *"I consider that our present sufferings are not worth comparing with the glory that will be revealed in us." (Romans 8:18).*

Suffering is the vehicle God uses to bring us to truth and freedom. As Chambers liked to say, *...the nature of this world is tragic.* Suffering is how God teaches us and changes us. It will purify us, if only we'll trust God.

The suffering of my journey propelled me to latch on to God like I had never latched on before. When he opened that black pit inside me, he had my full attention. I was motivated. And because I chose to look in his direction, he did the needed work. He purified my mind of the lies I believed about him, giving me the foundation I needed to trust him and surrender my life.

It was in the journey that I learned to transfer my reliance from myself to God. He revealed to me the reliability of his strength, provision, and protection. He and I tested it together over and over and over in my wilderness years until I finally got it. And when I did, I was ready to step into the role I was created for. I was now equipped for the job because God had emptied me of my self-sufficiency. (Well… maybe lessened it … it's still a battle!)

My relationship with God is the most intimate one in my life, and from that intimacy, life now flows in every direction.

I praise God for the path my life has taken. My suffering lasted for a moment (that's the true perspective), but the joy God has given me will last forever. I don't regret a minute of my healing journey or wish I hadn't gone to those hard places because today I'm free!

"Dear friends, do not be surprised at the painful trial you are suffering, as though something strange were happening to you. But rejoice that you participate in the sufferings of Christ, so that you may be overjoyed when his glory is revealed." (1 Peter 4:12-13)

The power of God that transformed my life reveals his glory to others. And if others will in turn see hope from my story and respond to him, their life will reveal his glory, too. *"And the God of all grace, who called you to his eternal glory in Christ, after you have suffered a little while, will himself restore you and make you strong, firm and steadfast." (1 Peter 5:10).*

I am not a different woman today. I am the woman he made me to be all along. Remembering that image of a portrait—the one God gave me so many years ago, the one covered in slime, mold, and refuse—his original design and creation is finally visible. The beauty was always there but obscured by the pain of my past. Not anymore!

I was born with all the traits and attributes needed to teach and lead a ministry. But because life played hardball, that original picture was severely marred, preventing me from stepping into that role. You could see those attributes poke out at various times, but they were distorted by trauma.

God's love for me revealed my true identity, purging the lies. Now I know he is my heavenly father and wants to be with me. God really likes me (and he likes you, too!) and sees me as worth his time and attention. Because God has made me a healthy person, someone secure in who she is, I am surrounded by healthier relationships. Every relationship is better, including the one with myself. Today I can honestly say that I like myself!

I am glad I took the healing journey. It did not make the world different, nor did it change my family or other relationships. But it did change me. And because of that, I find contentment in who I am, fulfillment in the incredible work God has given me to do, and satisfaction that I am a loved child of God. I am at peace.

Final Word

John Woolman, a Quaker who lived in colonial America, began his journal with these words: *I have often felt a motion of love to leave some hints in writing of my experience of the goodness of God.* If my story accomplishes anything, I hope it is to hint at the goodness of God.

List of Alters

1. Alex: 14-year-old boy. Protector, touchy, violent, full of rage, foul mouth, often wanted to scream, liked to drive fast, protector of Tammy, mistrusted men, felt abandoned. Held memories of physical abuse and cult ceremonies.
2. Barbara: 5 years old at first, then progressed to 17 during the healing process. Outgoing, dazzling, confident, energetic, irresistible, extroverted, performer, beautiful, did job interviews, impressive, flirtatious, loved music and singing. Held memories of being told she was special and of dancing with scarves.
3. Brenda (aka Bad Girl, a fragment of Brenda): 7 years old. Protector, tough but tender-hearted, scarred, worldly, strong, thought she was a bad girl, protected Little Cindy, knew a lot about the system inside us, nothing got to her, angry, hated involvement at church, hated abuse to Bree, hated marriage, liked dancing, drinking, and driving fast. Held memories of sexual abuse at home and cult rituals.
4. Cinderella: 17 years old. Idealistic, hopeful, confused, giving, homemaker, violated, full of pain, traumatized by separation. Held memories of violation and abuse in the first marriage.
5. Cynthia: Adult. Positive, upbeat, loved detail work like bookkeeping, loved accomplishing things, got identity from accomplishments, worked hard, loved order, lots of inner strength.
6. Jacob: 5-year-old boy. Hadn't been out/present since 1961, afraid to speak. Held the memory of a ritual ceremony.
7. JoAnn: 42 years old. In conflict with other women, didn't like schedules, wanted to have fun, free spirit.
8. Joey: 4-6-year-old boy. Angry, wanted to punch the bad people. Held memories of seeing children abused.
9. John: 6-8-year-old boy. Liked to build things and play with trucks. Sad, felt bad, carried guilt, was healed by Jesus. Held memories of cult rituals and abuse. Knew Dad abused us.
10. Judith Ann: 37 years old. Wise, had common sense, caring, motherly, powerless, helpful, encouraged exercise and healthy eating, tattled, like an inner self-helper, did what was right.

11. Little Cindy: 4-5 years old. Quiet, afraid of bad people, had stomach aches, felt abandoned, slept to avoid pain, hid, was vulnerable, liked sitting on Jesus' lap. Held memories of the satanic baptism and watching the cult rituals and abuse.
12. Marianne: 7 years old. Loving, spunky, playful, happy, terrified, wanted to stay home, cried a lot, slept to escape. Held memories of sexual abuse by church members and family.
13. Marie: 10 years old. Liked to bake, sing, go to the movies. Cleaned house, worked hard, feared hospitals and illness, felt shameful, a little mother and caretaker. Held memories of Mom almost dying in the hospital, worked hard to please Mom, wasn't nurtured.
14. Marilyn: 3 years old. Drew pictures because she didn't talk. Held memories of cult rituals and abuse and of being threatened if she talked.
15. Marine Corps: Adult. Protective, strong, steel-willed, disciplined, compulsive, tenacious, never gave up, powerful.
16. Matilda (Mattie): 13 years old. Hated her body, thought she was fat, ugly, and old, didn't eat at all or ate fattening food. Negative, alone, isolated, unhappy, angry.
17. Patty: 5 years old at first, then progressed to 17-18 during the healing process. Sexually aggressive, associated belonging with sex and violence. Held memories of sexual abuse with cult and family.
18. Sarah: 5 years old. Liked to color, play with dolls, and make paper dolls, got sick when she remembered abuse, didn't want to share her memories. Held memories of hiding and being physically abused.
19. Tammy: 14 years old. Thought she was bad. Hated her body. Thought she was fat. Shy, quiet, liked to be alone, felt tremendous pain, didn't want to be touched. Held memories of severe sexual abuse.
20. Teresa Lynn King: 25 years old. Protector, angry, tough, didn't take trouble from anyone—especially men. Wanted to run and start over, energized, decisive, intimidating, nothing stopped her.

21. Thomas: Angry with everybody, particularly men, wanted to kill Dad, frustrated with life, concerned about poor financial decisions, wanted to fix things and make good decisions.
22. Wendy: 6 years old. Terrified, easily spooked, loved animals. Held memories of animal sacrifices and of being confined.
23. Zora: Adult. Sensuous, sexy, loved being touched, loved men, enjoyed dancing, parties, and drinking. Referred to herself as Zora the Magnificent. Thought of herself as a gypsy, a flower in full bloom, radiant with color and fragrance. Sexually abused in cult rituals.

Glossary

Alters:

Alters (also called personalities or parts) are components of an individual's personality that are created as a result of extreme trauma. Those diagnosed with DID have two or more separate personalities, or parts of themselves, who come out, or choose to be present for certain situations. Sometimes they identify as being a certain age and having a different name or voice, but not always. Personalities or alters serve different purposes, including carrying the traumatic memory and fulfilling certain roles or functions, for instance, protecting the system. They have distinct behavioral and social patterns, often different from the host. They can also have different spiritual beliefs, likes and dislikes, etc.

Body memories:

When an abuse survivor begins to remember what happened to them, the emotional and physical wounds often reappear before the cognitive memory returns. It is common to re-experience any emotional reaction such as shame, fear, terror, anxiety, sadness, etc. The body remembers everything that happened to it, as well. So pain can appear anywhere in the body without a current-life explanation.

Co-consciousness and losing time:

Sometimes multiples are co-conscious, but not always. When a multiple is co-conscious, even when an alter is out, the host knows what is going on and will remember everything when they come back. If a multiple is not co-conscious, they will lose time, meaning the host or core personality may not remember what happened when certain alters were out. Losing time makes DID more difficult to navigate.

Come out or become the alter who is present:

When a part or alter comes out, it means they are the one experiencing and responding to whatever circumstances are occurring, including speaking.

Dissociation:

This is a normal human phenomenon where a person mentally and/or emotionally experiences a reality different from the one they are in physically. When someone dissociates, they detach or separate from what is currently happening.

- Example of mental separation: Someone walks into a room and doesn't remember why they are there. That person dissociated; their body is in the room, but their mind is somewhere else. Forgetting is mental separation.
- Example of emotional separation: Someone is being yelled at, causing strong feelings of fear and anxiety, so they dissociate by shutting down emotionally. They may zone out or become numb. This momentarily protects them from the pain of the words being spoken.

Dissociation is a continuum, beginning with the normal behavior described above. As it moves further down the continuum, it begins to interfere with the person's life, causing disruption. Chronic stress or a single traumatic event can cause someone to compartmentalize their life, yet not create separate personalities.

- Example of chronic stress: A woman is being emotionally battered by her husband. At home she is silent, sullen, and emotionally absent because she is living in a survival mode. At work, however, she is animated, chatty, and engaging with her co-workers because she has dissociated from her home life.
- Example of a single trauma: A parent lost their son when he committed suicide in their garage. Now every time they are in the garage or see the car, they feel physical paralysis for several minutes and are unable to complete the task they set out to do. The pain of losing their son has caused them to dissociate from their current reality.

In each of the above cases, even though they have dissociated, they do not have separate personalities, and, therefore, are not multiple.

Dissociative Identity Disorder (DID):

When dissociative behavior travels further down the continuum, one or more separate personalities are created. This is always the result of extreme stress occurring in childhood. Because children are not psychologically and emotionally equipped to process horrific events and ongoing abuse, they survive by compartmentalizing the trauma. It might stem from a single event, for example being the only surviving family member in a car accident. Or it can be the result of ongoing trauma, such as incest, physical or sexual abuse, ritual abuse, and many other types of painful events.

DID is a coping mechanism, not a mental illness. It is a God-created human phenomenon to help children survive unspeakable atrocities. By creating different personalities to hold the trauma, children are then able to go on living the other, so called normal parts of their life. While dissociation saves survivors when they are children, it ultimately breaks down in adulthood, interfering with their ability to function in normal life. This is when healing of the memories is needed to help restore them to wholeness.

Host:

The host is the original personality, sometimes called the core personality, the one that existed at birth, prior to the abuse or trauma.

Integration:

Integration is the process of incorporating alters back into the personality of the host, so they no longer operate independently. Integration can occur all at once, or over time, with one alter at a time. Before alters will be ready to integrate, they need to be seen, heard, believed/respected, and to have their needs met. When healing takes place for each alter in the system, it is then possible for integration to occur.

Mono-brain:

Mono-brain is a word I made up to describe someone who isn't multiple.

Multiple Personality Disorder (MPD): See Dissociative Identity Disorder

Multiples: People with two or more alters or parts.

Parts: See alters

Personalities: See alters

Post-Traumatic Stress Disorder (PTSD):

Sometimes when a person experiences a traumatic event, it interferes with their ability to function in normal day-to-day life. Experiencing or witnessing or participating in (e.g. First Responders) a traumatic event can cause PTSD along with many of the same problems that those with DID experience like flashbacks, nightmares, anger, and hypervigilance. Negative emotions and mood swings are also common to both. Those with PTSD often dissociate from the memory, but don't necessarily have alters or personalities. Everyone with DID also has PTSD, but not everyone with PTSD is multiple.

Satanic Ritual Abuse (SRA)

Satanic Ritual Abuse happens in religious ceremonies conducted for the purpose of worshiping Satan or other demonic beings and perverting the holiness of God and the Bible. The rituals are done in secret, hidden from the public, usually at night, and include every vile and deviant behavior imaginable.

Switching:

Whether it is the host or an alter, switching is when one personality goes back inside and another one comes out to be present.

System:

The system is a reference to all the alters or parts in one person who has DID.